**of F**

Everything you need to know to administer

MW00436003

I'd like to order the following *Essentials of Psychological Assessment:*

- ❑ WAIS®-IV Assessment (w/CD-ROM) / 978-0-471-73846-6 • $48.95
- ❑ WJ III™ Cognitive Abilities Assessment, Second Edition / 978-0-470-56664-0 • $38.95
- ❑ Cross-Battery Assessment, Second Edition (w/CD-ROM) / 978-0-471-75771-9 • $48.95
- ❑ Nonverbal Assessment / 978-0-471-38318-5 • $38.95
- ❑ PAI® Assessment / 978-0-471-08463-1 • $38.95
- ❑ CAS Assessment / 978-0-471-29015-5 • $38.95
- ❑ MMPI-2 Assessment, Second Edition / 978-0-470-92323-8 • $38.95
- ❑ Myers-Briggs Type Indicator® Assessment, Second Edition / 978-0-470-34390-6 • $38.95
- ❑ Rorschach® Assessment / 978-0-471-33146-9 • $38.95
- ❑ Millon™ Inventories Assessment, Third Edition / 978-0-470-16862-2 • $38.95
- ❑ TAT and Other Storytelling Assessments, Second Edition / 978-0-470-28192-5 • $38.95
- ❑ MMPI-A™ Assessment / 978-0-471-39815-8 • $38.95
- ❑ NEPSY®-II Assessment / 978-0-470-43691-2 • $38.95
- ❑ Neuropsychological Assessment, Second Edition / 978-0-470-43747-6 • $38.95
- ❑ WJ III™ Tests of Achievement Assessment / 978-0-471-33059-2 • $38.95
- ❑ Evidence-Based Academic Interventions / 978-0-470-20632-4 • $38.95
- ❑ WRAML2 and TOMAL-2 Assessment / 978-0-470-17911-6 • $38.95
- ❑ WMS®-IV Assessment / 978-0-470-62196-7 • $38.95
- ❑ Behavioral Assessment / 978-0-471-35367-6 • $38.95
- ❑ Forensic Psychological Assessment, Second Edition / 978-0-470-55168-4 • $38.95
- ❑ Bayley Scales of Infant Development II Assessment / 978-0-471-32651-9 • $38.95
- ❑ Career Interest Assessment / 978-0-471-35365-2 • $38.95
- ❑ WPPSI™-III Assessment / 978-0-471-28895-4 • $38.95
- ❑ 16PF® Assessment / 978-0-471-23424-1 • $38.95
- ❑ Assessment Report Writing / 978-0-471-39487-7 • $38.95
- ❑ Stanford-Binet Intelligence Scales (SB5) Assessment / 978-0-471-22404-4 • $38.95
- ❑ WISC®-IV Assessment, Second Edition (w/CD-ROM) / 978-0-470-18915-3 • $48.95
- ❑ KABC-II Assessment / 978-0-471-66733-9 • $38.95
- ❑ WIAT®-III and KTEA-II Assessment (w/CD-ROM) / 978-0-470-55169-1 • $48.95
- ❑ Processing Assessment / 978-0-471-71925-0 • $38.95
- ❑ School Neuropsychological Assessment / 978-0-471-78372-5 • $38.95
- ❑ Cognitive Assessment with KAIT & Other Kaufman Measures / 978-0-471-38317-8 • $38.95
- ❑ Assessment with Brief Intelligence Tests / 978-0-471-26412-5 • $38.95
- ❑ Creativity Assessment / 978-0-470-13742-0 • $38.95
- ❑ WNV™ Assessment / 978-0-470-28467-4 • $38.95
- ❑ DAS-II® Assessment (w/CD-ROM) / 978-0-470-22520-2 • $48.95
- ❑ Executive Function Assessment (w/CD-ROM) / 978-0-470-42202-1 • $48.95
- ❑ Conners Behavior Assessments™ / 978-0-470-34633-4 • $38.95
- ❑ Temperament Assessment / 978-0-470-44447-4 • $38.95
- ❑ Response to Intervention / 978-0-470-56663-3 • $38.95
- ❑ Specific Learning Disability Identification / 978-0-470-58760-7 • $38.95
- ❑ IDEA for Assessment Professionals (w/CD-ROM) / 978-0-470-87392-2 • $48.95
- ❑ Dyslexia Assessment and Intervention / 978-0-470-92760-1 • $38.95
- ❑ Autism Spectrum Disorders Evaluation and Assessment / 978-0-470-62194-3 • $38.95

Please complete the order form on the back.
To order by phone, call toll free 1-877-762-2974
To order online: www.wiley.com/essentials
To order by mail: refer to order form on next page

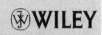

Essentials

of **Psychological Assessment** Series

ORDER FORM

Please send this order form with your payment (credit card or check) to:
John Wiley & Sons, Attn: J. Knott, 111 River Street, Hoboken, NJ 07030-5774

QUANTITY	TITLE	ISBN	PRICE
_____	_____	_____	_____
_____	_____	_____	_____
_____	_____	_____	_____
_____	_____	_____	_____
_____	_____	_____	_____

Shipping Charges:	**Surface**	**2-Day**	**1-Day**
First item	$5.00	$10.50	$17.50
Each additional item	$3.00	$3.00	$4.00

For orders greater than 15 items,
please contact Customer Care at 1-877-762-2974.

ORDER AMOUNT _____
SHIPPING CHARGES _____
SALES TAX _____
TOTAL ENCLOSED _____

NAME_____

AFFILIATION_____

ADDRESS_____

CITY/STATE/ZIP _____

TELEPHONE _____

EMAIL_____

❏ Please add me to your e-mailing list

PAYMENT METHOD:

❏ Check/Money Order   ❏ Visa   ❏ Mastercard   ❏ AmEx

Card Number _____ Exp. Date _____

Cardholder Name *(Please print)* _____

Signature _____

*Make checks payable to **John Wiley & Sons**. Credit card orders invalid if not signed.*
All orders subject to credit approval. • Prices subject to change.

To order by phone, call toll free 1-877-762-2974
To order online: www.wiley.com/essentials

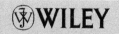

Essentials of Specific Learning Disability Identification

Essentials of Psychological Assessment Series

Series Editors, Alan S. Kaufman and Nadeen L. Kaufman

Essentials

of Specific Learning

Disability Identification

Dawn P. Flanagan
Vincent C. Alfonso

WILEY John Wiley & Sons, Inc.

Library of Congress Cataloging-in-Publication Data:
Flanagan, Dawn P.
    Essentials of specific learning disability identification / Dawn P. Flanagan, Vincent C. Alfonso.
        p. cm.—(Essentials of psychological assessment ; 82)
    Includes bibliographical references and index.
    ISBN 978-0-470-58760-7 (pbk.); 978-0-470-92058-9 (ePDF); 978-0-470-92059-6 (eMobi); 978-0-470-92060-2 (ePub)
    1. Learning disabilities—United States. 2. Learning disabled children—Education—United States. I. Alfonso, Vincent C. II. Title.
    LC4704.F575 2010
    371.9'043—dc22   2010026662

10 9 8 7 6 5 4

To my darling daughter, Megan:
For your wit, patience, and love;
For understanding beyond your years;
For finding the positive in every situation; and
For teaching me how to keep work in perspective.
You are a blessing.
I love you.
—Mom

In loving memory of my mother, Mary Alfonso—you are always on my mind!

CONTENTS

FOREWORD

Aᴄᴄᴏʀᴅɪɴɢ to the calculations of the United States Department of Education's National Center for Educational Statistics, the most frequently occurring disability among school-aged individuals in the United States is a specific learning disability (SLD). In fact, it accounts for nearly half of all disabilities in the school-aged population. It may well then come as a surprise to those who do not work in the field that in spite of the presence of a common definition of SLD, one that has essentially remained unchanged since 1975, there remains very little agreement about the best model or method of identifying students with SLD. Always controversial, since the passage of the Individuals with Disabilities Education Improvement Act (then known as IDEIA), the most recent reauthorization, in 2004, of the first version of the federal law requiring the public schools of the United States to provide a free and appropriate public education to students with disabilities (PL 94-142, the Education for All Handicapped Children Act), the disagreements over the best approach to identification of an SLD have grown. Prior to 2004, the Federal Regulations for implementation of the various versions of IDEA required, as a necessary but insufficient condition (except in special circumstances), the presence of a severe discrepancy between aptitude and achievement for a diagnosis of SLD. The regulations accompanying IDEA (all 307 small-print *Federal Register* pages of them), which retained the definition of SLD essentially as written in the 1975 law, dropped this requirement, and instead allow the schools to use one or a combination of three basic approaches to SLD identification: the severe discrepancy criteria of prior regulations, a process based on the response of a student to evidence-based (aka: science) interventions for learning problems (known popularly as the RTI approach), or any other approach the state or local education agency determines to be a scientifically or research-based approach to determination of an SLD.

The vagaries and ambiguities of the Federal Regulations and the pressure on schools to do what is new, and to do so quickly, has led to chaos in the field and fed considerable polemic debate over how to best determine an SLD. As if this were not enough controversy, note that the regulations concerning the determination of SLD in school-aged individuals (basically K–12) apply only to public schools and private schools that receive federal monies. Colleges and universities, the Social Security Administration, state departments of rehabilitation, the medical community, the courts, and other agencies that are involved in SLD identification and the provision of services and/or funding for these individuals can, and most do, apply different methods and have different rules for identification of an SLD. What is adopted then as the best method of diagnosis in the K-12 school systems will often be found unacceptable to other agencies, frustrating individuals who carry such a diagnosis, their parents, and the agencies themselves. This will lead to the very strong possibility that the federal judicial system will ultimately make the major decisions concerning how SLD is diagnosed. The vagaries of the Federal Regulations and the potential for extensive litigation in the absence of clear guidance from the USDOE are the primary reasons I so often refer to IDEIA as the "education lawyers' welfare act of 2004."

The issues of accurate and appropriate models from which to identify individuals with SLD sorely need attention from the academic community of scholars in a format that allows academics and practitioners to understand the many and diverse models now being promoted as best practice. *Essentials of Specific Learning Disability Identification* makes a practical foray into this arena, and does so succinctly, without sacrifice of a clear understanding of each model. And although this edited book is focused on the school-aged population, you will find educational, medical, psychometric, and neuropsychological models all present in the various chapters.

The opening chapters focus on descriptive efforts of the manifestations of SLD in the academically critical areas of reading, writing, math, oral expression, and listening, though some of the authors emphasize identification and some intervention in these chapters, as well. Some argue differences in neuropsychological organization of the brain; others argue specific deficits; and still others continue to call upon developmental delay as the essence of an SLD. There is less recognition in certain chapters than one might suppose that SLD is a very heterogeneous group of disorders, and that the underlying mechanism is not at all likely to be the same for everyone, although clearly most authors recognize this reality.

The second half of the work emphasizes models and methods of SLD identification, and herein we also find divergent views. After reading the volume, it is nothing less than striking the number of seemingly sound but incompatible models that are presented, especially knowing how many other models are in existence across the various state education agencies—not to mention the many other government agencies and programs using wholly different approaches. Every model presented in the latter half of this work has strengths in the approaches recommended for SLD identification, and each set of authors presents its case well. Nevertheless, the approaches, several of which are highly similar, will identify different children. Some are also just fundamentally incompatible; for example, while most emphasize the absolute necessity for a disorder in one or more of the basic processes underlying learning, at least one dismisses this aspect of the SLD definition as unnecessary to even assess or consider.

Fletcher leads off the chapters focused on diagnostic methods and models with a clear presentation of the RTI model as he and his colleagues perceive of it as best implemented. His well-reasoned approach has much to recommend it, but unfortunately many states are adopting a far more radical RTI-only approach, which, as Fletcher laudably notes, is not just poor practice but inconsistent with the Federal Regulations. Naglieri follows with a very different model, one that is more theory-driven than any of the other models, but providing good empirical support for his approach and practical advice on its implementation. Hale and his coauthors are next, with a model that, too, has a theoretical basis and that attempts to integrate RTI approaches with more traditional neuropsychological models. Berninger then treats us to a very accomplished work that takes on the complex issues of diagnosis and treatment of several types of SLD in the face of comorbidities, an issue dealt with poorly by most existing models, particularly RTI-only models. Her case for evidence-based models and ones that emphasize early identification and intervention is well made. Flanagan and Alfonso, the volume editors, follow with an articulation of the CHC approach to SLD identification, first describing how the CHC model would define SLD, and why, and then matching this approach to assessment in a CHC context. Last, Ortiz gives us guidance, to the extent possible, in differentiating cultural and linguistic differences from disabilities in the context of SLD determination. While this is often talked about, few give us this kind of concrete guidance to avoiding such diagnostic mistakes based on culture and language. We could all benefit still from reading the works of E. Paul Torrance from the 1970s on "differences not deficits" in such a context, as well.

This work then presents a strong reflection of the state of the field, and does a great service by putting theories of the development and etiology of SLD, commentary on interventions, and the dominant models of SLD identification between common covers. The editors have done a superb job in selecting authors to represent the viewpoints given and to elaborate with sufficient specificity the identification models, in most cases to the point at which they can be put into place upon reading this volume carefully. The greatest problem readers will face will be one of deciding which model(s) to follow, as all are appealing. There are authors of chapters in this work with whom I have had scholarly exchanges, and with whom I vehemently disagree on some issues but with whom I find myself in agreement on others. So I must count myself among those who will experience great dissonance in adopting and recommending a specific model of diagnosis to others based upon the models proffered herein. We have much to learn from the disagreements in this work, and it is indeed such disagreements and lack of compatibility of models and methods upon which science thrives. I suspect that as our science moves forward, we will find that all of these models have merit and utility for accurate and appropriate identification of individuals with SLD, but not for the same individuals. Individuals with SLD make up a heterogeneous group, and we truly need different models for their accurate identification (aka: different strokes for different folks) that are objective and evidence-based, such as provided in this work. Now, if we can just make them all part of a common, coherent system and stop the search for the one answer to the diagnosis of SLD for all students—that will be progress!

Cecil R. Reynolds
Bastrop, Texas

SERIES PREFACE

I n the *Essentials of Psychological Assessment* series, we have attempted to provide the reader with books that will deliver key practical information in the most efficient and accessible style. The series features instruments in a variety of domains, such as cognition, personality, education, and neuropsychology. For the experienced clinician, books in the series will offer a concise yet thorough way to master utilization of the continuously evolving supply of new and revised instruments, as well as a convenient method for keeping up to date on the tried-and-true measures. The novice will find in this series a prioritized assembly of all the information and techniques that must be at one's fingertips to begin the complicated process of individual psychological diagnosis.

Wherever feasible, visual shortcuts to highlight key points are utilized, alongside systematic, step-by-step guidelines. Chapters are focused and succinct. Topics are targeted for an easy understanding of the essentials of administration, scoring, interpretation, and clinical application. Theory and research are continually woven into the fabric of each book, but always to enhance clinical inference, never to sidetrack or overwhelm. We have long been advocates of "intelligent" testing—the notion that a profile of test scores is meaningless unless it is brought to life by the clinical observations and astute detective work of knowledgeable examiners. Test profiles must be used to make a difference in the child's or adult's life, or why bother to test? We want this series to help our readers become the best intelligent testers they can be.

IDEA 2004 and its attendant regulations provided our field with an opportunity to focus on the academic progress of all students, including those with specific learning disabilities (SLD). School psychologists, in particular, have moved from a wait-to-fail ability-achievement discrepancy model to a response to intervention (RTI) model for SLD identification. In adopting the latter method, the field has been encouraged by RTI proponents to give up cognitive and neuropsychological tests and, thus, ignore more than three decades of empirical research that has culminated in substantial evidence for the biological bases of learning disorders in reading, math, written language, and oral language. When RTI is applied in isolation, it fails to identify individual differences in cognitive abilities and neuropsychological processes and ignores the fact that students with SLD have different needs and learning profiles than students with undifferentiated low achievement. Most (but not all) of the distinguished contributors to this edited volume believe that without cognitive and neuropsychological testing, little can be known about the cognitive capabilities, processing strengths and weaknesses, nature of responses, and neurobiological correlates of students who fail to respond to evidence-based instruction and intervention.

This book, edited by the esteemed Dawn Flanagan and Vincent Alfonso, offers practitioners state-of-the-art information on specific learning disabilities in reading, math, writing, and oral language. The volume also provides practitioners with specific approaches for identifying SLD in the schools, including alternative research-based (or "third method") approaches, which share many common features. The alternative research-based approaches may be used within the context of an RTI service delivery model, with the goal of expanding (rather than limiting) the assessment methods and data sources that are available to practitioners. It is our belief, and the belief of the editors of this book, that when practitioners use these approaches in an informed and systematic way, they will yield information about a student's learning difficulties and educational needs that will be of value to all, but most especially, to the student with SLD.

Alan S. Kaufman, Ph.D., and Nadeen L. Kaufman, Ed.D.,
Series Editors
Yale University School of Medicine

ACKNOWLEDGMENTS

We thank Isabel Pratt, editor at John Wiley & Sons, Inc., for her encouragement and support of this project and for her assistance throughout the many phases of production. We express our appreciation to Kara Borbely, who worked diligently on countless, behind-the-scenes details necessary for publication, and Kim Nir and Janice Borzendowski for their skillful, thoughtful, and thorough copy editing of our manuscript. We are deeply indebted to Sabrina Ismailer for assisting us through every phase of this book and for often dropping everything to respond to our requests in a timely and complete manner. We also extend a heartfelt thank-you to the contributing authors, for their professionalism, scholarship, and pleasant and cooperative working style. It was a great pleasure to work with such an esteemed group of researchers and scholars! Finally, we wish to thank Alan and Nadeen Kaufman for their support, guidance, and friendship. They are not only the editors of the *Essentials of Psychological Assessment* series, but true leaders in the field. Indeed, like the majority of books in this series, the very ideas and methods espoused in this book, in one way or another, stem from and build on the decades of teaching, writing, and research Alan and Nadeen have provided practitioners the world over.

One

OVERVIEW OF SPECIFIC LEARNING DISABILITIES

Marlene Sotelo-Dynega
Dawn P. Flanagan
Vincent C. Alfonso

The purpose of this chapter is to provide a brief overview of the definitions and classification systems of and methods for identification of specific learning disabilities (SLD). Historically, children who did not perform as expected academically were evaluated and often identified as having a learning disability (LD) (Kavale & Forness, 2006). The number of children in the United States identified as having LD has tripled since the enactment of the Education for All Handicapped Children Act of 1975 (P.L. 94-142; Cortiella, 2009). This landmark legislation included criteria for the identification of exceptional learners, including children with LD, and mandated that they receive a free and appropriate public education (FAPE). Each reauthorization of P.L. 94-142 maintained its original intent, including the most recent reauthorization, the Individuals with Disabilities Education Improvement Act of 2004 (P.L. 108-446; hereafter referred to as "IDEA 2004"). Rapid Reference 1.1 highlights the most salient changes to this legislation through the present day.

The United States Department of Education (USDOE) has collected data on students who have qualified for special education services since 1975. The most current data show that 2.6 million school-aged children are classified as SLD. This figure represents nearly 4% of the approximate 66 million students currently enrolled in the nation's schools. Furthermore, of all students who have been classified with an educationally disabling condition, 43% are classified as SLD

≡ Rapid Reference 1.1

Salient Changes in Special Education Law From 1975 to 2004

1975	Education for All Handicapped Children Act (EHA) P.L. 94-142	Guaranteed school-aged (5–21 years) children with disabilities the right to a free and appropriate public education (FAPE).
1986	EHA P.L. 99-457	Extended the purpose of EHA to include children from birth to 5 years: • FAPE mandated for children ages 3–21 years. • States encouraged to develop early-intervention programs for children with disabilities from birth to 2 years.
1990	EHA renamed the Individuals with Disabilities Education Act (IDEA) P.L. 101-476	The term *handicapped child* was replaced with *child with a disability*. Autism and Traumatic Brain Injury classifications were added. Transition services for children with disabilities were mandated by age 16 years. Defined assistive technology devices and services. Required that the child with a disability be included in the general education environment, to the maximum extent possible.
1997	IDEA P.L. 105-17	Extended the Least Restrictive Environment (LRE) to ensure that *all* students would have access to the general curriculum. Schools are required to consider the inclusion of Assistive Technology Devices and Services on the Individualized Education Plans of all students. Orientation and mobility services were added to the list of related services for children who need instruction in navigating within and/or to and from their school environment.
2004	IDEA renamed the Individuals with Disabilities Education *Improvement* Act (IDEIA)[1] P.L. 108-446	Statute is aligned with the No Child Left Behind Act (NCLB) of 2001. Focus of statute is on doing what works and increasing achievement expectations for children with disabilities. Changes are made to the evaluation procedures used to identify specific learning disabilities.

[1]"IDEA" (rather than "IDEIA") is used most often to refer to the 2004 reauthorization and, therefore, will be used throughout this book.

≡ Rapid Reference 1.2

Students Ages 6–21 Years Served Under IDEA 2004

IDEA Disability Category	Percentage of All Disabilities	Percentage of Total School Enrollment
Specific Learning Disability	43.4	3.89
Speech or Language Impairment	19.2	1.72
Other Health Impairments	10.6	0.95
Mental Retardation	8.3	0.74
Emotional Disturbance	7.4	0.67
Autism	4.3	0.39
Multiple Disabilities	2.2	0.20
Developmental Delay Ages 3–9 years only	1.5	0.13
Hearing Impairments	1.2	0.11
Orthopedic Impairments	1.0	0.09
Visual Impairments	.44	0.04
Traumatic Brain Injury	.40	0.04
Deaf-Blindness	.02	0.00

Source: U.S. Department of Education, Office of Special Education Programs, Data Analysis System (DANS). Washington, DC: IES National Center for Educational Statistics. Available from http://nces.ed.gov/das.

(USDOE, Office of Special Education Programs, Data Analysis System [DANS], 2008). Rapid Reference 1.2 shows that none of the other 12 IDEA 2004 disability categories approximates the prevalence rate of SLD in the population, a trend that has been consistent since 1980 (USDOE, 2006).

A BRIEF HISTORY OF THE DEFINITION OF LEARNING DISABILITY

Definitions of LD date back to the mid to late 1800s within the fields of neurology, psychology, and education (Mather & Goldstein, 2008). The earliest recorded definitions of LD were developed by clinicians, based on their observations of individuals who experienced considerable difficulties with the acquisition of basic academic skills, despite their average or above-average general intelligence, or those who lost their ability to perform specific tasks after a brain injury that resulted from either a head trauma or stroke (Kaufman, 2008). Given that clinicians at that time did not have the necessary technology or psychometrically defensible instrumentation to test their hypotheses about brain-based LD, the medically focused study of LD stagnated, leading to the development of socially constructed, educationally focused definitions that *presumed* an underlying neurological etiology (Hale & Fiorello, 2004; Kaufman, 2008; Lyon et al., 2001).

In 1963, Samuel Kirk addressed a group of educators and parents at the *Exploration into the Problems of the Perceptually Handicapped Child* conference in Chicago, Illinois. The purposes of the conference were to (a) gather information from leading professionals from diverse fields about the problems of children who had perceptually based learning difficulties; and (b) develop a national organization that would lobby to secure services for these children. At this conference, Kirk presented a paper entitled "Learning Disabilities" that was based on his recently published book, *Educating Exceptional Children* (Kirk, 1962). In this paper, Kirk defined LD as

> a retardation, disorder, or delayed development in one or more of the processes of speech, language, reading, writing, arithmetic, or other school subjects resulting from a psychological handicap caused by a possible cerebral dysfunction and/or emotional or behavioral disturbances. It is not the result of mental retardation, sensory deprivation, or cultural and instructional factors. (p. 263)

Not only did the conference participants accept Kirk's term *LD* and corresponding definition, but they formed an organization that is now known as the Learning Disabilities Association of America (LDA). The LDA continues to influence the "frameworks for legislation, theories, diagnostic procedures, educational practices, research and training models" as they pertain to identifying and educating individuals with LD (LDA, n.d., ¶ 2).

Kirk's conceptualization of LD influenced other organizations' definitions of LD, including the Council for Exceptional Children (CEC), as well as federal legislation (e.g., P.L. 94-142). In addition, 11 different definitions of LD in use between 1982 and 1989 contained aspects of Kirk's 1962 definition. Therefore, it is not surprising that a comprehensive review of these definitions revealed more agreement than disagreement about the construct of LD (Hammill, 1990). Interestingly, none of the definitions strongly influenced developments in LD identification, mainly because they tended to focus on conceptual rather than operational elements, and focused more on exclusionary rather than inclusionary criteria. Rapid Reference 1.3 illustrates the salient features of the most common definitions of LD that were proposed by national and international organizations and LD researchers, beginning with Kirk's 1962 definition. The majority of definitions depict LD as a neurologically based disorder or a disorder in psychological processing that causes learning problems and manifests as academic skill weaknesses. In addition, most definitions indicate that LD may co-occur with other disabilities.

Although the definitions of LD included in Rapid Reference 1.3 vary in terms of their inclusion of certain features (e.g., average or better intelligence, evident across the life span), the most widely used definition is the one included in IDEA 2004 (Cortiella, 2009). Unlike other definitions, the IDEA 2004 definition refers to a *specific* learning disability, implying that the disability or disorder affects specific academic skills or domains. According to IDEA 2004, SLD is defined as follows:

> The term "specific learning disability" means a disorder in one or more of the basic psychological processes involved in understanding or in using language, spoken or written, which may manifest itself in the imperfect ability to listen, think, speak, read, spell, or do mathematical calculations. Such a term includes such conditions as perceptual disabilities, brain injury, minimal brain dysfunction, dyslexia, and developmental aphasia. Such a term does not include a learning problem that is primarily the result of visual, hearing, or motor disabilities; of mental retardation; of emotional disturbance; or of environmental, cultural, or economic disadvantage. (IDEA 2004, § 602.30, Definitions)

Because definitions of LD do not explicitly guide how a condition is identified or diagnosed, classification systems of LD were developed. Three of the most frequently used classification systems for LD are described next.

CLASSIFICATION SYSTEMS FOR LD

"Classification criteria are the rules that are applied to determine if individuals are eligible for a particular diagnosis" (Reschly, Hosp, & Schmied, 2003, p. 2). Although the evaluation of LD in school-aged children is guided by the mandate of IDEA 2004 and its attendant regulations, diagnostic

CAUTION

....

Because the three major classification systems use somewhat vague and ambiguous terms, it is difficult to identify SLD reliably and validly. Thus, multiple data sources and data-gathering methods must be used to ensure that children are diagnosed accurately.

Salient Features of Learning Disability Definitions

Source		Salient Features of LD Definitions								
	Ability-Achievement Discrepancy	Average or Above Average Intelligence	Neurological Basis	Disorder in a Psychological Process	Evident Across the Life Span	Listening and Speaking	Academic Problems	Conceptual Problems	Non-academic, language, or conceptual disorders as LD	Potential for Multiple Disabilities
Samuel Kirk (1962)	—	✓	✓	✓	✓	✓	✓	—	✓	✓
Barbara Bateman (1965)	✓	—	✓	✓	—	—	✓	—	—	✓
National Advisory Committee on Handicapped Children (1968)	—	—	✓	✓	—	✓	✓	✓	—	✓
Northwestern University (1969)	✓	—	—	✓	—	✓	✓	—	✓	✓
Council for Exceptional Children, Division for Children with Learning Disabilities (Late 1960s)	—	✓	✓	✓	—	✓	—	—	—	—
Joseph Wepman (1975)	—	—	—	✓	—	—	✓	—	—	—
	✓	—	—	✓	—	✓	✓	—	—	✓

Definition							
Education for All Handicapped Children Act (1975)	—	✓	✓	✓	✓	✓	✓
U.S. Office of Education (1977)	—	✓	✓	✓	✓	✓	✓
National Joint Committee on Learning Disabilities (1981)	—	✓	—	✓	✓	✓	—
Learning Disabilities Association of America (1986)	—	✓	✓	✓	✓	✓	✓
Interagency Committee on Learning Disabilities (1987)	—	✓	—	✓	✓	✓	✓
Individuals with Disabilities Education Act (1986, 1990, 1997, 2004)	—	✓	✓	✓	✓	✓	✓
National Joint Committee on Learning Disabilities (1990)	—	✓	—	✓	✓	✓	—
Kavale, Spaulding, and Beam (2009)	✓	✓	✓	✓	✓	✓	✓

Source: Adapted from Hammill (1990). On defining learning disabilities: An emerging consensus. *Journal of Learning Disabilities, 23,* 74–84.

criteria for LD are also included in the *Diagnostic and Statistical Manual of Mental Disorders, Fourth Edition, Text Revision (DSM-IV-TR;* American Psychiatric Association, 2000), and the *International Classification of Diseases* (ICD-10; World Health Organization, 2006). Rapid Reference 1.4 includes the type of learning disorders and classification criteria for LD in each system. Noteworthy is the fact that all three systems use somewhat vague and ambiguous terms, which interfere significantly with the efforts of practitioners to identify LD reliably and validly (Kavale & Forness, 2000, 2006).

Despite the existence of various classification systems, students ages 3 to 21 years who experience learning difficulties in school are most typically evaluated according to IDEA 2004 specifications (IDEA 2004, § 614) to determine if they qualify for special education services. Because the classification category of SLD as described in the IDEA statute includes imprecise terms, the USDOE published the Federal Regulations (34 CFR, Part 300) with the intent of clarifying the statute and providing guidance to State Educational Agencies (SEA) as they worked to develop their own regulations. The guidelines provided by the 2006 Federal Regulations were more detailed in their specifications of *how* an SLD should be identified.

METHODS OF SLD IDENTIFICATION AND THE 2006 FEDERAL REGULATIONS

Although the definition of SLD has remained virtually the same for the past 30 years, the methodology used to identify SLD changed recently. According to the 2006 Federal Regulations (34 CFR § 300.307–309), a state must adopt criteria for determining that a child has SLD; the criteria (a) must not require the use of a severe discrepancy between intellectual ability and achievement; (b) must permit the use of a process based on a child's response to scientific, research-based interventions; and (c) may permit the use of other alternative research-based procedures for determining whether a child has SLD. Many controversies have ensued since the publication of the three options for SLD identification. The controversies have been written about extensively as they pertain to the exact meaning of the guidelines, the specifications of a comprehensive evaluation, the implications of using response to intervention (RTI) as the sole method for SLD identification, and the lack of legal knowledge among decision makers and, therefore, will not be repeated here (see Fletcher, Barth, & Stuebing, this volume; Gresham, Restori, & Cook, 2008; Kavale, Kauffman, Bachmeier, & LeFever, 2008; Reschly et al., 2003; Reynolds & Shaywitz, 2009a, 2009b; Zirkel & Thomas, 2010 for a summary). The remainder of this chapter focuses on clarifying the three options for SLD identification, as these three options are currently being implemented across states (see Rapid Reference 1.5).

Rapid Reference 1.4

Three Frequently Used Diagnostic Classification Systems for Learning Disability

Classification System	Types of Learning Disorder	Examples of Classification Criteria[1]
Diagnostic and Statistical Manual of Mental Disorders, Fourth Edition, Text Revision (DSM-IV-TR, 2000)	Reading Disorder Mathematics Disorder Written Expression Disorder Learning Disorder NOS	Mathematics Disorder: A. Mathematical ability, as measured by individually administered standardized tests, is substantially below that expected, given the person's chronological age, measured intelligence, and age-appropriate education. B. The disturbance in Criterion A significantly interferes with academic achievement or activities of daily living that require mathematical ability. C. If a sensory deficit is present, the difficulties in mathematical ability are in excess of those usually associated with it. D. Must be differentiated from: normal variations in academic attainment, lack of opportunity, poor teaching, cultural factors, impaired vision and/or hearing, and mental retardation.
International Classification of Diseases (ICD-10, 2006)	Specific Reading Disorder Specific Spelling Disorder Specific Disorder of Arithmetical Skills Mixed Disorder of Scholastic Skills	Specific Reading Disorder: • A specific and significant impairment in the development of reading skills that is not solely accounted for by mental age, visual acuity problems, or inadequate schooling. • Reading comprehension skill, reading word recognition, oral reading skill, and performance of tasks requiring reading may all be affected.

(continued)

Classification System	Types of Learning Disorder	Examples of Classification Criteria[1]
	Other Developmental Disorders of Scholastic Skills Developmental Disorder of Scholastic Skills, Unspecified	• Spelling difficulties are frequently associated with specific reading disorder and commonly remain into adolescence even after some progress in reading has been made. • Specific developmental disorders of reading are commonly preceded by a history of disorders in speech or language development. • Associated emotional and behavioral disturbances are common during the school-age period. • Includes: Backward reading, developmental dyslexia, specific reading retardation. • Excludes: Alexia, dyslexia NOS, reading difficulties secondary to emotional distress.
Individuals with Disabilities Education Improvement Act (IDEA, 2004)	Specific Learning Disability in: Oral Expression Listening Comprehension Written Expression Basic Reading Skill Reading Fluency Reading Comprehension Mathematics Calculation Mathematics Problem Solving	Specific Learning Disability: 1. A disorder in one or more of the basic psychological processes. 2. Includes such conditions as perceptual disabilities, brain injury, minimal brain dysfunction, dyslexia, and developmental aphasia. 3. Learning difficulties must not be primarily the result of: • A visual, hearing, or motor disability • Mental retardation • Emotional disturbance • Cultural factors • Environmental or economic disadvantage • Limited English proficiency

[1] For the *DSM-IV-TR* and ICD-10 diagnostic classification systems, there are specific criteria for each disorder that are listed in the second column of this rapid reference. Criteria for only one of these disorders are included in this (third) column to serve as an example.

≣ Rapid Reference 1.5

National Investigation of State Education Agencies (Zirkel & Thomas, 2010)

- Surveyed the 51 State Education Agencies (including Washington, DC) to determine which of the three options included in the 2006 Federal Regulations was selected for SLD identification.
- The **severe discrepancy** approach remains viable, rather than prohibited, in the vast majority of states, with the choice delegated to the local district level.
- Twelve states have adopted **RTI** as the required approach for SLD identification, with seven states allowing the addition of a severe discrepancy and/or an alternative research-based approach.
- Twenty states appear to permit the **third option** or a research-based alternative.

Note. For state-by-state details regarding SLD eligibility determination, see Zirkel and Thomas (2010; Table 1, pp. 59–61).

Ability-Achievement Discrepancy

A discrepancy between intellectual ability and academic achievement continues, in one form or another, to be central to many SLD identification approaches because it assists in operationally defining *unexpected underachievement* (e.g., Kavale & Flanagan, 2007; Kavale & Forness, 1995; Lyon et al., 2001; Wiederholt, 1974; Zirkel & Thomas, 2010). Despite being a laudable attempt at an empirically based method of SLD identification, the traditional ability-achievement (or IQ-achievement) discrepancy method was fraught with problems (e.g., Aaron, 1997; Ceci, 1990, 1996; Siegel, 1999; Stanovich, 1988; Sternberg & Grigorenko, 2002; Stuebing et al., 2002), many of which are bulleted in Rapid Reference 1.6. The failure of the ability-achievement discrepancy method to identify SLD reliably and validly was summarized well by Ysseldyke (2005), who stated,

> Professional associations, advocacy groups, and government agencies have formed task forces and task forces on the task forces to study identification of students with LD. We have had mega-analyses of meta-analyses and syntheses of syntheses. Nearly all groups have reached the same conclusion: There is little empirical support for test-based discrepancy models in identification of students as LD. (p. 125)

≡ *Rapid Reference 1.6*
....

Salient Problems With the Ability-Achievement Discrepancy Method

- Fails to adequately differentiate between students with LD from students who are low achievers.
- Based on the erroneous assumption that IQ is a near-perfect predictor of achievement and is synonymous with an individual's potential.
- Applied inconsistently across states, districts, and schools, rendering the diagnosis arbitrary and capricious.
- A discrepancy between ability and achievement may be statistically significant, but not clinically relevant.
- Is a wait-to-fail method because discrepancies between ability and achievement typically are not evident until the child has reached the 3rd or 4th grade.
- Does not identify the area of processing deficit.
- Leads to overidentification of minority students.
- Does not inform intervention.

Thus, the fact that states could no longer require the use of a severe discrepancy between intellectual ability and achievement (IDEA 2004) was viewed by many as a welcomed change to the law. The void left by the elimination of the discrepancy mandate was filled by a method that allowed states to use a process based on a child's response to intervention to assist in SLD identification.

Response to Intervention (RTI)

The concept of RTI grew out of concerns about how SLD is identified. For example, traditional methods of SLD identification, mainly ability-achievement discrepancy, were applied inconsistently across states and often led to misidentification of students, as well as overidentification of minority students (e.g., Bradley, Danielson, & Hallahan, 2002; Learning Disabilities Roundtable, 2005; President's Commission on Excellence in Special Education, 2002). Such difficulties with

DON'T FORGET
....
Although RTI may be permitted under IDEA 2004, the driving force behind promoting RTI is found in No Child Left Behind (NCLB; 2001) legislation (PL 107-110).

traditional methods led to a "paradigm shift" (Reschly, 2004) that was based on the concept of *treatment validity*, "whereby it is possible 'to simultaneously inform, foster, and document the necessity for and effectiveness of special treatment' (L. S. Fuchs & D. Fuchs, 1998)."

At the most general level, RTI is a multitiered approach to the early identification of students with academic or behavioral difficulties. For the purpose of this chapter, we focus on RTI for academic difficulties only. The RTI process begins with the provision of quality instruction for all students in the general education classroom, along with universal screening to identify students who are at risk for academic failure, primarily in the area of reading (Tier I). Students who are at risk for reading failure—that is, those who have not benefitted from the instruction provided to all students in the classroom—are then given scientifically based interventions, usually following a standard treatment protocol (Tier II). If a student does not respond as expected to the intervention provided at Tier II, he or she may be identified as a *nonresponder* and selected to receive additional and more intensive interventions in an attempt to increase his or her rate of learning. When one type of intervention does not appear to result in gains for the student, a new intervention is provided until the desired response is achieved.

The inclusion of RTI in the law as an allowable option for SLD identification has created perhaps the most controversy since IDEA was reauthorized in 2004. This is because, in districts that follow an RTI-*only* approach, students who repeatedly fail to demonstrate an adequate response to increasingly intensive interventions are deemed to have SLD *by default*. Such an approach does not appear to be in compliance with the regulations. For example, according to the regulations, states must (a) use a variety of assessment tools and strategies to gather relevant functional, developmental, and academic information (34 CFR § 300.304[b][1]); (b) not use any single measure or assessment as the sole criterion for determining whether a child has a disability (34 CFR § 300.304[b][2]); (c) use technically sound instruments that may assess the relative contribution of cognitive and behavioral factors, in addition to physical or developmental factors (34 CFR § 300.304[b][3]); (d) assess the child in all areas related to the suspected disability (34 CFR § 300.304[c][4]); (e) ensure that the evaluation is sufficiently comprehensive to identify all of the child's special education and related services needs (34 CFR § 300.304[c][6]); and (f) ensure that assessment tools and strategies provide relevant information that directly assists persons in determining the needs of the child (34 CFR § 300.304[c][7]).

Although the use of RTI as a standalone method for SLD identification is inconsistent with the intent of the law, this type of service delivery model has been an influential force in the schools in recent years, particularly with respect to shaping Tier I and Tier II assessments for intervention in the general education setting. The emphasis in an RTI model on ensuring that students are benefitting from empirically based instruction and verifying their response to instruction, via a systematic collection of data, has elevated screening and progress monitoring procedures to new heights and has led many to embrace this type of service delivery model for the purposes of both prevention and remediation. In essence, RTI serves to improve accountability through data demonstrating whether or not learning has improved and sufficient progress has been made. Rapid Reference 1.7 highlights some of the most salient strengths and weaknesses of the RTI service delivery model regarding its use in the SLD identification process.

 *Rapid Reference 1.7*

Strengths and Weaknesses of RTI

Salient Weaknesses of RTI as a Standalone Method of SLD Identification	Salient Strengths of an RTI Service Delivery Model
• Lack of research on which RTI model works best, standard treatment protocol or problem-solving model, or under what circumstances each model should be used	• Focus is on the provision of more effective instruction
• Lack of agreement on which curricula, instructional methods, or measurement tools should be used	• Allows schools to intervene early to meet the needs of struggling learners
• Confusion surrounding what constitutes an empirically based approach	• Collected data better informs instruction than data generated by traditional ability-achievement discrepancy method
• Lack of agreement on which methods work across grades and academic content areas	• Helps ensure that the student's poor academic performance is not due to poor instruction
• Different methods of response/nonresponse, leading to different children being labeled as responders/nonresponders	• Holds educators accountable for documenting repeated assessments of students' achievement and progress during instruction
• No consensus on how to ensure treatment integrity	
• No indication of a true positive (SLD identification) in an RTI model	

Source: Learning Disabilities Association of America, White Paper (Hale et al., 2010).

Alternative Research-Based Procedures for SLD Identification

The third option included in the 2006 regulations allows "the use of other alternative research-based procedures" for determining SLD (§ 300.307[a]). Although vague, this option has been interpreted by some as involving the evaluation of a "pattern of strengths and weaknesses" in the identification of SLD via tests of academic achievement, cognitive abilities, and neuro-psychological processes (Hale et al., 2008, 2010; Zirkel & Thomas, 2010). Several empirically based methods of SLD identification that are consistent with the third option are presented in this book, such as Berninger's framework of assessment for intervention (Chapter 9), Flanagan and colleagues' operational definition of SLD (Chapter 10), Hale and Fiorello's Concordance-Discordance Model (Chapter 8), and Naglieri's Discrepancy/Consistency Model (Chapter 7). Readers may also be interested in the Response to the Right Intervention (RTRI) model proposed by Della Toffalo (2010).

Figure 1.1 provides an illustration of the three common components of third-method approaches to SLD identification (Flanagan, Fiorello, & Ortiz, 2010; Hale et al., 2008). The two bottom ovals depict academic and cognitive weaknesses, and their horizontal alignment indicates that the level of performance in

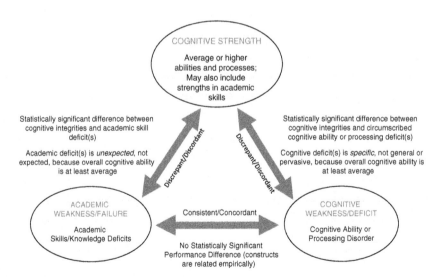

Figure 1.1. Common Components of Third-Method Approaches to SLD Identification

Source: Flanagan, Fiorello, and Ortiz (2010); Hale, Flanagan, and Naglieri (2008).

both domains (academic and cognitive) is expected to be similar or consistent. The double-headed arrow between the bottom two ovals indicates that the difference between measured performances in the weak academic area(s) is not significantly different from performance in the weak cognitive area(s). Again, in children with SLD there exists an empirical or otherwise clearly observable and meaningful relationship between the academic and cognitive deficits, as the cognitive deficit is the presumed cause of the academic deficit. The oval depicted at the top of Figure 1.1 represents generally average (or better) cognitive or intellectual ability. The double-headed arrows between the top oval and the two bottom ovals in the figure indicate the presence of a statistically significant or clinically meaningful difference in measured performance between general cognitive ability and the areas of academic and cognitive weakness. The pattern of cognitive and academic strengths and weaknesses represented in Figure 1.1 retains and reflects the concept of unexpected underachievement that has historically been synonymous with the SLD construct (Kavale & Forness, 2000).

CONCLUSION

In this chapter we reviewed briefly the prevailing definitions, diagnostic classification systems, and methods of identifying LD. The federal definition of SLD has remained virtually the same for the past 30 years, and SLD remains the most frequently diagnosed educationally disabling condition in our nation's schools. Despite no change in the definition of SLD in the most recent reauthorization of IDEA, the methods for identifying SLD, as per the 2006 Federal Regulations, have changed. For example, ability-achievement discrepancy can no longer be mandated, although it remains a viable option in the majority of states. RTI has been adopted by several states as the required approach for SLD identification, despite the fact that using this method alone is inconsistent with the federal law. Third-option or research-based alternatives to SLD identification are permitted in more than 20 states throughout the country and hold promise for identifying SLD in more reliable and valid ways than was achieved via previous methods (e.g., the traditional ability-achievement discrepancy method).

The remainder of this book addresses in greater detail the topics discussed briefly in this chapter. For example, Chapters 2 through 5 provide in-depth coverage of how SLD manifests in reading, math, writing, and oral language. Chapters 6 through 10 include discussions of RTI and several third-method approaches for SLD identification. Finally, Chapter 11 describes how practitioners can distinguish cultural and linguistic differences from SLD in the evaluation of English Language Learners. The confusion that has surrounded methods of SLD identification for many years, along with the obvious disconnect between the definition of SLD and the most typical methods of identifying it, continue to spark controversy. The chapters that follow, written by leading experts in the field, have the potential to shape future reauthorizations of IDEA and bring greater clarity to both the definition of and methods for identifying SLD.

RESOURCES

Council for Exceptional Children: www.cec.sped.org This Web site provides professional development resources, including a blog on response to intervention and a side-by-side comparison of the IDEA regulations and information about how the changes will impact students and teachers.

IDEA 2004: http://idea.ed.gov Statutes, regulations, and other documents related to IDEA 2004 are found here.

IDEA Partnership: www.ideapartnership.org This Web site offers resources developed by the IDEA Partnership (a collaboration of more than 55 national organizations, technical assistance providers, and organizations and agencies at state and local levels) and the Office of Special Education Programs (OSEP).

LD Online: www.ldonline.org This Web site provides comprehensive information about learning disabilities and ADHD, with valuable resources for parents, educators, and students.

National Association of School Psychologists (NASP): www.nasponline .org/about_nasp/positionpapers/SLDPosition_2007.pdf This is a position statement on the identification of students with specific learning disabilities (adopted in July 2007).

National Association of State Directors of Special Education (NASDSE): www.nasdse.org This is the official Web site of the NASDSE, with up-to-date information about projects and initiatives related to RTI, charter schools, and the IDEA Partnership.

National Center for Learning Disabilities: www.ld.org The NCLD works to ensure that the nation's 15 million children, adolescents, and adults with learning disabilities have every opportunity to succeed in school, work, and life.

National Center on Response to Intervention: www.rti4success.org The center provides technical assistance to states and districts and builds the capacity of states to assist districts in implementing proven models for RTI/EIS.

National Dissemination Center for Children with Disabilities (NICHCY): www.nichcy.org/resources/IDEA2004resources.asp NICHCY serves as a central source of information on IDEA 2004. It also provides a list of resources by state. See www.nichcy.org/states .htm.

National Early Childhood Technical Assistance Center: www.nectac .org/sec619/stateregs.asp This page provides links to state regulations and other policy documents (statutes, procedures, and guidance materials) for implementing Part B of IDEA.

National Joint Committee on Learning Disabilities (NJCLD): www .ldonline.org/njcld This Web site describes the mission of the NJCLD and its member organizations. It provides research articles and contact information for associations that offer assistance to individuals with SLD.

National Resource Center on Learning Disabilities (NRCLD): www .nrcld.org This Web site provides resources for educators and parents, including a toolkit on using response to intervention in SLD determination.

RTI Action Network: www.rtinetwork.org A Web site dedicated to the effective implementation of RTI in districts nationwide.

State Advisory Panels

Each state has a special education advisory panel that provides the state's Department of Education with guidance about special education and related services for children with disabilities. Check your own state's Department of Education Web site for specific information about your area.

U.S. Department of Education (USDOE): www.ed.gov This is the homepage of the USDOE, which provides current information about education policies and initiatives in the United States.

What Works Clearinghouse, Institute of Education Sciences: http:// ies.ed.gov.ncee/wwc This Web site offers scientific evidence about best practices in education.

 **TEST YOURSELF**

....

1. The number of children identified with **SLD** has doubled since the enactment of **P.L. 94-142 in 1975. True or False?**

2. Historically, definitions of LD have strongly influenced how we have identified LD. **True or False?**

3. In the public schools, **SLD** is identified primarily by the following:

   (a) DSM-IV criteria

   (b) IDEA and its attendant regulations

   (c) ICD-10

   (d) All of the above

4. According to the 2006 Federal Regulations, a district *must not require* use of the following procedure to identify **SLD:**

   (a) Response to intervention (RTI) process

   (b) Ability-achievement discrepancy model

   (c) Alternative research-based procedures

   (d) Psychoeducational assessments

5. Response to intervention has not been validated as a method for **SLD** identification. **True or False?**

6. Which of the following is not a salient strength of RTI:

   (a) Focus is on the provision of more effective instruction.

   (b) Allows schools to intervene early to meet the needs of struggling learners.

   (c) Collected data better informs instruction than data generated by traditional ability-achievement discrepancy method.

   (d) A true positive (SLD identification) is evident in an RTI model.

7. The number of states that appear to permit the third option, or a research-based alternative to **SLD** identification, is

   (a) 5.

   (b) 10.

   (c) 15.

   (d) 20.

8. **SLD** has an underlying neurological etiology. **True or False?**

9. According to **IDEA 2004**, a child may have **SLD** in any of the following except

   (a) written expression.

   (b) reading fluency skills.

   (c) mathematics calculation.

   (d) spelling.

10. A child can have an **SLD** in only one academic area. **True or False?**

Answers: 1. False; 2. False; 3. b; 4. b; 5. True; 6. d; 7. d; 8. True; 9. d; 10. False.

Two

HOW SLD MANIFESTS IN READING

Steven Feifer

DEFINING READING DISABILITY

The conceptualization of the term *learning disabled* (LD) has been at the forefront of school psychological debate, research, and practice since its inception as an educationally handicapping condition. Clearly, there has been a lack of sufficient clarity inherent within this overarching term, forcing scholars, practitioners, educational institutions, and public policy makers to craft their own interpretations and measurement techniques to best encapsulate the spirit of this disability. Today, there is little disagreement that learning disabilities represent an array of heterogeneous skill deficits in various academic domains such as reading, mathematics, written expression, and oral language. Nevertheless, most school systems have adopted inconsistent explanations and rather ill-conceived notions of how to define operationally, measure reliably, and intervene productively with children who manifest a learning disability in school. According to the United States Department of Education (2006), approximately 80% of students identified as having a learning disability primarily have deficits with reading skills. Consequently, most educational research has focused solely on reading disabilities, or what some refer to as *developmental dyslexia,* and delineated the disorder by using strict cut-points to classify students as either having or not having a disability (Fletcher, Lyon, Fuchs, & Barnes, 2007). Therefore, students with reading disabilities

> **DON'T FORGET**
> ····································
> Approximately 80% of students identified as having a learning disability have deficits in reading skills.

are viewed from a rather binary perch, with only those students manifesting a disability being eligible for support and accommodations through an Individual Education Plan (IEP).

The literature has been rife with numerous theoretical attempts and, at times, faulty conceptual notions to identify and measure underlying reading disabilities in children accurately. For instance, the *discrepancy model* had been the long-standing method that school systems have adopted to assist in identifying students with a specific learning disability (SLD). This method involves assessing academic achievement in one or more major curricular areas, such as reading, math, or written language, and determining whether or not the student's achievement is significantly discrepant from his or her overall intelligence. The discrepancy model does not focus on specific neurocognitive processes inherent in reading, but rather on more global attributes of cognition and achievement. The underlying assumption is that children with reading disabilities have the intellectual wherewithal to acquire functional reading skills, but are underachieving in school due to an inherent disability with learning.

There have been numerous shortcomings associated with the discrepancy model, including overreliance on a Full Scale IQ to capture the dynamic properties of an individual's reasoning skills (Hale & Fiorello, 2004) and the lack of agreement on the magnitude of the discrepancy at various ages and grades (Feifer & DeFina, 2000). According to Kavale and Forness (2000), nearly 50% of students classified as having a learning disability *do not* demonstrate a significant discrepancy between aptitude and achievement, due in part to the statistical imprecision of this method. Perhaps the most notable shortcoming of the discrepancy model was that it resulted in a wait-to-fail scenario, whereby students were forced to display a certain level of reading failure in order to qualify for special education services. This was especially at odds with the National Reading Panel's (2000) conclusion highlighting the importance of early intervention services for children with reading difficulties. Simply put, the discrepancy model propagates an age-old educational myth that views reading disabilities along a one-dimensional continuum between those students with the disability and those without.

According to Reynolds (2007), the biological basis of learning disabilities has been demonstrated through various neuropsychological studies of brain functioning, with various subtypes and precise diagnostic markers clearly emerging. Therefore, creating artificial cut-points through ability-achievement discrepancy models as the sole basis for identifying a learning disability merely denies students—most notably, students with lower IQs—from receiving special education support and services. As Goldberg (2001) noted, human cognition is a multidimensional phenomenon distributed throughout the cortex in a continuous and gradiential fashion, not in a linear and modular one. Hence, there are degrees of differences in learning and cognition, which must be explored through a multidimensional survey of brain functions, as opposed to simply contriving artificial cut-points in a distribution of achievement test scores. The fact remains that LD still has not been quantified with much exactitude, leaving Kavale and Forness (2000) to conclude that an operational definition of LD remains as elusive as ever, despite the neuropsychological literature providing a much more sophisticated and substantiated view of the cognitive processes involved in learning. Notwithstanding, there has been substantial movement in crafting a more operational definition of LD, which is delineated in subsequent chapters of this book (e.g., Naglieri, Chapter 7; Hale, Wycoff, and Fiorello, Chapter 8; Flanagan, Alfonso, and Mascolo, Chapter 10). Subsequent to the 2004 reauthorization of IDEA, states are no longer allowed to *require* school districts to use a discrepancy between IQ and achievement as being a necessary condition to identify students as having a reading disability. Among the many provisions in this law, states were finally allowed to opt out of using a discrepancy model to identify reading disabilities, and replace it by using a response to intervention (RTI) model. In other words, rather than comparing a student's overall intelligence with a nationally normed test of reading achievement to determine the presence of an educational disability, school districts were given the flexibility to craft a policy whereby, as part of a comprehensive evaluation, students who do not respond to evidence-based early reading programs may be considered eligible for special education services.

RTI is not new. It has been in use primarily as a schoolwide prevention program within various districts for several decades. What is new, however, is RTI's explicit support in federal special education law as a viable alternative to less effective traditional models of determining student eligibility for special education services (Canter, 2006). RTI has enjoyed considerable support, especially from such organizations as the National Association of School Psychologists (NASP), because it circumvents many of the shortcomings of the traditional discrepancy model. Additionally, RTI emphasizes the use of evidence-based approaches to instruction in hopes of eliminating academic problems that are frequently due to deficient curricula or poor instructional methodologies. In other words, the focus of RTI is more curriculum-centered than child-centered, with student underachievement in a core academic subject presumably due to poor instructional practices and implementation of inappropriate interventions. In summary, RTI refers to an expansive array of procedures that can be used in conjunction with a comprehensive evaluation to determine eligibility and need for special education services within a problem-solving model (Feifer & Della Toffalo, 2007).

There remains an inordinate amount of confusion regarding just how far the tentacles of RTI can stretch with respect to the identification of a specific reading disability. According to Reynolds (2007), a disability is recognized as constituting a particular condition residing intrinsically *within* the child, whereas RTI models focus more on extrinsic factors highlighting *child-school* interactions. In essence, RTI is more of a service delivery model, and not necessarily a diagnostic methodology to determine a specific reading disability. Though curriculum-based measurement (CBM) techniques are highlighted in most RTI models, and can be extremely useful in assisting educators to monitor progress effectively, CBM as a standalone measure is not sufficient to determine the presence of a disability. Consequently, the National Joint Committee on Learning Disabilities (NJCLD; 2005) concluded that using CBM within a core RTI framework in the absence of additional data is an insufficient means to diagnose a reading disability.

> ## DON'T FORGET
> ....
> CBM data alone cannot be used to diagnose a reading disability, even when gathered within an RTI service delivery model. A diagnosis of reading disability must be based on multiple data sources.

THE ROLE OF NEUROPSYCHOLOGY IN IDENTIFYING READING DISABILITIES

As Moats (2004) succinctly noted, conceptions of reading instruction, reading development, and, ultimately, the identification of a specific reading disability should take their lead from the neurosciences. In essence, cognitive neuropsychology may provide the best scientific rationale for the selection, implementation, and monitoring of reading programs designed to meet the needs of children who manifest early reading difficulty.

Current research in neuropsychology has revealed a number of important insights with respect to the neural underpinnings of literacy, and has begun to forge an alliance with educational research to develop a unifying theory of dyslexia. For instance, there are certain universal truths as to how the human brain acquires linguistic codes pertaining to reading. First, in all word languages studied to date, children with developmental reading disabilities (dyslexia) primarily have difficulties in both recognizing and manipulating phonological units at all linguistic levels (Goswami, 2007). Second, children of all languages initially become aware of larger acoustical units within the words themselves, such as syllable, onset, and rhyme. However, in a complex language such as

English, when one letter may map to as many as five distinct phonemes or sounds, English-speaking children tend to develop phonemic awareness more slowly than children in more phonologically consistent languages such as Spanish or Italian (Goswami). Last, specific neuroimaging techniques have demonstrated that phonological processing is a by-product of the functional integrity of the *temporal-parietal* junctures in the left hemisphere of the brain (McCandliss & Noble, 2003; Pugh et al., 2000; Sandak et al., 2004; Shaywitz, 2004). Most individuals with dyslexia have difficulty with phonological processing, which may indeed stem from disorganization of white-matter tracts connecting the temporal-parietal regions with other cortical areas involved in the reading process (Temple, 2002). In fact, Ramus (2004) suggested that microlesions in the perisylvan cortex along the left temporal regions are primarily responsible for phonological processing, and may be the primary cause of most reading disabilities.

Notwithstanding, not all children with reading disabilities suffer from the same types of deficits with respect to phonological processing disorders, or profit equally from all remediation techniques (Ramus, 2003). For instance, research studies have indicated that approximately one-third of all students will not make sufficient progress using Reading Recovery, though approximately two-thirds of low-achieving children will be able to return to regular reading groups in their classroom (Deford, Lyons, & Pinnell, 1991). Therefore, the question begs as to whether or not Reading Recovery would be considered an evidenced-based intervention. In essence, most reading interventions have some children who profit from them and others who do not. Therefore, another question looms even larger for both educators and psychologists alike; namely, is it possible to unravel different subtypes of reading disability based on certain neurocognitive differences in the brain in order to target more effective remediation strategies to assist *all* children who struggle with reading?

CAUTION

There is an inordinate amount of confusion regarding how far the tentacles of RTI can stretch with respect to the identification of a specific reading disability, because RTI is more of a service delivery model, and not necessarily a diagnostic methodology to determine a specific reading disability.

DON'T FORGET

Approximately one-third of all students will not make sufficient progress in Reading Recovery. More effective remediation strategies for these children may follow from an understanding of their neurocognitive differences, as may be garnered via a comprehensive cognitive or neuropsychological evaluation.

SUBTYPES OF READING DISABILITIES

The literature is rife with classification schemes purported to subdivide readers into various categories, and, to date, there have been differing opinions as to the most efficacious manner to catalog reading deficits (Heim et al., 2008). Nevertheless, there has been little disagreement among cognitive neuropsychologists that reading disabilities reflect the relative contribution, or lack thereof, of different cognitive processes in the brain. For instance, Heim et al. proposed three distinct subtypes of reading disabilities, one consisting mainly of phonological awareness deficits, a second consisting of poor visual attention deficits, and a third involving multiple cognitive deficits with both phonological awareness and visual perceptual deficits. Still other studies have shown even greater patterns of reading deficits manifesting from underlying neurocognitive processing deficits. For instance, Morris et al. (1998) identified seven clusters of reading disabilities based on phonological processing deficits in combination with rapid and automatic naming skills. King, Giess, and Lombardina (2007) found four specific subgroups of dyslexia based again on a combination of rapid naming tasks and phonological awareness, while Lachmann, Berti, Kujala, and Schroger (2005) divided reading deficits into two subgroups based on accurate word and nonword reading skills. Finally, Ho, Chan, Lee, Tsang, and Luan (2004) examined Chinese students with reading disabilities and noted deficiencies based on a combination of phonological memory skills, rapid naming skills, orthographic processing skills, and/or global deficiencies in all skills. In summary, most neuropsychological research is beginning to reconceptualize dyslexia as not being a unique entity, but rather a manifestation of a variety of neurocognitive pathologies (Pernet, Poline, Demonet, & Rousselet, 2009).

Due to the diversity and range of subtypes of reading-related deficits, reading disabilities most likely have a multifocal origin within the brain. In fact, most genetic-based studies of dyslexia have implicated an assortment of brain abnormalities. For instance, Grigorenko (2007) noted there were nine candidate chromosomal regions involved in developmental dyslexia, abbreviated as chromosomes 15q, 6p, 2p, 6q, 3cen, 18p, 11p, 1p, and Xq. Pernet et al. (2009) also cited genetic studies revealing multiple loci for chromosomal abnormalities in the dyslexic brain, specifically implicating chromosomes 16, 6, and 2. These genetic studies are suggestive of a multifactorial origin of dyslexia and provide a theoretical framework for specific subtypes of reading disabilities (Pernet et al.). In essence, each of these genetic transcriptions lays down the bylaws for the subsequent development and overall functional integrity of the reading brain. According to Cao, Bitan, and Booth (2008), reading disabilities ultimately derive

Dyslexia

≡ *Rapid Reference 2.1*

Four Subtypes of Reading Disorders

1. *Dysphonetic dyslexia:* Difficulty sounding out words in a phonological manner.
2. *Surface dyslexia:* Difficulty with the rapid and automatic recognition of words in print.
3. *Mixed dyslexia:* Multiple reading deficits characterized by impaired phonological and orthographic processing skills. This is probably the most severe form of dyslexia.
4. *Comprehension deficits:* The mechanical side of reading is fine but difficulty persists deriving meaning from print.

from faulty genetic transcriptions, which distort the functional connectivity within various sites of the reading brain. Feifer and Della Toffalo (2007) have summarized four general subtypes of dyslexia stemming primarily from the contribution of multiple brain regions and the functional interplay of each. These subtypes are defined in Rapid Reference 2.1.

The first reading disability subtype, *dysphonetic dyslexia,* is characterized by an inability to utilize a phonological route to successfully bridge letters and sounds. Instead, there tends to be an overreliance on visual and orthographic cues to identify words in print. Interestingly, newborns have the capability to discriminate phonemes in unfamiliar languages; then, between 6 and 10 months, the brain develops improved sensitivity toward discriminating phonemes within the native language to which it is routinely exposed (Posner & Rothbart, 2007). Since there is little reliance on letter-to-sound conversions, these readers tend to guess frequently on words based on the initial letter observed. For instance, the word *cat* may be read as *couch,* or perhaps *corn.* These students have tremendous difficulty incorporating strategies to allow them to crash through words in a sound-based manner, are often inaccurate oral readers, and tend to approach reading simply by memorizing whole words. According to Noble and McCandliss (2005), poor phonological processing in the early years leads to inefficient neural mappings between letters and sounds. The *supramarginal gyrus,* located at the juncture of the temporal and parietal lobes, appears to be the key brain region responsible for phonological processing (McCandliss & Noble, 2003; Shaywitz, 2004; Sandak et al., 2004).

The second reading disability subtype is often referred to as *surface dyslexia* and is the direct opposite of the dysphonetic subtype. Students with this disability are readily able to sound out words but lack the ability to recognize words in print automatically and effortlessly. Consequently, these students tend to be letter-by-letter and sound-by-sound readers, as there is an overreliance on the phonological properties of the word, and an underappreciation of the orthographical or spatial properties of the visual-word form. Most words are painstakingly broken down to individual phonemes and read very slowly and laboriously. Fluency tends to suffer the most, though phonological processing skills remain relatively intact. According to Cao et al. (2008), the left *fusiform gyrus*, a key brain region that automatically recognizes words, tends to be weaker for children with reading disabilities. Since this brain region is particularly sensitive toward the orthographic representation of words, children with reading disabilities often struggle with fluency and speed. In addition, children with reading disabilities have difficulty recognizing word pairs having similar orthography but different phonology (e.g., *pint/mint*) (Cao et al., 2008). Specific interventions should focus on automaticity and fluency goals, and not necessarily an explicit phonological approach.

The third reading disability subtype, often referred to as *mixed dyslexia*, constitutes the most severe type of reading disability for students. Generally, these readers have difficulty across the language spectrum, and are characterized by a combination of poor phonological processing skills, slower rapid and automatic word recognition skills, inconsistent language comprehension skills, and bizarre error patterns in their reading. The term *double-deficit hypothesis* often applies here, as there are numerous deficits that disrupt the natural flow of rapidly and automatically recognizing words in print. According to Cao et al. (2008), children with severe reading difficulties showed weaker modulatory effects from the left *fusiform gyrus* to the left inferior parietal lobes, suggesting deficits integrating both the phonological representation and orthographical representation of words. Hence, these students have difficulty with phonological processing tasks, rapid naming skills, verbal memory, and with reading fluency (Feifer & Della Toffalo, 2007). Most interventions should focus on a *balanced literacy* approach, which targets multiple aspects of the reading process in order to yield the best opportunity for success.

The final reading disability subtype involves deficits in *reading comprehension* skills. It has been estimated that some 10% of all school-aged children have good decoding skills but have specific difficulties with reading comprehension skills (Nation & Snowling, 1997). In essence, these readers struggle to derive meaning from print despite good reading mechanics. A school psychological assessment should measure constructs such as *executive functioning*, which involves the strategies students use to organize incoming information with previously read material; *working memory*, which is the amount of memory needed to perform a given cognitive task; and *language foundation* skills, which represent the fund of words with which a student is familiar, to determine the underlying causes for comprehension deficits (Feifer & Della Toffalo, 2007).

As previously noted, children with reading comprehension difficulties often display marked deficits on selected aspects of *executive functioning* skills, especially working memory skills (Reiter, Tucha, & Lange, 2004; Vargo, Grosser, & Spafford, 1995; Wilcutt et al., 2001). Working memory involves the ability to hold representational knowledge of the world around us, and works in tandem with executive functioning. Simply put, the longer the information is available, the greater the mental flexibility to manipulate, store, and arrange this information in a manner that facilitates retrieval. According to Cutting, Materek, Cole, Levine, & Mahone (2009), not only do poor visual and verbal working memory skills hinder reading comprehension, but also executive functioning attributes such as the capacity to plan, organize, and self-monitor incoming information. Therefore, school psychologists should focus their assessments on cognitive constructs such as verbal IQ, executive functioning, working memory, attention, and reading fluency measures when testing for deficits in reading comprehension. In summary, specifying the underlying linguistic and cognitive factors associated with poor reading comprehension skills may be helpful toward developing more effective intervention strategies to assist children throughout their learning journey.

Some cognitive attributes actually enhance both phonological and orthographical skills and build automaticity in deciphering words in print. For instance, Posner and Rothbart (2007) have stressed the importance of the brain's *executive attention network* in facilitating the reading process. According to Posner and Rothbart, a necessary prerequisite for the automatic recognition of words is the ability to visually attend to the unique features of the printed word. Therefore, reading interventions that simply rely on remediating phonological processing skills do not necessarily translate into more productive reading unless some emphasis is also placed on the recognition of the visual-word form itself. Consider the following example: The average adult is capable of reading approximately 250 words per minute, or approximately 4 words per second. According to Stein (2000), during the reading process, the eyes remain fixated on an individual word for up to 300msec before very subtle but rapid eye movements, called *saccades*, shift the eyes toward the next visual stimulus. This leaves precious little time to labor over the visual-word form itself, thus placing an increased burden on attention mechanisms to automatically code each visual stimulus in a linguistic manner. Further complicating the process is the English language, in which there are more than 1,100 ways of representing 44 sounds (phonemes) using a series of different letter combinations (Uhry & Clark, 2005). By contrast, in Italian there is no such ambiguity, as just 33 graphemes are sufficient to represent the 25 phonemes. This means that the same letter groups in Italian almost always represent the same unique sound, which makes the language more logical, consistent, and much easier to read.

Simply put, when there is less emphasis on deciphering subtle differences on the orthographical word unit, there is also less emphasis placed upon the executive attention network. According to Posner and Rothbart (2007), the executive attention network is more of a *top-down* type of attention system, modulated primarily by the *anterior cingulate gyrus* in the frontal lobes of the brain. This attention network contributes to the reading process by assisting readers to instantly recognize a word through a direct visual-to-semantic route, instead of a slower paced phonological route. In addition, most beginning readers also use the brain's executive attention network to take in the visual-word form and compare this unique configuration with stored exemplars from previously read material in order to automatically recognize words in print (Harm & Seidenberg, 2004).

REMEDIATION STRATEGIES FOR READING DISABILITIES

The National Reading Panel (2000) identified more than 100,000 published research articles in reading since 1966 in order to determine the most effective research-based intervention strategies for students with reading disabilities. Unfortunately, the overwhelming majority of these studies were discarded due to methodological failures. The rigorous standards set forth by the National Reading Panel included articles published only in English, articles that used an experimental or quasi-experimental design with a control group or multiple baseline method, articles that clearly detailed characteristics of the normative sample, articles with specific interventions that allowed for replication, and, finally, articles containing a detailed analysis of how long treatment effects lasted. Still, the conclusions reached by the National Reading Panel have served as the gold standard for evidence-based intervention by identifying five linguistic skills children need to become functionally independent readers. The five pillars for reading success involved the explicit and direct instruction of *phonemic awareness* (the manipulation of spoken syllables in words), *phonics* (letter-sound correspondences), *fluency* (reading speed and accuracy), *vocabulary* (lexicon of known words), and

> **DON'T FORGET**
> ....
> Reading success involves explicit and direct instruction in five areas: phonemic awareness, phonics, fluency, vocabulary and comprehension skills.

comprehension skills (deriving meaning from print). Furthermore, the panel concluded that all students, including those with and without disabilities, would benefit from instructional techniques involving explicit teaching of phonemic awareness and phonics. Hence, the genesis for a *balanced literacy* instructional approach was set in motion.

The specific findings of the National Reading Panel were largely based on a meta-analytic review of the literature, but in many respects did not differ from previous landmark research. For instance, Adams (1990) also carried out an extensive review of the literature and concluded that not only must letter-sound connections be taught in the early grades but they should also be linked to the actual reading process so students have direct application of these connections to text. In addition, Snow, Burns, and Griffin (1998) concluded that direct instruction in phonemic awareness and phonics was more effective in teaching reading than other forms of instruction. As Adams observed, there is a certain hierarchical structure in the development of phonemic awareness that should be helpful in targeting specific intervention strategies for the early reader. Berninger and Richards (2002) expanded on this hierarchy to link specific brain regions to the subsequent development of phonological processing. Rapid Reference 2.2 depicts these specific brain regions and their correlations with phonological development (Feifer & Della Toffalo, 2007).

≡ *Rapid Reference 2.2*

Developmental Sequence of Phonological Processing

Activity	Ages	Purpose	Brain Development
1. Response to Rhymes	3–4	Three- and 4-year-old children can memorize nursery rhymes, rhyming songs, and provide the final word in rhyming text.	The myelination of the auditory cortex in the temporal lobes allows children at approximately age 3 years to more closely discriminate speech sounds (Berninger & Richards, 2002).
2. Classifying Phonemes	4–5	Children at this age begin to match similar sounds together and can pick the sound	Brain development tends to progress from the right hemisphere to the left. By age 4 *(continued)*

		that does not belong (e.g., *book, look, took, cat*).	years, children can begin to take sound discriminations from the right hemisphere and classify them in the left, as the brain now allows for crosstalk between the hemispheres (Berninger & Richards, 2002).
3. Segmenting Words	5–6	Five-year-olds can isolate sounds at the beginning and end of words and are capable of inventive spelling (e.g., "KT" for *cat*).	Cross-modal associations now become more automatic, allowing for visual or orthographic representation of words (*parietal lobes*) being stored in an auditory manner (*temporal lobes*).
4. Phoneme Segmentation	6–7	By 1st grade, children can tap out the number of phonemes in a word, and can often represent all the sounds in a word by inventive spelling.	Brain development and myelination also proceeds from back to front, especially in language zones. Posterior regions code the sounds while anterior structures arrange them sequentially (Berninger & Richards, 2002).
5. Phoneme Deletion	6–8	Depending on the complexity of the word, children can delete or can substitute the sound of one word to create another word (e.g., say, *sting* without the "t").	The instructional environment is crucial in sculpting the tertiary regions of the brain for higher-level thinking and the manipulation of phonemes.

Phonological Strategies

One of the most long-standing and traditional methodologies of teaching specific phonological processing skills is the Orton-Gillingham Multisensory Method, developed in the early 1930s by Anna Gillingham and Dr. Samuel Orton. The initial goal of the program was to create a sequential system of reading that is multisensory and continues to build on itself by depicting how sounds and letters are related. The program is based on the assumption that 80% of the 30,000 most commonly used English words follow a predictable code, and are therefore phonologically consistent or regular (Uhry & Clark, 2005). Feifer and Della Toffalo (2007) referred to this program as a *bottom-up,* or synthetic method, of teaching reading because the theoretical foundation of the program is hierarchically structured and sequenced based on a set of learned rules and correspondences for letters and sounds. Progress monitoring is documented by benchmark measures examining letter knowledge, alphabetizing skills, reading, spelling, and handwriting. There is great emphasis on utilizing diacritical markers for coding the 44 phonemes and 68 graphemes in various reading situations. Rapid Reference 2.3 summarizes the five basic steps in teaching reading from a sound-to-word framework, or in essence, a bottom-up approach to reading (Barton, 1998).

≡ *Rapid Reference 2.3*

Five Steps in Teaching Phonology (Barton, 1998)

Step 1: Phonemic awareness involves teaching students how to properly listen to a single word or syllable and break it into individual phonemes. The English language has 44 phonemes, which represent the smallest unit of sound in the language. Children are also taught blending strategies, as well as sound substitutions, sound deletions, and sound comparisons.

Step 2: Phoneme/grapheme correspondence involves the introduction of the alphabet system representing a visual component to link with phonemes. Children are explicitly taught that specific sounds are represented by a variety of letter combinations; emphasis is also placed on how to blend letters into single-syllable words.

Step 3: The six types of syllables that compose English words are introduced. If students are aware of a specific type of syllable, then the sound should be automatic. These syllable subtypes include:

a. Closed syllables (just one vowel; e.g., *cat*)

b. Open syllables (ends in long vowel; e.g., *baby*)

c. Vowel-consonant "e" syllables (silent "e" elongates vowel; e.g., *make*)

d. Vowel-team syllables (two vowels make one sound; e.g., *caution*)

e. R-controlled syllables (vowel followed by "r" changes sound; e.g., *hurt*)

f. Consonant-"le" syllables (word ends in "le"; e.g., *turtle*)

Step 4: Probabilities and rules are explicitly taught. The English language provides several ways to spell the same sounds. For instance, the word *caution* has the sound /SHUN/, which can be spelled either /TION/, /SION/, or /CION/.

Step 5: Roots and affixes, as well as morphology, are taught, to expand a student's vocabulary and ability to comprehend unfamiliar words.

Fluency Strategies

Some children struggle with reading fluency skills, and not necessarily phonological processing skills; they simply have difficulty rapidly and automatically recognizing the orthography of print. While the temporal-parietal circuit is vital for developing phonemic awareness and phonological processing skills, the occipital-temporal regions of the brain constitute the essence of what Shaywitz (2004) referred to as the *visual-word form area*. The visual-word form area is primarily responsible for the rapid and automatic recognition of words, and to a certain extent is very much dependent on the work of the temporal-parietal region. In other words, effective phonological mapping of sounds greatly enables the visual-word form area to perform its job. Hence, there appears to be a certain symbiosis between phonological awareness and rapid and automatic processing of the visual-word form. According to Schatschneider and Torgeson (2004), there are three ways phonemic awareness skills support the growth of accurate word reading, each of which is described in Rapid Reference 2.4.

The following interventions are more suitable for students who have difficulty with reading fluency but may not necessarily struggle with phonological aspects of reading:

Read Naturally (Read Naturally, Inc.) focuses on building reading fluency and speed, as well as fostering more accurate comprehension skills. The program uses repeated exposures to modeled reading and progress

---

≡ *Rapid Reference 2.4*

Three Ways Phonemic Awareness Skills Support Accurate Word Reading (Schatschneider & Torgeson, 2004)

1. *They help children understand the alphabetic principle.* Without some ability to identify sounds in words, it is difficult to see further relationships between letters in print and individual phonemes in spoken words.

2. *They facilitate the generation of possible words in context that are only partially sounded out.* For instance, if a child knows the sound that is represented by the first two letters in the word (e.g., "ch"), he or she is more likely able to guess the correct word.

3. *They help children notice the regular ways letters represent sounds in words.* If children can hear three sounds in the word *cat*, it helps them notice the way letters correspond to sounds. This reinforces certain spelling patterns and serves as almost a mnemonic device so the child can automatically recognize words simply by glancing at them.

monitoring to increase overall fluency skill. It is designed for students who fall below the mean level oral fluency rates for 2nd grade (51 wpm) through 8th grade (133 wpm). There is an initial placement test that determines the level at which each student begins the program. Next, the student and teacher agree on a reading fluency goal, which is typically 30 to 40 words correct per minute higher than the student's current level of performance. The student must master rate, accuracy, prosody, comprehension, and retell/summary goals for at least 8 of the 24 stories in each level before moving up to the next half-grade reading level.

All Read Naturally tasks follow a structured sequence whereby the student first selects a story of interest, subvocalizes vocabulary terms and meanings along with a recording, and formulates a prediction about the story. Second, the student then attempts a "cold read" of the story, and graphs the number of words read correctly in one minute. Next, each student reads the story aloud with the tape recording, at least three times. The rate of the recorded reading level increases with each successive reading. The student then attempts a "hot read" of the passage as the teacher records errors, monitors prosody, and times the reading for one minute. A variety of comprehension questions, including main idea, details, vocabulary, drawing inferences, and a short-answer question are answered either before or after the hot read is completed. Last, the student is then given 5 to 8 minutes to retell the story, either orally or in writing.

Read Naturally is usually recommended for a minimum of 30 minutes per day, three to five days per week. Both cold and hot reads are recorded and graphed, along with comprehension scores and retell points.

Great Leaps Reading (Diarmuid, Inc.) was designed as more of a supplementary reading program and requires just 10 minutes per day, for a minimum of three days per week. The program is divided into three major sections:

1. *Phonics*, for developing basic sound awareness skills.
2. *Sight-phrases*, for mastering sight words skills.
3. *Fluency*, which uses age-appropriate stories designed to build oral reading fluency and automaticity, as well as to enhance student motivation.

The heart and soul of the program are the strategies used to enhance fluency. Great Leaps argues against teaching high-frequency words in isolation, and instead relies on "sight phrases" to be mastered within the context of a story. The program is highly scaffolded, meaning that mastering one skill leads to the next. In fact, students literally "leap" to the next page once mastery on timed one-minute tests is attained. The goal of Great Leaps is to develop fluent and independent reading skills up to a 5th grade level. There are two practical advantages to utilizing Great Leaps in the public school setting. First, the cost of the program is relatively inexpensive; second, Great Leaps requires little training and can be used by a teacher, parent, instructional assistant, tutor, or school volunteer. A typical training session takes about 3 hours, though most experienced teachers will find the instructions are more than adequate to begin implementation without training.

READ 180 (Scholastic) is truly a balanced literacy program designed to meet the needs of students who are struggling on one or more of the five pillars of reading as outlined by the National Reading Panel (2000). The 90-minute instructional model begins with a 20-minute whole-group teacher-directed instruction; then students rotate between three smaller groups during the next 60 minutes. The first group involves small-group instructional activities that allow teachers to better differentiate instruction. The second group is what makes the program unique, in that students use highly interactive and adaptive software that systemically directs the learner through the four learning zones.

1. The *Reading Zone* includes phonics, fluency, and vocabulary instruction as students read through passages.
2. The *Word Zone* provides systematic instruction in decoding and word recognition skills as 6,000 words are defined and analyzed.
3. The *Spelling Zone* allows students to practice spelling and receive immediate feedback.
4. The *Success Zone* focuses on comprehension once the other zones have been mastered.

The software component of the program is highly adaptive, offering opportunities to repeat oral readings, to hear models read with fluency, and to watch videos that provide background knowledge and introduce vocabulary. Based on how the student reads, the software continually adjusts the level of instruction to adapt to the individual learner. Following the computer training, students meet for another small-group instructional activity, which involves building reading comprehension using both paperback and audiobooks. The session ends with a 10-minute whole-group wrap-up period.

Wilson Reading System (Wilson Language Training) is one of the few reading programs developed specifically for adolescents and adults with dyslexia (Uhry & Clark, 2005). It was developed by Barbara Wilson and is based on an Orton-Gillingham approach to reading, meaning that it is a multisensory and synthetic phonics approach to teaching reading for students with language-based difficulties. The Wilson Reading System was developed for students in Grades 3 through adults, and may also be appropriate for bilingual students who have adequate English skills but continue to have difficulties with written language skills. According to Uhry and Clark, there are three unique features of the Wilson program that can be extremely helpful for older students with dyslexia.

■ First, there is an immediate emphasis on the six syllable types, though complex diacritical markers are not a component of the program. Instead, students create their own system of coding syllables using underlining instead of slash marks.

■ A second feature of the program is the use of a unique finger-tapping system to analyze spoken words into phonemes to assist with spelling. For example, in teaching the word *map*, three lettered cards are put on the table to represent the three sounds in the word. The students are taught to say each sound while tapping a different finger against their thumb.

■ Third, the Sound Cards in the program are color-coded: Consonants are yellow, vowels orange, and word families green.

The program recommends students receive 45 to 90 minutes of instruction per day, and it may take more than one day to complete any given lesson. It should be noted that all steps in the program are laid out in a very structured format, with students starting at the same level. While the lessons are not scripted per se, teacher training begins with an initial 2-day overview.

Reading Comprehension Strategies

There is a great deal of support in the literature that children with poor reading comprehension skills also have deficits in receptive vocabulary development, as well as limited semantic processing (Catts, Adlof, & Weismer, 2006; Nation & Snowling, 1997; Nation et al., 2004). Furthermore, these children tend to have relatively normal phonological processing abilities, thus illustrating the dissociation, not association, between phonology and comprehension at the later elementary grades. Therefore, the intervention focus should be at the *language* level, not at the *phonological* level, for students with poor reading comprehension skills. The ability to utilize background knowledge and draw inferences from the text also facilitates the comprehension process and allows for a deeper and enriched engagement of the passage. Clearly, executive functioning skills represent a student's ability to stitch together relevant aspects of the text in order to derive meaning from print.

Soar to Success (Houghton Mifflin) is a relatively fast-paced, small-group instructional program, designed to accelerate reading for students in Grades 3 through 6. The program focuses mainly on language-based strategies aimed at improving reading comprehension skills. Specific instructional strategies involve the use of graphic organizers to help students visually construct meaning from print. In addition, reciprocal teaching uses four strategies—Summarize, Clarify, Question, and Predict—as teachers model the use of these strategies while the text is being read. There are 18 books, sequenced from simple to complex, as part of the process of scaffolding instruction.

The Lindamood-Bell Learning Process Center offers various products to assist with reading comprehension by enhancing working memory skills. Working memory subserves the reading process by temporarily suspending previously read information while simultaneously allowing the reader to acquire new information. Deficits in working memory can certainly disrupt a student's ability to make appropriate linkages among information in the text. For instance:

- *Lindamood Visualizing and Verbalizing for Language Comprehension and Thinking* was developed to use concept imagery as a means to assist students with reading comprehension, critical thinking, and connecting meaning to conversation.

- *Seeing Stars: Symbol Imagery for Phonemic Awareness, Sight Words and Spelling* was designed to develop symbol imagery skills in order to facilitate sight-word development and comprehension of the orthography of print. The program begins by visualizing the sequence of letters for the sounds within words, and extends into multisyllabic and contextual reading and spelling.

FUTURE INTERVENTIONS

With the advent of modern neuroimaging procedures, scientists can actually observe physiological changes in the brain with each passing thought, fleeting memory, or random cognitive endeavor. For better than 100 years, neuroscientists have recognized that changes in blood flow and blood oxygenation in the brain (known as *hemodynamics*) are closely linked to specific neural activity. Thus, listening to music or passively watching a reality television program will demand less cognitive energy and thereby use less oxygen than a demanding cognitive activity such as performing mental math or reading a piece of literature (Bremner, 2005). Shaywitz and Shaywitz (2005) demonstrated that children with reading disabilities who received explicit types of phonics instruction on a daily basis had alterations within the temporal-parietal regions of their brain as measured by fMRI technology. This groundbreaking research illustrated how specific teaching techniques can fundamentally alter specific neural connections, resulting in greater academic performance. Incredibly, modern neuroscience is beginning to reveal how evidence-based interventions involving the explicit teaching of phonology can facilitate the development of neural systems that underlie reading (Shaywitz & Shaywitz).

Future research is expounding on the idea that enhanced neural connections in the temporal-parietal region of the brain may lead to more efficacious reading skills. Neurofeedback research has led the charge in studying brain-wave patterns (i.e., EEG) and demonstrated that children can indeed self-regulate their own brain-wave activity (Swingle, 2008). For instance, when the brain is engaged in a highly demanding activity such as reading, the EEG patterns should not slow down, which is common with deficits in attention, but rather speed up to handle the increased cognitive load. However, Arns, Peters, Breteler, and Verhoeven (2007) showed increased slow wave activity (delta and theta) in the frontal and temporal regions for children with dyslexia. This was consistent with prior research (Backes, et al., 2002; Shaywitz, 2004) that demonstrated dyslexic readers had less activation of both the temporal and prefrontal cortex during phonological processing tasks and failed to use brain areas normally specialized in language processing. If children with reading disabilities show slower brain activation in these language areas, then do advanced readers show more rapid neural activations in these brain regions? In fact, some research has suggested that precocious readers' peak alpha frequency tends to be 5.2% faster than grade-level readers (Suldo, Olson, & Evans, 2001). According to Demos (2005), all forms of neurofeedback have the potential for changing EEG coherence, or the functional connectivity between two brain regions. As Shaywitz and Shaywitz (2005) noted, the brain systems for reading are very malleable, and their disruption in dyslexic children may be remediated through evidence-based intervention programs. Perhaps neurofeedback will be the wave of the future to strengthen neural connections and enhanced coherence in vital regions of the brain to facilitate the bevy of interventions showing promise in remediating reading disabilities in all children.

🐟 TEST YOURSELF 🐟

1. **The subtype of dyslexia that is characterized by an overreliance on sound/ symbol relationships, poor fluency and speed, and difficulty with rapid word recognition is**

   (a) dysphonetic dyslexia.

   (b) surface dyslexia.

   (c) mixed dyslexia.

   (d) phonemic dyslexia.

2. **Which of the following constructs has little bearing on reading comprehension skills?**

   (a) Executive functioning

   (b) Working memory

   (c) Language foundation skills

   (d) Performance IQ scores

3. **Which of the following are disadvantages of the discrepancy model?**

   (a) Views reading along a one-dimensional continuum.

   (b) Little agreement as to what the discrepancy should be.

   (c) Promotes a wait-and-fail policy.

   (d) All of the above

4. **Teaching phonological processing skills to children involves all of the following except**

   (a) teaching phoneme/grapheme correspondence.

   (b) using a whole-word approach to reading.

   (c) teaching six-syllable subtypes.

   (d) teaching phonemic awareness.

5. **All of the following are clear advantages of utilizing an RTI process except that it**

   (a) allows for earlier intervention.

   (b) provides an excellent method to monitor progress.

   (c) emphasizes evidence-based approaches to interventions.

   (d) is excellent at diagnosing a reading disability.

6. **The subtype of dyslexia that is characterized by an overreliance on visual cues to decode words, frequent guessing, and poor letter-to-sound conversion skills is called**

   (a) dysphonetic dyslexia.

   (b) surface dyslexia.

   (c) mixed dyslexia.

   (d) semantic dyslexia.

7. **An example of a bottom-up type of reading intervention for a younger student with poor phonological processing skills is**

   (a) the whole-word approach.

   (b) Orton-Gillingham methods.

   (c) biofeedback.

   (d) Read Naturally.

8. **All of the following are good strategies for students with poor reading comprehension except**

   (a) the Soar to Success program.

   (b) the Lindamood Visualizing and Verbalizing for Language Comprehension and Thinking program.

   (c) enhancement of language and vocabulary skills.

   (d) all of the above.

9. **An effective intervention for poor reading fluency skills is**

   (a) Read Naturally.

   (b) blood oxygenation.

   (c) self-esteem tests.

   (d) cognitive functioning tests.

10. **The five pillars of reading delineated by the National Reading Panel are:**

    (a) Working memory, personality functioning, language skills, cognitive functioning, phonemic awareness

    (b) Language skills, executive functioning skills, socioeconomic status, reading fluency, teacher training

    (c) Phonemic awareness, phonics, fluency, vocabulary, comprehension skills

    (d) Content affinity, working memory, executive functioning, language skills, automaticity

Answers: 1. b; 2. d; 3. d; 4. b; 5. d; 6. a; 7. b; 8. d; 9. a; 10. c.

Three

HOW SLD MANIFESTS IN MATHEMATICS

David C. Geary
Mary K. Hoard
Drew H. Bailey

Many children find learning mathematics difficult not because they have a learning disability, but because mathematics is a complex and nuanced field that requires effort and focus for most people to learn. There are, nonetheless, about 7% of children and adolescents who have specific learning disabilities in mathematics (MLD) due to underlying deficits or developmental delays in the cognitive systems that support mathematics learning (Barbaresi, Katusic, Colligan, Weaver, & Jacobsen, 2005), and another 5% to 10% of children and adolescents who have persistent low achievement in mathematics (LA) despite average cognitive ability and reading achievement. There is much less research on children with MLD and their LA peers than there is on children with reading disability (RD), but considerable progress has been made in the past 15 years (Gersten, Clarke, & Mazzocco, 2007). In this chapter, we provide a brief review of this progress; specifically, how MLD and LA are defined and what is known about their etiology and incidence; the different ways in which MLD and LA can be expressed in the areas of number, counting, and arithmetic; the cognitive correlates and potential diagnostic markers of MLD and LA; the components of an assessment of MLD and LA; treatment protocols; and, finally, practical resources.

During preparation of this chapter, the authors were supported by grant R37 HD045914 from the National Institute of Child Health and Human Development (NICHD).

43

DEFINITION, ETIOLOGY, AND INCIDENCE
OF MATHEMATICS LEARNING DISABILITY AND
LOW ACHIEVEMENT IN MATHEMATICS

Definition

Currently, there is no agreed-upon test or achievement cutoff score used to diagnose MLD or LA (Gersten et al., 2007; Mazzocco, 2007). A consensus is beginning to emerge among researchers, however, at least with respect to the importance of distinguishing between MLD and LA (Geary, Hoard, Byrd-Craven, Nugent, & Numtee, 2007; Murphy, Mazzocco, Hanich, & Early, 2007). When children score below the 10th percentile on standardized mathematics achievement tests for at least two consecutive academic years they are categorized as MLD, and children scoring below the 25th or 30th percentile (but above the 10th percentile) across two consecutive years are categorized as LA. These two groups clearly differ in the severity and breadth of their mathematical difficulties, as well as in the underlying sources of these difficulties, as described in the "Cognitive Correlates" and "Diagnostic Markers" sections below.

As a group, children with LA typically have average IQs, and children with MLD have low-average IQs. The IQ difference across these two groups contributes to some aspects of their mathematics learning, but does not appear to be the primary source of MLD. As a result, the usefulness of a discrepancy between mathematics achievement and IQ as a diagnostic criterion for MLD has not been established (Mazzocco, 2007).

CAUTION

There is no agreed-upon test or achievement cutoff score for MLD or LA diagnosis, and the usefulness of IQ-achievement discrepancy as a diagnostic criterion for MLD has not been established.

Etiology

As with other forms of specific learning disability (SLD), twin and family studies suggest both genetic and environmental contributions to MLD (Kovas, Haworth, Dale, & Plomin, 2007; Light & DeFries, 1995; Shalev et al., 2001). Shalev and her colleagues found that family members (e.g., parents and siblings) of children with MLD are 10 times more likely to be diagnosed also with MLD than are members of the general population. In a large twin study of academic learning in elementary school, Kovas et al. found genetic as well as shared (between the pair of twins) and unique environmental contributions to individual differences in mathematics achievement and MLD. Depending on the grade and mathematics test used, from one half to two thirds of the individual variation in mathematics achievement was attributable to genetic variation, and the remainder to a combination of shared and unique experiences.

The same genetic influences affect individual differences across the entire range of mathematics performance. In other words, the genetic influences responsible for the low performance associated with MLD were responsible for individual differences at all levels of performance (Kovas et al., 2007; Oliver et al., 2004). These results suggest that there are not MLD genes, but rather the genetic influences on MLD are the same as those that influence mathematics achievement at the average- to high-end levels of performance. Of the genetic effects, one third were shared with general cognitive ability, one third with reading achievement independent of cognitive ability, and one third were unique to mathematics. Thus, about two thirds of the genetic influences on mathematics achievement and MLD are the same as those that influence learning in other academic areas, and one third only affect mathematics learning.

The shared genetic influences on academic achievement may explain why many children with MLD have RD or other difficulties that interfere with learning in school, such as attention deficit hyperactivity disorder (ADHD; Barbaresi et al., 2005; Shalev et al., 2001). Barbaresi et al. found that between 57% and 64% of individuals with MLD also had RD, depending on the diagnostic criteria used for MLD. These genetic influences, however, do not necessarily tell us about how effective future interventions may be, because changes in the individuals' environment may alter the relative extent of genetic and environmental influences on MLD status and/or related outcomes. In any event, the studies to date indicate important environmental influences on mathematics learning and MLD. For example, schooling influences mathematics achievement in general, and interventions for MLD improve the mathematics achievement of these children above and beyond the influence of general education, even if they do not eliminate individual differences.

Incidence

On the basis of several population-based, long-term studies and many smaller-scale studies, about 7% of children and adolescents will be diagnosable as MLD in at least one area of mathematics before graduating

DON'T FORGET
....
Approximately 7% of children and adolescents will be diagnosable as MLD before graduating high school.

from high school (Barbaresi et al., 2005; Lewis, Hitch, & Walker, 1994; Shalev, Manor, & Gross-Tsur, 2005). An additional 5% to 10% of children and adolescents will be identified as LA (Berch & Mazzocco, 2007; Geary et al., 2007; Murphy et al., 2007).

SUBTYPES OF MLD AND HOW THEY MANIFEST DEVELOPMENTALLY

We do not yet know if there are distinct groups of students with discrete types of MLD, but individuals diagnosed with MLD have deficits in several domains. The three most consistently found deficits involve number sense, semantic memory, and procedural competence (Geary, 1993). Children with MLD and children with LA may have deficits in one or more of these domains; children may differ in the severity of one type of deficit or another; and children may differ in the developmental course of the deficit. These findings have been based largely on the study of number, counting, and arithmetic development. Different forms of deficit may be found in the future as cognitive studies expand to include other areas of mathematics, such as algebra and geometry.

> **DON'T FORGET**
> ....
> Mathematical disabilities: Cognitive, neuropsychological, and genetic components.
> **Author:** David C. Geary
> **Publication Date:** 1993
> **Findings:** First review that identified semantic memory and procedural components of MLD, as well as a spatial component.
> **Journal:** *Psychological Bulletin*, 114, 345–362.

NUMBER SENSE

Typical Development

Children's number sense includes an implicit and potentially inherent understanding of the *exact quantity* of small collections of objects and of symbols (e.g., Arabic numerals) that represent these quantities (e.g., 3 = ■ ■ ■), and of the *approximate magnitude* of larger quantities (Butterworth & Reigosa, 2007; Dehaene, Piazza, Pinel, & Cohen, 2003; Geary, 1995). This implicit knowledge is manifested in children's ability to (a) apprehend the quantity of sets of 3 to 4 objects or actions without counting, that is, by *subitizing* (Mandler & Shebo, 1982; Starkey & Cooper, 1980; Strauss & Curtis, 1984; Wynn, Bloom, & Chiang, 2002); (b) use nonverbal processes or counting to quantify small sets of objects and to add and subtract small quantities to and from these sets (Case & Okamoto, 1996; Levine, Jordan, & Huttenlocher, 1992; Starkey, 1992); and, (c) estimate the magnitude of sets of objects and the results of simple numerical operations (Dehaene, 1997).

DON'T FORGET

Subitizing means to judge the number of objects in a group rapidly, accurately and confidently without counting them. Children and adults can subitize for sets of 1 to 3, sometimes 4, objects, but not more than this.

Sensitivity to differences in the quantity of small sets of objects (e.g., ■■ versus ■■■) is evident during infancy (Antell & Keating, 1983), and shows modest improvement for some children during the preschool years. The approximate representational system is assessed by infants' ability to discriminate between *more than* and *less than* when comparing large collections of objects. Six-month-olds can discriminate sets that differ by a ratio of 2:1 (e.g., $16 > 8$, but not $14 > 8$), that is, when the larger quantity is 100% more than the smaller one. Eleven-month-olds can determine ordinal sequences of sets of items that differ by large amounts (A < B < C; Brannon, 2002; Xu & Spelke, 2000). The ability to approximate relative quantity improves rapidly, due to some combination of brain maturation and experience, during the preschool years such that 6-year-olds can discriminate quantities that differ by 20% and reach the adult level of discrimination (12%) later in childhood (Halberda & Feigenson, 2008). These fundamental numerical competencies provide the foundation for many aspects of children's early mathematics learning (Geary, 2006, 2007). For instance, the exact representational system appears to be built from the ability to subitize, and is important for children's initial understanding that Arabic numerals and number words represent distinct quantities (e.g., ■■■ = 3 = three); and the approximate system supports learning of the mathematical number line.

Geary et al. (2007) created the *Number Sets Test* as a means to assess fluency in accessing exact representations of small quantities and in combining and decomposing them. An example is shown in Figure 3.1. Students are asked to combine pairs or triplets of Arabic numerals (e.g., 1 4) or sets of objects (e.g., ■■ ◆◆◆) and circle the rectangles that match a target number (e.g., 5). One strategy is dependent on subitizing, that is, determining the numerosity of small sets and then adding the associated quantities (e.g., ■■ ◆◆◆ = 5; Geary & Lin, 1998). Other strategies involve a combination of subitizing and counting, or simply counting (counting may contribute to the development of representations of quantity). The speed with which typically achieving children (TA) can access these representations and combine them increases steadily

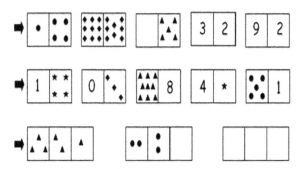

Figure 3.1. Example Items From the *Number Sets Test*

from 1st to 4th grade. Their ability to determine that 3 = ◆◆◆ does not change, but they access this knowledge more rapidly and learn to combine these basic representations of quantity into larger ones.

For schoolchildren, the number line is often used to assess the approximate representational system. Making placements on a physical number line that are based on use of this system results in a pattern that conforms to the natural logarithm (*Ln*) of the number (Feigenson, Dehaene, & Spelke, 2004; Gallistel & Gelman, 1992); specifically, the placements that are compressed for larger magnitudes such that the perceived distance between 8 and 9 is smaller than the perceived distance between 2 and 3, as shown for the bottom number line in Figure 3.2. With schooling, children who are TA quickly develop number-line placements that conform to the linear mathematical system (Siegler & Booth, 2004); the difference between two consecutive numbers is identical regardless of the distance between them on a number line (see top, Figure 3.2).

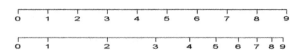

Figure 3.2. The top number line is the mathematic representation where the distance between successive whole numbers is equal. The bottom number line shows how children represent numbers before learning the mathematical number line. For them, the difference between 1 and 2 seems larger than that between 2 and 3. As numerals get larger, they seem less and less different from one another.

Children With MLD and LA

There is evidence that children with MLD and, to a lesser extent, children with LA have deficits or developmental delays for both subitizing and the ability to represent approximate quantities (Butterworth, 2005; Geary, Hoard, Nugent, & Byrd-Craven, 2008; Koontz & Berch, 1996; Landerl, Bevan, & Butterworth, 2003). Koontz and Berch conducted the first study of the exact representational system of children with MLD. Children in the 3rd and 4th grades with MLD, and children who are TA, were administered a variant of Posner, Boies, Eichelman, and Taylor's (1969) physical and name identity task. For instance, children were asked to determine if combinations of Arabic numerals (e.g., 3 − 2), number sets (■■ − ■■■), or numerals and sets were the same (2 − ■■) or different (3 − ■■). In keeping with previous studies (Mandler & Shebo, 1982), reaction time patterns for the children who are TA indicated fast subitizing, that is, automatic access to representations for quantities of 2 and 3, regardless of whether the code was an Arabic numeral or a number set. The MLD children showed fast access to numerosity representations for the quantity of 2, but appeared to rely on counting to determine quantities of 3. The results suggest that some children with MLD might not have an inherent representation for numerosities of 3, or the representational system for 3 does not reliably discriminate it from 2.

The performance of MLD children on the *Number Sets Test* is consistent with this finding and, in comparison to the TA peers, suggests about a three-year delay in their fluency in accessing representations of small exact quantities and in combining and recombining them (Geary et al., 2007; Geary, Bailey, & Hoard, 2009). The performance of children with LA is between that of MLD and children who are TA but closer to that of children who are TA.

To assess the approximate representational system, Geary et al. (2008) examined the pattern of placements of children with MLD, children with LA, and children who are TA of numbers on a 0 to 100 number line at the beginning of 1st grade and the end of 2nd; the number 50, for instance, should be placed exactly halfway between 0 and 100. The pattern of placements reveals how children understand the sequence of numbers: Do their placements conform to the mathematical number line at the top of Figure 3.2 or the compressed line at the bottom? The placements of children who, as a group, were largely linear-conforming to the mathematical number line in 1st grade became increasingly so by the end of 2nd. The placements of the children with MLD were logarithmic-conforming to the compressed number line, suggesting dependence on the approximate magnitude system; they had not modified this system to conform to the mathematical number line. The placements of the children with LA were largely linear by the end of 2nd grade, and at this point similar to children who are TA. This is not the whole story, however, because the placements of children with MLD suggested more "compression" (e.g., the distance between 8 and 9 was very small) than those of the children with LA and children who are TA—the children with MLD showed less discrimination among smaller-valued numbers than did the other children, independent of IQ and working memory. The findings suggest a one-year developmental delay in the acuity of the approximate magnitude representational system for children with LA, and a more substantial delay and perhaps a deficit in this system for children with MLD (also Halberda, Mazzocco, & Feigenson, 2008).

COUNTING KNOWLEDGE

Typical Development

Most schoolchildren quickly learn to count by rote, and this in and of itself is not a useful indicator of MLD or LA status. What is more interesting is whether these children understand the core principles of counting. Gelman and Gallistel (1978) proposed that children's counting behavior is guided by five inherent and implicit principles that mature during the preschool years, as shown in the top portion of Rapid Reference 3.1. The principles of one-one correspondence, stable order, and cardinality define the initial "how to count" rules, which provide the potentially inherent skeletal structure for children's emerging counting knowledge (Gelman & Meck, 1983). Whether or not there are inherent constraints to children's emergent counting knowledge, children make inductions about the basic characteristics of counting by observing others' counting (Briars & Siegler, 1984; Fuson, 1988). One result is a belief that certain unessential features of counting are essential, as shown in the bottom portion of Rapid Reference 3.1. The unessential features of standard direction and adjacency are common sources of error in children's counting.

CAUTION

The ability to count by rote is not in and of itself a diagnostic marker for MLD or LA. Most of these children can count by rote.

One way to assess children's counting knowledge is to ask them to help a puppet learn how to count. The child is asked to monitor the puppet's counting of objects and to tell the puppet if the count was "okay" or "not okay" (Briars & Siegler, 1984; Gelman & Meck, 1983). On some counts the puppet counts correctly and on others the puppet violates one of Gelman and Gallistel's

≡ *Rapid Reference 3.1*

Implicit Counting Principles and Unessential Features of Counting

Implicit Principle	Description
One-one correspondence	One and only one word tag (e.g., *one, two*) is assigned to each counted object.
Stable order	Order of the word tags must be invariant across counted sets.
Cardinality	The value of the final word tag represents the quantity of items in the counted set.
Abstraction	Objects of any kind can be collected together and counted.
Order irrelevance	Items within a given set can be tagged in any sequence.

Unessential Feature	Description
Standard direction	Counting proceeds from left to right.
Adjacency	Consecutive count of contiguous objects.
Pointing	Counted objects are typically pointed at, but only once.
Start at an end	Counting starts at one of the end points of an array of objects.

(1978) implicit principles or Briars and Siegler's unessential features. If the child detects a violation of one of Gelman and Gallistel's principles, it is assumed that the child at least implicitly understands the principle. If the child states that correct counting from right to left, for instance, is okay, then the child knows that the standard left-to-right counting is unessential (i.e., you can count in other ways and still get the correct answer, as long as each item is tagged only once with a counting word). Children's knowledge of counting principles and unessential features of counting and sensitivity to violations of these principles and features (e.g., while watching a puppet count) emerge during the preschool years and mature during the early elementary-school years (LeFevre et al., 2006).

Children With MLD and LA

Using the puppet task, we have found that children with MLD and children with LA in elementary school understand most basic counting principles, but they are sometimes confused when counting deviates from the standard left to right counting of adjacent objects (Geary, Bow-Thomas, & Yao, 1992; Geary, Hoard, Byrd-Craven, & Desoto, 2004). A more consistent finding is that children with MLD, but not children with LA, fail to detect errors when the puppet double-counts the first object in an array of objects; that is, this single object is tagged "one, two." They detect these double counts when they occur with the last item, indicating they understand one-one correspondence; but when the double count occurs on the beginning item, they have difficulty retaining a notation of the counting error in working memory during the count (Geary et al., 2004; Hoard, Geary, & Hamson, 1999). The forgetting of miscounts is potentially problematic for children who are learning to use counting to solve arithmetic problems. Ohlsson and Rees (1991) predicted that children who are skilled at detecting counting errors would more readily learn to correct these miscounts and thus eventually commit fewer errors when using counting to solve arithmetic problems. The evidence for this prediction is mixed (Geary et al., 1992, 2004), but detection of these double-counting errors may still be a good empirical indicator of risk for MLD (Geary et al., 2007; Gersten, Jordan, & Flojo, 2005).

ARITHMETIC

Typical Development

By the time children enter kindergarten they have coordinated their number sense and counting skills with an implicit understanding of addition and subtraction. The result is an ability to use number words to solve formal addition and subtraction problems (Groen & Resnick, 1977; Siegler & Jenkins, 1989). The most thoroughly studied improvement in arithmetical competency is change in the mix of strategies children use during problem solving (Ashcraft, 1982; Carpenter & Moser, 1984). A common early strategy for solving simple addition problems is to count both addends. These counting procedures are sometimes executed with the aid of fingers, the *finger counting strategy*, and sometimes without them, the *verbal counting strategy* (Siegler & Shrager, 1984). The two most commonly used procedures, whether children use their fingers or not, are called *min* (or counting on) and *sum* (or counting all; Fuson, 1982; Groen & Parkman, 1972). The min procedure involves stating the larger-valued addend and then counting a number of times equal to the value of the smaller addend, such as counting 5, 6, 7, 8, to solve 5 + 3. With the sum procedure (also called *max* procedure), children start with the smaller addend and count the larger one; for example, 3, 4, 5, 6, 7, 8. The sum procedure involves counting both addends starting from 1. The development of procedural competencies is related, in part, to improvements in children's conceptual understanding of counting (Geary et al., 1992).

The use of counting results in the development of memory representations of basic facts (Siegler & Shrager, 1984). Once formed, these long-term memory representations support the use of memory-based processes. The most common of these processes are *direct retrieval* of arithmetic facts and *decomposition*. With direct retrieval, children state an answer that is associated in long-term memory with the presented problem, such as stating "eight" when asked to solve 5 + 3. Decomposition involves reconstructing the answer based on the retrieval of a partial sum; for example, 6 + 7 might be solved by retrieving the answer to 6 + 6 and then adding 1 to this partial sum. The general pattern of change is from use of the least sophisticated problem-solving procedures, such as sum counting, to the most efficient retrieval-based processes. However, development is not simply a switch from use of a less sophisticated strategy to use of a more sophisticated one. Rather, at any time children can use each of the strategies to solve different problems; they may retrieve the answer to 3 + 1 but count to solve 5 + 8. What changes is the mix of strategies, where more sophisticated strategies are used more often, and less sophisticated ones less often (Siegler, 1996).

DON'T FORGET

Development of arithmetic problem solving does not progress linearly from less sophisticated strategies to more sophisticated ones. Rather, as children develop, more sophisticated strategies are simply used more often than less sophisticated ones.

Children With MLD and LA

Research on the development of arithmetic competencies in children with MLD and children with LA reveals that they use the same types of strategies during problem solving as their TA peers (e.g., Geary, 1990; Geary & Brown, 1991; Jordan & Montani, 1997; Ostad, 1997). However, children with MLD and children with LA differ in their procedural competence and in the development of long-term memory representations of basic facts (semantic memory; Geary, 1993).

Semantic Memory

Children with MLD and a subset of children with LA have difficulties learning basic arithmetic facts or retrieving them from long-term semantic memory once they are learned (Barrouillet, Fayol, & Lathuliére, 1997; Geary, 1990; Geary, Hamson, & Hoard, 2000; Jordan, Hanich, & Kaplan, 2003a). It is not that these children never correctly retrieve answers. Rather, they show a persistent difference in the frequency with which they correctly retrieve basic facts, and in the pattern of retrieval errors.

There are, at least, two potential sources of these retrieval difficulties, a deficit in the ability to represent phonetic/semantic information in long-term memory (Geary, 1993) and a deficit in the ability to inhibit irrelevant associations from entering working memory during problem solving (Barrouillet et al., 1997). The former has not been systematically studied, but is implied by the difficulties some children with MLD have in learning basic facts, even with repeated practice (e.g., Goldman, Pellegrino, & Mertz, 1988). The latter form of retrieval deficit was first discovered by Barrouillet et al., based on the memory model of Conway and Engle (1994), and has been confirmed in our laboratory (Geary et al., 2000).

One way to assess this form of retrieval problem (i.e., inability to inhibit irrelevant associations from entering working memory) is to ask children to solve a series of addition problems but instruct them to remember only the answer; that is, not to use counting (Jordan & Montani, 1997). Geary et al. (2000) administered this task to a mixed group of 2nd graders with MLD and LA and compared them to a group of children who were TA. The children with MLD/LA committed more retrieval errors, and between 17% and 29% of these errors were counting string associates of one of the addends; for example, the child retrieved 7 for the problem $4 + 6$ (7 follows 6 in the counting string). In a longitudinal study of MLD, Geary, Bailey and Hoard (submitted) administered the same task to MLD, LA, and children who are TA in 2nd, 3rd, and 4th grade. For a subgroup of children with LA (hereafter, LA-R; defined based on the high percentage of retrieval errors), 85% of their retrieved answers were incorrect in all three grades, with little across-grade improvement. The remaining children with LA showed 55% retrieval errors in 2nd grade and 37% by 4th. The MLD children showed 78% retrieval errors in 2nd grade and 59% by 4th. The children who are TA had the fewest errors; 37% to 34% across grades. The most intriguing finding was for the pattern of counting-string intrusion errors (e. g., retrieving 5 to solve $3 + 4$). These were rare among the children who are TA (5% of retrieval errors in 2nd grade), more common among the children with LA (9%), and especially frequent among children with LA-R (21%) and MLD (21%). Unlike most other tasks in which children with LA outperform children with MLD, the children with LA-R showed no across-grade drop in the percentage of intrusion errors, but the percentage dropped to 8% by 4th grade for the children with MLD.

DON'T FORGET
....
Children with MLD and some children with LA can have two types of memory problems that affect their ability to learn basic arithmetic combinations. One form results in difficulties memorizing the answers at all. With the other, the children may memorize the correct answer but when they try to remember it, other related numbers pop into their mind (e.g., 5 when asked to solve 3 + 4), and they become confused.

The overall pattern suggests that difficulties learning basic arithmetic facts are common among children with MLD, and that for some as yet unknown percentage of these children, extended practice may not be sufficient to overcome this deficit. Even when basic facts are committed to memory, many children with MLD and a subset of children with LA have more functional memory deficits. Specifically, when asked to retrieve an answer to a basic problem (e.g., 5 + 9), they retrieve several numbers from long-term memory, which results in a high percentage of retrieval errors.

Procedural Competence
Children with MLD and children with LA commit more procedural errors when they solve simple arithmetic problems (4 + 3), simple word problems, and complex arithmetic problems (e.g., 745 – 198) compared to their TA peers. Even when these children do not commit errors, they often use developmentally immature procedures in relation to their TA peers (Geary, 1990; Hanich et al., 2001; Jordan et al., 2003a; Jordan, Hanich, & Kaplan, 2003b; Raghubar et al., 2009). During the solving of simple addition problems, children with MLD use the sum-counting strategy more frequently and for more years than their TA peers, but most eventually become competent in using the min strategy. The pattern is especially pronounced for children with MLD and comorbid RD. Many of the children with LA also show a delay in the development of procedural competence, but do not show as severe a deficit in the solving of simple word problems, presumably because their reading

DON'T FORGET
....
The procedural competence of children with MLD is 2 to 3 years behind that of children who are TA. The procedural competence of children with LA is in between that of children with MLD and their TA peers, and represents about a one-year delay in comparison to children who are TA.

comprehension is better than that of most children with MLD (Jordan et al., 2003b). In all, the procedural competence of children with MLD is two to three years behind that of children who are TA (e.g., Geary et al., 2004; Ostad, 1998). The procedural competence of children in the LA group is in between that of children in the MLD and TA groups, and represents about a one-year delay in comparison to children who are TA (Geary et al., 2007).

The deficits and delays in children with MLD and children with LA when solving simple arithmetic problems become more evident when solving complex arithmetic problems (Fuchs & Fuchs, 2002; Jordan & Hanich, 2000). During the solving of multistep arithmetic problems, such as 45×12 or $126 + 537$, Russell and Ginsburg (1984) found that 4th grade children with MLD committed more errors than their IQ-matched TA peers. The errors involved the misalignment of numbers while writing down partial answers or while carrying or borrowing from one column to the next. Raghubar et al. (2009) confirmed this finding and found that it was more pronounced for subtraction than for addition. Common subtraction errors included subtracting the larger number from the smaller one (e.g., $83 - 44 = 41$), failing to decrement following a borrow (e.g., $92 - 14 = 88$; the 90 was not decremented to 80), and borrowing across 0s (e.g., $900 - 111 = 899$). These patterns were found for children with MLD and children with LA, regardless of their reading achievement.

Cognitive Correlates and Diagnostic Markers

The most commonly studied cognitive correlates of MLD and LA are working memory, speed of processing, and overall intelligence (e.g., IQ). Studies of the cognitive correlates of MLD and LA have attempted to determine whether deficits in one or more of these basic cognitive areas cause or modify the expression of MLD and LA.

Working Memory and Speed of Processing

A core function of working memory is to hold mental representations of information in mind while simultaneously engaging in other mental processes. Working memory is composed of a central executive function expressed as attention-driven control of information in two representational systems (Baddeley, 1986). These two representational systems are a language-based phonetic buffer and a visuospatial sketch pad. It has been well established that children with MLD do not perform as well as children who are TA on working memory tasks (Bull, Johnston, & Roy, 1999; Geary et al., 2004; McLean & Hitch, 1999; Swanson, 1993; Swanson & Sachse-Lee, 2001), but it is not fully understood which component or components of working memory contribute to the math cognition deficits of these children. Geary et al. (2007) simultaneously assessed the central executive, phonological loop, and visuospatial sketch pad components of working memory and sought to determine if these components are potential mediators of the math cognition deficits of children with MLD.

Geary et al. (2007) found that for the children with MLD, the central executive function was implicated as a potent source of their deficits across math cognition tasks that involved counting, number representation, and several aspects of addition. Phonological and visuospatial working memory contributed to more specific math cognition deficits, as did speed of processing. The children in the MLD group scored a full standard deviation below their LA peers—the average child with MLD was at the 16th percentile—on measures of each of the working memory systems, and showed a deficit of about the same magnitude on the speed of processing measure, consistent with Swanson and colleagues' findings of pervasive working memory deficits in children with MLD (Swanson, 1993; Swanson & Sachse-Lee, 2001). However, as described previously, children with LA have mild number-sense deficits, and the subset of children with LA-R have persistent difficulties in remembering basic addition facts. Neither of these LA groups has working memory deficits as assessed by standard central executive, phonological loop, or visuospatial sketch pad tests. The memory problems of the children with LA-R, nonetheless, suggest a deficit in one specific component of the central executive—the ability to inhibit irrelevant associations from entering conscious awareness—that is not assessed by many standard working memory measures (see also Raghubar, Barnes, & Hecht, in press).

DON'T FORGET

Children with MLD have pervasive working memory deficits, especially in the central executive.

Tasks that assess the central executive require children to hold one or several pieces of information in mind, while performing another mental task. For instance, an experimenter might say "3, 6, 9, 2" and the child is asked to repeat the sequence backwards. Tasks that assess the phonological loop just require memory for sounds, without mental manipulation; for example, repeating a string of three words verbatim. One task that assesses the visuospatial sketch pad involves the brief presentation of a maze, with a route drawn from start to finish; the child is then asked to reproduce the route on a blank maze.

The potential contributions of working memory to math cognition deficits are further complicated by speed of processing. Children with MLD and children with LA process information more slowly than children who are TA (Bull &

Johnston, 1997; Murphy et al., 2007; Swanson & Sachse-Lee, 2001), which in turn may result in performance deficits in many areas, including measures of working memory and mathematics. The relation between speed of processing and working memory, however, is debated and awaits full resolution. The issues center on whether individual differences in working memory are driven by more fundamental differences in speed of neural processing (Kail, 1991), or whether the attentional focus associated with the central executive speeds information processing (Engle, Tuholski, Laughlin, & Conway, 1999). Either way, children with MLD and children with LA are slower at executing many basic processes, such as identifying and naming numbers, which likely makes the learning of mathematics that involves these processes more difficult for these children.

Intelligence

Scores on standardized intelligence (IQ) tests are the best single predictors, though not the only predictors, of academic achievement (e.g., Walberg, 1984). Individuals who score poorly on tests of mathematical achievement are also likely to have lower than average IQs, but interest in the subject and a belief that effort is important can also influence mathematics achievement (Blackwell, Trzesniewski, & Dweck, 2007; Spinath, Spinath, Harlaar, & Plomin, 2006). Children with MLD typically have low-average IQs, which contributes to their slower learning of mathematics. However, most of the preceding described mathematical cognition deficits are found in children with MLD, independent of IQ. Children with LA typically have average IQ scores, and thus this cannot be a factor in their difficulties with number sense and fact retrieval.

COMPONENTS OF THE MULTIMETHOD DIAGNOSTIC APPROACH

Standard achievement and IQ measures should be part of the diagnostic assessment. Children with MLD typically score below the 10th percentile on nationally standardized mathematics achievement tests for more than one grade (Geary et al., 2007; Murphy et al., 2007); many children who score poorly in one grade may score in the average range the next, which is not associated with MLD or LA (Geary, 1990). The importance of IQ for diagnosing MLD has not yet been determined, but researchers will often exclude children who score below 85 (16th percentile) on IQ tests, with a typical IQ between 90 and 95 (average range). Children with LA tend to have mathematics achievement scores between the 10th and 25th national percentile and average IQs. Again, low mathematics achievement scores have to be observed across several grades before the child should be considered LA.

CAUTION
....

Low mathematics achievement scores must be observed across several grades before a child should be considered MLD or LA. Children with MLD will typically have IQs of 90 to 95 (about the 30th percentile), but mathematics achievement scores consistently below the 10th national percentile. Children with LA typically have average IQs (typically above the 30th percentile), but mathematics achievement scores consistently around the 20th national percentile.

Tests that are specifically designed to diagnose MLD and LA are still in the early stages of development (Geary et al., 2009; Jordan, Glutting, & Ramineni, in press; Locuniak & Jordan, 2008). Jordan and her colleagues have developed a number sense test that assesses kindergarten children's understanding of numbers, counting, and their implicit understanding that addition increases quantity and subtraction decreases it. They have shown that performance on these core number-sense competencies, assessed in their battery, are predictive of later mathematics achievement, above and beyond the influence of IQ and working memory. Geary et al. developed a potentially useful screening measure, the *Number Sets Test*.

The *Number Sets Test*: Useful Diagnostic Tool?

The *Number Sets Test* was designed as a group-administered pencil-and-paper measure of the speed and accuracy with which children can identify number and quantity of sets of objects and combine these with quantities represented by Arabic numerals. The combination of stimuli potentially taps critical features of number sense (Geary et al., 2007; see Rapid Reference 3.2).

Administering the Number Sets Test
Children are asked to determine as quickly and accurately as possible if pairs or trios of object sets, Arabic numerals, or a combination of these matched a target number (5 and 9). As shown in Figure 3.1, the object sets or numerals were combined to create dominolike rectangles; specifically, two types of stimuli were developed: 0 to 9 small objects (circles, squares, diamonds, and stars) in a half-inch square, and one Arabic numeral (18-point font) in a half-inch square. Each test page also includes two lines of three three-square rectangles for each combination. The target numbers are listed in a large font (36 point) at the

≡ Rapid Reference 3.2

....

Predicting Mathematical Achievement and Mathematical Learning Disability With a Simple Screening Tool: The *Number Sets Test*

Authors: David C. Geary, Drew H. Bailey, and Mary K. Hoard

Publication Date: 2009

Findings: Performance on the *Number Sets Test* was predictive of 3rd grade mathematics achievement scores and, in 1st grade, identified two thirds of children diagnosed as MLD in 3rd grade and nine-tenths of individuals without MLD.

Journal: *Journal of Psychoeducational Assessment, 27,* 265–279

top of each page. On each page, 18 items match the target, 12 are larger than the target, 6 are smaller than the target, and 6 contain 0 or an empty square.

Two items matching a target number of 4 are first explained for practice. Then, using 3 as the target number, four lines of two items are administered as practice. For test pages, the child is instructed to move across each line of the page from left to right without skipping any and to "circle any groups that can be put together to make the top number, 5 (9)" and to "work as fast as you can without making many mistakes." The child is given 60 seconds and 90 seconds per page for the targets 5 and 9, respectively. The test yields information on the number of items correctly identified (i.e., circles) as matching the target value—*hits*; the number of correct matches that were not identified—*misses*; the number of incorrect items that were not circled and thus rejected as matches—*correct rejections*; and, the number of incorrect items that were identified as matching the target—*false alarms*.

Scoring the Number Sets Test

The test is designed to allow for a signal detection analysis of children's accuracy (Macmillan, 2002). The key variable is sensitivity (d'), which represents the child's sensitivity in the detection of target quantities (i.e., 5 or 9) independent of tendency to circle items or not. For instance, one child might circle many correct items—that is, get many hits—but only because he or she has a bias to circle any item that looks close. This child will also have many false alarms. Another child may only circle items that he or she is certain are correct and will thus also have many hits but very few false alarms. The two children may have the same number of hits but the first child will have a lower sensitivity score (d') than the second child. The second child will get many items right and many items wrong, suggesting that he or she is guessing for a lot of the items. The sensitivity score controls for this tendency to guess.

Predictive Utility of the Number Sets Test

First graders' d', or sensitivity score, was highly correlated with mathematics achievement in 1st, 2nd, and 3rd grade, above and beyond the influence of working memory, speed of processing, and IQ (Geary et al., 2009). To assess the utility of the test for predicting MLD status, Geary et al. defined MLD as scoring at or below the 15th national percentile on the Numerical Operations mathematics achievement test (Wechsler, 2001) in 2nd and 3rd grade, with respective scores at the 8th and 7th percentiles. First-grade d' scores were a better predictor of MLD status at the end of 3rd grade than were 1st grade math achievement scores. Using statistical techniques to maximize the diagnostic sensitivity (ability to predict MLD) and specificity (ability to rule out MLD), the 1st grade mathematics achievement test scores identified 51% of children who were later diagnosed as MLD at the end of 3rd grade, and the d' scores identified 66% of these children. First-grade mathematics achievement and d' scores correctly identified 96% and 88%, respectively, of children who would not be diagnosed as MLD at the end of 3rd grade. Although more work remains to be done, the *Number Sets Test* has promise as a potential screening tool for identifying children at risk for MLD.

Treatment Protocols

There are few scientifically validated treatment protocols designed specifically to address the mathematical cognition deficits of children with MLD and their LA peers. The National Mathematics Advisory Panel conducted a meta-analysis of high-quality mathematics interventions for students with learning disabilities, broadly defined, and found that direct, teacher-guided explicit instruction on how to solve a specific type of mathematics problem was the most effective intervention (Gersten et al., 2008). The interventions were always for multiple sessions extending over several weeks to six months and resulted in large improvements in students' ability to solve mathematical word problems, computational arithmetic problems, and novel word and arithmetic problems.

Fuchs and her colleagues are developing cognitively motivated interventions for children at risk for MLD and LA (e.g., Fuchs et al., 2006; Fuchs et al., in press). They are designing these interventions to specifically focus on the mathematical cognition deficits described earlier. As an example, Fuchs et al. (in press) developed an intervention to increase the frequency and accuracy with which children with MLD use the min counting procedure to solve addition problems, and a corresponding procedure to solve subtraction problems. A combination of explicit instruction and deliberate practice of the counting procedures resulted in improved competence in solving simple addition and subtraction problems and more complex problems in which simple ones were embedded (e.g., 34 + 62 involves 4 + 2 for the units column and 3 + 6 for the tens column).

CONCLUSION

Research on the causes and treatment of MLD and LA has grown tremendously over the past 15 years. Although a consensus has not yet been reached, the field is moving toward a diagnostic cutoff for MLD at the 15th percentile on a mathematics achievement test for more than one grade, which effectively results in identifying children who score below the 10th percentile in most grades (e.g., Murphy et al., 2007). Some children who score below the 15th percentile in one grade may score higher in the next, but many other children score lower than this across successive grades, and many of these children will have scores below the 10th percentile in many of these grades. The cutoff for children with LA is more liberal but typically below the 25th or 30th percentile across several grades, which effectively results in identifying children who score at about the 20th percentile in most grades (Geary et al., 2007). Children with MLD and, to a lesser extent, children with LA show a deficit or delay in their number sense, learning of arithmetic procedures, and in memorizing basic arithmetic facts. These learning difficulties are related in part to their IQ (i.e., range of 90 to 95) and poor working memory for children with MLD, but not for children with LA.

Whatever the underlying causes, the number sense and procedural difficulties appear to be more of a developmental delay (improves across grades) than a deficit (shows little grade-to-grade improvement), with children with LA about one year behind TA peers and children with MLD about three years behind (e.g., Geary et al., 2004). The difficulties remembering arithmetic facts are more persistent for children with MLD and for a subset of children with LA. Recent research has also led to the development of assessment and screening measures that have the potential to be more effective than mathematics achievement tests for the identification of children at risk for MLD and LA (Geary et al., 2009; Locuniak & Jordan, 2008). Well-designed intervention studies that focus on the specific mathematical cognition delays and deficits of these children are also yielding promising results (e.g., Fuchs et al., in press). There is much that remains to be learned about MLD and LA, but if the past 15 years is any indication, in coming years we will witness the emergence of a mature field, with specific cognitively-informed diagnostic measures to pinpoint specific areas of deficit and corresponding treatment protocols.

RESOURCES

- Berch and Mazzocco's (2007) edited volume, *Why Is Math So Hard for Children?* provides an authoritative review of the current state of the field.
- Resources for parents and teachers can be found on the website for the National Center for Learning Disabilities (www.ncld.org), and updates on research on MLD and LA can be found on our MU Math Study website (http://mumathstudy.missouri.edu) and that of Lynn Fuchs at Peabody College, Vanderbilt University (http://peabody.vanderbilt.edu/x4751.xml).
- Technical reviews of the Gersten et al. (2008) learning disability intervention studies and of the cognitive processes underlying mathematical learning in general and in children with MLD (Geary et al., 2008) can be found on the website of the National Mathematics Advisory Panel (www .ed.gov/about/bdscomm/list/mathpanel/reports.html).
- The United State Department of Education What Works Clearing House provides a variety of research-based resources for parents, teachers, and principles (http://ies.ed.gov/ncee/wwc). These resources range from reviews of the effectiveness of mathematics curricula to practice guides for implementing specific instructional approaches for students having difficulty with mathematic

🐾 TEST YOURSELF 🐾

1. Individuals with low mathematics achievement scores, on average, have deficits in
   (a) number sense.
   (b) IQ.
   (c) working memory.
   (d) reading achievement.
   (e) all of the above.
2. Low mathematics achievement is _____ associated with genetic factors than typical and high mathematics achievement, suggesting that MLD is _____ "genetic," compared to typical mathematics achievement.
   (a) more; more
   (b) more; similarly

(c) less; less

(d) equally; similarly

(e) equally; more

3. **Individuals with MLD**

(a) use arithmetic strategies less efficiently than typically achieving individuals and execute them less efficiently.

(b) use arithmetic strategies less efficiently than typically achieving individuals, but execute them as efficiently.

(c) use arithmetic strategies as efficiently as typically achieving individuals and execute them as efficiently.

(d) use arithmetic strategies as efficiently as typically achieving individuals, but execute them less efficiently.

4. **The *Number Sets Test* is an especially useful predictor of later mathematics achievement and MLD status, consistent with the claim that impaired _____ is the key feature of MLD.**

(a) IQ

(b) peripheral vision attentional memory

(c) number sense

(d) manual dexterity

5. **Sources of arithmetic fact retrieval deficits include**

(a) insufficient encoding of facts in long-term memory.

(b) lack of experience with number lines.

(c) inability to inhibit irrelevant associations in working memory.

(d) both a and c

6. **Which of these is not an implicit principle of counting?**

(a) Cardinality

(b) Order-irrelevance

(c) Start-at-an-end

(d) One-one correspondence

7. **Which of the following statements is supported by recent research on number-line understanding?**

(a) TA and LA placements are linear by the end of 2nd grade.

(b) MLD placements are logarithmic by the end of 2nd grade.

(c) MLD placements are more compressed for larger numbers than LA and TA.

(d) All of the above

Answers: 1. e; 2. d; 3. a; 4. c; 5. d; 6. c; 7. d

Four

HOW SLD MANIFESTS IN WRITING

Nancy Mather
Barbara J. Wendling

DEFINITION, ETIOLOGY, AND INCIDENCE OF WRITING DISABILITIES

Like the writing process itself, writing disabilities are complex and multifaceted. Writing requires the linking of language, thought, and motor skills. A writer must employ and integrate many diverse abilities to write legibly, spell, and translate thoughts into writing. Difficulty in any one aspect of writing can contribute to difficulty in another. For example, poor fine-motor skill will directly impact handwriting, and then poor handwriting will impact the quality and quantity of written output. Thus, writing is a highly demanding task that has been described as "an immense juggling act" (Berninger & Richards, 2002, p. 173).

Definition

A disorder of written expression is defined in the *Diagnostic and Statistical Manual of Mental Disorders, Fourth Edition, Text Revision* (DSM-IV-TR; American Psychiatric Association, 2000) as writing skills substantially below expectation based on the individual's age, intelligence, and age-appropriate education. Furthermore, the disorder must significantly interfere with academic achievement or activities of daily living that require writing. In the Individuals with Disabilities Education Improvement Act (IDEA, 2004), written expression is identified as one of the eight areas for eligibility under the category of specific learning disability (SLD). Under the guidelines of both the *DSM-IV-TR* and IDEA, poor handwriting or poor spelling alone is insufficient for a diagnosis of a written expression disorder. The writing difficulties must interfere with the ability to express oneself in writing. Many times, however, lower-level skills, such as handwriting and spelling, are the reasons for an individual's difficulty with written expression. Early identification of writing problems requires that attention be given to children who are struggling with the development of handwriting and spelling, as these are the foundational skills of writing in the primary grades.

Etiology

Individuals with writing disabilities comprise a heterogeneous group. The causes for poor writing stem from a variety of factors, including medical, neuro-biological, neuropsychological, and/or environmental. Medical conditions such as carbon monoxide poisoning or fetal alcohol syndrome (FAS) have been linked to writing disorders (Bernstein, 2008), as has trauma to the parietal lobe of the brain (National Institute for Neurological Disorders and Stroke [NINDS], 2009). Results from family and twin studies indicate that a genetic component is involved (e.g., Bernstein; Raskind, 2001). Individuals with specific language impairments and delays are certainly at risk for writing difficulties. Neuropsychological causes may include difficulties with fine-motor skills, language, visual-spatial abilities, attention, memory, or sequencing skills. In addition, the causes of writing problems will vary based on the type of writing difficulty. For example, a problem with spelling may occur because of a limited ability to recall the orthography (written symbols) of a language, whereas a problem in written expression is more likely to stem from inadequate oral language development.

In some cases, writing difficulties may not be noted until some time after 1st grade, as more emphasis in the classroom may be placed on reading development. In fact, an individual's writing difficulties may not be observed until the student transitions from 3rd to 4th grade, when the writing demands increase dramatically and state testing often occurs.

Incidence

The prevalence of students with some type of learning disability is typically estimated to be between 5% and 6% of the total U.S. school-age population (National Center for Education Statistics, 2009). For writing disability, the prevalence appears similar to that of reading disability; problems with written expression are estimated to occur in 2% to 8% of school-aged children, with a

higher prevalence of boys than girls (Katusic, Colligan, Weaver, & Barba
2009; Wiznitzer & Scheffel, 2009). The number of individuals with only a specific
writing disability is difficult to pinpoint because individuals with writing disability
often have comorbid conditions, such as disorders in reading, math, attention, or
behavior. In a study addressing the incidence of written language disorders,
Katusic et al. found that 75% of the sample of students with written language
disorders ($N = 806$) in a large birth cohort were also experiencing problems in
reading. Thus, only about one-fourth of students with writing disabilities did not
have a reading disability.

Teachers, however, have reported a much higher incidence of handwriting
difficulties, estimating that nearly one-third of their male students and about 10%
of their female students struggle with
handwriting (Rosenblum, Weiss, &
Parush, 2004). These findings suggest that writing disabilities have
been underdiagnosed. This is partially due to comorbidity issues, but
also to the lack of emphasis on written language by researchers and edu-
cators alike. Evidence of the lack of instructional focus on writing in the U.S.
schools can be found in reviewing the National Assessment of Educational
Progress (NAEP) findings. According to the Nation's Report Card: Writing 2007
(Salahu-Din, Persky, & Miller, 2008), less than one-third of 4th and 8th graders
and less than one-fourth of 12th graders were found to be proficient in writing.

> **DON'T FORGET**
> ....
> Writing disabilities tend to be
> underdiagnosed even though the
> prevalence rate is similar to that of
> reading disabilities.

SUBTYPES OF WRITING DISABILITY

Individuals who struggle with writing may have difficulty with one or more aspects
of written language. Berninger (1996) suggested that when assessing writing, an
evaluator should consider the various "constraints" impacting writing. Understanding the multidimensional impact of constraints such as limited instruction,
specific cognitive or linguistic weaknesses, limited cultural experiences, and poor
motivation can help inform the type and extent of accommodations and
instruction needed, as the various constraints affect different aspects of writing
skill. In some cases, the problem is primarily with motor skills, which affects the
development of handwriting. Other times, the problem is primarily code-based,
impacting spelling; and in still others, it is primarily language-based impacting
composition. Frequently, the problems are combined, which complicates the
diagnosis and treatment of the individual's writing difficulties.

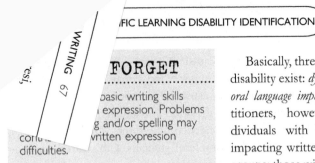

FORGET
....
basic writing skills
expression. Problems
g and/or spelling may
written expression
difficulties.

Basically, three subtypes of writing disability exist: *dysgraphia, dyslexia,* and *oral language impairments.* Many practitioners, however, categorize individuals with learning disabilities impacting written language into two groups: those with basic writing skills difficulties and those who experience difficulty with written expression. Difficulties with basic writing skills include the transcription skills of handwriting and spelling. Dysgraphia and dyslexia primarily impact these transcription skills. Difficulties with written expression, or text generation, primarily stem from oral language impairments or significant problems with executive functioning.

Dysgraphia

Dysgraphia has been described as a neurological disorder characterized by writing disabilities (NINDS, 2009), but definitions of dysgraphia vary. Some indicate that dysgraphia is essentially a type of motor disorder that manifests itself in poor-quality script (Deuel, 1994; Hamstra-Bletz & Blote, 1993). Other definitions associate dysgraphia with the inability to spell both familiar and novel words (Miceli & Capasso, 2006). Still other definitions indicate that dysgraphia is not a unitary disorder and that an individual may demonstrate poor functioning in any or all of the different facets of writing performance (Wiznitzer & Scheffel, 2009).

For the purposes of this chapter, dysgraphia is viewed as a primary impairment in graphomotor skills and the production of written forms, which can then affect handwriting and spelling development. Individuals with dysgraphia struggle with the motoric aspects of writing, having weaknesses in motor control and the execution of specific motor movements. They often have difficulty with letter-writing skills, difficulty with legibility (how easily others can recognize their letters), delayed automaticity (how many letters they can write in 15 seconds), and/or speed (the amount of time required to complete a writing task) (Berninger & Wolf, 2009a,b). These handwriting difficulties are often accompanied by problems in orthographic coding with or without graphomotor control or planning issues that result in poor spelling (Berninger, 2004; Gregg, 2009). Individuals with dysgraphia may have any level of intellectual and oral language abilities. They may have no difficulty in reading, or mathematics, with the exception of writing numbers. Figure 4.1 illustrates the writing of Toby, a 22-year-old college senior with dysgraphia who has average reading ability, but nearly illegible handwriting.

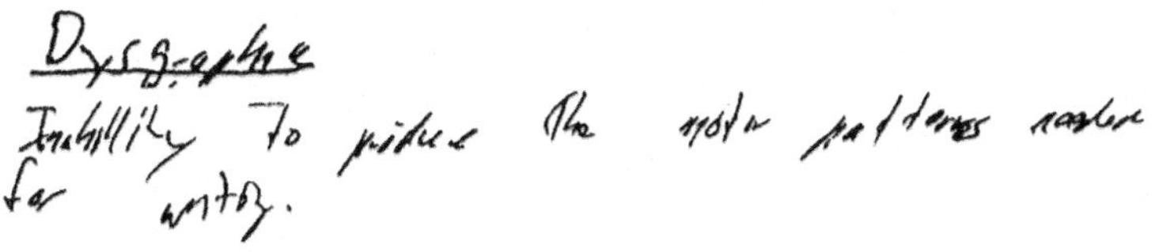

Dysgraphia

Inability to produce the motor patterns needed for writing.

Figure 4.1. Translation: Dysgraphia, the inability to produce the motor patterns needed for writing.

Dyslexia

A number of individuals with writing disabilities may be diagnosed with dyslexia, a disorder that affects both reading and spelling. In fact, poor spelling is often described as the hallmark of dyslexia (Gregg, 2009). Decoding (word reading) and encoding (word spelling) involve many of the same processes. These skills require mastery of the alphabetic principle or knowing how sounds and symbols correspond. For many individuals, problems in decoding and encoding stem from the same primary roots: poor phonological and/or orthographic abilities. Dyslexia and dysgraphia involve difficulties with the symbolic aspects of language—reading or writing words. Often, individuals with dyslexia or dysgraphia have average intellectual abilities and adequate oral language skills.

> # CAUTION
> Poor spelling with adequate ability to express ideas in writing is often typical of dyslexia and/or dysgraphia. Even though IDEA 2004 includes only the one broad category of written expression, poor spelling and handwriting are often symptomatic of a specific writing disability and should not be ignored.

Oral Language Impairments

Students with oral language impairments frequently exhibit difficulties with written expression because they lack the necessary lexical, morphological, orthographic, and syntactic knowledge to express their thoughts in writing. (See Rapid Reference 4.1 for definitions of these terms.) These students may also have difficulty with handwriting, and/or spelling. When limited language is the primary problem, the individual will have difficulties in both oral and written expression. When language is not the primary problem, the individual will be more capable in oral expression than in written expression. In these cases, it is important to explore the individual's

≡ *Rapid Reference 4.1*

Definitions of Terms

Lexical knowledge: Vocabulary; knowledge of the meaning of words and the relationships among words.

Morphology: The meaning units of language (i.e., prefixes, suffixes, and roots).

Orthography: The system of marks, including graphemes, that makes up written language.

Syntactic knowledge: Knowledge of grammar and the rules governing sentence structure.

DON'T FORGET

One feature of a specific learning disability in the area of written expression is that the individual is far more capable with oral expression than with written expression (Kronenberger & Dunn, 2003).

performance in basic writing skills, as well as his or her abilities to employ the executive functions required to plan, organize, and revise writing. Poor basic writing skills or poor executive functions could be possible reasons or contributing factors for problems in written expression.

HOW WRITING DIFFICULTIES MANIFEST DEVELOPMENTALLY

Handwriting, spelling, and written expression all follow different developmental courses, although a problem in one area can influence development in another area. A student with poor handwriting has fewer opportunities to practice spelling; a student with poor spelling may limit word choices to only those he or she knows how to spell; and a student with problems in ideation or expression may write simple sentences and repetitive ideas, resulting in slow development of spelling and vocabulary. Often, students who have difficulties with writing seem to become stuck in a developmental phase, until appropriate feedback and interventions are provided.

Handwriting

Warning signs of future writing difficulties are visible in the earliest writing attempts of children. Awkward pencil grips, illegible writing, saying words aloud while writing, avoiding writing tasks, or fatiguing quickly can all signal potential writing problems. According to Levine (1987), handwriting proficiency typically develops in the following stages: (a) *imitation* (preschool to kindergarten), when children pretend to write by copying others; (b) *graphic presentation* (1st and 2nd grade), when children learn how to form letters and to write on a line with proper spacing; (c) *progressive incorporation* (late 2nd to 4th grade), when letters are produced with less effort; and (d) *automatization* (4th through 7th grade), when children write rapidly, easily, and efficiently. In the final stages, students develop personalized styles and increase their writing rates. Students who struggle with handwriting often initially have difficulty learning to form letters and then have trouble writing with ease. In general, when compared to their classmates, students with learning disabilities demonstrate slower rates of handwriting speed (Weintraub & Graham, 1998).

Spelling

For most children, knowledge of phoneme-grapheme correspondences develops naturally over the preschool and early elementary years, progressing from the skill of knowing letter names and letter sounds to being able to break apart (segment) the individual sounds within words. As general guidelines, the majority of 1st grade students can segment words into syllables; by 2nd grade, most children can segment words into individual phonemes, and orthography, morphology, and syntax begin to increase in importance (see Rapid Reference 4.1 for definitions). Once a writer is able to sequence sounds correctly, he or she must then pay attention to various letter patterns and spelling options. As students' knowledge of orthography develops, they recognize and use permissible letter sequences, and they are able to sequence common letter strings in the correct order (e.g., *ight*). Although unexpected letters and irregular spelling patterns may be memorized, securing these images is more difficult than securing words that conform to common, regular spelling patterns (Ehri, 2000).

As spelling improves, the writer develops increasing awareness of the spelling of irregular words, affixes (prefixes and suffixes), as well as the spellings of words derived from Greek, Latin, or other languages. Several researchers have studied how spelling skill evolves and have proposed various models to explain the stages or phases of spelling development (e.g., Bear, Invernizzi, Templeton, & Johnston, 2008; Ehri, 2000; Gentry, 1982; Henderson, 1990). Rapid Reference 4.2 illustrates the phases of spelling development as proposed by Bear et al.

In addition, one must consider spelling development within the context of a specific language (e.g., Spanish has more regular grapheme-phoneme correspondence than English). Thus, children learning more consistent orthographies learn

≡ Rapid Reference 4.2

An Overview of Phases of Spelling Development

Letter-Name Alphabetic Spelling: Ages 5 to 8
- Progresses from using scribbles to using the names of the letters as cues to represent the sound.
- Learns to segment the sounds within words.
- Comprises three periods: early (prephonemic to semiphonemic), middle (phonetic), and late (transitional to correct).

Within Word Pattern Spelling: Ages 7 to 10
- Spells preconsonantal nasals (e.g., the "m" in *jump*), consonant blends (e.g., *bl-* and *-st*) and consonant and vowel digraphs (e.g., *ph* or *oa*).
- Spells most consonant-vowel-consonant-silent "e" (CVCe) words correctly (e.g., *five*).
- Spells some vowel teams correctly (e.g., *ea, oa, ai*).
- Spells some homophones correctly (e.g., *bear* and *bare*).

Syllables and Affixes: Ages 9 to 14
- Spells words of more than one syllable.
- Starts to consider syllables and affixes.
- Makes errors at place where the syllables and affixes meet (e.g., *hopful* for *hopeful*)
- Makes errors on unaccented second syllables (e.g., *mountin* for *mountain*)

Derivational Relations Spelling: Age 10 to Adulthood
- Spells common word derivations (e.g., *big, bigger, biggest*).
- Spells words of Greek and Latin origin correctly (e.g., *psychology* or *aquatic*).
- Uses spelling rules correctly when adding suffixes (e.g., doubling the final consonant (*stop → stopped*) or dropping the final "e" (*like → liking*) when adding a suffix that begins with a vowel).

to spell more quickly than those who are learning to spell less consistent orthographies. Phonological development may be universal to the development

DON'T FORGET

A child's primary language must be considered when analyzing his or her spelling development.

of all alphabetic languages, whereas the way sounds are mapped to letters is more language specific, making spelling in some languages easier than others (Goswami, 2006). In addition, the nature of the orthography of the native language will influence how children attempt to spell the English words that they are learning (Joshi, Hoien, Feng, Chengappa, & Boulware-Gooden, 2006).

Written Expression

As noted, one area of written language can affect development and performance in another area. If a writer has to stop and think about how to spell a word, an already developed idea may be forgotten (Graham, Berninger, Abbott, Abbott, & Whitaker, 1997). For the development of written expression, beginning writers often progress from scribbles to strings of letters, to single words, to lists and un-

> **DON'T FORGET**
> ....
> Ignoring problems in basic writing skills may delay the identification of a disability in written expression.

connected complete sentences, and then to complete connected sentences that are integrated to produce stories, paragraphs, or essays. Sentence syntax increases in complexity, as does the use of a variety of sentence structures that include embedded clauses. Whereas a less skilled writer may just use simple sentences or compound sentences, more advanced writers use different types of sentence structures to help maintain a reader's interest. As written language skills develop, students increase their knowledge of awareness of audience, organization, cohesion (unity of the ideas), and text structure. Because the nature of writing requirements changes as students progress in school, problems in written expression may not be noted until 3rd or 4th grade.

COGNITIVE CORRELATES AND DIAGNOSTIC MARKERS OF A SPECIFIC LEARNING DISABILITY IN WRITING

Writing involves the integration of many different cognitive and linguistic factors at several levels: *subword* (e.g., phonology, orthography, and morphology), *word* (e.g., spelling and vocabulary), *sentence* (e.g., syntax), and *text* (e.g., cohesion and type of text structure) (Englert & Raphael, 1988; Gregg, 1995, 2009; Gregg & Mather, 2002). These factors then influence the writer's ability to plan, draft, and edit (Englert, Raphael, Anderson, Anthony, & Stevens, 1991; MacArthur & Graham, 1993). Text generation and text revising, the most complex of the writing skills, involves numerous cognitive and linguistic capacities (e.g., idea generation, reasoning, oral language, and knowledge of syntax and vocabulary) (McCloskey, Perkins, & Van Divner, 2009). Careful analysis of the processing requirements of writing tasks can help determine which aspects of cognitive processing are involved; differential diagnosis requires careful examination of multiple subcomponent processes (Hale & Fiorello, 2004). The quality of written products can be increased or constrained by a multitude of factors (Hooper et al., 1994).

Over the last 25 years, Berninger (2009) and colleagues have carefully examined the various predictors of handwriting, spelling, and composing. In a review of the findings from their years of research, the best predictors of handwriting have been orthographic coding, the ability to form mental representations of written words, and graphomotor planning for sequential finger movements, which controls motor output. The best predictors of spelling have been measures of phonological and orthographic coding, as well as vocabulary knowledge in 1st through 3rd grade. The best predictors of composition fluency, the number of words written within a time limit, and composition quality have been orthographic coding, handwriting automaticity, and working memory. Spelling had a significant relationship to compositional fluency only in the primary grades, whereas handwriting automaticity had a significant relationship from 1st through 6th grade. In fact, automatic letter writing has been identified as the best predictor of composition length and quality for both elementary and high school students (Connelly, Campbell, MacLean, & Barnes, 2006; Jones, 2004). Thus, competence in written language is based on both the fluency and quality of the response (Hale & Fiorello, 2004).

Using contemporary CHC theory, the cognitive abilities related to written expression include the broad abilities of auditory processing (*Ga*), long-term retrieval (*Glr*), processing speed (*Gs*), crystallized intelligence (*Gc*), short-term memory (*Gsm*), and fluid reasoning (*Gf*) (Floyd, McGrew, & Evans, 2008). Auditory processing, in particular the narrow ability of phonetic coding, is important in segmenting sounds for spelling. Associative memory (a narrow *Glr* ability) and perceptual speed (a narrow *Gs* ability) are involved in mapping the sounds to their corresponding letters, another skill essential for spelling. Crystallized intelligence is a store of acquired knowledge and includes orthographic knowledge, knowledge of morphology, and lexical knowledge, all of which contribute to spelling and written expression. Short-term memory, which includes both memory span and working memory, is engaged during the writing process. For example, short-term memory is involved in maintaining the idea to be communicated while transcribing the words. Fluid reasoning includes the ability to think logically and to apply acquired knowledge to new situations, both of which are essential for written expression.

In addition, the process of expressing oneself in writing requires executive functions, such as attention, working memory, planning, and self-regulating behaviors. Ineffective or inconsistent use of executive function capacities can affect any aspect of the writing process and may be at the core of many written language problems (Dehn, 2008; Hale & Fiorello, 2004; McCloskey et al., 2009). These executive functions are also often impaired in individuals with attention deficit disorders, which helps explain the high prevalence of writing disabilities in that population (Mayes & Calhoun, 2006, 2007).

COMPONENTS OF THE DIAGNOSTIC APPROACH TO IDENTIFYING A SPECIFIC LEARNING DISABILITY IN WRITING

An assessment of written language disorders requires a multisource, multimethod diagnostic approach that includes both standardized assessments, as well as informal assessments, including curriculum-based measurements (CBMs) and classroom work samples. The evaluator should be clear about the reasons for testing, as well as the types of questions being asked so that the assessment is designed to address all major domains of concern (Hooper et al., 1994). Because writing leaves a permanent record of performance, the individual's difficulties can be easily observed and analyzed. The purpose of a comprehensive evaluation is to identify the basis for the impairment in handwriting, spelling, or written expression and then recommend the most appropriate interventions (Fletcher, Lyon, Fuchs, & Barnes, 2007). The evaluator's goal is to pinpoint the specific areas of writing difficulty and to identify the specific cognitive and/or linguistic correlates that are impeding the development of writing skills. Rapid Reference 4.7 lists assessment resources for practitioners.

Prior to conducting a comprehensive evaluation, valuable information about the student's writing skills can be gathered through the use of formative assessments, such as CBMs. Specific procedures are incorporated into CBMs to assess and monitor a student's performance in spelling or written expression. Instructional decisions are made using the data collected from administered CBM probes with criteria for goals and progress rates determined by comparison to a normative group (Deno, Fuchs, Marston, & Shin, 2001). Progress monitoring is then paired with instructional modifications, and data-based decision rules are used for interpreting graphed CBM data to determine the effectiveness of the instructional interventions (Stecker, Fuchs, & Fuchs, 2005). If a response to intervention (RTI) model is in place, this type of information should be readily available. However, even without an RTI model in place, information from CBMs may be incorporated as part of prereferral data or as a means to monitor progress after an evaluation has been conducted.

Handwriting

Three types of graphomotor disorders are prevalent in the adolescent and adult population with SLD and ADHD: *symbolic deficits*, *motor speed deficits*, and *dyspraxia*

(Deuel, 1992; Gregg, 2009). Gregg explains these different disorders as follows. With symbolic deficits, the writer has specific phonemic, orthographic, and morphemic weaknesses that affect only writing, not drawing. These linguistic problems often co-occur in individuals with dyslexia. With motor speed deficits, the writer is capable of good handwriting, but letters and words are produced slowly. Individuals with ADHD often exhibit motor speed deficits (Deuel). With dyspraxia, the writer has limited ability to learn and perform voluntary motor activities, which affects both writing and drawing.

In assessing handwriting, it is important to consider overall legibility, letter formation errors, and writing rate. Legibility is often best determined by attempting to read a student's papers. Letter formation errors are identified by examining words and letters more closely. Writing speed is often measured by asking a student to copy a short passage for one minute, or to write the letters of the alphabet as quickly as possible. In younger children, difficulties with handwriting usually result from a combination of fine-motor problems, limited ability to revisualize letters, and difficulty remembering the motor patterns for making the letter forms. With older children, problems often center on overall legibility and the fluency and automaticity of writing speed. A skill is automatic when it is mastered so well that minimal conscious attention and effort are required (Dehn, 2008). The speed and automaticity of graphomotor processing is the cornerstone for developing fluent text generation skills, as the automatic motor routines free up cognitive resources needed for generating ideas into text (McCloskey et al., 2009). Quick and accurate letter formation is often measured by the speed at which a student can write the alphabet and/or copy sentences.

> **DON'T FORGET**
> ....
> Fluent writing skills require automaticity and ease with graphomotor production.

Basic Writing Skills

Many standardized tests are available for assessing aspects of basic writing skills, such as the Woodcock-Johnson III Tests of Achievement (Woodcock, McGrew, Schrank, & Mather, 2001, 2007) or the Kaufman Test of Educational Achievement, Second Edition (Kaufman & Kaufman, 2004). In addition, analyses of classroom writing samples can help determine a student's knowledge of punctuation and capitalization rules, as well as the types and frequency of spelling errors. If spelling difficulties are present, which is often the case in students with SLD in writing, it is important to consider the student's knowledge and use of phonology, orthography, and morphology.

Phonology

Phonological processes are critical for the development of spelling skills because spelling requires an awareness of the internal structure of words (Bailet, 1991; Blachman, 1994). Even spelling problems in high school students and young adults reflect specific deficits in the phonological aspects of language (Bruck, 1993; Moats, 1995). The most important phonological

> **DON'T FORGET**
> ....
> Segmentation skill is critical to spelling ability.

awareness ability for spelling is segmentation, the ability to break apart the speech sounds (Ehri, 2006; Smith, 1997). This ability allows an individual to place the graphemes representing the phonemes in correct order. Segmentation can be tested using standardized tests or informal procedures. In addition, an individual's ability to spell nonsense words conforming to English spelling patterns can help reveal his or her knowledge of phoneme-grapheme connections.

Orthography

Students with weaknesses in orthography have particular difficulties remembering letter sequences and spelling words that contain irregular spelling patterns (e.g., *once*) because they do not have mental images of words stored in memory or word specific memory (Ehri, 2000). Results from a recent study suggested that high-functioning college students with dyslexia use phonological skills to spell familiar words, but they still have difficulty memorizing orthographic

> **CAUTION**
> ....
> Spelling nonsense words involves both phonological and orthographic knowledge. Difficulty may be caused by weaknesses in one or both aspects of linguistic knowledge.

patterns and recalling spelling rules, which results in inconsistent spellings of irregular and less familiar words (Kemp, Parrila, & Kirby, 2009). Orthography can be measured with standardized tests, such as the Test of Orthographic Competence (Mather, Roberts, Hammill, & Allen, 2008), or with informal procedures, such as having a student spell words that contain irregular elements, for example, *once*, *said*, and *again*.

Morphology

Morphology also interacts with phonology and orthography to affect the spelling of words. Students with weaknesses in morphology, the meaning elements of words, often have trouble with word endings (e.g., verb tense, plurals), as well as the spelling of prefixes and suffixes. Morphology also influences how words are spelled, as the spelling often preserves meaning, rather than letter-sound connections (e.g., *music* and *musician*, *hymn* and *hymnal*). As a component of orthographic knowledge, the evaluator should explore the writer's knowledge and use of varied morphological patterns.

Written Expression

Unfortunately, poor writers tend to lack knowledge about the entire writing process and are less likely than others to revise text to improve clarity (Hooper et al., 1994). Because reciprocal influences exist between oral and written language, oral language abilities will affect an individual's abilities to compose written text (Berninger & Wolf, 2009b). Thus, when evaluating a person's ability to express ideas, an assessment should also include measures of both receptive and expressive oral language. In addition, an evaluator should explore how the person performs on tasks requiring working memory and/or executive functioning. Individuals with good memory abilities are able to write more complex sentences and juggle multiple writing tasks (Dehn, 2008; Swanson & Siegel, 2001). Furthermore, an evaluator should consider a writer's declarative knowledge (e.g., knowledge of topics), procedural knowledge (e.g., knowledge of strategies used to produce various text genres), and conditional knowledge (e.g., which strategies or text structures to employ for a particular audience) (Hooper et al., 1994).

Cognitive/Linguistic Abilities

A comprehensive evaluation of the individual's cognitive and linguistic abilities is an important component of the diagnostic approach. Determining which abilities are intact and which are impaired is necessary to understanding why the individual is struggling with writing and is helpful in planning the most effective instructional program. Using a test such as the Woodcock-Johnson III Tests of Cognitive Abilities (Woodcock, McGrew, & Mather, 2001, 2007) provides comprehensive assessment of the underlying abilities related to writing. For example, the evaluator can assess many of the cognitive correlates mentioned previously: working memory, processing speed, comprehension-knowledge, fluid reasoning, long-term retrieval, and auditory processing. In addition, executive functions, such as attention, are very important to writing performance and should be explored.

DON'T FORGET
....
Oral language is the cornerstone of written language.

EXAMPLES OF TREATMENT PROTOCOLS

Many students who have been diagnosed as having a learning disability in written expression are spending all of their day in general education classrooms. Similar to their peers, they are being asked to produce clear, coherent writing to a variety of topics and demands in a timely fashion. In contrast to oral language and reading disabilities, less is known about the treatment of writing disabilities (Fletcher et al., 2007; Graham & Perin, 2007). This may explain why many students who struggle with writing make little improvement in skill across the grades. Poor writing cannot just be attributed to SLD; in fact, 2 out of 3 children in 4th grade do not write well enough to meet class expectations, and as many as 70% of students in grades 4 through 12 are deficient in writing skills (Persky, Daane, & Jin, 2003). Some teachers may not devote enough time to integrating writing into the curriculum, whereas others may focus too much on preparing students to pass writing exams rather than developing the writing skills that they will need in high school and postsecondary education. Thus, an effective writing curriculum requires that both general and special education teachers are knowledgeable about writing instruction and work together to help students improve their writing skills.

In selecting treatments for individuals with writing disabilities, one first has to consider: (a) the area or areas of written language that are affected, (b) the severity of the writing difficulties, and (c) how and where services will be delivered. For example, a student with dysgraphia is likely to benefit from instruction to improve keyboarding skill or the use of voice-recognition software, whereas a student with weaknesses in written expression will need to learn strategies to help with ideation and organization. Isaacson (1989) differentiated between the roles of the secretary and author in the writing process. Interventions geared to the improvement of basic writing skills are directed toward the secretary, whereas interventions directed toward improving composition ability address the role of the author.

Rapid Reference 4.3 includes seven recommendations provided by Cutler and Graham (2008) to improve primary grade writing instruction, followed by recommendations by Graham and Perin (2007) for improving writing instruction in middle and high schools. Several types of evidence-based programs have also been shown to result in beneficial outcomes for struggling writers. After an intervention or interventions have been selected, the duration and intensity of the services must be determined, as well as the specific ways to monitor and document an individual's progress.

Handwriting

In many school districts, handwriting instruction begins with manuscript writing and progresses to cursive writing, at the end of the 2nd or beginning of the 3rd

≡ Rapid Reference 4.3

....

Recommendations for Improving Writing Instruction

Recommendations for Primary Grade Writing Instruction
(Cutler & Graham, 2008)

1. Increase the amount of time students spend writing.
2. Have students spend more time writing expository text.
3. Teach both skills and writing strategies (e.g., teaching text structures explicitly).
4. Foster students' interest in and motivation for writing.
5. Encourage connections for writing between home and school.
6. Make computers a central part of the writing program.
7. Provide professional development for teachers.

Recommendations for Middle and High School Writing Instruction
(Graham & Perin, 2007)

1. Teach students strategies for planning, revising, and editing their compositions (e.g., Self-Regulated Strategy Development (SRSD) see Rapid Reference 4.6).
2. Teach students how to summarize texts.
3. Have adolescents work together to plan, draft, revise, and edit their compositions.
4. Encourage students to set specific, reachable goals for the writing that they are to complete.
5. Use computers and word processors as instructional supports for writing assignments.
6. Use sentence-combining activities to help students construct more complex sentence structures.
7. Engage students in prewriting to help them generate or organize their ideas.
8. Engage students in analyzing concrete information and data to help them develop ideas and content for a particular writing task.
9. Use a process writing approach that combines a number of writing instructional activities, which stress extended writing opportunities and writing for authentic audiences, and provides individualized instruction.
10. Provide students with models of good writing to read and analyze.
11. Use writing as a tool for learning content material.

grade. A general consensus does not exist regarding whether children with handwriting difficulties should be taught manuscript or cursive writing first; some children find printing to be easier, whereas others find cursive to be easier. Methods that teach manu-cursive (e.g., D'Nealian), a continuous-stroke method

≡ *Rapid Reference 4.4*

··

Common Elements for Handwriting Instructional Programs

1. Opportunities to practice handwriting: With older students, practice can include functional opportunities for writing (e.g., filling out job applications, bank forms, etc.).
2. Teacher modeling of correct letter formation with direct instruction of how to form the letters.
3. Opportunities to practice letter formation by tracing over models (e.g., dotted letters), with gradual fading of the models.
4. For younger students, provide primary paper with a middle line to foster the correct size of letters. As skill develops, provide the student with standard paper.

that is a mixture of the two styles, are probably the most effective, because a student has to master only one writing style. Instructional programs for handwriting have several common elements, which are summarized in Rapid Reference 4.4.

The following four principles are effective for teaching children letter formation: (1) forming letters with verbal cues and tracing until the letters and the patterns become automatic; (2) copying letters and then practicing writing letters in isolation and then within words; (3) encouraging students to evaluate their own handwriting; and (4) helping students until they acquire a clear, legible writing style (Mather, Wendling, & Roberts, 2009). Berninger (2009) describes the results from a prior large-scale study where the most effective method for teaching letter formation was the use of number arrow cues combined with writing letters from memory.

Word processors can help students bypass handwriting difficulties, allowing them to produce neat, clean copies of their written work. Because of their severe difficulties with handwriting, some students should begin word processing instruction as early as 2nd or 3rd grade. To become efficient at word processing, students require instruction in both keyboarding skills and how to operate the various functions of a word processing program.

Basic Writing Skills

Because of the pervasiveness of spelling problems among students with SLD, quality spelling instruction is essential. Traditional approaches to spelling, such as having

≡ Rapid Reference 4.5

Research-Based Principles for Effective Spelling Instruction

1. Present spelling words in lists, rather than in sentences.
2. Encourage students to pronounce the sounds in the words slowly as they attempt to spell the words.
3. Provide students with frequent and systematic review of the words they are learning.
4. Determine words that are appropriate for the students by analyzing their present level of skill development.
5. Do not ask students to write words several times as a study technique. Instead, have them write a word from memory without looking at the word.
6. Pay special attention to the teaching of irregular words, those that do not conform to English spelling patterns (e.g., *once*). Some students will benefit from tracing, saying, and then writing these types of words from memory.

students study for and take weekly spelling tests, or more holistic approaches, such as assuming children will learn to spell by writing, are ineffective for students who struggle. Although orthographic knowledge and knowledge of linguistic principles increase developmentally, many students with SLD develop more slowly in spelling skill than their peers. Thus, spelling is the major area of focus for instruction in basic writing skills. In addition, some students also require direct teaching of syntax and punctuation and capitalization rules. To determine appropriate spelling interventions, first it is necessary to assess and determine a student's level of underlying lexical or orthographic knowledge (Baumann & Kame'enui, 2004). Rapid Reference 4.5 describes the general research-based principles that will result in the most effective spelling instruction.

Written Expression

In general, teaching children explicit strategies that focus on planning, problem solving, and self-monitoring improves composition ability (Fletcher et al., 2007). It is difficult, however, for students to use strategies if they are not fluent in the lower-level skills of handwriting and spelling (Graham & Perin, 2007).

Self-Regulated Strategy Development
One well-researched example of a model for strategy training is self-regulated strategy development (SRSD), which has been tested in more than 40 instructional

≡ Rapid Reference 4.6

Stages of SRSD Instruction

Stage 1: Develop and activate background knowledge. At this beginning stage, the teacher models and explains any preskills that the students need to learn to understand the strategy. Sample compositions are read and discussed.

Stage 2: Discuss it. Students and teachers discuss the goals and benefits of strategy use.

Stage 3: Model it. The teacher models how the strategy is used, sets goals for what he or she plans to achieve, and then assesses whether the goals were met.

Stage 4: Memorize it. Students engage in activities to help them memorize the strategy steps.

Stage 5: Support it. The teacher provides scaffolds, prompts, and guidance, as students apply the strategies to their writings.

Stage 6: Independent performance. At this final stage, students are able to use the strategy correctly on their own.

---

writing studies with both elementary and secondary students (Graham & Harris, 2009; Harris & Graham, 1992; Harris, Graham, Mason, & Friedlander, 2008). Numerous applications of SRSD have been created to help students enrich their writing vocabularies, improve their abilities to produce both narrative and expository written text, and enhance their understandings of the higher-level cognitive processes required for composition. Rapid Reference 4.6 presents the stages of SRSD instruction as developed by Graham and Harris.

CAUTION

When students with SLD are taught strategies in general education settings, they may not receive explicit, intensive instruction that provides ample opportunities for practice and review (Schumaker & Deshler, 2009). They often do not receive individualized feedback on their practice attempts, and because mastery is not required, they do not acquire the writing strategies. Thus, specific instructional conditions must be in place, if students with SLD are to improve their writing abilities.

Teaching Text Structure

Another example of a method for helping students learn to recognize and use common organizational patterns is direct instruction in the different types of text structures, both narrative (e.g., story grammar) and expository (e.g., compare/

> **DON'T FORGET**
> ....
> Students with writing disabilities require instruction that is individualized, sequential, explicit, and systematic.

contrast, cause/effect, or sequential paragraphs and essays). This type of instruction helps students learn to plan and organize their compositions. To teach students about various text structures, teachers provide direct, explicit instruction by modeling different text structures and then show students how to use text structure models and graphic organizers to plan, generate, and monitor their writing. One example of a research-based approach for teaching text structure is Cognitive Strategy Instruction in Writing (CSIW) developed by Englert and her colleagues (Englert, 2009). The CSIW curriculum incorporates think sheets and graphic organizers to help students understand and self-evaluate their compositions.

CONCLUSION

Writing is one of the most complex human functions; it is a critical communication skill for academic success, as well social and behavioral well-being (Katusic et al., 2009). Because of the importance of writing throughout the life span, educators and psychologists concur that the early detection of writing difficulties is critical for school and vocational success (Hamstra-Bletz & Blote, 1993). Unfortunately, writing, referred to as the "neglected R" (National Commission on Writing in America's Schools and Colleges, 2003, 2004), has not received the same level of attention as has reading, from educators and researchers alike. Perhaps this helps explain why writing disabilities are underdiagnosed and, in many cases, addressed long after the onset of the individual's difficulties. Hopefully, additional research in the coming years will increase our knowledge regarding the identification of subtypes of writing disorders, as well as the most efficacious methods of assessment and intervention.

RESOURCES

Practitioners need to be aware of the assessment tools as well as the instructional materials for written language. Rapid Reference 4.7 lists several assessment tools for evaluating aspects of writing. Rapid Reference 4.8 lists examples of instructional materials for writing, and is organized into handwriting, spelling, and composition categories, followed by assistive technology and professional books.

≡ *Rapid Reference 4.7*

....

Assessment Resources for Practitioners

Motor/Handwriting

Beery-Buktenica Developmental Test of Visual-Motor Integration, Fifth Edition: www.psychcorp.pearsonassessments.com

Bruininks-Oseretsky Test of Motor Proficiency, 2nd Edition: www.psychcorp.pearsonassessments.com

Peabody Developmental Motor Scales, 2nd Edition: www.proedinc.com

Process Assessment of the Learner-Second Edition (PAL-II) Diagnostics for Reading and Writing: www.psychcorp.pearsonassessments.com

Informal checklists for observing and analyzing handwriting

Spelling

Subtests from Kaufman Test of Educational Achievement, Second Edition (KTEA-II) and Wechsler Individual Achievement Test, Third Edition (WIAT-III): www.psychcorp.pearsonassessments.com

Subtests from Woodcock-Johnson III Tests of Achievement (WJ III ACH): www.riversidepublishing.com

Subtest from Wide Range Achievement Test, Fourth Edition (WRAT-4): www3.parinc.com

Word Identification and Spelling Test (WIST): www.proedinc.com

Test of Written Spelling, Fourth Edition (TWS-4): www.proedinc.com

Test of Orthographic Competence (TOC): www.proedinc.com

Informal spelling inventories

Curriculum-based measures

Composition

Oral and Written Language Scales (OWLS) Written Expression Scale: www.psychcorp.pearsonassessments.com

Test of Written Expression (TOWE): www.proedinc.com

Test of Written Language, Fourth Edition (TOWL-4): www.proedinc.com

Writing Process Test (WPT): www.proedinc.com

Writing rubrics

Curriculum-based measures

Subtests from the Kaufman Test of Educational Achievement, Second Edition (KTEA-II)

Subtests from the Wechsler Individual Achievement Test, Third Edition (WIAT-III): www.psychcorp.pearsonassessments.com

Tests from the Woodcock-Johnson III Tests of Achievement (WJ III ACH): www.riversidepublishing.com

(continued)

Cognitive Abilities Related to Writing
Differential Ability Scales, Second Edition (DAS-II): www.psychcorp
.pearsonassessments.com

Kaufman Assessment Battery for Children, Second Edition (KABC-II): www
.psychcorp.pearsonassessments.com

Stanford Binet Intelligence Scales, Fifth Edition (SB5): www.proedinc.com

Wechsler Intelligence Scale for Children, Fourth Edition (WISC-IV): www
.psychcorp.pearsonassessments.com

Woodcock-Johnson III Tests of Cognitive Abilities (WJ III COG): www.riverside
publishing.com

≡ *Rapid Reference 4.8*

Instructional Resources for Practitioners

Handwriting or Keyboarding
Fonts4Teacher: www.fonts4teachers.com

Handwriting without Tears: www.hwtears.com

Read, Write, and Type: www.talkingfingers.com

Start Write: Handwriting Software: www.startwrite.com

The Handwriting Worksheet Wizard™: www.startwrite.com

Writing aids (e.g., pencil grips, raised line paper): www.thepencilgrip.com www
.theraproducts.com

Spelling
Franklin Spelling Tools: www.franklin.com

Patterns for Success in Reading and Spelling: www.proedinc.com

Phonics and Spelling through Phoneme-Grapheme Mapping: www.sopriswest.com

Scholastic Spelling: www.scholastic.com

Sitton Spelling Sourcebook Series: www.sittonspelling.com

Spellography: www.sopriswest.com

Word Journeys: Assessment-Guided Phonics, Spelling, and Vocabulary Instruction:
www.guilford.com

Words Their Way: Word Study for Phonics, Vocabulary, and Spelling Instruction,
Fourth Edition: www.phschool.com

Wordy Qwerty: www.talkingfingers.com

Composition
Draft Builder® www.donjohnston.com

Excellenceinwriting: Excellenceinwriting.com

Inspiration®: www.inspiration.com
Kidspiration®: www.inspiration.com
Write: Outloud®: www.donjohnston.com

Assistive Technology
Co-Writer® Solo: www.donjohnston.com
Dragon Naturally Speaking: www.nuance.com
Neo or Neo2 Portable Word Processors: www.alphasmart.com
WordQ® and SpeakQ®: www.wordq.com

Examples of Recent Professional Books
Best Practices in Writing Instruction (Graham, MacArthur, & Fitzgerald, Eds., 2007)

Handbook of Writing Research (MacArthur, Graham, & Fitzgerald, Eds., 2006)

Helping Students with Dyslexia and Dysgraphia Make Connections: Differentiated Instruction Lesson Plans in Reading and Writing (Berninger & Wolf, 2009a).

Teaching Basic Writing Skills: Strategies for Effective Expository Writing Instruction (Hochman, 2009)

Teaching Students with Dyslexia and Dysgraphia: Lessons from Teaching and Science (Berninger & Wolf, 2009b)

Writing Assessment and Instruction for Students with Learning Disabilities (Mather, Wendling, & Roberts, 2009)

Writing Better: Effective Strategies for Teaching Students with Learning Difficulties (Graham & Harris, 2005)

🐾 TEST YOURSELF 🐾

1. **IDEA 2004 indicates that a student can be identified as having a specific learning disability in either basic writing skills or written expression. True or False?**

2. **An individual with a specific learning disability in written expression always has limited oral language. True or False?**

3. **Why is it important to consider the individual's handwriting skills?**

   (a) Handwriting is predictive of the quality of written expression.

   (b) Handwriting automaticity is an important predictor of composition fluency.

   (c) Poor handwriting can interfere with spelling and composition.

   (d) All of the above

   (e) None of the above

4. **The most important phonological skill for spelling is**
   (a) blending.
   (b) segmenting.
   (c) deleting.
   (d) substituting.

5. **Awareness of the letters and letter strings is**
   (a) phonological awareness.
   (b) morphological awareness.
   (c) orthographic awareness.
   (d) phoneme-grapheme knowledge.

6. **Spelling is developmental in nature. True or False?**

7. **Difficulties in written expression may not be noted until the transition between 3rd and 4th grades. Why?**

8. **Dysgraphia is a disorder that always impacts just handwriting. True or False?**

9. **When evaluating an individual for a specific learning disability in written expression, consider**
   (a) performance on handwriting tasks.
   (b) performance on spelling tasks.
   (c) performance on oral language tasks.
   (d) all of the above.
   (e) b and c.

10. **Effective instruction for written expression should**
    (a) be explicit.
    (b) teach strategies.
    (c) teach text structures.
    (d) address all of the above.

Answers: 1. False; 2. False; 3. d; 4. b; 5. c; 6. True; 7. Writing demands change from single-word responses and filling in blanks to composition; or, emphasis is on reading not writing.; 8. False; 9. d; 10. d.

Five

HOW SLD MANIFESTS IN ORAL EXPRESSION AND LISTENING COMPREHENSION

Elisabeth H. Wiig

INTRODUCTION

Children and adolescents with language disabilities present a variety of symptoms and have different needs for assessment and intervention. It is the responsibility of the educational diagnostician to determine which tests and assessments to use to identify students' language strengths and weaknesses. This requires thought, and should be based on decisions concerning the variables that influence oral expression and listening comprehension that may need to be explored.

Intrapersonal variables describe what the child or adolescent brings to the process of using language for learning and social interaction. They include linguistic skills and competencies, brain-behavior and cognitive and emotional variables. The development and influence of these variables on oral expression and listening comprehension are explored in this chapter. The intrapersonal linguistic and neuropsychological variables related to oral expression and listening comprehension are addressed in many standardized, norm-referenced tests. Features of tests and assessments that evaluate the contributions of these variables are also discussed in this chapter.

Interpersonal variables are determined by the environment and culture in which the child or adolescent is raised and has to function. They include the educational setting of school, the culture within the school, the curriculum objectives and expected educational outcomes and the community and society at large. The interaction between language disabilities and the demands for using language in social contexts will be discussed. Educational and academic assessments focus on the student's interactions with the curriculum, and these are discussed in greater detail in other chapters included in this volume. This chapter will touch only briefly on assessing academic achievement.

DEFINITION, ETIOLOGY, AND INCIDENCE OF LANGUAGE DISABILITIES

Definition

Language-based learning disabilities are specific learning disabilities (SLD) that reflect disorders in one or more of the psychological processes involved in learning and using the linguistic system for academic pursuits and social interactions. They are often described as involving primarily oral expression (oral language) or as a combination of difficulties in oral expression and listening comprehension. The Individuals with Disabilities Education Improvement Act (IDEA) (U.S. Department of Education, 2004) subsumes language disabilities under the broader category of specific learning disabilities. A language disability is considered to exist if a student does not achieve adequately for age or does not meet state-approved grade-level standards in the areas of oral expression or listening comprehension.

The *Diagnostic and Statistical Manual of Mental Disorders, Fourth Edition, Text Revision* (DSM-IV-TR) (American Psychiatric Association, 2000) defines language disabilities from a clinical perspective as being either of the "Expressive" (code 315.31) or "Mixed Receptive-Expressive" (code 315.32) type. Expressive language disabilities are identified by the following criteria: (a) development of oral expression is significantly below the development of listening comprehension and nonverbal intellectual ability, (b) language disabilities interfere with academic, vocational, and professional achievement and/or social communication, (c) the language difficulties are in excess of those usually observed in cases with cognitive, sensory, or motor deficits or environmental deprivation, and (d) symptoms do not meet criteria for a combined disability in oral expression and listening comprehension or pervasive developmental disorders (DSM-IV- TR, pp. 58–61). "Mixed Receptive-Expressive" language disabilities are defined by the following criteria: (a) oral expression and listening comprehension are significantly below nonverbal intellectual ability, (b) language disabilities interfere with academic, vocational, and professional achievement and social communication and (c) symptoms do not meet criteria for pervasive developmental disorders (DSM-IV-TR, pp. 62–64).

The *International Statistical Classification of Diseases and Related Health Problems, Tenth Revision* (ICD-10) (World Health Organization, 2005) categorizes language disabilities as either "Expressive" or "Receptive" (codes F80.1 and F80.2). In both definitions (DMS-IV-TR and ICD-10), oral expression disabilities are considered to constitute a separate clinical, diagnostic category, a concept that is challenged by Leonard (2009).

The modality-based categorization systems for language disabilities featured in DSM-IV-TR and ICD-10 are reflected in many standardized language tests. Thus, vocabulary tests traditionally separate receptive and expressive abilities, and even recent language tests feature composite or index scores for receptive (listening comprehension) versus expressive language (oral expression) abilities. This reflects a long-standing tradition in standardized assessments that clinicians and publishers are reluctant to abandon, but that this author, albeit in vain, has argued to discontinue. My colleagues and I agree with Leonard's (2009) view that "expressive language disorders" cannot be uniquely separated from "receptive language disorders." Some of the reasons separate categories have been challenged are summarized in Rapid Reference 5.1. We also agree that a "receptive-expressive" (listening comprehension and oral expression) diagnostic category may be more accurate due to overlaps in the processing requirements for understanding and using oral language for communication.

In clinical/educational practice, language disabilities are commonly identified by the language domains or the neuropsychological functions that are affected. The general approach used by speech-language pathologists to describe language disabilities uses the domains of language affected as a reference. In this system, language disabilities are classified as affecting primarily content (meaning/semantics), structure (phonology, morphology and syntax), use (contextual

≡ Rapid Reference 5.1

Reasons Why Separate Categories of Language Disabilities Have Been Challenged

- Details of oral language that are important for identifying language disabilities, such as using morphology grammatically (e.g., verb tense, auxiliary "is"), are difficult to evaluate through comprehension.
- Many children classified by tests as having an expressive language disability were reclassified as having a receptive-expressive disability a year later (Conti-Ramsden & Botting, 1999).
- Using factor analysis on standardized language test results, a single-dimension model (receptive-expressive) best explained the nature of language disabilities (Tomblin & Zhang, 2006).

≡ *Rapid Reference 5.2*

Language Domain Definitions

- *Phonology* refers to the rules used to combine speech sounds to make meaningful words.
- *Morphology* refers to the rules for using small units of meaning (morphemes) to indicate, among others, the third person (-s) and tense of verbs (-ed), auxiliary verb (*is*), and comparisons (-er and -est).
- *Syntax* refers to the rules used for combining words into simple sentences with one clause or complex sentences with multiple clauses.
- *Semantics* refers to the word content (vocabulary) and rules for using this to form meaningful units of expression.
- *Pragmatics* refers to the rules for using words, sentences and expressions in informal or formal social interactions. An example is asking for permission by saying, "May I . . . "

use/pragmatics) or combinations of these (see Rapid Reference 5.2 for definitions). This categorization system results in identification of individual profiles of strengths and weaknesses across language domains. It is reflected in standardized language tests that provide composites or index scores for abilities related to language content versus language structure. Some standardized language tests also include behavioral rating scales to establish criterion-referenced measures for language use in context (pragmatics).

When the domain-specific categorization system is used to identify the nature of a language disability, primary deficits in the acquisition and use of structure (grammar) appear more common than deficits in content (vocabulary). Deficits in both domains, as well as in the use of language in context (pragmatics), are characteristics of severe language disabilities. One advantage of using a linguistic classification system in educational practice is that targeted outcomes for intervention/education can be developed to correspond to grade-level curriculum objectives for, among others, English and Language Arts. A second advantage is that published methods and materials, both traditional and evidence-based, tend to target a specific linguistic domain, either content, structure, or use, for intervention.

The neuropsychological categorization system uses measures of immediate and working memory, verbal fluency for semantic categories (e.g., animal names), processing speed for naming familiar visual input (e.g., colors, shapes, numbers,

≡ Rapid Reference 5.3

....

Identifying Absolute and Relative Strengths and Weaknesses

In norm-referenced testing, a student's absolute and relative strengths and weaknesses on subtests can be identified to form a profile.

- *Absolute* (normative) strengths and weaknesses are judged against peer performance on standardized, norm-referenced subtests having a mean of 10 and a standard deviation of 3. Subtest scaled scores at or above 10 + 3 (or 13) can be judged as absolute strengths, and scores at or below 10 − 3 (or 7) as absolute weaknesses (Semel, Wiig, & Secord, 2004).
- *Relative* strengths and weaknesses can be judged against the average of a set of subtest scaled scores. Any deviation of 3 or more scaled score points from the mean of the subtests is judged as either a relative strength or weakness, depending on the direction of the deviation from the mean (Semel et al., 2004).

letters), and other executive functions related to self-regulation as reference. These measures may be included in standardized language tests (Semel et al., 2004). The diagnostic advantage of identifying absolute or relative strengths and weaknesses (see Rapid Reference 5.3) within executive functions relates directly to the determination of, among others, possible compensatory strategies, using multimodal input or providing structured approaches that develop critical thinking to support executive functions.

Etiology

Language acquisition and maturation involve a complex process, and the functional systems engaged can easily be disrupted by genetic, neuroanatomical, neurological, medical, and environmental factors (Brown & Hagoort, 1999). Language disabilities can also be secondary in nature. For example, language and communication disabilities are part of genetic syndromes such as the Down, Fragile X, and Tourette spectrum syndromes (Dornbush & Pruitt, 1995; Prestia, 2003). In addition, language disabilities are a core part of autism spectrum disorders, and co-occur with attention deficit/hyperactivity disorder (ADHD), executive function disorders (EFD) such as obsessive-compulsive disorder, and psychiatric disorders such as bipolar and anxiety disorders and psychosis (Barkley, 1997; Brown, 2000; Culatta & Wiig, 2002; Pinborough-Zimmerman et al., 2007; Ottinger, 2003; Wetherby, 2002). Language disabilities can also result from traumatic brain injury at any stage of development. Environmental factors, such as exposure to toxic elements, prenatal factors such as psychosocial stress exposure during gestation, and very low birth weight can also cause language disabilities (Breslau, Chilcoat, DelDotto, Andreski, & Brown, 1996; Entringer et al., 2009).

It is generally accepted that children and adolescents with language disabilities represent a heterogeneous group whose disabilities result from a variety of factors. The group becomes more heterogeneous with age and as cognitive demands and language requirements for academic pursuits and social interaction increase. As a result, language disabilities are expressed differently across the life span (Larson & McKinley, 2003; Paul, 2000).

Neuroanatomical Bases

Research of neurological bases for language disabilities points to variations from the average or normal in the development of critical neuroanatomical structures. Thus, neurologists have developed an anatomical risk index that combines measures of brain volume, asymmetrical development, and other anatomical differences that are either specific or nonspecific for language disabilities, dyslexia, and/or schizophrenia (Leonard et al., 2001; Leonard et al., 2008). Children with high negative risk index scores show inferior performance on listening comprehension, oral expression, and reading measures (Leonard et al., 2002; Leonard, Eckert, Given, Virginia, & Eden, 2006; Leonard, Eckert, & Kuldau, 2006). These findings link language disabilities and dyslexia through shared neurological risk factors, a link that is often seen in educational practice.

With advances in neuroimaging, the earlier emphasis on anatomical and gray-matter cerebral factors and functions has shifted to focus on white-matter development and associated cerebral functions (Fields, 2008). The brain's white matter contains millions of axons that are covered with myelin, a fatty substance that surrounds and insulates the axon of some nerve cells. The axons connect neurons in different regions of the brain, and neural impulses travel about 100 times faster along neurons when the axons are adequately covered with myelin. Specific cells regulate myelination, and defects in these cells have been associated with mental disorders and are assumed to be present in language disabilities with executive dysfunction. Higher levels of myelination of white-matter structures have also been associated with higher IQ (Fields). Knowledge of white-matter development and functions opens new avenues for explaining why we observe executive function disorders in many children with language disabilities and why these become increasingly prominent during adolescence.

Incidence

Prevalence reports for language disabilities vary, depending on factors such as severity and type of disability, age of identification, and criteria used for inclusion and definition. A study of children in kindergarten reported an overall prevalence rate of 7.4%, with a higher rate among boys (8%) than girls (6%) (Tomblin, Mainela-Arnold, & Zhang, 2007). Other studies indicate prevalence rates from 6% to 8% of school-age children (Gilger & Wise, 2004), and an estimated 50% of children with early language disabilities later experience reading difficulties. A recent study of 8-year-olds estimated the prevalence rate for language disabilities to be 6.3%, and the ratio of boys to girls to be nearly double (1.8 to 1) (Pinborough-Zimmerman et al., 2007). The percentage of language disabilities associated with autism spectrum disorders has been estimated at 3.7%, with intellectual disability (i.e., IQ < 70) at 4%. The prevalence rates for mental health disorders that co-occur with language disabilities are reported at 6.1% for ADHD, 2.2% for anxiety disorders, and 1.7% for conduct disorders (Pinborough-Zimmerman et al.).

LANGUAGE DISABILITY SUBTYPES

Searches for syndrome clusters in children with language disabilities, referred to by speech-language pathologists (SLPs) as *specific language impairments* (SLI), indicate clusters that are common for English- and Dutch-speaking children (Botting & Conti-Ramsden, 2004; van Daal, Verhoeven, & Van Balkom, 2004; Haskill & Tyler, 2007). One common cluster identifies children with phonological and concurrent oral expression deficits. Children in this group have difficulties articulating speech sounds and show delays from age-level expectations for intelligibility in oral expression. A second common cluster identifies children with phonological, syntactic, and lexical deficits. Children in this group have delays in phonological awareness that may include, among others, problems in blending or substituting sounds or rhyming. They also have problems acquiring the rules for combining words into grammatical sentences, especially when clauses are combined into longer, complex sentences. These

DON'T FORGET

The term *specific language impairment* (SLI) is generally used to label school-age children, adolescents, and young adults for whom language disabilities are of a primary nature, and do not result from emotional disorders, cognitive delays, sensory impairments, or language differences (Leonard, 1998; National Joint Committee on Learning Disabilities, 1994).

children may have limited vocabularies and difficulties in making the transition from using words for concrete references (i.e., referring to specific objects, actions, or attributes) to using the words for abstract references or in figurative expressions. Children in the latter cluster exhibit the most severe language learning disabilities.

DEVELOPMENTAL MANIFESTATIONS

The linguistic system is complex and a child must acquire and store a large repertoire of words, phrases, and sentences (vocabulary and grammar) in long-term memory. Because language is combinatorial, allowing us to create an infinitely large number of utterances of varying lengths, a set of combinatorial principles or rules (mental grammar) must be learned to create novel utterances and messages. This requires adequate working memory to be able to process, interpret, and produce language in real time (i.e., at normal rates of speech). To develop language competence, the brain must process information from several linguistic domains. Processing must occur rapidly and synchronously within the functional neural networks involved in creating and/or expressing meanings and intentions. This results in a complex process of acquisition that takes more than a decade for the normally developing child and occurs in predictable steps and stages. In the following discussions, the representational language system will be divided into structure, content, and use.

Acquisition of Structure

At the level of phonology, the child must learn rules for processing speech-sound sequences and combining speech sounds (phonemes) into words. This is important because the phonological system interfaces with syntactic structure (morphology and syntax), and phonological skills support listening and speaking and the acquisition of literacy skills for reading and writing. In normally developing children, phonemic skills develop in infancy and interface with meaning so that by 18 months most children understand about 150 and use about 50 words for communicating. This learning process requires language-specific listening (i.e., categorical perception) and computational strategies for recognizing repeated speech-sound (phonemic) patterns and combinations of speech sounds into words (Kuhl, 2004).

The child must also acquire linguistic rules for interpreting and expressing number, tense, comparison, and reference marked by pronouns (morphology). The morphological rule system is generally acquired during the preschool and early elementary school years and is normally well established by Grades 3 through 4. The early syntactic rule system applies to forming simple sentences with a single clause, and the typical child acquires these rules during the preschool years concurrently with the acquisition of morphology. Coordinated clauses with the words *and, but, or* develop during the late preschool years. Typical children at age 5 develop complex sentences with subordinated clauses: adverbial (e.g., "She left before . . . "), nominal (e.g., "She decided that . . . "), and relative (e.g., "She told the woman who . . . "). These sentence structures are later refined by increasing length and degree of abstraction and by increases in knowledge bases (Nippold, Hesketh, Duthie, & Mansfield, 2005; Nippold, Mansfield, & Billow, 2007).

CAUTION

It is often assumed that late-talking children will have significant language difficulties or develop a language disability. This assumption has not been supported by several studies (Rice, Taylor, & Zubrick, 2008; Weismer, 2007). For example, Weismer reported that only 8.8% of late talkers end up with impaired language at age 5 years. The same study indicated that a late-talking child's comprehension of language at 2½ years of age is the best predictor of language production at age 4½ years.

During the preschool and early grades, children with language disabilities exhibit difficulties in acquiring rules for using, among others, the auxiliaries *be* and *do*, third-person singular *-s*, regular past-tense endings (e.g., *-ed*), and irregular forms of nouns and verbs. They use word endings inconsistently compared to typically developing children, and the percentage of accurate identifications of children with and without language disabilities (predictive values), based on the use of morphology, approximate or exceed 80% (Bedore & Leonard, 1998; Joanisse, 2004). School-age children and adolescents with language disabilities show deficits in the use of complex syntax during conversation and in narrative and expository dialogue. They typically produce shorter and simpler sentences and use fewer subordinate clauses (Nippold, Mansfield, Billow, & Tomblin, 2008). Among 15-year-olds with a history of early language disabilities (Grade 1), the syntactic competence still differs from that of typically developing children (Nippold, Mansfield, Billow, & Tomblin, 2009). The language disabilities of these adolescents are reflected by lower density in number of clauses and use of nominal clauses in discourse and by syntactic deficits on a standardized language test. Moreover, the discourse and standardized measures of use of syntax correlate significantly, indicating that errors in the spontaneous use of syntax for socialization also occur on formal tasks featured in standardized tests.

Acquisition of Content

During the preschool and school years, children must develop large vocabularies, associated concepts, and combinatorial rules (i.e., semantics) that interface with the syntactic structures. This level of the linguistic system develops and is modified throughout a speaker's lifetime. The structural and semantic language systems are acquired through analogical comparisons that are common for learning in all cognitive domains. The required comparisons develop from an initial focus on concrete similarities to comparisons of abstract relational similarities in a process of progressive alignment (Gentner & Namy, 2006). Problems in the understanding and use of prepositions, space and time references (e.g., using *forward* for space or time), antonyms (e.g., *inward* and *outward*), synonyms (e.g., *configuration* for *pattern*), abstract words (e.g., *ethics*) and figurative expressions (e.g., *bridging the generation gap*) are among typical characteristics of individuals with language disabilities.

Acquisition of Use

The rule system for communication in context (pragmatics) is driven by the human need for expressing intentions, controlling self and others, and adapting to cultural-linguistic expectations. Because the system is exceedingly complex and requires adequately functioning interactive neuronal networks, much can go wrong if one or more of the components of the network is damaged. One of the important pragmatic functions is to elicit and share information through questioning. Children with language disabilities tend to have problems understanding and using higher-level *wh*-questions (e.g., "why?" "how?"), even when asked in the context of illustrations (Deevy & Leonard, 2004).

When asked *wh*-questions that require inferential thinking (i.e., going beyond the facts given in a simultaneously spoken and read text), they have significant difficulties (Wiig & Wilson, 1994). In addition, children and adolescents with language disabilities have difficulties interpreting intentions that are expressed indirectly to control the environment and others (e.g., "Shouldn't you take your shoes off?"). They also have difficulties engaging in interactions that require complex intentions such as apologizing, persuading, and negotiating terms.

COGNITIVE CORRELATES AND DIAGNOSTIC MARKERS

Attention

Attention has been described as concentration, focalization, and consciousness, and is considered the aspect of human cognition that can be controlled in the presence of limited capacity or resources (Anderson, Anderson, & Anderson, 2006). The functional system involved in executive attention is formed by several interactive components. The nature and degree of attentional deficits vary across disorders, depending on which underlying brain structures are involved (See Rapid Reference 5.4).

Attentional capacities increase throughout childhood with the maturation of the central nervous system and frontal lobes (Manly et al., 2001). Selective attention develops early, between ages 6 and 13 years. Stable sustained attention develops later, with growth in all aspects of attention between ages 8 and 10 years and a spurt in development occurring around age 11 years. Impaired attention, especially response inhibition, is prevalent in ADHD and is associated with frontal lobe dysfunction (Semrud-Clikeman et al., 2000). In a recent study, children with ADHD performed poorly on all measures of attention featured in a continuous processing test, indicating pervasive deficits in the integrity of the attentional system (Anderson et al., 2006). Deficits in sustained attention and processing speed are also prevalent after moderate or severe traumatic brain injury (TBI), and children with moderate TBI show mild attentional deficits, involving primarily selective and sustained attention (Anderson et al.). Because language disabilities co-occur with ADHD and TBI, it is important to assess the degree and nature of attentional deficits to provide appropriate support during language intervention and in the classroom.

≡ Rapid Reference 5.4

....

Different Types of Attention

Sustained attention maintains attention over time and is controlled by the reticular formation, brain stem, and frontal regions of the brain.

Selective attention allows us to focus on a single stimulus and block distracters, and is mediated by temporal, parietal, and striatal regions of the brain.

Inhibiting responses, dividing and shifting attention comprise the executive level of the attentional system, mediated by the frontal lobes.

Processing Speed

Processing speed refers to the rate at which a child or adolescent can respond to a series of simple auditory or visual stimuli. Processing speed deficits have emerged as contributing factors in, among others, language disabilities, dyslexia, and other reading disabilities in children, adolescents, and adults (Leonard et al., 2007; Miller et al., 2006; Tallal, 2003; Wiig, Zureich, & Chan, 2000; Wolf, Bowers, & Biddle, 2000). Frontal and/or temporal-parietal brain regions and subcortical structures mediate processing speed, depending on whether the input is auditory or visual. Processing speed appears related to the extent of myelination, dendritic branching, and neurochemical or biophysical factors (Colombo, 2004). Higher levels of processing speed have been linked to greater working memory capacity and to inductive reasoning abilities (Kail, 2007). Thus, the ability to learn novel, nonnative speech sounds has been linked to the extent of white matter in the left temporal-parietal brain region, and dyslexia has been linked to abnormalities in the white-matter connections between the temporal and parietal regions. The evidence suggests that processing speed is not domain specific, but rather affects many domains and represents activation of integrative neuronal networks, as suggested by observed associations between general intelligence and processing speed (Ho, Baker, & Decker, 2005).

In the auditory-processing speed domain, Tallal (2003) reports that infants who respond fast and accurately to rapidly changing auditory input, develop language normally. In other words, the acoustic patterns for phonemes in a language are learned through repeated experience at normal conversational rates. The repetitions set up distinct neural firing patterns in the brain regions that mediate rapid auditory processing. In contrast, infants who respond correctly only when auditory stimuli are presented at slower speeds are at risk for language disabilities (Tallal). That is, the language-learning process is slowed down when the acoustic properties of natural speech change too rapidly for a child to process and because demands differ as a function of the linguistic context in which a phoneme is produced.

In the visual-processing speed domain, differences in processing speed affect the early development of reading skills and fluency in reading. In infants, toddlers, and young preschoolers between ages 5 and 36 months, visual-processing speed develops in similar linear patterns in full- and preterm infants. However, levels of performance differ (Rose, Feldman, & Jankowski, 2002). Full-term infants require shorter time, in seconds, for attention, and need fewer repetitions for familiarization, than preterm infants, both positive precursors for effective processing speed.

≣ *Rapid Reference 5.5*

Speed of Processing

Single-dimension naming (e.g., colors or forms) measures reaction + retrieval + response time, or "perceptual speed."

Dual-dimension naming (e.g., color-form combinations) measures perceptual speed + cognitive overhead that results from increased demands on attention, visual working memory, and set shifting, or "cognitive speed."

Neuroimaging of regional cerebral blood flow (rCBF) during rapid naming of color-form combinations reveals that cortical blood flow increases significantly in the temporal-parietal regions bilaterally, and decreases in frontal regions (Wiig Nielsen, Minthon, & Warkentin, 2002).

Functional magnetic resonance imaging (fMRI) validates rCBF and shows concurrent activation of subcortical regions, including the hippocampus (Wiig, Nielsen, Minthon, & Jacobson, 2008).

Processing and naming speed for familiar visual stimuli (e.g., colors and shapes) can differentiate children with normal language development and with language disabilities. Children and adolescents with and without language disabilities show similar, linear patterns of increase in visual processing speed and naming speed (i.e., decreased naming time) for single- (colors or forms) and dual-dimension (color-form combinations) stimuli (Wiig et al., 2000; Wiig, Langdon, & Flores, 2001) (see Rapid Reference 5.5). In normally developing children, processing speed and naming speed for color-form combinations stabilize between ages 13 and 15 years. In contrast, processing speed and naming speed, especially for dual-dimension stimuli (e.g., a red circle), remain significantly slower in children with language disabilities. Among children with significant processing speed and naming speed deficits for color-form combinations (i.e., with longer naming times), close to 50% exhibit severe language disabilities (i.e., total language standard scores at 70 or below) (Wiig et al., 2000).

Among behavioral indices, processing speed and naming speed for visual input are not significantly related to the cortical anatomical risk index described earlier (Leonard et al., 2002; Leonard, Eckert, & Kuldau, 2006). That index did not account for variations in myelination and white matter. This suggests that variations in white-matter cerebral development may be involved in both language disabilities and reading disabilities. The findings also lead us to conclude that processing speed deficits are among significant factors in predicting language disabilities. Other significant markers include deficits in auditory processing and phonological awareness, attention, short-term auditory memory, auditory and visual working memory, and set shifting (i.e., cognitive flexibility).

Short-Term Memory

Short-term (immediate) capacities are central in language acquisition and use. Auditory short-term memory is used to retain spoken language for a short time, lasting only a few seconds, to process for comprehension (see Rapid Reference 5.6). It is used to maintain small amounts of information, while integrating linguistic aspects for language comprehension.

A child or adult's short-term auditory memory is directly related to the number of language units (i.e., sounds, syllables, or words) he or she can produce in 2 seconds. More importantly, the relationship between production speed and time remains stable throughout life (Cowan, 1996; Cowan et al., 1992). Children with language disabilities tend to have inadequate short-term auditory memory capacities for real-time processing and chunking, and, therefore, interpreting what is heard. While short-term auditory memory deficits do not necessarily translate directly into severe early language disabilities, they interfere with processing and understanding lengthy or complex information such as sentences with multiple subordinated and/or embedded clauses (e.g., relative clauses). Procedural memory, involved in sequential learning, such as for acquiring syntax, is also inadequate in children with language disabilities, and the deficits affect learning beyond the linguistic domain (Tomblin, Mainela-Arnold, & Zhang, 2007; Ullman & Pierpoint, 2005).

≡ Rapid Reference 5.6

....

Short-Term Memory

Short-term auditory memory is limited to 7, plus or minus 2 units in adults (Miller, 1956). Auditory memory capacity can be improved by: (a) controlling word length by using shorter words (word length effect), (b) developing conscious mental rehearsal, (c) using priming to set up expectations (Cowan, 1996; Cowan et al., 1992), and (d) developing linguistic structure to group into meaningful units (chunking).

Visual short-term memory, important for reading and other visual processing tasks, is limited to four units in adults (Awh, Barton, & Vogel, 2007). Similar intervention principles can be applied to facilitate visual memory capacity.

≡ Rapid Reference 5.7

Working Memory

Baddeley (1986, 1996) proposed a model for working memory with distinct subsystems: (a) A phonological loop, activating verbal information in memory (e.g., content and structure), (b) a visual-spatial sketchpad, activating visual information in memory (e.g., reading and writing), and (c) a modality-free central executive.

Working Memory

Working memory is a neural activation resource with limited capacity and of limited duration (see Rapid Reference 5.7). It serves to hold information in mind, as in a buffer store, while processing, interpreting, or responding. Adequate working memory capacities are essential for interpreting spoken language as well as for integrating thought and language for complex oral expression. Research supports a connection between language disabilities and inadequate working memory for spoken language (Adams & Gathercole, 1995, 2000; Leonard et al., 2007; Weismer, Evans, & Hesketh, 1999; Weismer, Plante, Jones, & Tomblin, 2005).

There is evidence of developmental relationships between working memory and inhibitory control, general-purpose functions that guide complex cognition and behavior (Roncadin, Pascual-Leone, Rich, & Dennis, 2007). In typically developing children, working memory and inhibitory control interact and develop similarly in boys and girls, but show distinct age-related differences. Dual-task efficiency, as in shifting between two tasks or dimensions, correlates positively with working memory activation in children ages 6 through 11 years. Dual-task efficiency correlates positively with inhibition efficiency, as in inhibiting responses to nonessential stimuli, in children ages 12 through 17 years. This indicates that with age and experience, strategic processes, rather than general-purpose resources, determine performance on complex tasks with competing stimulus or response demands. In children with language impairments, the maturation and integration of working memory and inhibitory cognitive control to form strategic processes appear delayed to a degree that negatively affects the acquisition and use of complex sentence structures and cognitive content.

Word Retrieval

Dysnomia is the general term used for difficulties in retrieving words from long-term memory store. These difficulties are commonly observed in children with language disabilities during tasks that require controlled access to the stored lexicon, such as naming objects on confrontation, associative naming, verbal fluency, sentence completion, and thematic speaking and writing (German & Newman, 2004; German & Simon, 1991; McGregor, Newman, Reilly, & Capone, 2002). Typically, responses to associative naming tasks, such as naming animals, lack the organized semantic grouping that facilitates retrieval. Unsuccessful attempts at retrieving a specific word to fit a controlled verbal context result in typical error patterns. A common pattern for dysnomia is to circumlocute by describing the entity to be named (e.g., " . . . the thing that . . . "). Other naming errors involve substituting highly associated words (e.g., *fork* for *knife*) or words with shared prefixes (e.g., *telephone* for *television*). Spontaneous speech is often interrupted by prolonged pauses and the use of placeholders (e.g., " . . . well, well, you see . . . ") to maintain audience attention. Word-finding difficulties are greatest when there are few cues for retrieval or the associative links are weak.

DON'T FORGET

Dysnomia is a medical term that refers to a developmental disability that interferes with rapid and accurate recall and retrieval of names, especially for object names. Anomia is the medical term used when word retrieval deficits occur after a stroke or traumatic brain injury.

Accurate and speedy word retrieval is the result of activation of a neural network that includes the left posterior parietal cortex and frontal brain regions (Buckner, 2003). The left parietal cortex determines whether the information required has been stored during memory formation. The frontal regions provide the neural resources required for controlled access. Neuroimaging indicates that naming the same animals or objects from visual or auditory stimulation activates the same left inferior-temporal region (Tranel, Grabowski, Lyon, & Damasio, 2005). This suggests that the mediation between word forms and their conceptual representations is independent of input modality. These findings may explain the pervasive nature of word-retrieval deficits in children with language and reading disabilities.

COMPONENTS OF A MULTISCORE, MULTIMETHOD DIAGNOSTIC APPROACH

Objectives

The objective of an expert diagnostician of language disabilities is to obtain reliable and valid measures and observations that can describe a student's difficulties

≡ Rapid Reference 5.8

Intra- and Interpersonal Variables

Intrapersonal variables can be related to (a) linguistic knowledge (e.g., phonology, morphology, syntax, semantics, and pragmatics), (b) cognitive factors (e.g., memory, executive functions, reasoning, and problem solving), and (c) emotional variables (e.g., self-awareness, confidence, self-regulation, and personality type).

Interpersonal variables that control language and communication relate to, among others, (a) the school setting (e.g., environment, interactions, and culture), (b) the curriculum (e.g., grade level, curriculum objectives, and learning outcomes), and (c) society in general (e.g., culture, religion, societal roles, functions, and settings).

dynamically in relation to the contexts in which the student is expected to perform. A student's performance in any given context is controlled by intrapersonal (i.e., what the student brings to the context) as well as interpersonal variables (i.e., what is expected by a context). Rapid Reference 5.8 provides examples of intra- and interpersonal variables. Because of the complexity of controlling and interactive variables, multidimensional, multimethod, and multiscore assessments are required to identify strengths and weaknesses in performance.

The assessment of language disabilities may or may not take place within a response to intervention (RTI) framework (Fuchs, Mock, Morgan, & Young, 2003), depending on factors such as age, previous identification/diagnosis, severity, or setting (clinical/educational). Responsiveness to intervention emphasizes naturalistic assessment in a three-tiered process, and progress monitoring should use curriculum-based evaluations. In Tier I, teachers provide quality academic instruction and support within the general education program. If educational objectives are not met after tracking progress during a specified time period, often for nine weeks, students are referred to a study team for intervention. In Tier II, students receive evidence-based intervention, often in small groups, that supplements the core curriculum. If expected progress is not documented by curriculum-based evaluations, students are referred for intensive individualized and research-based intervention in Tier III.

The main issue in special education, including speech-language pathology, is now whether or not norm-referenced language testing will have a place in public school settings in the future. Let us consider some perspectives for standardized assessment of students with language impairments, as each perspective requires different methods and approaches.

Clinical Perspectives

From a clinical perspective, the speech-language pathologist (SLP) must determine whether a student shows evidence of having a language disability. Norm-referenced tests have traditionally been used to compare a given child's performance to that of a large group of age/grade peers based on a normal curve distribution, identify the degree and nature of the disorder, and determine eligibility for speech and language services. These tests can focus on specific aspects of linguistic development, as do tests of receptive and expressive vocabulary (e.g., Dunn & Dunn, 2004), basic concepts (e.g., Bracken, 2006a, 2006b; Wiig, 2004) or syntactic development (e.g., Rice & Wexler, 2001). They can also be broad in scope and contain several subtests and tasks that may cover linguistic domains, such as semantics, morphology, and syntax and interactions between them (Semel, Wiig, & Secord, 2004). Norm-referenced tests provide different types of scores, some of which are more reliable and appropriate than others (see Rapid Reference 5.9 for an explanation). In comprehensive language tests, subtest scores can be summed to form a total language score. The scores on two or more subtests can be summed to form a composite score, or factor analysis can be used to develop index scores. The advantages of the total, composite, and index scores are that they are the most reliable and show the

≡ Rapid Reference 5.9

Scores on Norm-Referenced Tests

Raw scores represent the actual point scores earned on a test/subtest.

Percentile-rank scores indicate the relative standing based on the percentage of scores that occur above and below the child's standing.

Standard scores are derived with a mean of 100 and standard deviation of 15 for the total test or composites, and a mean of 10 and standard deviation of 3 for subtests.

Age-equivalent scores represent the raw score that is the average for chronological age. They define a child that does not exist. They can be misleading and cause parents or others to modify their interactions to fit the supposed age expectations.

Percentile-rank and standard scores can be compared across ages to indicate growth.

The total test and composite scores are the most reliable in test/retest situations and provide the highest sensitivity, specificity, and predictive values for differentiating between children with and without language disabilities.

highest sensitivity (i.e., accuracy in identifying children with disorders) and specificity (i.e., accuracy in identifying children without disorders) values (Semel et al., 2004). Furthermore, when the constructs that underlie two composite/ index scores are relatively distinct, these scores can be compared to determine intrapersonal strengths and weaknesses.

CAUTION
....

Many norm-referenced tests of intelligence, language, and learning provide composite or index scores. There can be a temptation to compare composite or index standard scores based on the examiner's perceived needs. This can lead to faulty interpretations of a student's strengths or weaknesses. The standard scores on two sets of composite or index scores should be compared only when there is no overlap in subtest content (i.e., when they are orthogonal). This caution is essential for valid assessment.

Cognitive Perspectives

Cognitive perspectives on assessment are exemplified by psychological or neuropsychological tests (Lezak, Howieson, & Loring, 2004). The traditional tests of intelligence, the Stanford-Binet Intelligence Scale, now in its fifth edition (Roid, 2003), and the Wechsler Intelligence Scale for Children, now in its fourth edition (Wechsler, 2003), are the best-known examples of broad-based assessments of cognition and reasoning. These tests must be administered and interpreted by certified (or in some cases, licensed) psychologists. For the speech-language pathologist, evidence of comorbidities and executive dysfunctions is of greater value for planning long-term intervention than is a judgment of overall intellectual ability. With advances in neuroimaging, tests and subtests with a brain-behavior perspective are more frequently used in assessing individuals with suspected language disabilities to identify executive function disorders. Evidence of executive function disorders can be seen in, among others, difficulties in initiating tasks, setting goals, planning, sequencing, organizing and prioritizing, impulsivity, inhibiting responses and self-monitoring, and flexibility in shifting the focus of tasks. Tests with a brain-behavior perspective are more often included in assessing individuals with learning disabilities to identify executive function disorders (e.g., Delis, Kaplan, & Kramer, 2001).

The SLP must question whether there is evidence of comorbidities, such as auditory-processing, attention, memory, or other executive function deficits, and identify cognitive strengths and weaknesses in the student's intrapersonal cognitive profile. One of the aspects of cognition that plays a primary role in language acquisition is memory, as discussed earlier. A second aspect relates to the acquisition of critical executive functions such as attention, cognitive set shifting, and immediate and working memory.

Tests of cognition may be comprehensive or highly specific in focus, and psychologists have traditionally administered these tests. However, executive function tasks are now included in a broad-based language test (e.g., Semel et al., 2004). These tasks include rapid naming to evaluate processing speed (e.g., naming color-shape combinations), producing word associations (e.g., animal names), digit span forward and backward recall, and familiar sequence recall (e.g., naming months of the year). As a result, SLPs can identify some of the underlying neuropsychological deficits commonly associated with language disabilities. As neuroscience provides us with increasing evidence of brain-behavior relationships, we may expect that executive function assessment will play an increasingly important role in differentiating environmentally caused language disabilities from neurologically based language disabilities.

Educational Perspectives

These perspectives focus on assessing the acquisition of the basics for academic achievement. Academic achievement tests are often broad in scope, and evaluate listening, reading, writing and written language, math skills, conceptual knowledge, and reasoning (e.g., Woodcock, McGrew, & Mather, 2001). School psychologists and special educators use these tests to assess academic skill and strategy levels in students with learning difficulties. From an educational perspective, the SLP needs to identify which aspects of language and academic performance in context are compromised by language disabilities and/or by comorbidities. Specifically, the SLP must identify those curriculum objectives that are compromised and those that are not. Behavioral observations and rating scales that focus on language and communication (e.g., listening, speaking, reading, and writing) can also be used to evaluate the student's ability to respond to grade-level curriculum objectives (Semel et al., 2004; Wiig & Secord, 2003). This knowledge must be integrated with the expected learning outcomes so that language intervention can ameliorate areas of weakness while strengthening existing areas that are not compromised for compensation.

Social/Societal Perspectives

From a social/societal perspective, the SLP must identify which aspects of social communication and peer relations are compromised, whether verbal pragmatics, nonverbal communication, perspective taking, friendships, or interactive sharing and participation in conversation, discussion, or games. Aspects of student-adult relationships in school and at home must also be examined. Among these are developing and expressing mutual respect, following directions and instructions, managing own and others' behaviors, and establishing trust relationships. Behavioral observations and rating scales of pragmatic abilities can assist the SLP in identifying objectives for language intervention, counseling, and/or psychological services.

EXAMPLES OF TREATMENT PROTOCOLS

The case studies presented here provide representative examples of treatment protocols for preschool and early school-age children. The intervention methods and approaches used for the children in the protocols reflected evidence-based practice (American Speech-Language-Hearing Association, 2005; Johnson, 2006).

The first treatment protocol was for a boy age 3 years and 7 months, with an SLI diagnosis. The boy was given two age-appropriate, norm-referenced language tests. On the first, the Preschool Language Scale, Fourth Edition (Zimmerman, Steiner, & Pond, 2002), the total language standard score was 64, the receptive language standard score 61, and the expressive language standard score 71. On the second, the CELF-Preschool–2 (Semel et al., 2004), the core language standard score was 69, the receptive and expressive language standard scores 73, the language content standard score 79, and the language structure standard score 67. Regarding subtests, the scaled scores for morphology and syntax (3 and 4, respectively) indicated severe difficulties (i.e., standard was at or below $-2\ SD$ of the mean). Behavioral ratings with a norm-referenced pragmatics checklist indicated performance in the 1st to 5th percentile. Based on the combined test scores, the child's language impairment was considered of the receptive-expressive type, and linguistic content acquisition was considered a relative strength. Based on these and other test results, the child qualified for language intervention, and physical and occupational therapy.

The primary objective for language intervention was to develop comprehension and use of linguistic rules for structure (morphology and syntax). The

≡ *Rapid Reference 5.10*

....

Narrative-Based Approach to Language Intervention

In narrative-based approaches to language intervention with young children, the clinician/educator selects age-appropriate children's stories with illustrations. The story is read to the child as he or she looks at illustrations for context and comprehension. The child is then engaged interactively by asking open-ended *wh*-questions, retelling parts of the story or imitating the dialogue of the characters.

secondary objective was to strengthen the acquisition of vocabulary to maintain the area of relative strengths. A narrative-based approach was chosen for language intervention (see Rapid Reference 5.10). Age-appropriate stories, such as "Goldilocks," provided content, context, and models for morphology, syntax, pragmatics, and narrative structure. Strategies such as story retelling and story generating with related and familiar content and topics were used to elicit expressive language. Procedures such as providing models for sentence imitation and recasting by modifying or expanding the child's utterances to include the intended linguistic targets (e.g., verb forms and sentence structure) were used during interactive storytelling. The child's sentence length, measured by the numbers of meaningful units, increased. Focusing on features of meaning and relationships between familiar and unfamiliar words (e.g., *baby bear/little bear, little, bigger*, and *biggest*) also expanded the child's vocabulary use. In combination, this resulted in improved and increased use of language (pragmatics) to express intentions such as expressing personal needs (e.g., asking for help) in interactions with parents, siblings, and other children.

The second treatment protocol was for a girl 6 years, 1 month old, entering Grade 1. She was also tested with two age-appropriate norm-referenced language tests. On the first, the Test of Early Language Development–3 (TELD-3; Hresko, Reid, & Hammill, 1999), she obtained a Listening quotient of 74 and a Spoken Language quotient of 66. On the second test, Clinical Evaluation of Language Fundamentals–4 (CELF-4; Semel et al., 2004), the Core Language standard score was 63, the Receptive Language standard score 83, and the Expressive Language standard score 65. The discrepancy between the Receptive and Expressive Language standard scores (i.e., 18 points) was statistically significant. The Language Content standard score was 79 and the Language Structure standard score 69. Regarding subtest performance, word and sentence structure and expressive vocabulary received low scaled scores (3 and 4, respectively), while word relationships were understood at an above-average level (SS = 11). In the profile it is notable that the child's expressive vocabulary score was in the low range and receptive content scores in the typical range. This discrepancy may indicate word-finding difficulties, often found in mixed language disabilities with listening and oral expression difficulties, and language-based academic learning disabilities. The performance on a phonological awareness rating scale was in the low developmental range (6th to 9th percentile), indicating a need for phonological awareness training to strengthen the acquisition of early literacy skills and decoding for reading. Based on these and other test results, she received language intervention, occupational therapy for motor skills development, and learning disability services for literacy development in Grade 1.

Language intervention focused on developing morphological and syntactic language skills in structured therapy and academic text-based receptive-expressive activities. Developing structural rules for sentences with subordination, and establishing meaning relationships for spatial, temporal, and other conjunctions were primary goals for intervention. Modeling, recasting, and parallel production, among other procedures, strengthened the morphological and syntactic rules systems. Rephrasing and restructuring sentences by, among others, changing statements to questions and changing the order of clauses in complex sentences strengthened syntactic and pragmatic flexibility. Vocabulary instruction, including robust vocabulary instruction (Beck, Perfetti, & McKeown, 1982), was used to develop meaning features and word associations, and understanding word relationships within semantic categories strengthened vocabulary development and word-finding abilities.

RESOURCES

American Speech-Language-Hearing Association (2004). *Evidence-based practice in communication disorders: An introduction.* [Technical report]. Available from www.asha.org/members/deskref-journals/deskref/default.

American Speech-Language-Hearing Association (2006). *New roles in response to intervention: Creating success for schools and children.* [Position paper]. Available from www.asha.org/nr/rdonlyres/52cd996a-16a9-4dbe-a2a3-eb5fa0be32eb/0/rtiroledefinitions.pdf#se.

Johnson, C. J. (2006). Getting started in evidence-based practice for childhood speech-language disorders. *American Journal of Speech-Language Pathology, 15,* 20–35.

🐦 TEST YOURSELF 🐦

1. **Receptive and expressive language disabilities are easy to differentiate with standardized language tests. True or False?**

2. **In the search for language disability clusters, researchers found**
   (a) clusters that occurred across languages.
   (b) children with only lexical deficits.
   (c) distinct receptive-expressive contrasts.
   (d) none of the above.

3. **Neuroanatomical risk indexes have established**
   (a) no similarities between language disabilities and dyslexia.
   (b) similarities between language disabilities and schizophrenia.
   (c) separate and distinct risk patterns in language disabilities, dyslexia, and schizophrenia.
   (d) similarities between listening comprehension, oral expression, and reading disabilities.

4. **Differences in the rate of development and degree of myelination**
   (a) are related to the neuroanatomical risk index for language disabilities.
   (b) can account for processing and naming speed differences.
   (c) have little influence on intelligence.
   (d) are eliminated with age.

5. **The prevalence of language disabilities is estimated to be 2% higher among girls than boys. True or False?**

6. **Among advantages of using a linguistic domain reference system for assessing language disabilities are**
   (a) educational outcomes can be linked to grade-level curriculum objectives for English and language arts.
   (b) published, evidence-based interventions target specific linguistic skill areas.
   (c) areas of weakness can be related directly to curriculum objectives that are at risk.
   (d) all of these

7. **The early acquisition of phonological skills and semantics requires**
   (a) primarily computational strategies.
   (b) primarily categorical perception.
   (c) a combination of categorical perception and computational strategies.
   (d) extensive rule learning.

8. **Research has established links between**
   (a) auditory processing speed deficits and language disabilities.
   (b) working memory deficits and language disabilities.

(c) visual processing speed deficits and severe language disabilities.

(d) a and b

(e) none of the above.

9. Dysnomia is a common characteristic of learning disabilities that involve

(a) listening comprehension.

(b) oral expression.

(c) delayed vocabulary development.

(d) responses to visual input.

10. Intrapersonal variables that affect language abilities

(a) are influenced by cultural standards.

(b) include neuropsychological and emotional factors.

(c) are determined by classroom demands for language.

(d) none of the above.

11. Standardized language tests commonly reflect the receptive and expressive dichotomy featured in DSM-IV-TR and ICD-10. True or False?

Answers: 1. False; 2. a; 3. d; 4. a; 5. False; 6. d; 7. c; 8. a; 9. b; 10. b; 11. True.

Six

A RESPONSE TO INTERVENTION (RTI) APPROACH TO SLD IDENTIFICATION

Jack M. Fletcher
Amy E. Barth
Karla K. Stuebing

CLASSIFICATION AND IDENTIFICATION

From the beginning of the history of the concept of specific learning disabilities (SLD), defining and identifying children and adults with SLD has been controversial (Doris, 1993). The controversies have emerged regardless of the label, beginning with terms like *organic driveness syndrome, dyslexia* and *dyscalculia, minimal brain dysfunction* (or injury), and now *SLD.* The fundamental issue, regardless of the descriptive label, is how to identify a subgroup of people from a larger population of people with learning, achievement, and (historically) behavioral difficulties that are representative of the concept of SLD (Fletcher, Lyon, Fuchs, & Barnes, 2007). In this chapter, we focus on approaches to identification of SLD that are implemented as part of a response to intervention (RTI) framework.

Classification

Fundamental to understanding any approach to identification of SLD is an understanding of classification, an area of research that has spanned many areas of science for many centuries. Classifications permit the assignment of a larger set of observations

Supported in part by grant P50 HD052117, "Texas Center for Learning Disabilities," from the Eunice Kennedy Shriver National Institute of Child Health and Human Development (NICHD). The content is solely the responsibility of the authors and does not necessarily represent the official views of the NICHD or the National Institutes of Health.

into smaller subgroups based on a set of attributes that define how the observations are similar and dissimilar. The assignment of the observations to the smaller subgroups is *identification* and represents an operationalization of the definitions that emerge from the classification. The relation of classification and identification is apparent in biology by virtue of assigning plants to species. *The Diagnostic and Statistical Manual of Mental Disorders* (DSM-IV-TR), produced by the American Psychiatric Association (1994), is an example of a hypothetical classification of mental and behavioral disorders that, as in other areas of medicine, is largely categorical and uses signs and symptoms for identification (also called *diagnosis*). For SLD, classifications operate when the child's difficulties in school are identified as SLD and not as an intellectual disability or oral language problem. The different identification models outlined in this book vary in how criteria for identification of SLD are operationalized, but they don't really vary in the underlying classification of major disorders or the critical aspect of SLD that serves to differentiate it from other academic problems, which is *unexpected underachievement*. The differences are in how the classification is operationalized as a set of criteria for identification of children into subgroups.

Thus, any approach to identification derives from a classification that provides a characterization of the attributes specific to the subgroups to be identified. These attributes may be used to differentiate specific subgroups from the many different subgroups of the larger population of people who experience learning, achievement, and behavioral difficulties (Morris & Fletcher, 1988). At the heart of the classification are hypothesized constructs that represent the nature of the different subgroups, such as SLD, intellectual disability, attention-deficit/hyperactivity disorder (ADHD), and other subgroups that may experience learning, achievement, and behavioral difficulties (e.g., children with depression or motivational difficulties). The result is a classification of different disorders that, in turn, lead to identification (or diagnostic) criteria that are then operationalized into a measurement system (definition) that permits determination of subgroup membership. The classification, and the resultant operational definitions and criteria, are also hypotheses that require continual evaluation. The measurement model is observable, and operationalizes subgroups that are inherently unobservable. Thus, SLD is not directly observable, but is operationalized by articulating the classification and the measurement model used to operationalize it. See Rapid Reference 6.1 for definitions of important terms used in this chapter.

Classifications tend to describe subgroups and, sometimes, individuals that represent ideal types, or prototypes. They are usually hierarchical and arranged in terms of larger to smaller classes that all share at least one common attribute, but differ on other attributes. However, especially for subgroups like SLD in which the primary attributes are dimensional—that is, exist on a continuum with

≡ Rapid Reference 6.1

Classification Terminology

Taxonomy: The science of classification.

Classification: An organization of entities into classes, usually hierarchical, and proceeding from larger to smaller subgroups based on shared and nonshared attributes. The classes may not be observable, representing hypothetical prototypes of each class.

Identification (or Diagnosis): The assignment of entities to a classification.

Definition: A method for operationalizing identification into a classification.

no natural demarcations (see Fletcher et al., 2007)—deciding about subgroup membership involves the placement of individuals along a set of multiple, correlated dimensions. Because there are no natural demarcations, the decisions that stem from the measurement model are inherently arbitrary and significantly influenced by the measurement error inherent in the procedures used to operationalize the classification. Measurement error

DON'T FORGET

SLD is fundamentally a dimensional classification that exists on a continuum and for which there are no natural demarcations of specific categories. Other dimensional disorders include ADHD and, in medicine, obesity and hypertension. In any dimensional disorder, categories are arbitrary and there is measurement error in making group distinctions.

is an especially significant problem, if rigid cut-points are applied and no considerations are made for the correlations among dimensions (Francis et al., 2005).

Good classifications are reliable and not dependent on the specific measurement model, so that they can be replicated despite variations in the measurement model. They also identify most of the people of interest (i.e., have adequate coverage). Most importantly, good classifications are valid not simply because subgroups can be identified but because the subgroups making up a valid classification can be differentiated on variables not used to establish the subgroups (Skinner, 1981). For example, if SLD is identified as a discrepancy between IQ and achievement, there should be systematic differences between low achievers who meet IQ-discrepancy criteria and low achievers who do not meet criteria for intellectual disabilities on cognitive, behavioral, and other variables not used to define the subgroups (e.g., intervention response). Good classifications that meet these criteria facilitate communication, prediction, and other activities (see Rapid Reference 6.2).

≡ *Rapid Reference 6.2*

Characteristics of Good Classifications

- *Reliable:* Replicate across different approaches to operationalizations (internal validity).
- *Valid:* Classes can be differentiated on variables not used to define them (external validity).
- *Coverage:* Identifies the majority of the entities of interest.
- *Effective:* Facilitates communication and prediction.

In this chapter, the identification of SLD in the context of an RTI framework will be presented with these ideas about classifications, measurement models, and their reliability and validity as guiding principles. First, the concept of SLD will be discussed as a classification hypothesis. Second, identification will be discussed in the context of how an RTI service delivery framework aligns with this concept. We present an approach to identification that aligns with the 2004 Individuals with Disabilities Education Improvement Act (IDEA 2004) not because it is a gold standard, but because the concepts in IDEA are aligned with a classification that includes the essential components of the SLD concept. IDEA 2004 also explicitly includes the idea that multiple sources of data must be considered, an essential part of any approach to identification. We then review some of the available reliability and validity evidence involving identification of SLD in an RTI framework.

WHAT IS SLD?

Historically, the SLD construct has been invoked in reference to the idea of "unexpected underachievement." Although early efforts to implement a classification of SLD based on this construct were too broad and included children with primary behavior problems (Doris, 1993), the construct has always attempted to represent people who struggle to master reading, writing, and mathematics, despite the absence of conditions known to interfere with mastery of academic skills, such as a sensory disorder, intellectual disability, emotional and

DON'T FORGET

Exclusionary criteria represent attributes that, by definition, preclude membership in a class (e.g., intellectual disability precludes SLD). Inclusionary criteria are attributes that indicate membership in a class, but are usually necessary and not sufficient (e.g., low achievement is necessary, but not sufficient for identification of SLD).

behavioral difficulties that interfere with motivation or effort, and factors such as economic disadvantage, minority language status, and poor instruction. In the next few sections, the evolution of the concept of SLD based on diagnosis by exclusion, toward identification criteria that are more inclusionary, will be discussed.

Exclusionary Definitions

Early attempts to identify SLD focused on excluding "known" causes of low achievement. The exclusionary clauses in the federal statutory definition of SLD, which involved absence of sensory or motor disorders, intellectual disability, and behavioral disorders of presumed environmental origin, have their roots in the earliest attempts to identify behavior disorders in children that were due to brain disorders (Still, 1902). Similarly, early descriptions of dyslexia as "word blindness" in a seemingly bright child attending a good school also used evidence of adequate intellectual functioning and educational opportunities to exclude certain forms of reading disabilities (Morgan, 1896). The first formal definitions of *minimal brain dysfunction* (Clements, 1966) included the exclusionary criteria present in the U.S. federal statutory definition of SLD: "The term does not include children who have learning disabilities, which are primarily the result of visual, hearing, or motor handicaps, or mental retardation, or emotional disturbance, or of environmental, cultural, or economic disadvantage" (U.S. Office of Education, 1968, p. 34).

The notion inherent in these early attempts to define and operationalize SLD is that "unexpected underachievement" can be identified simply by specifying conditions in which underachievement is due to presumably known causes that are excluded as factors in SLD. The classification underlying this approach to identification distinguishes SLD from sensory disorders, mental retardation, behavioral problems, and environmental factors related to low achievement. However, the provisions about environmental factors related to low achievement (e.g., environmental disadvantage) were originally in place in the federal definition of SLD to prevent pooling of funds provided under special education and civil rights legislation (i.e., Title I; Doris, 1993). Not surprisingly, this approach to operationalizing a classification of SLD was not successful because the resulting subgroup was heterogeneous (Rutter, 1978) and assumptions about environmental factors, such as "cultural disadvantage," were difficult to operationalize (Kavale & Forness, 1985). As Ross (1976) stated,

Stripped of clauses which specify what a learning disability is not, this definition is circular, for it states, in essence, that a learning disability is an

≡ Rapid Reference 6.3

Models for SLD Identification

Aptitude-achievement discrepancy: SLD is identified in the presence of a "significant" discrepancy between aptitude (different IQ scales, listening comprehension) and achievement, usually with exclusionary criteria and often with no criterion for absolute low achievement.

Low achievement: SLD is indicated by the presence of absolute low achievement relative to chronological age expectations, usually with exclusionary criteria.

Cognitive discrepancy: SLD is indicated by a pattern of intraindividual strengths and weaknesses on measures of cognitive processes, usually with some linkage to expected relations of achievement and cognitive function (weakness) and evidence of strengths in other cognitive processes.

Hybrid model: SLD is indicated by two inclusionary criteria, inadequate instructional response, and absolute low achievement, with exclusionary criteria representing other disorders.

inability to learn. It is a reflection of the rudimentary state of knowledge in this field that every definition in current use has its focus on what the condition is not, leaving what it is unspecified and thus ambiguous. (p. 11)

Examples of common models for SLD Identification are provided in Rapid Reference 6.3.

Moving Toward Inclusionary Definitions

The changes since early efforts to define SLD on the basis of exclusionary criteria can be understood as an effort to identify inclusion criteria that specify which people meet criteria for SLD. What is important is that the underlying notion of SLD as "unexpected underachievement" and the classification framework that distinguishes SLD from mental retardation and behavior disorders is unchanged. The challenge is determining a set of inclusionary criteria that reliably and validly identify people with SLD, as opposed to another form of achievement problem.

DON'T FORGET

Moving from exclusionary to inclusionary definitions of SLD does not change the underlying notion of SLD as "unexpected underachievement" or the classification framework that distinguishes SLD from other disorders.

Aptitude-Achievement Discrepancy Models

Early efforts to use a discrepancy of higher aptitude and lower achievement have long been proposed. Although the most well-known model uses IQ scores to operationalize aptitude, variations in which IQ composite is used (e.g., verbal IQ, nonverbal or performance IQ, composite or full-scale IQ), even in listening comprehension, have been proposed and evaluated (Fletcher et al., 2007). The use of an aptitude-achievement discrepancy as an inclusionary criterion has failed in part because this approach to measurement does not yield a subgroup of children who are poor achievers that can be validly differentiated from other low achievers on the basis of attributes not used to define the subgroups. Using IQ-achievement discrepancies in the reading domain as an example, Hoskyn and Swanson (2000) compared the cognitive skills of poor readers who met and did not meet IQ-achievement discrepancy criteria across 19 studies. They reported negligible to small differences on measures involving reading sight words (−.02), automaticity (.05) and memory (.12), small effects for phonological processing (.27) and pseudoword reading (.29), and larger differences on measures of vocabulary (0.55) and syntax (0.87). The authors concluded that most cognitive abilities assessed in the meta-analysis, especially those closely related to reading, showed overlap between the two groups, although Swanson (2008) seemed to temper these conclusions because of some of the larger effect sizes. However, some of the effect size differences were inflated because Hoskyn and Swanson incorporated variables used to define the groups into the determination of effect sizes, which inflated some of the differences on pseudoword reading and vocabulary.

In a second meta-analysis of 46 studies that included most of the 19 studies identified by Hoskyn and Swanson (2000) but did not include definitional variables in the effect size estimates, Stuebing et al. (2002) reported negligible aggregated effect size differences on behavioral (−0.05) and achievement variables (−0.12). There was a small effect size difference on cognitive variables (0.30) not used to define the subgroups, but negligible differences on measures of phonological awareness, rapid naming, verbal memory, and vocabulary. They also reported that the heterogeneity in estimates of effect sizes could be explained by variations in how IQ-discrepancy and low achievement were defined.

In other domains, the long-term prognosis of reading disabilities does not vary with IQ-discrepancy (Francis, Shaywitz, Stuebing, Shaywitz, & Fletcher, 1996). In the area of intervention response, Fuchs and Young (2006) concluded from a review of 13 studies that IQ was a good predictor of intervention response. However, an empirical meta-analysis of these 13 articles, along with nine additional studies, found that IQ accounts for only small amounts (<1%) of the unique variance in response to reading intervention (Stuebing, Barth, Molfese, Weiss, & Fletcher, 2009). Thus, there is little evidence that supports classifications of SLD based on IQ-achievement discrepancy criteria.

DON'T FORGET

IQ-achievement discrepant and low-achieving readers do not show robust differences in external validity studies, including behavior, achievement, cognitive processes, prognosis, and intervention response. Aptitude-achievement models have been studied in relation to a variety of indices of aptitude, including listening comprehension, and in relation to math and other domains, and in speech and language disorders, with little evidence of validity (Fletcher et al., 2007).

Low Achievement Models

Given the concerns about the validity of classifications based on IQ-achievement discrepancy, some have proposed that SLD be identified on the basis of absolute low achievement, so that anyone scoring below the 25th percentile may belong to the SLD subgroup (Siegel, 1992). The problem with this argument is that it departs from the original concept of SLD as "unexpected underachievement" since the SLD group would include children with various forms of poor achievement. However, grouping students according to achievement strengths and weaknesses (e.g., reading versus math disabilities) does lead to subgroups that can be reliably and validly differentiated. Indeed, the strongest evidence for the validity of the SLD construct comes from research studies on cognition, genetics, and brain function that demonstrate differentiation of children with reading and math difficulties from children with intellectual disabilities, ADHD and no achievement problems, and typically developing children (Fletcher et al., 2007). As such, *low achievement is a necessary but not sufficient condition for identification of SLD*, and represents a clear inclusionary criterion.

CAUTION

The mere presence of low achievement does not necessarily indicate SLD.

If the SLD classification is multidimensional, then multiple measurements are needed to identify SLD. In this context, low achievement is stipulated as the inclusionary criterion and exclusionary criteria are added to rule out the presence of other disabilities and the environmental factors associated with low achievement, resulting in a subgroup that has different kinds of SLD (e.g., basic reading, reading fluency, reading comprehension, mathematics computations and problem solving, written language). Thus, the task is to rule out other disabilities and environmental factors as "causes" of underachievement and specify the domain(s) in which underachievement may occur. In fact, a review of the literature on the classification of SLD using the criteria for reliable and valid classifications provided earlier suggests that this approach to SLD identification has the strongest evidence of any measurement model (Fletcher et al., 2007).

The weakness of the low achievement model for SLD identification is its inability to sort people according to putative causes of low achievement. For example, it is difficult to demonstrate major differences in the cognitive and neural correlates of low achievement between economically advantaged and disadvantaged children. In addition, it does not seem reasonable to stipulate that children for whom environmental factors seem to operate cannot also possess the attributes of SLD. The issue is still whether there are additional inclusionary criteria that would help identify people as SLD and also have a relation with intervention planning and response (Kavale & Forness, 1985).

> **DON'T FORGET**
> ....
> Low achievement is a necessary but not sufficient condition for SLD identification and should be considered an inclusionary criterion.

> **CAUTION**
> ....
> Children from environmentally disadvantaged backgrounds may possess the attributes of SLD; therefore, the extent to which such disadvantage may be a contributing or primary cause of learning difficulties should be evaluated carefully.

Cognitive Discrepancy Models

Proponents of identification models that assess cognitive strengths and weaknesses typically do not place their hypothesized measurement models in a classification context, focusing instead on criteria for identification. If they did put these proposals into a classification context, there would be a body of research comparing low-achieving students who met criteria for SLD based on a cognitive discrepancy with low-achieving students who did not meet these criteria. Nonetheless, the proposal that such strengths and weaknesses are markers for SLD is an argument that they represent as an inclusionary criterion. This argument builds upon a large body of research indicating that specific cognitive difficulties lead to specific achievement difficulties (Fletcher et al., 2007). The federal statutory definition of SLD indicates that:

The term "specific learning disability" means a disorder in one or more of the basic psychological processes involved in understanding or in using language, spoken or written, which may manifest itself in an imperfect ability to listen, speak, read, write, spell, or to do mathematical calculations. (USOE, 1968, p. G1042)

The controversy about an assessment of cognitive processes involves the value that such assessments add to intervention planning and outcomes for students identified with SLD. Part of the problem is that cognitive processes are correlated with achievement, which begs the question of why measure the correlates (psychological processes) when the "manifestations" (achievement) are part of the measurement model? It is difficult for a correlate to contribute independently of the manifestations. Contrary to recent assertions (Reynolds & Shaywitz, 2009), there is not a strong evidence base suggesting that classifications based on cognitive strengths and weaknesses yield a unique subgroup of students representative of SLD, or that such assessments are strongly related to intervention response (Gresham, 2009; Pashler, McDaniel, Rohrer, & Bjork, 2009). In their elegant revisiting of this decades-old issue, Pashler et al. reviewed the literature on different approaches to matching individual characteristics to intervention, including learning styles, aptitude-by-treatment interactions, and personality-by-treatment interactions. They found a fragmented evidence base that largely did not find the interactions of person-level attributes and differential response to intervention that these hypotheses would predict. However, they noted that there were few methodologically adequate studies.

> ## CAUTION
> ....
> The evidence-base supporting cognitive discrepancies as a valid tool for identifying SLD subgroups that respond differentially to interventions is weak.

The framework is viable, and the strongest evidence for the aptitude-by-treatment interactions posited by advocates of a cognitive discrepancy model actually comes from studies that operationalize strengths and weaknesses in the achievement domain. For example, Connor, Morrison, Fishman, Schatschneider, and Underwood (2007) showed that when teachers geared reading interventions based on strengths and weaknesses in decoding and comprehension, differential outcomes were apparent. More generally, the fact that children with SLD in reading

> ## DON'T FORGET
> ....
> Planning interventions based on strengths and weaknesses in the achievement domain has a strong evidence base.

show improved reading performance when provided reading and not math instruction (Morris et al., in press) may seem trivial, but in fact supports the idea of aptitude-by-treatment interactions and is strong support for the concept of SLD. Whether such findings extend to cognitive discrepancies has not been established. These are hypotheses that warrant continued investigation, especially in the context of a measurement framework that involves multiple attributes.

Provision of Adequate Instruction

In addition to low achievement, the other potential attribute of an approach to the classification of SLD is the evaluation of instructional response. Most definitions of SLD indicate that inadequate instruction is one of the environmental factors that should be treated as an exclusionary factor (Fletcher et al., 2007). For example, IDEA 2004 states that children may not be identified as SLD if there is no evidence of adequate instruction in reading or math. Concerns about the adequacy of instruction component has taken on a new emphasis in the last decade because of consensus reports indicating that many children are identified as SLD and placed in special education despite inadequate core instructional programs (Donovan & Cross, 2002). Perhaps the most significant change in IDEA 2004 is the provision that indicates that regardless of the identification model:

> To ensure that underachievement in a child suspected of having a specific learning disability is not due to lack of appropriate instruction in reading or math, the group must consider, as part of the evaluation . . . (1) Data that demonstrate that prior to, or as a part of, the referral process, the child was provided appropriate instruction in regular education settings, delivered by qualified personnel; and (2) Data-based documentation of repeated assessments of achievement at reasonable intervals, reflecting formal assessment of student progress during instruction, which was provided to the child's parents.

Under this language, instructional response is not just exclusionary. Because data can be collected that measure progress and the quality of instruction, instructional response becomes an inclusionary criterion, with inadequate instructional response representing evidence that underachievement is unexpected.

DON'T FORGET
....
Inadequate instructional response is an inclusionary characteristic of SLD in models derived from RTI service delivery frameworks.

A Hybrid Model for SLD Identification

This discussion of history, classification, and the development of multicriteria identification models is prefatory to any discussion of an identification model for SLD. The issue is not which model is best, or even which attributes must be measured, but rather the alignment with the SLD construct. Fletcher et al. (2007) argued that the evidence supports a hybrid model of classification consistent with a consensus group of researchers convened by the U.S. Department of Education Office of Special Education Programs (Bradley, Danielson, & Hallahan, 2002). This group suggested three primary criteria, the first two of which are clearly inclusionary (Bradley et al., p. 798):

1. Student demonstrates low achievement.
2. There is insufficient response to effective research-based interventions. A systematic plan for assessing change in performance must be established prior to intervention.
3. Exclusion factors such as mental retardation, sensory deficits, serious emotional disturbance, language minority children (where lack of proficiency in English accounts for measured achievement deficits), and lack of opportunity to learn should be considered.

Rapid Reference 6.4 lists criteria for SLD identification that are consistent with those outlined by Bradley et al. (2002).

Identifying people with SLD, whether as part of the process stipulated in IDEA 2004, a clinic outside of school, and in research, requires multiple criteria. Researchers and practitioners may argue about how these attributes are

---

≡ *Rapid Reference 6.4*

....

Criteria for Identification of SLD in a Hybrid Model That Integrates Low Achievement and Components of RTI

- Insufficient response to effective research-based interventions, based on assessments of progress and the quality/fidelity of instruction.
- Demonstration of absolute low achievement in word reading, reading fluency, reading comprehension, mathematics computation, mathematics problem solving, and/or written expression.
- Exclusionary factors such as intellectual disability, sensory deficits, serious emotional disturbance, language minority status, and lack of opportunity to learn do not explain inadequate instructional response.

operationalized and whether other attributes are needed, but these three sets of criteria seem to align with the notion of unexpected underachievement. The difference in this hybrid model relative to other cognitive dis-

CAUTION

No matter which model is used for identification, a single criterion is never adequate to indicate SLD.

crepancy and low achievement models is that the primary criterion for "unexpected" is based on instructional response. *What better evidence for unexpected underachievement is there than evidence that the person has not responded to quality instruction?*

In this hybrid model and in models that emerge in the context of RTI implementations, intractability to quality instruction is a marker for unexpected underachievement and an inherent component of identification and, as in all the classification models reviewed in this chapter, intrinsic to the concept of SLD. As such, intractability constitutes an *inclusionary* attribute. Moreover, this component is essential whether the identification model stems from an RTI process or a process that includes some form of cognitive discrepancy. Only if an achievement deficit is present and the child demonstrates intractability in response to adequate instruction is there evidence that the low achievement is unexpected.

DON'T FORGET

No child should be identified as SLD without evidence of intractability in response to adequate instruction.

RTI AND SLD IDENTIFICATION

The advantage of identifying SLD from an RTI service delivery system is that the instructional response components are embedded in the identification process, streamlining eligibility decisions and directly linking special education services with those provided in general education. RTI service delivery frameworks also permit a more flexible approach to assessment where tools are selected according to hypotheses about the basis for inadequate instructional response. Individual educational plans stem directly from the comprehensive evaluation. Consistent with IDEA 2004, identification incorporates multiple sources of data.

What Is an RTI Framework?

The most important consideration in understanding RTI models is that they are not primarily for the identification of SLD (see Rapid Reference 6.5).

≡ Rapid Reference 6.5

What Is RTI?

The primary goal of RTI is to improve academic and behavioral outcomes for all students by eliminating discrepancies between actual and expected performance. RTI also:

- Offers a set of processes for coordinating high-quality service delivery in schools.
- Takes a multitiered, layered instructional approach that prevents problems first, and then brings increasingly intense interventions to students who don't respond.
- Facilitates making instructional decisions based on data.
- Integrates entitlement programs with general education.

Rather, the primary goal is the prevention and remediation of academic and behavioral difficulties through effective classroom and supplemental instruction, including those provided by all entitlement programs. As such, RTI is a framework for effectively delivering and coordinating services in schools. RTI frameworks provide data that are relevant to identification of SLD and that lead to different approaches to referral and placement decisions related to SLD (Fletcher & Vaughn, 2009a).

CAUTION

RTI is a framework for service delivery. Identification is a secondary objective, which derives from screening and progress monitoring, but also requires additional criteria.

In an RTI framework, universal screening of students for achievement and behavioral difficulties occurs 2 to 3 times yearly. Children who are at risk have access to tiered, or layered, interventions that begin in the general education classroom and increase in intensity depending on the students' instructional response. Intensity is increased by providing more time, teaching in smaller groups, and varying curricula and interventions to meet the needs of the individual student. Rapid Reference 6.6 includes common characteristics of most RTI frameworks.

The need for more intense interventions is measured by brief assessments of progress, often based on a curriculum-based measurement (CBM) framework (Fuchs & Fuchs, 1998; VanDerHeyden & Burns, 2010). If a child progresses through multiple layers of intervention and does not show adequate instructional response relative to some benchmark established by the school, district, or state,

≡ *Rapid Reference 6.6*

Characteristics of Most RTI Frameworks

- Universal, population-based screening and progress monitoring; decision-making based on data to modify instruction
- Implementation of evidence-based interventions in the general education classroom with supplemental and intensive intervention
- A coordinated, seamless system of service delivery, connecting prevention and remediation
- Data that provide information relevant to eligibility for special education
- Parent involvement and team-based decision making

the child may be considered for special education because of the evidence that instruction within the general education curriculum has not been adequate to meet the student's instructional needs. At this point, a comprehensive evaluation would occur. Controversy attends the issue of appropriate benchmarks. However, the interpretation of these benchmarks is facilitated by links with some sort of national reference, as well as state requirements for annual yearly progress, which is clearly possible from a CBM framework (Fuchs & Fuchs, 2004). For instructional decision making, tying measures to the curriculum where progress is indexed to local benchmarks is reasonable. Nevertheless, care should be taken in using local standards for a legal eligibility requirement, unless there is a clear link with national standards and evidence of reliability and validity.

DON'T FORGET

The primary goal of an RTI framework is the prevention and remediation of academic and behavioral difficulties through effective classroom and supplemental instruction, including those provided by all entitlement programs.

DON'T FORGET

Benchmarks are most interpretable when linked to a national reference as well as state requirements for annual yearly progress.

One myth about RTI models is that they require a child to complete multiple levels of intervention before special education is considered. In fact, a child can be referred for special education evaluation at any point in the RTI process (VanDerHeyden & Burns, 2010). Referral, however, begs the question of what special education can provide. In some instances, the child may need the

DON'T FORGET
....
A child may be referred for special education at any point in the RTI process.

civil rights protections afforded by IDEA 2004, or may have problems that are not addressed by the RTI framework (e.g., a speech and language disorder, or concerns about a pervasive developmental disorder). Even in identification approaches to SLD implemented before IDEA 2004, the question emerged of what identification for special education would provide by way of services and protections when a child was referred for special education. The difference is that in RTI, a primary goal is to identify treatment needs, and eligibility determination is not isolated from efforts at intervention.

Implementation Frameworks
There are many approaches to the implementation of RTI frameworks, which are best considered not as a single model, but as a set of processes, with variation in how the processes are implemented (Fletcher & Vaughn, 2009a). These approaches have at least two historical origins, both representing efforts to implement prevention programs in schools. The first origin represents efforts to prevent behavior problems using a schoolwide prevention approach (Donovan & Cross, 2002; Walker, Stiller, Serverson, Feil, & Golly, 1998). These models often utilize a *problem-solving* process, whereby a team identifies a behavioral or academic problem, chooses an intervention to address the problem, evaluates the outcome of the intervention, and then proposes new interventions if the problem has not been resolved (Reschly & Tilly, 1999).

The second origin derives from research on preventing reading difficulties in children. These approaches use *standardized protocols* to deliver interventions that increase in intensity and differentiation depending on the child's instructional response. An example of such an approach is the 3-tier model of instructional delivery in reading that begins in general education (Tier 1); adds supplemental instruction in the form of additional small group instruction for 20 to 40 minutes per day for about 20% of students who do not respond to enhanced general education instruction (Tier II); and more intensive instruction for longer periods of time, usually in smaller groups, for about 5% of students who do not respond to general education and supplemental intervention (Tier III). The problem-solving and standardized treatment protocol models reflect the impact of public health models of healthcare delivery that distinguish primary, secondary, and tertiary levels of intervention and increase intensity and differentiation (and cost) depending on the individual's response

≡ *Rapid Reference 6.7*

Overarching Approaches to RTI Implementation

- *Problem-solving model:* A shared decision-making team is organized at a school, composed of administrators, teachers, and itinerant professionals. Based on screening and progress-monitoring data, the team identifies a behavioral or academic problem and an intervention to address the problem, evaluates the outcome of the intervention, and then proposes new interventions if the problem has not been resolved. This model has its origins in RTI implementations involving behavioral difficulties, but is also used for academic problems.

- *Standard protocol:* Based on universal screening and progress-monitoring data, children are identified as at risk. Interventions are usually standardized at each tier and increase in intensity and differentiation depending on the child's instructional response. These models originated in efforts to enhance reading instruction outcomes.

to treatment (Vaughn, Wanzek, Woodruff, & Linan-Thompson, 2006). Rapid Reference 6.7 summarizes approaches to RTI implementation, and Rapid Reference 6.8 identifies specific issues that schools should consider when implementing RTI.

≡ *Rapid Reference 6.8*

Sampling of Issues School Districts Should Consider When Implementing RTI Frameworks

- Leadership, from superintendent to teacher and community, must be on board
- Role of parents
- How to screen and monitor progress
- Criteria for inadequate response
- Number of tiers
- Organization of curriculum and relation to tiers
- How to target professional development
- Standard protocol versus problem-solving model
- Role of special education and assessment professionals
- What constitutes the comprehensive evaluation?

These models share common features, including (a) universal screening, to identify students at risk for academic and behavioral difficulties; (b) progress monitoring, to evaluate response to interventions; and (c) increasingly intense interventions that begin with high-quality, differentiated general education instruction and subsequent supplemental programs, which increase time in, and differentiation of, instruction (VanDerHeyden & Burns, 2010). These three components provide data that lead to referral for special education and a *comprehensive evaluation* to determine eligibility for SLD or another category of special education or other entitlement programs. The objectives of RTI models hinge on the provision of quality, evidence-based instruction, which again is true for any identification model.

RTI frameworks have been adopted by school districts for many reasons, most of which are focused on improved outcomes for all students, and not just because of concerns revolving around special education (Spectrum K12, 2008). When districts adopt RTI models, there is evidence of improved achievement and behavioral outcomes, as well as a reduction in special education referrals (Jimerson, Burns, & VanDerHeyden, 2007; VanDerHeyden, Witt, & Gilbertson, in press). Unfortunately, much of the controversy is over identification, and there is a general failure by critics to recognize that the concerns raised about approaches derived from an RTI framework also plague more traditional models of identification (Fletcher & Vaughn, 2009b).

CAUTION

Implementation of RTI frameworks may require considerable discussion and negotiation at a district level, and may take several years to scale effectively. The administrative hierarchy, from the superintendent to the teacher, must be on board.

Applications to Identification of SLD

The difference in the referral and eligibility process in an RTI framework versus a traditional approach is demonstrated in Figure 6.1 (Fletcher et al., 2007). The first difference is the importance placed on universal screening and continuous progress monitoring. On the left side, the traditional approach does not involve universal screening or progress monitoring, both of which are apparent in the model on the right side of the figure based on RTI. The second difference involves how students are referred for special education. An educator or parent initiates the referral in a traditional model, an approach known to relate to gender and minority disproportionality (Donovon & Cross, 2002). In an RTI framework, referral emerges because of inadequate instructional response, and progress

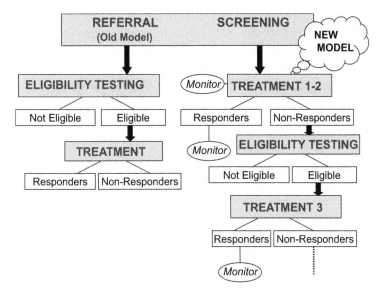

Figure 6.1. Comparison of a Traditional Model of Identification for SLD With a Model Based on Response to Instruction (RTI)

monitoring continues whether the student is identified with SLD or not. The third difference is the idea of multiple treatments and modification of instruction based on progress. Both multiple treatments and modifying instruction based on progress are implicit in the traditional model, but explicit in the RTI model. The fourth difference relates to special education. The traditional model sets aside special education as a separate service; the RTI model links general and special education and continues progress monitoring.

> **DON'T FORGET**
> ....
> Any model for SLD identification requires a comprehensive evaluation, including those provided in the context of RTI, as well as evidence of inadequate instructional response.

Other differences occur in the comprehensive evaluation. In a model based on RTI, much is already known about the student because of screening, progress monitoring, and the nature of interventions that have not been effective. As such, the student comes to the eligibility process with data and specific questions that represent hypotheses about the basis for effective instructional response, which form the basis for the comprehensive evaluation. Assessments are tailored to specific questions about the instructional needs of the child and the basis for inadequate response. As part of the evaluation, the child can be given IQ tests, assessments of cognitive processes, behavioral assessments, or any procedure deemed necessary to understand inadequate instructional response and to determine whether special education services are appropriate interventions (Fletcher et al., 2007; VanDerHeyden & Burns, 2010). There is no requirement or expectation that the same evaluation be done with each and every child.

The Comprehensive Evaluation

The flexibility around assessment, which should occur regardless of the identification framework, leads to the concern that identification is based solely on the data used to screen students and monitor progress (Reynolds & Shaywitz, 2009). Not only is this illegal in terms of the provisions of IDEA 2004, it is also inconsistent with the classification of SLD and the fact that multiple criteria are needed. However, in some instances, the only formal data may be that based on instructional response data (VanDerHeyden & Burns, 2010). There is no requirement in IDEA 2004 that all the components of identification be formally assessed (vision, hearing, limited English proficiency, intellectual disability, behavioral problem, etc.), but the evaluation still should consider these components and make eligibility decisions based on multiple sources of information.

Eligibility decisions could be made when the only formal data are based on instructional response, but it is recommended that additional formal assessment be included for evaluations of SLD. The comprehensive evaluation should formally address the two attributes that are necessary for identification of SLD-low achievement and instructional response. In addition, the comprehensive evaluation needs to address the presence of other disabilities and contextual factors that may influence achievement. For these reasons, it is recommended that a comprehensive evaluation for SLD include a brief evaluation using norm-referenced achievement tests; data on instructional response; and, at a minimum, assessments of developmental and medical history and teacher/parent rating scales to screen for behavioral factors that may contribute to low achievement.

CAUTION

Data on inadequate instructional response are rarely sufficient to satisfy requirements of IDEA 2004, much less identify SLD. However, this does not mean that every possible attribute or concern must be formally evaluated.

Establish Low Achievement

Firmly establishing low achievement should be part of most comprehensive evaluations for SLD. As outlined in Fletcher et al. (2007, Chapter 4), norm-referenced assessments of achievement can be used that are brief and based on hypotheses about the nature of academic impairment for the specific child. The addition of norm-referenced assessments of achievement is important because the use of instructional response data as the sole criterion for the identification of inadequate responders may have lower reliability, and specific measures based on progress monitoring may overidentify children as inadequate responders (i.e., false positive errors; Barth et al., 2008; Fuchs & Deshler, 2007). In addition, assessments of inadequate response should have cut-points set to minimize errors where a "true" inadequate responder is identified as an adequate responder (i.e., false negative errors). In this context, norm-referenced achievement tests nicely complement data on instructional response and provide additional information supporting identification of a child as SLD. Progress-monitoring data assessing instructional response may not be as strong for all eight domains in IDEA (e.g., reading comprehension). Also, there is no need to assess all eight domains of IDEA if the nature of the achievement problem is easily established. Why complete extensive assessments of reading comprehension and written expression for children who have problems with word recognition and spelling? In sum, use of norm-referenced assessments of academic achievement in the hybrid model should be brief and based on hypotheses about the nature of academic impairment (Fletcher et al., 2007).

Another reason to include norm-referenced assessments of achievement is that the resultant patterns of difficulty can be tied to the research base on different types of SLD (Fletcher et al., 2007). There is a great deal known about the cognitive and neural correlates of reading, math, and written expression difficulties. By identifying the achievement domains in which the student has weaknesses, decisions about instruction can be aligned with the evidence base. Some students have problems in multiple domains and need a more comprehensive intervention plan.

DON'T FORGET

There is an extensive body of research on SLD and different academic skills, spanning the range from cognitive processes to neural correlates and genetics, as well as emotional and behavioral correlates and environmental factors. This research has fueled investigation on intervention over the past decade (Fletcher et al., 2007).

≡ *Rapid Reference 6.9*

**Methods for Assessing Instructional Response
(Fuchs & Deshler, 2007)**

- *Final status:* Compares norm-referenced and/or criterion-referenced postintervention achievement scores to a benchmark.
- *Slope-discrepancy:* Compares rates of growth to the average rate for a reference group, usually with a progress-monitoring assessment.
- *Dual-discrepancy:* Compares both rates of growth and level of performance on a progress-monitoring assessment to identify inadequate response.

Assess Intervention Response

Fuchs and Deshler (2007) identified three major approaches to identifying students as meeting one criterion for SLD based on instructional response, including (1) final status, (2) slope-discrepancy, and (3) dual-discrepancy (see Rapid References 6.9 and 6.10). Final status methods compare norm-referenced and/or criterion-referenced postintervention achievement scores to a benchmark. *Slope-discrepancy* methods compare rates of growth to the average rate for a reference group, while *dual-discrepancy* methods use both rates of growth and level of performance on a progress-monitoring assessment to identify inadequate response. (For more information on these approaches, see VanDerHeyden & Burns, 2010.)

≡ *Rapid Reference 6.10*

**Characteristics Differentiating Adequate and Inadequate
Responders to Reading Instruction**

- Inadequate responders tend to be older, more economically disadvantaged, more likely male, and more likely to have repeated grades.
- Behavioral difficulties are more common in inadequate responders, especially inattention.
- Assessments of phonological awareness, rapid naming, and different oral language skills may more reliably differentiate adequate and inadequate responders.
- IQ scores are weaker discriminators of responder status relative to more specific assessments of cognitive processes.

As with any cut-point-based criterion used to identify a component of SLD, the cut-points associated with these methods are arbitrary. Much of the controversy involves whether benchmarks can be local or based on some type of national standardization. The use of intervention response data to monitor progress and adjust instruction, for which local benchmarks are at the discretion of the district, is very reasonable and strongly supported by research (Stecker, Fuchs, & Fuchs, 2007). For identification purposes, intervention response criteria should have some form of national standardization whenever possible. All three approaches are examples of discrepancy models, but the latter two incorporate assessments of change (Fuchs & Fuchs, 1998) and use progress-monitoring assessments.

Assess Contextual Factors
If the concerns that lead to referral involve other disabilities, the assessment may need to be more comprehensive and address the presence of other disabilities and the exclusionary criteria, which are better considered as contextual factors impacting treatment planning. A more comprehensive evaluation could involve assessments of IQ and adaptive behavior, to identify intellectual disabilities, determine procedures for identifying pervasive developmental disorders, evaluate limited English proficiency, and/or conduct speech and language assessments. Behavior rating scales from parents and teachers should be routinely completed as screening measures for comorbid disorders (e.g., ADHD), and other contextual factors that may explain low achievement; they certainly need to be considered in formulating a treatment plan. Not every child needs to be assessed for every potential problem; in an RTI framework, there will be hypotheses about why the student is not responding to intervention that will lead to assessments specific to the child, and hopefully to an intervention plan that is individualized.

More generally, disability determination is two-pronged. If the student is evaluated outside of an RTI framework, additional consideration of evidence that an identified disorder (first prong) leads to adaptive impairment (i.e., educational need; second prong) must also be considered, since disability determination always has these two prongs. In an RTI framework, adaptive impairment is determined first (i.e., evidence that the child does not achieve at grade level despite quality instruction), and the

DON'T FORGET
....
Disability determination has two components. There must be evidence of a problem and evidence that the problem has consequences for adaptation, or an educational need. In an RTI framework, the adaptive consequences are identified first, and then the problem is specified.

establishment of eligibility involves determining the basis for this intractability. In other identification models, the assessment of adaptive impairment may be subjective and partly responsible for the confusion that emerges when an interdisciplinary team denies eligibility despite a diagnosed disorder that sometimes, but not always, interferes with school performance. Just having a disorder is not sufficient to identify the disorder as a disability.

Reliability Issues

The coverage of classifications based on an RTI approach is difficult to address because there is no gold standard for determining an inadequate response (or a child with SLD). This concern also applies to any identification approach to SLD, as identification will always depend on how the model is operationalized. In general, various methods used to identify inadequate instructional response show more congruence in identifying students who respond adequately than inadequately (Barth et al., 2008). In some respects, since the goal is to avoid missing students who need additional intervention, we would suggest that false negative errors (missing an inadequate responder) should be minimized, even if the false positive rate (identifying an adequate responder as inadequate) will increase.

> **CAUTION**
> ....
> Because SLDs are dimensional, there is no gold standard or true positive for any classification model. Identification is always relative to the criteria used to operationalize the classification.

Regardless of whether identification is based on the assessment of instructional response, low achievement, or some type of cognitive discrepancy, any psychometric approach based on cut-points is a discrepancy model and will not identify the same students as inadequate responders, (Francis et al., 2005). This is certainly true for the assessment of intervention response (Barth et al., 2008; Burns & Senesac, 2005; Speece, Case, & Molloy, 2003). Some of the variance across approaches reflects uneven cut-points and the use of different assessments across methods. Even if these factors are controlled, the lack of overlap should not be surprising, as the distinctions are dimensional, likely exist on a continuum, and reflect the measurement error of the assessment, which makes it difficult to reliably identify those above and below a rigid cut-point on a

> **CAUTION**
> ....
> Many studies find poor overlap across methods used to identify inadequate responders, suggesting a need for multiple criteria.

dimension (Cohen, 1983). Indeed, children who cluster around the cut-point are usually similar to one another.

To illustrate, Barth et al. (2008) evaluated intervention response in 399 Grade 1 students in relation to cut-points, measures, and approaches frequently cited for the identification of inadequate responders to instruction from a Grade 1, Tier 2 intervention (Mathes et al., 2005). Measures of association ($n = 808$) were computed to address the agreement of different operationalizations of instructional response. Agreement between methods was generally weak, especially for identifying inadequate responders, although agreement for identifying adequate responders was stronger. Speece et al. (2003) found that dual-discrepancy models identified children as inadequate responders who were not identified by simple low achievement or level of performance measures, even when the latter controlled for the cutoff score, all at the 25th percentile. Although Speece et al. (2003) argued in favor of a dual-discrepancy model because of its focus on growth, a recent study questioned whether assessments of growth add to the information provided by level of performance at the end of the year on the same progress-monitoring assessment (Schatschneider, Wagner, & Crawford, 2008). Altogether, these issues with overlap, which occur for any model for LD identification, suggest that multiple criteria should be used, which is why the use of norm-referenced assessments of achievement in a hybrid model is encouraged.

Validity Issues

Hypothetical classifications are also evaluated by comparing the emergent subgroups on variables not used to identify the members. Thus, identification from an RTI framework should yield subgroups that are unique. Al Otaiba and Fuchs (2002) summarized 23 studies of elementary schoolchildren (preschool through Grade 3) who received reading interventions. They reported that most studies identified difficulties with phonological awareness as a major characteristic of inadequate responders. However, difficulties with rapid naming, phonological working memory, verbal ability, attention and behavior problems, orthographic processing, and demographic variables related to inadequate response.

In a subsequent meta-analysis of 30 studies, Nelson, Benner, and Gonzalez, (2003) found several dimensions on which adequate and inadequate responders were different, with moderate to small effect size differences in the following order (larger to smaller): rapid naming, problem behavior, phonological awareness, letter knowledge, memory, and IQ.

Stage, Abbott, Jenkins, and Berninger (2003) compared cognitive functions in children who responded "faster" or "slower" to a Grade 1 intervention. In a univariate context, faster responders had higher scores on verbal IQ, phonological and orthographic awareness, rapid naming, and verbal reasoning. The slower responders were rated as more inattentive. Verbal IQ and discrepancies of verbal IQ and reading achievement did not contribute uniquely to responder differentiation.

Al Otaiba and Fuchs (2006) compared groups of children who met adequate response criteria across kindergarten and Grade 1. Students consistently identified as inadequate responders performed more poorly on measures of morpholology, vocabulary, rapid naming, sentence repetition, and word discrimination, with more behavioral difficulties. Phonological segmentation was a weak discriminator of responder status.

DON'T FORGET

Validity studies show consistent differences between adequate and inadequate responders in cognitive and demographic characteristics.

CAUTION

Cognitive differences between adequate and inadequate responders may represent a continuum of severity, as opposed to qualitatively different subgroups.

In a series of intervention studies in kindergarten through Grade 3, reported in Vellutino, Scanlon, Zhang, and Schatschneider (2008), relations of IQ and nonverbal processing with responder status were weak in contrast to assessments of phonological awareness and oral language. They noted that the differences were not qualitative, but representative of a continuum of severity that aligned with the severity of reading skills before and after the intervention. The issue of whether cognitive and instructional differences between adequate and inadequate responders are qualitative or quantitative clearly requires additional research.

CONCLUSION

The validity results reviewed in this chapter are certainly in need of replication, and may not hold if other cognitive assessments are completed with different measures or using other models of cognitive skills. The results may differ if other operationalizations of inadequate response are used, although method variation had little effect on the shape of the profiles. This is true regardless of the identification model. However, when comparing identification models stemming from RTI frameworks with other identification models based on low achievement or some form of IQ or cognitive discrepancy, it is important to recognize that the differences are at the measurement level, not the underlying conceptualization of the SLD construct.

Other concerns about identification of students as SLD in an RTI framework have been identified (Fuchs & Deshler, 2007; Fiorello, Hale, & Snyder, 2006; Kavale & Flanagan, 2007; Reynolds & Shaywitz, 2009) and addressed elsewhere (e.g., Fletcher, Coulter, Reschly, & Vaughn, 2004; Fletcher & Vaughn, 2009b; Gresham, 2009; VanDerHeyden & Burns, 2010). It is common to argue that an assessment of cognitive processes is required because the statutory definition of SLD in Federal Regulations identifies SLD as "a disorder of psychological processes." In addition to the discussion in the section in this chapter on cognitive discrepancy models of identification, it is important to recognize that word reading, math computations, and so on are *cognitive processes* that have been specifically studied from cognitive, neuroimaging, and genetic frameworks. Identification in an RTI framework does not routinely include assessments of IQ or cognitive processes when the concern is SLD because of the weak evidence that such assessments contribute to intervention planning.

Concerns that identification in an RTI framework will not identify "gifted" children with SLD (Reynolds & Shaywitz, 2009) hinges on whether the construct of "giftedness" can be reliably measured and whether the idea that a person can be gifted and have characteristics of SLD is valid. The specific concern is whether children identified in any model must demonstrate characteristics of absolute low achievement. The question only emerges if the identification model posits the existence of some general attribute that represents aptitude for learning and predicts treatment response, which is not supported by evidence (Fletcher et al., 2007; Fletcher & Vaughn, 2009a, 2009b; Stuebing et al., 2009). As Fletcher and Vaughn (2009b) discussed, if some type of composite IQ score is the measure of aptitude, a regression-corrected discrepancy *may be* meaningful for students in the upper ranges of IQ. However, discrepancies involving very high IQ and lower achievement that is not demonstrative of absolute low achievement (e.g., < the 25th percentile) is often a regression artifact (Reynolds, 1984). Assuming a population correlation of .60 for IQ and achievement, a 1.5 standard error discrepancy would require achievement scores 32 points lower at IQ levels of 130 (Fletcher et al., 1994). As opposed to relying on IQ-achievement discrepancies, it may be more reasonable to ensure that achievement domains are broadly measured using norm-referenced assessments. In particular, many students may have problems with automaticity that can be identified with fluency assessments. In sum, the identification of students as gifted tends to be driven by a reliance on IQ and a failure to correct for correlations of IQ and achievement and to

CAUTION

....

Although children considered "gifted" and SLD may exist, research has not found effective approaches to identifying these students. Many students identified because of high IQ and relative achievement discrepancies reflect a failure to account for regression to the mean.

CAUTION

....

The idea that slow learners can be identified on the basis of IQ scores in the 70 to 80 range does not have much research support.

broadly assess achievement domains as recommended in the hybrid model. It may well be that "gifted" students with SLD exist. But IQ-discrepancy by itself does not indicate SLD (Kavale & Flanagan, 2007), just as poor instructional response by itself is not adequate to identify SLD.

Similarly derived concerns exist about whether children with IQ scores in the borderline-low-average range (70 to 80) (so-called slow learners) are misplaced. As summarized previously, IQ is not strongly associated with treatment response, prognosis, or other attributes that would make it an important attribute requiring routine measurement. The best way to assess aptitude for learning is to put a person in an intervention and measure his or her growth. Slow learners learn more slowly.

More generally, identification of SLD within RTI service delivery frameworks is not a panacea for the issues with measurement and determination of discrepancies that have longed plagued psychometric models of identification. Approaches that incorporate assessments of instructional response are based on discrepancies with age and treatment response, but are simpler because they do not require the use of difference scores between two or more psychometric tests. These methods are also no better than the quality of the instructional services provided, but this is also true for any model of SLD identification. Regardless of the identification model, the SLD construct requires multiple criteria for identification; these criteria must include instructional response as an inclusionary criterion; and the use of rigid cut-points that attempt to treat SLD as a categorical distinction will perpetuate the identification issues of great concern to educational practitioners, policy makers, and parents. At the very least, confidence intervals should be used to account for the measurement error of the tests. It is disheartening to see many states adopt criteria purporting to derive from RTI models that specify a rigid cut-point, which likely will have the effect of perpetuating adversarial relations of schools and parents around the issue of who is eligible, as opposed to what services are being provided and how much growth the student is showing. SLD is a supportable and defensible construct that can be reliably and validly identified, but there is a need to anchor research on identification in a classification framework and constantly evaluate the reliability and validity of the classification.

🐟 TEST YOURSELF 🐟
....

1. **In SLD, classification is what happens when someone is diagnosed with LD. True or False?**

2. **Which of these are true for aptitude-achievement discrepancy?**
   (a) Differences in cognitive functions between IQ-discrepant and nondiscrepant poor readers are small for cognitive variables not used to define the groups.
   (b) Children with an IQ-achievement discrepancy have a better response to intervention.
   (c) The long-term development of reading is better in IQ-discrepant than nondiscrepant poor readers.
   (d) A variety of measures have been used to operationalize aptitude in aptitude-achievement discrepancy models.

3. **Which statements are true for low achievement models of identification?**
   (a) Low achievement per se is a reliable indicator of SLD.
   (b) Low achievement is necessary but not sufficient for identification of SLD.
   (c) There is a strong evidence base supporting the validity of classifications of SLD based on low achievement models.
   (d) Absolute low achievement is a requirement for any model of SLD identification.

4. **The primary goal of RTI models is the identification of the right child as SLD. True or false?**

5. **Which statements best characterizes referral for special education in an RTI model?**
   (a) Children are never referred; they are screened and identified at the end of the RTI process.
   (b) Referral is made in the context of universal screening, progress monitoring, and intervention response, with special education as part of the continuum of service delivery.
   (c) Referral is not needed because RTI models do not require a comprehensive evaluation.
   (d) RTI models are often recommended for districts that have gender and minority disproportionality in special education.

6. **Comprehensive assessments in an RTI model and a traditional model may not differ for some children. True or false?**

7. **Identification in an RTI model is more straightforward than a traditional model because no discrepancy scores are involved. True or false?**

8. **Which of these items is not a component of most RTI models?**

    (a) Universal screening

    (b) Progress monitoring

    (c) Increasingly intense interventions

    (d) Assessment of cognitive strengths and weaknesses

9. **There is a strong evidence base supporting classifications of SLD based on cognitive strengths and weaknesses. True or false?**

10. **Issues with RTI models for identification include**

    (a) weak overlap of different methods for identifying inadequate responders.

    (b) insufficient development of evidence-based interventions in some academic domains.

    (c) that scaling an RTI model is an intensive process requiring close collaborations between administrators, teachers, school professionals, and parents.

    (d) absence of reliable screening tools and measures for progress monitoring

Answers: 1. False; 2. a, d; 3. b, c; 4. False; 5. b, d; 6. True; 7. False; 8. d; 9. False; 10. a, b, c.

Seven

THE DISCREPANCY/CONSISTENCY APPROACH TO SLD IDENTIFICATION USING THE PASS THEORY

Jack A. Naglieri

There are many reasons why children experience academic failure (e.g., poor instruction, lack of motivation, visual or auditory problems, lack of exposure to books and reading, instruction that does not meet a child's particular style of learning, overall limited intellectual ability, a specific intellectual ability deficit, etc.). This chapter focuses on those children who have a disorder in one or more of the basic psychological processes that underlie academic success and failure; that is, children with scores on a reliable and well-validated multidimensional test of cognitive processes that vary from the average to the well below-average ranges, with corresponding variability in standardized achievement test scores. These children can only be identified via a comprehensive assessment using nationally normed tests that uncover the processing deficit(s) and associated academic failure, despite adequate instruction and a consideration of other exclusionary factors. These types of children would meet the criteria for a specific learning disability (SLD) as defined by the 2004 reauthorization of the Individuals with Disabilities Education Improvement Act (IDEA; see Hale, Kaufman, Naglieri, & Kavale, 2006).

This chapter is about children who have a disorder in one or more of the basic psychological processes. These children's academic failure may be exacerbated by poor instruction, but inadequate teaching did not cause the problem. These children would likely benefit from frequent progress monitoring, but ongoing progress monitoring is not enough to ensure academic success. In order to understand the reasons for academic failure, these children need to be carefully evaluated by a qualified professional who can identify SLD on the basis of a disorder in one or more of the basic psychological processes. Children with cognitive and academic processing deficits also require instruction that is tailored to their unique learning needs.

This chapter examines the issues related to assessment of cognitive processing, diagnosis, and intervention for children with SLD. The goal is not to compare this method to other possible options, such as response to intervention (RTI), but rather to clarify exactly how identification of children with a *specific* learning disability can be accomplished with recognition of the requirements stipulated by IDEA 2004 and the Federal Regulations (for more information see Hale et al., 2006, and Kavale, Kaufman, Naglieri, & Hale, 2005). In the remainder of this chapter the question of how to measure basic psychological processes is discussed, and details about how measuring basic psychological processes fits the federal law are provided. Next, the Discrepancy/Consistency Model is presented (with a case study), followed by a discussion of the validity of this approach.

DON'T FORGET

SLD is defined by IDEA as a "disorder in one or more of the basic psychological processes," so these must be measured for a diagnosis to be rendered.

BASIC PSYCHOLOGICAL PROCESSES

The Kaufman Assessment Battery for Children (K-ABC; Kaufman & Kaufman, 1983) was the first well-developed measure of ability to be conceptualized and developed using a cognitive processing perspective. The second test to be specifically developed using a neuropsychological perspective on ability was the Cognitive Assessment System (CAS; Naglieri & Das, 1997a). These tests provided the tools necessary to document a disorder in basic psychological processes central to SLD. That is, the "identification of a core cognitive deficit, or a disorder in one or more psychological processes, that is predictive of an imperfect ability to learn, is a marker for a specific learning disability" (p. 5), as stated by the U.S. Department of Education Roundtable (American Institutes for Research, 2002). In order to utilize a cognitive processing approach to SLD identification, three main components are needed. First, the child must have significant intraindividual differences among the basic psychological processes such that the lowest processing score is substantially below average. Second, there needs to be a significant difference between average processing scores and achievement. Third, there needs to be consistency between poor processing scores and academic deficits (Hale & Fiorello, 2004; Naglieri, 1999, 2005). This is referred to as a Discrepancy/Consistency Model by Naglieri (1999).

≡ *Rapid Reference 7.1*

Discrepancy/Consistency Model Criteria for Determining SLD

SLD is suggested when the following criteria are met:
1. There is a discrepancy among processing scores.
2. There is a discrepancy among achievement scores.
3. There is a consistency between low processing and low achievement scores.
4. The low scores are substantially below average.

The Discrepancy/Consistency Model could be applied using any measure of ability (see Rapid Reference 7.1). However, in this chapter the focus is on a theory of basic psychological processes called Planning, Attention, Simultaneous, and Successive (PASS) as it is measured by the CAS (Naglieri & Das, 1997a). This is intended to provide an example of how SLD can be operationalized, and the findings used for diagnostic and instructional decision making. Although this is not intended to be the only way to define what the important cognitive processes may be, PASS is a theory that has been carefully validated along several dimensions. This theory is used to present a method of examining evidence for SLD determination that is intended to be used as a part of a larger collection of data obtained within a problem-solving context. The section that follows begins with a discussion of what cognitive processes are and how they should be measured; then the PASS processing abilities will be presented, followed by a brief review of the validity of the theory.

What Is a Cognitive Process?

Before discussing the basic psychological processes called PASS, the concept of a "cognitive process" needs to be examined. The term *cognitive process* refers to a foundational, neuropsychologically identified ability that provides the means by which an individual functions in this world. A specific cognitive process provides a unique ability to function. For example, Successive processing is used to manage information that is arranged in a specific sequence. A group of cognitive processes is needed to meet the multidimensional demands of our complex environment. That is, multiple processes (e.g., Successive and Attention) provide the ability to notice (attend) the slight difference in the sequence of letters that make up two similar words, for example, *weird* and *wired*. Having several cognitive

DON'T FORGET
....

The cognitive demands of a task determine the type of processing needed.

processing abilities affords the capability of completing the same task using different types or various combinations of processes (this is important for intervention planning). For example, reading a word requires blending the separate sounds that make the word, which involves Successive processing; but seeing the word as a whole involves Simultaneous processing.

Cognitive processes underlie all mental and physical activity. Through the application of cognitive processes humans acquire all types of knowledge and skills. However, it is very important to recognize that skills, such as reading decoding or math reasoning, are *not* examples of cognitive processes; these are sets of specific knowledge and skills acquired by the application of cognitive processes. Further, specific skills such as blending sounds together in order to make a word are not a special type of cognitive processing, but instead, a basic psychological process that is specifically used for working with serial information to perform this act (e.g., Successive processing). It is the interaction of basic cognitive processes with instruction (and related factors such as motivation, emotional status, quality of instruction, etc.) that leads to learning and social competence.

The separation of cognitive processes from knowledge and skills is critical for effective assessment of the basic psychological processes. Assessment of achievement must be accomplished with tests that adequately evaluate the domain of interest (e.g., reading, math, etc.). Assessment of cognitive processes must be conducted using tests that are as free of academic content as possible. Having separate measures of achievement and cognitive processes maximizes the extent to which scores reflect the processing construct efficiently, rather than the combination of processing and academic skill. Moreover, it is critical to recognize that while achievement domains can be defined effectively by the content of the test, processing tests are defined by the cognitive demands of the test questions or tasks. For this reason, cognitive processes should *not* be defined by the content or modality of the task. For example, a test that is often described as an "auditory processing test" requires repetition of digits in the same sequence that was presented orally by an examiner. The essential requirement of this task is that the child retain the order of the numbers spoken by the examiner long enough to repeat them in the correct order; which means that the task requires successive (from CAS) or sequential (from K-ABC) processing. But the same task can be given visually (e.g., K-ABC Hand Movements subtest) and it still can measure sequential processing. How can two tasks using different modalities (e.g., auditory and visual) measure the same process? The answer is that the underlying cognitive processing demand is the same—that is, the child's ability to work with information in order—regardless of modality.

Finally, the question of how the processes themselves are identified should be considered. Researchers have used many different ways for determining what the important cognitive processes may be. Some have relied on the experimental literature to define the constructs of interest; others have utilized statistical methods such as factor analysis to discover underlying dimensions; and some rely on abilities defined in the cognitive or neuropsychological literature (e.g., working memory, rationality, etc.). Naglieri and Das (1997a, 2005) defined the essential psychological processes on the basis of an understanding of how the brain functions. This allowed them to be unencumbered by what is included in traditional IQ tests and build explicitly on a theory derived from Luria (1966, 1973, 1980). The next important task was to systematically examine the validity of these constructs, which we have summarized in several sources (Naglieri, 2005; Naglieri & Conway, 2009; Naglieri & Das, 2005) and which will be done briefly in this chapter. First, however, the origins of the PASS theory are described.

DON'T FORGET
....
Measurement of the "basic psychological processes" must be made using tests that are reliable and valid for that specific use.

PASS Theory

Luria's theoretical description of how the human brain functions is considered one of the most complete (Lewandowski & Scott, 2008). In his seminal works *Human Brain and Psychological Processes* (1966), *Higher Cortical Functions of Man* (1980), and *The Working Brain* (1973), he described the brain as a functional mosaic, with parts that make specific contributions to a larger interacting network. Luria stressed that no area of the brain functions without input from other areas so that cognition and behavior result from an interaction of complex brain activity across various areas. Luria's research on the functional aspects of the brain provided the basis for the neuropsychological processing theory of intelligence called PASS, initially described by Das, Naglieri, and Kirby (1994) and operationalized by the CAS (Naglieri & Das, 1997a). The four PASS processes represent a fusion of cognitive and neuropsychological constructs such as executive functioning (Planning and Attention), selective, sustained, and focused activity (Attention), processing of information into a coherent whole

(Simultaneous), and serial processing of information (Successive) (Naglieri & Das, 2005). These four neuropsychologically defined intellectual processes are described more fully in the following sections.

Planning

Planning is a frontal lobe function, especially the prefrontal cortex, and one of the prominent abilities that differentiates humans from other primates. Goldberg (2002) wrote that Planning

> plays a central role in forming goals and objectives and then in devising plans of action required to attain these goals. The cognitive processes required to implement plans, coordinate these activities, and apply them in a correct order are subserved by the prefrontal cortex. Finally, the prefrontal cortex is responsible for evaluating our actions as success or failure relative to our intentions. (p. 23)

Planning helps us achieve goals through the development and use of strategies to accomplish tasks for which a solution is required. Planning is an essential ability for all activities that requires someone to figure out how to solve a problem. The task of problem solving includes self-monitoring and impulse control as well as making, evaluating, and implementing strategies to achieve a goal. Thus, Planning allows for the generation of solutions, discriminating use of knowledge and skills, as well as control of Attention, Simultaneous, and Successive processes (Das, Kar, & Parrila, 1996).

Attention

Attention is a cognitive processing ability that is associated with Luria's first functional unit (the reticular formation), which allows an individual to selectively focus cognitive activity toward a stimulus over a period of time without being distracted by other competing stimuli. The longer attention is needed, the more difficult maintenance of focused activity will be. Intentions and goals (e.g., Planning process) are responsible for control of Attention, which is why measures of these two processes correlate strongly. The attention work of Schneider, Dumais, and Shiffrin (1984) and the attention selectivity work of Posner and Boies (1971), which relates to deliberate discrimination between stimuli, is similar to the way that the Attention process, included in PASS theory and operationalized by the CAS, was conceptualized.

Simultaneous Processing

Simultaneous processing is needed for organizing information into groups or a coherent whole. The ability to recognize patterns as interrelated elements is made possible by the parietal-occipital-temporal brain regions. Due to the substantial spatial characteristics of most Simultaneous tasks, there is a visual-spatial dimension to activities that demand this type of process. Conceptually, the examination of Simultaneous processing is achieved using tasks that could be described as involving visual-spatial reasoning found in progressive matrices tests like those originally developed by Penrose and Raven (1936).

Simultaneous processing is not, however, limited to nonverbal content, as demonstrated by the important role it plays in the grammatical components of language and comprehension of word relationships, prepositions, and inflections (Naglieri, 1999), as is illustrated by the Verbal-Spatial Relationship subtest included in the CAS (Naglieri & Das, 1997a). Matrices tests have been included in so-called nonverbal tests such as the Wechsler Nonverbal Scale of Ability (Wechsler & Naglieri, 2006) and the Naglieri Nonverbal Ability Test, Second Edition (NNAT-II; Naglieri, 2008a), or nonverbal portions of intelligence tests, such as the Wechsler Intelligence Scale for Children–Fourth Edition (WISC-IV; Wechsler, 2003), the Stanford-Binet Intelligence Scales–Fifth Edition (SB5; Roid, 2003), or a Simultaneous processing scale, as found on the Kaufman Assessment Battery for Children, Second Edition (KABC-II; Kaufman & Kaufman, 2004) and the CAS.

Successive Processing

Successive processing is needed when working with stimuli arranged in a defined serial order. Successive processing is an integral ability involved with the serial organization of sounds, such as learning sounds in sequence (e.g., phonological skills) and early reading. In fact, Successive processing has been conceptually and experimentally related to the concept of phonological coding (Das, Mishra, & Kirby, 1994). When serial information is grouped into a pattern, however, (like the number 553669 organized into 55–3–66–9), then successful repetition of the string may be related to Planning (i.e., the decision to use a chunking strategy) *and* Simultaneous (organizing the numbers into related groups) *and* Successive (retaining the order of the numbers) processes. *Chunking* is often used by older children and can be used as an effective strategy for those who are weak in Successive processing (see Naglieri & Pickering, 2010). Young children with poor Successive processing often have difficulty following directions or comprehending what is being said to them when sentences are too lengthy (Naglieri, 2005). Teachers and parents often misinterpret this weakness as a failure to comply or as a problem with Attention. The concept of Successive processing is similar to the concept of Sequential processing included in the KABC-II (Kaufman & Kaufman, 2004), and tests that require recall of serial information such as Digit Span Forward on the WISC-IV (Wechsler, 2003).

Operationalization of the PASS Theory

The PASS theory was operationalized on the CAS (Naglieri & Das, 1997a). This instrument is thoroughly described in the *CAS Interpretive Handbook* (Naglieri & Das, 1997b) and other sources (e.g., Naglieri, 1999; Naglieri & Conway, 2009). Naglieri and Das (1997a, 1997b) generated tests to measure the PASS theory following a systematic and empirically based test development program designed to obtain efficient measures of the processes for individual administration. The PASS theory was used as the foundation of the CAS, so the content of the test was determined by the theory and not by previous views of ability. The CAS was standardized on a sample of 2,200 children ages 5 to 17 years who were representative of the U.S. population on a number of important demographic variables. The sample is a nationally representative, stratified sample based on gender, race, ethnicity, region, community setting, classroom placement, and parental education (see Naglieri & Das, 1997a, for more details). The CAS yields four separate standard scores, one for each of the Planning, Attention, Simultaneous, and Successive scales, and a Full Scale standard score, each having a normative mean of 100 and *SD* of 15.

HOW TO USE PROCESSING FOR SLD DETERMINATION

IDEA 2004 describes several important criteria of a comprehensive evaluation that should be used for SLD eligibility. First, a variety of assessment tools and strategies must be used to gather relevant information about the child. Second, the use of any single measure or assessment as the sole criterion for determining whether a child has SLD is not permitted. Third, practitioners must use technically sound instruments to assess the relative contribution of cognitive and behavioral factors. Fourth, assessments must be selected and administered so as not to be discriminatory on the basis of race or culture, and these tests are administered in a form most likely to yield accurate information. Fifth, the measures used are reliable and valid for the purposes for which they were intended.

> **DON'T FORGET**
> ....
> IDEA is unambiguous about the nature of a comprehensive assessment. A variety of assessment tools and strategies must be used.

The Federal Regulations (2006) clarified that states are not allowed to prohibit the use of a severe discrepancy between ability and achievement for

SLD determination, but use of the traditional ability-achievement discrepancy was discouraged. Also clarified was the following: Screening to determine appropriate instructional strategies for curriculum implementation shall not be considered an evaluation for special education eligibility. RTI may be used as a part of the SLD eligibility process but "determining why a child has not responded to research-based interventions *requires* [italics added] a comprehensive evaluation" (p. 46647) and "RTI does not replace the need for a comprehensive evaluation" (p. 46648). What RTI does provide is greater assurance that (a) adequate learning experiences have been provided before initiating a comprehensive evaluation; and (b) the child's failure to respond is not the result of inadequate instruction. These regulations also further clarify that assessments used in the comprehensive evaluation "include those tailored to assess specific areas of educational need and not merely those that are designed to provide a single general intelligence quotient" (p. 43785). Despite these changes in the methodology for identifying SLD, the definition of this disorder remains a "disorder in one or more of the basic psychological processes" (see Rapid Reference 7.2).

The definition of SLD and the method used to identify children with this disorder should be consistent (Hale et al., 2006; Kavale et al., 2005). Because IDEA 2004 clearly specifies that children must have a disorder in "one or more of the basic psychological processes," which is the underlying cause of SLD,

---

≡ *Rapid Reference 7.2*

Definition of SLD

Section 602 of IDEA defines an SLD as follows:

(A) *In general*: The term specific learning disability means a disorder in one or more of the basic psychological processes involved in understanding or in using language, spoken or written, which disorder may manifest itself in the imperfect ability to listen, think, speak, read, write, spell, or do mathematical calculations.

(B) *Disorders included*: Such term includes conditions as perceptual disabilities, brain injury, minimal brain dysfunction, dyslexia, and developmental aphasia.

(C) *Disorders not included*: Such term does not include a learning problem that is primarily the result of visual, hearing, or motor disabilities, of mental retardation, of emotional disturbance, or of environmental, cultural, or economic disadvantage.

cognitive processes must be measured. A comprehensive evaluation of the basic psychological processes unites the statutory and regulatory components of IDEA 2004, and ensures that the methods used for identification more closely reflect the definition. Any defensible eligibility system would demand continuity between the statutory and regulatory definitions, and for this reason alone SLD determination requires the documentation of a basic psychological processing disorder. Moreover, the tools used for this assessment must meet the technical criteria included in IDEA 2004. There is ample evidence that the CAS, and the theory it was based on, meets these requirements (Naglieri & Conway, 2009).

The PASS theory as operationalized by the CAS provides a means to define the basic psychological processes included in the definition of SLD. In order to apply this approach, an individual child's PASS profile must be examined to determine if a relative or cognitive weakness exists. A *relative weakness* is found when at least one PASS scale standard score is significantly lower than the child's mean PASS score. Because the PASS scores are compared to the individual child's average (and not the normative mean of 100), a "relative" strength or weakness indicates that there is variability in the cognitive profile. For example, a child who has standard scores of 114 (Planning), 116 (Simultaneous), 94 (Attention), and 109 (Successive) has a relative weakness in Attention because this score is 14.25 standard score points below the child's mean of 108.25. A relative weakness is not sufficient for identification of a disorder in processing. In contrast, a dual criterion is used to determine if a *cognitive weakness* is found. That is, the score is significantly below the child's mean *and* that score is also well below average. For example, a child who has standard scores of 102, 104, 82, and 97 for Planning, Simultaneous, Attention, and Successive, respectively, has a cognitive weakness in Attention. This is determined because the Attention score is 14.25 standard score points below the child's mean of 96.25 *and* the 82 is well below average (12th percentile) in relation to the norm.

DON'T FORGET

A "cognitive weakness" provides the strongest evidence of a "disorder in one or more of the basic psychological processes" because it is relatively lower than the child's mean and lower in relation to the national norm.

DISCREPANCY/CONSISTENCY MODEL

Naglieri (1999) suggested that evidence of a disorder in one of the four PASS basic psychological processes should be based on a cognitive weakness because (a) the child's ipsative weakness is evidence of a *specific* disorder in processing and (b) the score is low relative to a national norm and therefore unusual.

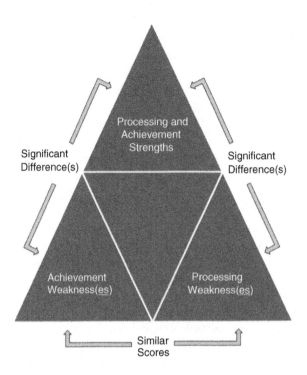

Figure 7.1. Discrepancy/Consistency Model for SLD Diagnosis

Additionally, the child must have deficient academic performance in a specific area to be considered eligible for programming for children with a *specific* learning disability. The relationship among the variables is illustrated in Figure 7.1. This figure includes a significant *discrepancy* between the child's high cognitive processing scores and some specific academic achievement, a significant *discrepancy* between the child's high and low cognitive processing scores, and *consistency* between the child's low processing and low achievement scores.

The Discrepancy/Consistency Model for the identification of specific learning disabilities was described first by Naglieri (1999). The goal of the method is to obtain a systematic examination of variability of both cognitive and academic achievement test scores. Determining whether the cognitive processing scores differ significantly is accomplished using the method originally proposed by Davis (1959), popularized by Kaufman (1979), and modified by Silverstein

(1993). This so-called, ipsative method determines when the child's scores are reliably different from the child's average score. This technique has been applied to a number of tests including, for example, the WISC-IV (Naglieri & Paolitto, 2005), the CAS (Naglieri & Das, 1997a), and the SB5 (Roid, 2003). It is important to note that in the Discrepancy/Consistency Model described by Naglieri (1999), the ipsative approach is applied to the PASS scales, which represent four neuropsychologically defined constructs, *not* the subtests as is usually done, for example, with the Wechsler scales. This changes the method from one that demands considerable clinical interpretation of the meaning of *subtest* variability to analysis of *scales* that have been theoretically defined and have higher reliability and validity. This distinction is important because the criticisms of the ipsative method (McDermott, Fantuzzo & Glutting, 1990) have centered around subtest-, not scale-level, analysis.

Naglieri (1999) and Flanagan and Kaufman (2004) stressed the importance of recognizing that because a low score relative to the child's mean could still be within the average range, adding the requirement that the weakness in a processing test score is also well below average is important. In a study of PASS profiles for the CAS standardization and validity samples Naglieri (2000) found that those students who had a cognitive weakness were likely to have significantly lower achievement scores and more likely to have been identified as in need of special education. That study was described by Carroll (2000) as one that illustrated what a more successful profile method could be. Davison and Kuang (2000) suggested that "adding information about the absolute level of the lowest score improves identification over what can be achieved using ipsative profile pattern information alone" (p. 462).

The utility of PASS profiles was examined in a recent study by Huang, Bardos, and D'Amato (2010). They studied PASS profiles on the CAS for large samples of students in general education ($N = 1,692$) and students with learning disabilities ($N = 367$). They found 10 core PASS profiles for those in regular education and eight unique profiles from students with SLD. Huang et al., concluded that "a student with a true LD has a relatively high chance of being accurately identified when using profiles analysis on composite [PASS] scores (p. 28)." They added that their "analysis has provided evidence for the use of the PASS theory and that it appears that it has sufficient applications for diagnosis for students suspected of having a LD" (p. 28).

DON'T FORGET

The Discrepancy/Consistency Model is used to determine whether the child has a cognitive weakness and academic failure that are consistent with a specific learning disability.

In summary, there are important data suggesting that PASS scale discrepancies that are significant relative to the child's overall level (the ipsative method) and substantially below what would be considered typical (normative) provide evidence that a child has "a disorder in the basic psychological processes" necessary for SLD identification (Naglieri, 2005). Finding a specific cognitive processing weakness and evidence of academic failure provide information that contributes to the diagnosis of SLD, especially if other inclusionary/exclusionary conditions are also met. The steps to apply this method are provided in Figure 7.2 and are demonstrated in the case that follows.

Case Illustration

This case illustration (provided by Linda Marcoux, school psychologist, Charles County, Maryland) is intended to demonstrate how the Discrepancy/Consistency Model can be applied as part of a comprehensive evaluation. Rather than provide an entire case study with all the details ordinarily included with such an evaluation, the essential elements that illustrate how the PASS theory can be used to understand a child's past and present behavior and test scores are provided.

Background

Daniel is a 5th grader who was referred for testing after problems with reading and writing persisted following participation in interventions at school. The majority of Daniel's difficulties are related to spelling and writing, and he experiences some difficulties with decoding unfamiliar words. When Daniel is unable to read an unfamiliar word in a sentence he is often able to use context clues to make reasonable guesses at the words, but resists using decoding strategies he has been taught. Daniel's parents and teachers report that he often reverses letters within words on spelling tests, and writes letters, and occasionally numbers, backwards. In class, there are times when he refuses to sound out words by combining letter sounds, or implement other decoding strategies he has learned. Decoding is typically very labor-intensive for Daniel, and when he has to decode several words within a sentence he does not necessarily comprehend what he reads. Overall comprehension is not problematic for Daniel, but on occasion his poor decoding interferes with his understanding of written material. The evidence of difficulty decoding unfamiliar words and resistance to using decoding strategies suggests a possible weakness in Successive processing, and the tendency to use context clues to gain meaning from text implies good Simultaneous processing ability.

Daniel's parents and teachers report that Daniel is readily able to comprehend and draw meaningful inferences from spoken information and that he performs

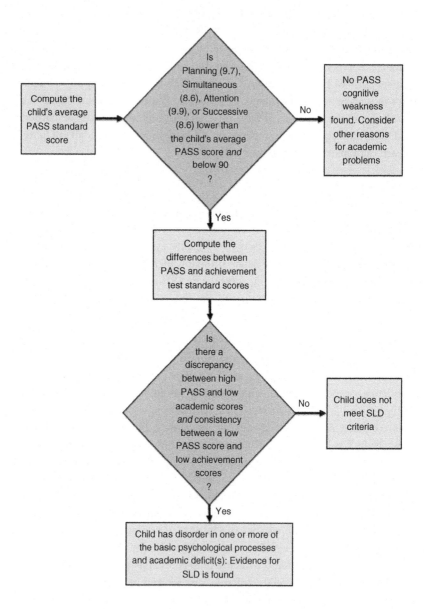

Figure 7.2. Flowchart for Planning, Attention, Simultaneous, and Successive (PASS) and Achievement Comparisons

Source: Values needed for significance when comparing PASS scale standard scores are from Naglieri (1999). Copyright © Jack A. Naglieri, 2010. All rights reserved.

well in math. He participates enthusiastically in class discussions and often provides meaningful insight. The ability to connect pieces of information into a whole (Simultaneous processing) underlies Daniel's ability to make insightful inferences. However, when Daniel is given a written assignment to complete, he often acts out and can become extremely disruptive. Historically, Daniel's problematic behavior has often been a primary concern, but strong academic and behavioral interventions have helped to decrease the outbursts. Nevertheless, his problems with decoding and writing persist.

During administration of the various tests, Daniel became noticeably agitated during tasks that required him to write or otherwise use information in a specific linear order. He shook his head and occasionally rubbed or closed his eyes while listening to information that required him to rely on the order of the words to complete the task. At times, he even refused to respond.

Selected Assessment Results

Daniel's performance on the CAS showed considerable variability across his PASS scale scores (see Rapid Reference 7.3). His Simultaneous standard score (114) is significantly above his average, and his Successive standard score (73) is significantly below his average and well below the Average range. Daniel's cognitive weakness in Successive processing is also consistent with his performance on academic tasks. For example, he earned low scores on spelling and memory tasks that demanded he work with information in a specific linear order. On the spelling subtests Daniel frequently reversed the order of letters within words. Similarly, he had considerable difficulty on the Understanding Directions subtest when directed to "Point to the chair if the TV is on, and if the TV is off,

≡ Rapid Reference 7.3

Selected Scores for the Case of Daniel

	Standard Scores	Difference From Child's Mean
Planning	106	9.25
Simultaneous	114	17.25
Attention	94	−2.75
Successive	73	−23.75
Child's Mean	96.75	

point to the table after pointing to the cat." Instructions like these require that he recall the sentence in the correct order and obtain meaning based on the sequence of the information provided—which demands considerable Successive processing. At times, Daniel refused to attempt a response, and at other times he pointed to the correct objects but in the incorrect order. Additionally, Daniel performed poorly on the Memory Index from a test of phonological processing (see Figure 7.3), which required him to remember words and numbers in a specific linear order. He also performed poorly when he was asked to repeat a word without a designated sound or syllable. Daniel had considerable difficulty completing these tests accurately because they rely on Successive processing ability.

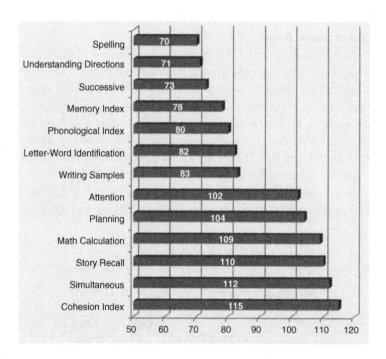

Figure 7.3. Planning, Attention, Simultaneous, and Successive (PASS) and Achievement Standard Scores for Daniel

Source: Planning, Attention, Simultaneous and Successive scores from CAS; Spelling, Understanding Directions, Letter-Word Identification, Writing Samples, Math Calculation from Woodcock-Johnson III Tests of Achievement (WJ III ACH; Woodcock, McGrew, & Mather, 2001); and Phonological Index, Memory Index, and Cohesion Index from the Test of Auditory Processing Skills–Third Edition (TAPS-3; 2005). Standard scores are based on a mean of 100 and *SD* of 15.

Daniel demonstrated a strength in Simultaneous processing (standard score of 114), which was also consistent with his good performance on certain academic tasks. For instance, Daniel performed well on a test that required him to listen to and recall spoken information from a story, as well as several other tasks that do not primarily rely on Successive processing. It is likely that Daniel's cognitive strength in Simultaneous processing, coupled with his behavior problems, masked his difficulties with tasks that demand Successive processing.

Daniel's standard scores on the CAS and the achievement tests fit the Discrepancy/Consistency Model. He has a significant cognitive weakness in Successive processing (standard score of 73), which is significantly lower than his PASS mean score and well below average for children his age. Similarly, Daniel scored in the 70s and 80s on a variety of academic tasks that rely heavily on Successive processing ability, such as spelling, following directions in order, and remembering phonological information in a specific sequence. His score on the Successive processing scale is consistent with his low scores on certain academic tasks. Moreover, there is a discrepancy between Daniel's low academic scores and his average to high average scores on the other PASS scales.

Although Daniel's overall Full Scale standard score on the CAS was in the average range, his standard score on the Successive processing scale indicates a deficit in a basic psychological process. This processing deficit, along with his academic failure that has not been managed through typical and additional academic interventions in the classroom, indicates that more specialized instruction will be necessary for Daniel to make sufficient academic gains (see Figure 7.4). It is also likely that Daniel's deficit in Successive processing led him to be very frustrated in the classroom. Interventions that take this weakness into consideration are needed (see Naglieri & Pickering, 2010).

CORRESPONDENCE BETWEEN IDEA AND THE DISCREPANCY/CONSISTENCY MODEL

According to Kavale et al. (2005), SLD identification procedures should address the components in the conceptual definition in a systematic manner to accurately identify the presence of SLD. Importantly, they argued that the identification of children with SLD should include a comprehensive evaluation that ensures students who have a learning disability are accurately identified. The Discrepancy/Consistency Model provides an important

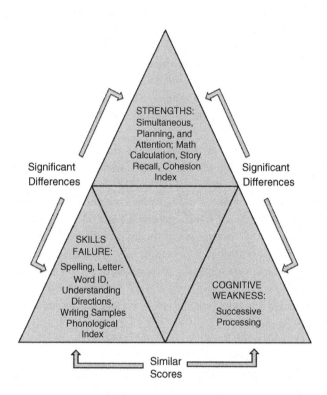

Figure 7.4. Discrepancy/Consistency Results for Daniel

component of the procedure for identifying SLD. Perhaps most importantly, using this method unifies the definition of SLD and the method used to identify children as suggested by Kavale et al., (2005) and Hale et al. (2006).

These authors further argued that because IDEA 2004 clearly states that children with SLD have a disorder in "one or more of the basic psychological processes," a comprehensive evaluation of the basic psychological processes unites the statutory and regulatory components of the law.

> **DON'T FORGET**
> ....
> The Discrepancy/Consistency Model should be part of a larger comprehensive assessment process to identify a child with SLD. No one method alone is sufficient.

Does the Discrepancy/Consistency Model Meet IDEA Requirements?

In recent years there had been an increasing emphasis on empirically supported methods, as evidenced by several requirements that appear in IDEA. In order to understand the science behind any proposed method of SLD diagnosis, as well as the tests used to obtain important information, each of the requirements found in IDEA should be carefully considered. The validity of the PASS theory vis-à-vis SLD diagnosis and intervention has been presented in several sources (Naglieri, 1999, 2005, 2008b; Naglieri & Das, 1997a, 2005; Naglieri & Conway, 2009; Naglieri & Otero, in press) and, therefore, only a few points relevant to the Discrepancy/Consistency Model are briefly summarized here. The first relates to nondiscriminatory assessment, and the second to using measures that are valid for the purposes they were intended.

Is Cognitive Processing Assessment Nondiscriminatory?

The need for fair assessment of diverse populations of children has become progressively more important as the U.S. population continues to become more diverse. Recognizing this change, IDEA stresses that assessments (this includes measures of basic psychological processes as well as methods such as RTI) must not discriminate on the basis of race, culture, or language background. Appropriate assessment of children who may have SLD from all race and ethnic groups must be accomplished using tools that are nondiscriminatory. At the heart of this issue is selection of the tool that can be most effectively used within a diverse context. Fagan (2000) and Suzuki and Valencia (1997) argued that because processing tests do not rely on test items with language and quantitative content they are more appropriate for assessment of culturally and linguistically diverse populations. Ceci (2000) suggested that a processing approach could (a) allow for early detection of disabilities before academic failure is experienced, (b) have better diagnostic utility, and (c) provide a way to better understand children's disabilities. All of these authors suggest that traditional IQ tests that yield large mean score differences among ethnic groups should be avoided and measures of cognitive processing used instead.

> **CAUTION**
>
> Always ask the question "What empirical evidence is there that supports a particular approach to measuring basic psychological processes?"

There is evidence that PASS cognitive processing scores differ minimally between race and ethnic groups and when the test is given in different languages. For example, PASS cognitive processing scores of 298 African American children and 1,691 white children were compared by Naglieri, Rojahn, Matto, and Aquilino (2005). Controlling for key demographic variables, they found that regression analyses showed a CAS Full Scale mean standard score difference of 4.8 points in favor of white children. Naglieri et al. also found that correlations between the CAS scores and the achievement tests of the Woodcock-Johnson Psych-educational Battery–Revised (WJ-R; Woodcock & Johnson, 1989, 1990) were very similar for African Americans (.70) and whites (.64), suggesting that the PASS scales show little predictive bias. Similarly, Naglieri, Rojahn, and Matto (2007) examined the utility of the PASS theory with Hispanic children by comparing performance on the CAS of Hispanic and white children from the standardization sample. The study showed that the two groups differed by 4.8 standard score points when demographic differences were statistically controlled. They also found that the correlations between achievement and the CAS scores did not differ significantly for the Hispanic and white samples (Naglieri et al., 2007). The results of these studies are consistent with suggestions by Fagan (2000) and Suzuki and Valencia (1997) that processing tests are more appropriate for assessment of culturally and linguistically diverse populations because language and quantitative content are not included.

Comparisons of PASS scores obtained for different linguistic versions of the CAS have also been conducted. Naglieri et al. (2007) compared PASS standard scores on the CAS administered in English and Spanish to bilingual children referred for reading problems. The children earned similar Full Scale scores on the English and Spanish versions of the CAS (using norms based on the original standardization sample) that were highly correlated ($r = .96$). Importantly, deficits in Successive processing were found on both versions of the test (consistent with the view that children with reading disabilities are poor in this process); and 90% of children who had a cognitive weakness on the English version of the CAS also had the same cognitive weakness on the Spanish version of the CAS. Natur (2009) compared Arabic-speaking Palestinian students using the Arabic version of the CAS to a matched sample of children from the United States. He found a very small difference between the Arab (Full Scale standard score mean of 101.0) and U.S. (Full Scale standard score mean of 102.7) scores using the U.S. norms. Similarly, Taddei and Naglieri (2006) found that Italian children's ($N = 809$) Full Scale standard score of 100.9 on the Italian version of the CAS (Naglieri & Das, 2006) was very similar to the Full Scale of 100.5 for a matched sample of U.S. children ($N = 1,174$) from the original standardization sample. The small mean score differences between the performance of U.S. versus Arabic and U.S. versus Italian children, as well as the similarity in findings when the English and Spanish versions of the CAS are administered to the same children,

DON'T FORGET
....

There is considerable evidence that the PASS theory as measured by the CAS can be appropriately used for culturally and linguistically diverse populations.

suggests that the neuropsychologically based PASS theory as measured by the CAS appears to be robust across cultures and languages.

Do Exceptional Children Have Specific PASS Profiles?

The Discrepancy/Consistency Model for SLD diagnosis requires that a child shows a *specific* PASS cognitive weakness and academic failure. For this reason, research on intraindividual differences in PASS scores related to the specific disability is important. Research on the profiles found for children with different types of disabilities is an important source of validity for the discrepancy and consistency procedures. The profiles of the PASS processing standard scores obtained from children with reading disabilities and attention deficit hyperactivity disorder (ADHD) was summarized by Naglieri (2005). Children with specific reading decoding problems obtain low Successive processing standard scores (Naglieri, 1999; Naglieri, et al., 2007). In contrast, children diagnosed with ADHD hyperactive/impulsive (ADHD-H) type earned low standard scores in Planning (Dehn, 2000; Naglieri, Salter, & Edwards, 2004). Children with an autism spectrum disorder had low standard scores on the Attention scale (Goldstein & Naglieri, 2009). These groups are graphically described in Figure 7.5.

Reading decoding is a common problem for many children, and this disorder has been related to a cognitive weakness in Successive processing. Das et al. (1994) suggest that a Successive processing deficit underlies a phonological skills deficit and associated reading decoding failure. Successive processing involvement increases if the word is not easily recognized, and this process is even more important if the words are to be read aloud, because articulation also requires a considerable amount of Successive processing. For this reason, a test of phonemic skills, such as phonemic separation, is sensitive to reading failure (Das, Parrila, & Papadopoulos, 2000). Several studies on the relationship between PASS and reading disability have shown that Successive processing, in particular, is an important ability that underlies phonological skills (Das et al., 2000).

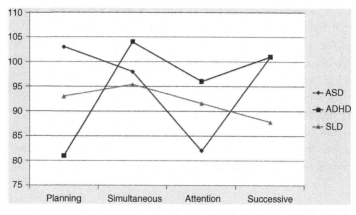

Figure 7.5. Planning, Attention, Simultaneous, and Successive (PASS) Profiles From the Cognitive Assessment System (CAS) for Children With Specific Learning Disabilities (SLD), Attention Deficit Hyperactivity Disorders (ADHD), and Autism Spectrum Disorders (ASD)

Note. Standard scores are based on a mean of 100 and SD of 15.

Does PASS Have Relevance to Reading Instruction?

The connection between assessment of psychological processes and intervention is an important one, especially for children with SLD. There is a line of research that illustrates how the PASS theory can be used within an instructional environment and for academic remediation. The PASS Remedial Program (PREP; Das, 1999) and the Planning Strategy Instruction, also known as Planning Facilitation, are described by Naglieri and Pickering (2010) as the two main approaches that have been studied. These methods are described in the sections that follow.

PREP is a remedial program based on the PASS theory and supported by several initial studies beginning with Krywaniuk and Das (1976), Kaufman and Kaufman (1979), and Brailsford, Snart, and Das (1984). These researchers demonstrated that students could be taught by the regular education teacher to more effectively apply Successive processing to reading, for example, by paying attention to the sequences of the sounds and letters. Subsequently, considerable research support for PREP has been reported (Boden & Kirby, 1995; Carlson & Das, 1997; Das, Mishra, & Pool, 1995; Das et al., 2000; Parrila, Das, Kendrick, Papadopoulos, & Kirby, 1999). PREP is a structured program of tasks designed to improve the use of Simultaneous and Successive processes that underlie reading and integrate these processes into word reading skills such as phoneme segmentation and sound blending. Each PREP task was designed to facilitate the development and use of strategies such as rehearsal, monitoring performance, revision of expectations, and sound blending. Children's ability to use these strategies is improved through experience with the tasks. Importantly, children are encouraged to use strategies, rather than being explicitly taught these strategies by the teacher.

Two studies particularly illustrate the value of PREP. First, Parrila et al., (1999) compared PREP with a whole-language reading program using two carefully matched groups of 1st grade children. The results showed a significant improvement of reading (Word Identification and Word Attack from the Woodcock Reading Mastery Test–Revised [WRMT–R]; Woodcock, 1987) for the PREP group, and the gain in reading was greater than it was for the whole-language control group. They also found that children with a higher level of Successive processing as measured by the CAS at the beginning of the program benefited the most from the PREP instruction; but those with the greatest improvement in the whole-language program had higher levels of Planning. The second study by Das et al. (2000) found 23 children who were taught using PREP improved significantly more in Word Attack and Word Identification from the WRMT–R (Woodcock, 1987) than did the 17 children in the control group. In total, these studies suggest that teaching children to better utilize PASS processes as delivered by the PREP program appears to be effective for remediating deficient reading skills during the elementary school years, as suggested by Ashman and Conway (1997).

Does PASS Have Relevance to Math Instruction?

The Planning component of the PASS theory has been shown to be important to classroom performance in math in a series of intervention studies. These investigations showed that children can be taught to better utilize their planning ability to be more strategic when they complete math tasks, and that the facilitation of plans improves academic performance. The initial concept for Planning Strategy Instruction was based on the research of Cormier, Carlson, and Das (1990) and Kar, Dash, Das, and Carlson (1992) within a mediated learning experience context. This means that an environment is created that encourages children to discover the value of strategy use without being specifically instructed on what to do. This is accomplished by asking the children questions about how they completed the tasks, what they noticed about the questions, which methods worked for them, and what would they do in the future to be more successful. These authors found that students who performed poorly on measures of Planning from the CAS demonstrated significantly greater gains than those with higher Planning standard scores. A series of studies followed that showed that the so-called Planning Strategy Instruction method improved children's performance in math calculation (Naglieri & Gottling, 1995, 1997). The students with learning disabilities who participated in these studies learned to recognize the need to plan and use strategies when completing math computation problems. (More details about the method are provided by Naglieri and Gottling [1995, 1997] and by Naglieri and Pickering [2010]).

Naglieri and Johnson (2000) further extended this Planning Strategy Instruction research with students who had learning disabilities and mild mental impairments. They found that children with a cognitive weakness in Planning improved considerably over baseline rates while those with no cognitive weakness improved only marginally. Similarly, children with cognitive weaknesses in Simultaneous, Successive, and Attention showed substantially lower rates of improvement. The importance of this study was that the five groups of children responded very differently to the same intervention, that is, the PASS processing standard scores were predictive of the children's response to this math intervention. In summary, these studies of PASS and math illustrate a connection between CAS Planning standard scores and instruction.

Children With ADHD

Iseman and Naglieri (in press) examined the effectiveness of teaching strategies to students with ADHD randomly assigned to an experimental group who received the Planning Strategy Instruction method, or a control group that received additional math instruction. They found large prepost effect sizes for students in the experimental group (.85), but not the control group on classroom math worksheets (.26), as well as standardized test score differences in Math Fluency (1.17 and .09, respectively) from the Woodcock-Johnson III Tests of Achievement (WJ III ACH; Woodcock, McGrew, and Mather, 2001) and Numerical Operations (.40 and −.14, respectively) from the Wechsler Individual Achievement Test (WIAT-II; Wechsler, 2001). One year later, the experimental group continued to outperform the control group. These findings suggest that students in the experimental group outperformed the control group on (a) math computation worksheets, (b) standardized tests of math at the end of the study, and (c) standardized tests of math one year later. This study further illustrated the importance PASS processes have to the acquisition of academic skills.

The Planning Strategy Instruction method was also applied to reading comprehension by Haddad et al. (2003). Their study involved 45 children in regular education programs who were encouraged to be more strategic when completing reading comprehension tasks. They found that children with a Planning weakness benefited substantially (effect size of 1.4) from the instruction designed to encourage the use of strategies and plans. In contrast, children with no PASS weakness or a Successive weakness only showed smaller effect sizes (.52 and .06, respectively). Their re-

DON'T FORGET
....
ADHD is described as a failure of self-control associated with the frontal lobes, and this is why these children perform poorly on the Planning Scale of the CAS.

sults suggested that PASS profiles are relevant to instruction and, specifically, that teaching children to be more strategic improved reading comprehension the most for those children with low Planning ability.

PASS Theory and Game-Based Learning

Computer games are often considered a form of entertainment, but a growing body of research suggests that these activities can be effective learning tools (e.g., Flowers, 2007; Pivec, 2007). The underlying rationale behind Digital Game-Based Learning (DGBL) is that humans learn through observation, imitation, and play. Perhaps most importantly, DGBL may be an effective learning tool because it engages and immerses the learner in the tasks, while traditional classrooms are more restricted to lectures and books that limit the learning to an audience-based experience (Fore-man, 2004). In fact, researchers have found that DGBL can help literacy development (Flowers; Segers & Verhoeven, 2005). One such pro-gram called Skatekids (SKO; www .skatekids.com) is linked to the PASS theory.

DON'T FORGET
....
One may think that children don't learn academic skills from video games, but there are "serious games" designed to teach children to read, and they work.

The designers of SKO built this game with recognition of the cognitive processing demands of reading, similar to the efforts made when PREP was constructed. This type of so-called, serious game teaches children to (a) use strategies, (b) attend to details, (c) focus on the sequences of letters and sounds, and (d) focus on the relationships among information while also learning reading skills. This combination of skill training and processing-based instruc-tion has recently been tested in a series of studies. Naglieri, Conway, and Rowe (2010) found that 3rd grade students' Dynamic Indicators of Basic Early Literacy Skills (DIBELS; Good & Kaminski, 2002) Oral Reading Fluency (ORF) scores improved more for those with high usage of SKO than for the students in the low usage group. In a second study, Naglieri, Rowe, and

Conway (2010) found that DIBELS ORF scores from a high usage group of 2nd grade students improved significantly more than medium and low usage groups. The third study (Rowe, Naglieri, & Conway, 2010) found evidence that the amount of time students spent playing SKO was related to posttest reading scores, over and above the effects of pre-test reading scores. Finally, Naglieri et al. (2010) found that students at risk (based on DIBELS ORF scores at the beginning of the school year) who were exposed to SKO improved by midyear substantially more than a no-use control group. In total, these studies of this innovative way to help improve children's reading skills suggest that a game-based method has considerable promise. Due to the fact that children with SLD often have associated anxiety, and typically resist reading, an engaging game that is highly motivating and also improves reading skills offers considerable promise.

CONCLUSION

The purpose of this chapter was to describe a procedure that can be used to identify children with SLD in a manner consistent with the definition of SLD found in IDEA, something neither the ability-achievement discrepancy model nor the RTI method do. Importantly, there is good evidence that the Discrepancy/Consistency Model described in this chapter, when operationalized using the CAS, is nondiscriminatory and has good validity for the purposes that it was intended. That is, there is strong evidence showing that the CAS measures of cognitive processing correlate strongly with achievement (see Naglieri & Rojahn, 2004), which indicates that the PASS scores derived from the CAS assist in explaining academic success and failure. Research also shows small differences between African American and white groups, Hispanic and white groups, as well as Hispanic bilingual children and cross-cultural populations. This evidence suggests that the CAS measures of PASS cognitive processes are appropriate for nonbiased assessment of diverse groups. The PASS cognitive processing abilities also appear to vary with the type of disability in predictable ways; for example, reading decoding problems are associated with Successive processing scores, and children with ADHD are low in Planning. The evidence of specific PASS profiles for children with different disabilities is important for eligibility determination as well as instructional planning, and suggests that, when used within a larger context of a comprehensive assessment, information about a child's basic psychological processes can provide a vital source of information for determining if SLD exists and how greater academic gains can be achieved.

🐟 TEST YOURSELF 🐟

1. **The first two intelligence tests explicitly developed to measure ability from a processing perspective were**

   (a) WISC-III and WJ-R.

   (b) WISC-IV and K-ABC.

   (c) K-ABC and CAS.

   (d) K-ABC and WISC-III.

   (e) SB-V and CAS.

2. **The definition of a specific learning disability in IDEA is based on**

   (a) a specific academic deficiency.

   (b) a disorder in one or more of the basic psychological processes.

   (c) failure to respond to instruction.

   (d) a and b

   (e) a and c

3. **The definition of a cognitive process presented here is based on**

   (a) the cognitive demands of the task.

   (b) the content of the task.

   (c) the modality of the task.

   (d) curriculum-based measurement.

   (e) the procedural demands of the task.

4. **Which of the following criteria of a comprehensive evaluation are included in IDEA?**

   (a) A variety of assessment tools must be used.

   (b) No single measure or assessment can be used to determine SLD.

   (c) Technically sound tests of cognitive and behavioral factors must be used.

   (d) Assessments must be nondiscriminatory.

   (e) All of the above.

5. **Kavale, Kaufman, Naglieri, and Hale (2005) suggested that**

   (a) RTI is an acceptable first step in SLD determination.

   (b) the ability achievement discrepancy method is best for determining SLD.

   (c) determining whether a disorder in a basic psychological process is essential for SLD determination.

   (d) a and c

   (e) a and b

6. **Which of the following are true about a relative weakness and a cognitive weakness?**

   (a) A relative weakness is not sufficient for SLD diagnosis.

   (b) A cognitive weakness is a relative weakness with a processing score that is also well below average.

(continued)

(c) A cognitive weakness is based on subtest level ipsative analysis and clinical judgment.

(d) a and c

(e) a and b

7. **Federal law (IDEA 2004) and the Federal Regulations (2006) state that the long-standing approach of using an ability-achievement discrepancy to determine whether a child has SLD is not permitted. True or False?**

8. **Children with specific learning disabilities, attention deficit hyperactivity disorder and autism spectrum disorder have different PASS profiles on the CAS. True or False?**

9. **Researchers have found that the phonological skill deficit that underlies specific reading disability is related to**

(a) planning processing.

(b) attention processing.

(c) simultaneous processing.

(d) successive processing.

10. **There is research evidence that PASS theory as measured by the CAS has relevance to intervention and instruction. True or False?**

Answers: 1. c; 2. d; 3. a; 4. e; 5. d; 6. e; 7. False; 8. True; 9. d; 10. True.

Eight

RTI AND COGNITIVE HYPOTHESIS TESTING FOR IDENTIFICATION AND INTERVENTION OF SPECIFIC LEARNING DISABILITIES

The Best of Both Worlds

James B. Hale
Kirby L. Wycoff
Catherine A. Fiorello

THE ENIGMA OF SPECIFIC LEARNING DISABILITIES: AN INTRODUCTORY ANALYSIS

Children who have specific cognitive processing strengths and deficits that lead to poor academic achievement may have a *specific learning disability* (SLD) (Hale, Kaufman, Naglieri, & Kavale, 2006). In the landmark 1975 Public Law 94-142, the U.S. Department of Education first formalized ability-achievement discrepancy in an attempt to define the essence of SLD and achieve consensus among stakeholders (e.g., Mercer, Jordan, Allsopp, & Mercer, 1996). The focus of researchers and practitioners alike was placed on discrepancy, with less consideration given to the essential SLD statutory definition that specifies *children with SLD have a deficit in the basic psychological processes that adversely affects academic achievement.*

Growing dissatisfaction with the SLD definition and discrepancy method has ignited a firestorm among seemingly polarized factions, who support either summative or formative evaluation (see Batsche, Kavale, & Kovaleski, 2006), suggesting a paradigm shift in practice is necessary (e.g., Reschly & Ysseldyke,

2002). Theoretical, political, and practical considerations are surely relevant, but serving children's needs must be our consummate priority, and this necessitates incorporating all empirically based practices in the schools, including those that represent the best of both these worlds.

The problem with SLD identification and service delivery is clear. SLD has become anything but "specific," with different practices in identification leading to an explosion in SLD prevalence (Reschly & Hosp, 2004), increasing by as much as 150% to 200% since 1997 (e.g., Macmillan, Gresham, Lopez, & Bocian, 1996; Macmillan & Speece, 1999) and representing 50% of all students receiving special education services (Kavale, Holdnack, & Mostert, 2005). Concerns over the use of traditional ability-achievement discrepancy for SLD identification are numerous, with the lack of sensitivity and specificity (see Rapid Reference 8.1) in measurement frequently leading to misclassification (e.g., Macmillan, Siperstein, & Gresham, 1996), which makes it difficult to establish appropriate intervention and remediation strategies for children who are struggling in school (e.g., Hale, Fiorello et al., 2008).

Problems with the traditional ability-achievement discrepancy set the stage for new ways of identifying and serving children with learning problems (Reschly & Hosp, 2004; VanDerHeyden, Witt, & Gilbertson, 2007), with response to intervention and/or instruction (RTI) being the leading candidate for replacing discrepancy. This change from summative standardized evaluation to ongoing formative assessments of academic achievement, currently epitomized in the RTI approach, was codified into law as a method for determining SLD eligibility in the

☰ Rapid Reference 8.1

Defining Sensitivity and Specificity

If a disorder or disability is defined accurately, then we know what it is and who has it. An individual who has the disorder or disability is known as a *true positive*. If a true positive for a disorder or disability is known, then we can determine how *sensitive* and *specific* the tests are in diagnosing the condition.

Sensitivity: If a test is sensitive, then it will help us determine whether a child has a disorder or not; a poor score on the test could indicate a child has the disorder, whereas a good score makes the diagnosis unlikely.

Specificity: If a test is specific, it will help determine whether a child has a particular disorder as compared to other possible disorders. Thus, a poor score on the test could indicate a child is likely to have a particular disorder, but not any other disorders; whereas a good score makes the diagnosis unlikely.

Individuals with Disabilities Education Improvement Act (IDEA; 2004), with those unresponsive to RTI approaches considered eligible for special education services under the SLD category.

This chapter discusses the advantages of an RTI approach for serving children's needs, with some advocates arguing it should be mandated (Hale, 2006). Despite its empirical allure for ongoing monitoring of student achievement, and its humanistic appeal for serving all children in the prevention of learning problems (e.g., Fletcher & Vaughn, 2009), we argue that its use for SLD identification is fraught with methodological shortcomings *that cannot be resolved*, including the fact that there is no *true positive* in an RTI model. In other words, when a child fails to respond to intervention, practitioners can be sure of one thing: The child did not respond according to the idiosyncratic criteria chosen by the team (e.g., Reynolds & Shaywitz, 2009). These criteria are idiosyncratic because there are no mandated or mutually agreed upon RTI curricula, instructional methods, measures, or decision rules regarding response (Hale, Flanagan, & Naglieri, 2008).

There is a plethora of reasons why children do not respond to our best attempts at intervention, only one of which is SLD (Hale et al., 2006). Identifying a child as having SLD only because he or she did not respond to intervention is essentially a *diagnosis by default*—something that most researchers and practitioners can agree is not scientifically or empirically sound practice. While RTI is an appropriate and necessary model of service delivery, we argue that evaluation methods need to be comprehensive and individualized at Tier 3 in an RTI model (i.e., after standard and/or problem-solving RTI approaches were found to be ineffective or marginally effective). These evaluations must include cognitive and neuropsychological measures, and other data sources for accurate differential diagnosis of SLD and other disorders, not only for purposes of identification, but ultimately for developing more effective interventions.

Given the limitations of RTI for SLD identification first enumerated in 2004 (Hale, Naglieri, Kaufman, & Kavale), the Office of Special Education and Rehabilitative Services (OSERS) scrambled to incorporate what has been coined the *third method* for determining SLD in the final IDEA regulations published in 2006. Although the third method language was vague, many states (Zirkel & Thomas, 2009) and even recent achievement tests (e.g., Wechsler Individual Achievement Test–Third Edition [WIAT-III]; Wechsler, 2009), have interpreted this regulatory requirement to reflect an increasing awareness of, and interest in, identification of psychological and neuropsychological processing strengths and deficits as the preferred method of determining SLD (Hale, Fiorello et al., 2008).

DON'T FORGET

The difference between a child with low achievement (i.e., learning delay) and a child with a *specific* learning disability (i.e., learning deficit) is particularly relevant for SLD classification and service delivery. If a child has a learning *delay*, then a more intensive instructional approach can be used to help him or her, because he or she learns similarly to others, but needs more instruction to accomplish the same learning objectives. If a child has a learning *deficit*, then a more *individualized* instructional approach can be used to help him or her, because he or she learns *differently* than others, and needs instruction designed to meet his or her unique needs.

Although empirical alternatives for identifying SLD using a third method are available (and discussed in other chapters in this book), such as the Flanagan, Ortiz, Alfonso, and Mascolo's (2002, 2006) Operational Definition of SLD, and the Naglieri (1999) Discrepancy/Consistency Model, we focus on our Concordance-Discordance Model (C-DM; Hale, Fiorello, Bertin, & Sherman, 2003; Hale & Fiorello, 2004). The interested reader is referred to Hale, Flanagan et al. (2008) for a description of the similarities and differences among these empirically based third method approaches for SLD identification. The one thing all three approaches have in common is the identification of a cognitive strength, a cognitive deficit, and an achievement deficit associated with the cognitive deficit (Hale, Flanagan et al.).

This chapter provides practitioners with a cursory understanding of how the C-DM fits within the Cognitive Hypothesis Testing (CHT) approach to assessment and intervention (Hale & Fiorello, 2004). The CHT approach, discussed in detail later, is basically a logical series of steps of hypothesis generation and testing about a child's difficulties (Hale & Fiorello). This model recognizes the value of RTI approaches for preventing learning problems and for addressing the educational needs of most children. But for those who do not respond, comprehensive evaluations to determine *why* they are not learning well, and *what* can be done to help them learn is important, not only for the learning and psychosocial needs of children with SLD, but for *all* children (Fiorello, Hale, Snyder, Forrest, & Teodori, 2008; Fiorello, Hale, Decker, & Coleman, 2009; Fuchs & Deshler, 2007; Hain, Hale, & Glass-Kendorski, 2009; Hale, Fiorello, Miller et al., 2008; Miller & Hale, 2008).

The Balanced Practice Model (Hale, 2006), discussed later in this chapter, encourages widespread adoption of RTI, not only to serve children's learning needs, but also to reduce referrals for comprehensive evaluation and special education services. However, the Balanced Practice Model also recognizes that children with *true* SLD have brain-based processing assets and deficits that lead to a learning disability and that require individualized instruction designed to meet their unique needs (Hale, Fiorello, Miller et al., 2008). This Balanced Practice Model does not suggest that brain-based deficits in SLD are solely due to intrinsic factors, as disability is always the result of individual and environmental determinants, but rather it acknowledges that the interaction of individual and environmental influences is what has led to the SLD—an interaction that should be acknowledged in practice.

Truly individualized interventions cannot happen if an RTI-only approach is used for identifying SLD, because all children with learning problems—those who have learning delays and those with learning deficits—are clumped into a single heterogeneous SLD categorical model (Fiorello et al., 2009). For nonresponders to RTI service delivery, we argue here that comprehensive evaluation of brain-behavior relationships using the CHT and C-DM approaches will not only lead to better identification of SLD, but also more effective interventions targeted to an individual child's needs.

INITIAL ATTEMPTS AT DEFINING AND DETERMINING SPECIFIC LEARNING DISABILITY

In 1975, with the signing into law of P.L. 94-142, public schools were mandated to provide a Free and Appropriate Public Education (FAPE) to all students, including those with SLD. When the act was fully implemented in 1977, the U.S. Department of Education drew from the National Advisory Committee on Handicapped Children (NACHC; 1968) definition:

> The term "specific learning disability" means a disorder in one or more of the psychological processes involved in understanding or in using language, spoken or written, which may manifest itself in an imperfect ability to listen, speak, read, write, spell, or to do mathematical calculations. The term does not include children who have LD which are primarily the result of visual, hearing, or motor handicaps, or mental retardation, or emotional disturbance, or of environmental, cultural, or economic disadvantage (U.S. Office of Education, 1977).

DON'T FORGET
....
The idea of unexpected underachievement or discrepancy between ability and achievement was first formally noted when Barbara Bateman posited children's learning disorders were characterized by "an educationally significant discrepancy between their estimated potential and actual level of performance related to basic disorders in the learning process."

As part of the SLD definition movement, Samuel Kirk's student Barbara Bateman noted that children with SLD were not delayed learners, but rather showed an imperfect ability to learn, presumably due to processing deficits. Bateman's (1964) definition operationalized this notion:

> Children who have learning disorders are those who manifest an *educationally significant discrepancy* between their estimated potential and actual level of performance related to basic disorders in the learning process, which may or may not be accompanied by demonstrable central nervous system dysfunction, and which are not secondary to generalized mental retardation, educational or cultural deprivation, severe emotional disturbance or sensory loss.

Since its inception, the ability-achievement discrepancy model in SLD identification has come under increasing criticism as a useful or valid SLD identification method (e.g., Fletcher et al., 1998; Hale & Fiorello, 2004; Kavale et al., 2005; Vellutino, Scanlon & Lyon, 2000). Nevertheless, in response to inconsistency among SLD definitions, the U.S. Department of Education formalized the discrepancy between expected and actual achievement as the primary criterion for determining the presence of SLD (e.g., Mercer et al., 1996).

A discrepancy between ability and achievement, or *unexpected underachievement*, is central to most definitions of SLD (e.g., Kavale & Forness, 1995; Lyon et al., 2001; Wiederholt, 1974). Although this approach was a laudable attempt at an empirically based approach to SLD identification, the model itself is fraught with problems (e.g., Aaron, 1997; Ceci, 1990, 1996; Siegel, 1989; Stanovich, 1988a; Sternberg & Grigorenko, 2002; Stuebing, Fletcher, & LeDoux, 2002), which are detailed below.

Problem 1: Ability-achievement discrepancy does not discriminate well between low achievers and children with SLD. Ability-achievement discrepancy discriminates poorly between children with SLD and those who are low achieving (e.g., Epps, Ysseldyke, & McGue, 1984; Francis, Shaywitz, Stuebing, Shaywitz, & Fletcher, 1996; Fuchs, Mathes, Fuchs, & Lipsey, 2001; Kavale, Fuchs, & Scruggs, 1994; Stanovich & Siegel, 1994; Ysseldyke, Algozzine, Shinn, & McGue, 1982). Groups of IQ-discrepant (cognitively strong and academically weak) and IQ-consistent (low cognitive and academic achievement) children often demonstrate significant overlap, suggesting that many low achievers are classified as SLD inappropriately (e.g., Fuchs, Mock, Morgan, & Young, 2003). Alternatively, some processing deficits may lower IQ and achievement scores in children with SLD, presenting the illusion of consistent low performance, when in actuality the lower IQ reflects the average of the processing strengths and weaknesses (i.e., the Mark Penalty; Willis & Dumont, 1998).

Traditional ability-achievement discrepancy poorly distinguishes between low-IQ and high-IQ poor readers, with both groups often demonstrating similar underlying problems at the word-recognition level, yet high-IQ poor readers are more likely to be identified as having SLD (e.g. Aaron, 1997; Fletcher et al., 1994; Flowers, Meyer, Lovato, Wood, & Felton, 2001; O'Malley, Francis, Foorman, Fletcher, & Swank, 2002; Stanovich & Siegel, 1994; Stuebing et al., 2002; Stanovich, 2000, 2005).

Problem 2: Ability-achievement discrepancy is applied inconsistently across local and state educational agencies, leading to variable classification rates and data that undermine the SLD construct. Despite the fact that the discrepancy method has been the primary way to legally classify a student as SLD for nearly 30 years, regulations, policies, and procedures for implementing the discrepancy method have varied across states and local education agencies (e.g., Reschly & Hosp, 2004; Mastropieri & Scruggs, 2005). Districts used a variety of discrepancy procedures, including grade-level deviation, expectancy algorithms based on regression analysis, and/or standard-score differences (e.g., Berninger & Abbott, 1994; Reynolds, 1984; Reschly & Hosp, 2004). Further, practitioners working in schools were given much professional license regarding the degree to which they adhered to the district's SLD identification policy, which caused wide variability in SLD identification, even within a single district (e.g., Vaughn, Linan-Thompson, & Hickman, 2003), and low achievers were often identified as needing services even when they did not demonstrate a discrepancy (e.g., Gottlieb, Alter, Gottlieb, & Wishner, 1994; MacMillan et al., 1998). Implementation differences across districts and states undermine the SLD construct, especially as it relates to classification accuracy, access to services, and generalizability of research findings.

Problem 3: Intelligence testing and ability-achievement discrepancy have led to overrepresentation of ethnic, cultural, linguistic, and racial minorities in special education and the

SLD category. The overrepresentation of students from diverse ethnic, cultural, and linguistic backgrounds in special education is well documented (e.g., Deno, 1970; Dunn, 1968; Macmillan & Hendrick, 1993). Since the days of *Brown vs. Board of Education*, minority groups have been underserved academically and, later, overrepresented in special education. Dunn reported an alarmingly high number of students (60% to 80%) from minority or "low status backgrounds" in special education, a problem that has continued for some time (Artiles & Trent, 1994; Hosp & Reschly, 2004). Disproportionate representation of minority children in special education classes is not only related significantly to minority status, both also demographic and socio-economic variables (e.g., Finn, 1982; Hosp & Reschly, 2004; Oswald, Coutinho, Best, & Singh, 1999). The recurring theme of intelligence testing is that these tests are unfair for children of cultural, ethnic, racial, and linguistic difference (Hale & Fiorello, 2004). While an exploration of test bias and cultural loading in assessment is beyond the scope of this chapter, the overrepresentation of minorities in special education remains an important phenomenon.

Problem 4: Use of rigid cutoff scores for establishing an ability-achievement discrepancy does not take into account profile variability, the relationship between ability and achievement measures, the standard error of measurement, and reasons for variable performance. The discrepancy method relies on a difference between the predicted or expected "ability" of a child (e.g., IQ) and his or her underachievement (e.g., poor grades, standardized achievement test scores) (Reynolds, 1984). This model fails to identify those children who have lower IQs due to profile variability and who also have lower achievement scores (Willis & Dumont, 1998), as this pattern of cognitive strengths, weaknesses, and achievement deficits would be expected, given the SLD definition (Hale, Flanagan et al., 2008; Stuebing et al., 2002). While there are still some stalwart proponents of global IQ interpretation (e.g., Watkins, Glutting, & Lei, 2007), the methods used to support this position have been empirically challenged, with results suggesting profile analysis is required for children with SLD and other disabilities (Hale, Fiorello, Kavanagh, Holdnack, & Aloe, 2007).

Hale and colleagues (e.g., Elliott, Hale, Fiorello, Moldovan, & Dorvil, in press; Fiorello, Hale, McGrath, Ryan, & Quinn, 2001; Fiorello, Hale, & Snyder, 2006; Fiorello et al., 2007; Hale, Fiorello,

Kavanagh, Hoeppner, & Gaither, 2001; Hale et al., 2007; Hale, Fiorello et al., 2008) demonstrated that there is significant profile variability in children with ADHD, SLD, and traumatic brain injury, and that the most achievement variance is accounted for by subtests, not factors, with the least amount of variance accounted for by a global composite, such as overall IQ. They argue this profile variability and the limited achievement predictive validity precludes global IQ interpretation for most children with disabilities. Instead, careful empirically based profile analysis, based on knowledge of subtest factor loadings and substantiated through cross-battery interpretive approaches (Fiorello et al., 2009), must be accomplished for assessment and intervention purposes.

CAUTION

Profile variability precludes global IQ interpretation in children with SLD, and limits the predictive validity of the cognitive/intelligence test. Best practices requires careful examination of "psychological processes" based on empirical profile analysis to determine SLD, and how the processes are interfering with academic achievement, for identification and intervention purposes.

While a child might demonstrate discrepancy on one measure, he or she might not on another because of different technical characteristics of the measures, different construct coverage of the measures, or differences in administration and scoring (Hale & Fiorello, 2004). In addition, two children may have similar profiles and needs, but only a 1- or 2-point difference between them may determine who receives needed services. As such, cutoff scores are essentially arbitrary numbers (e.g., Aaron, 1997; Gresham, 2001; Siegel, 1999; Sternberg & Grigorenko, 2002), making SLD determination somewhat capricious (e.g., Reynolds, 1984).

Problem 5: Ability-achievement discrepancy is not a model of prevention addressing which children need early intervention.
As such, it has been referred to as a "wait-to-fail" paradigm. It is not uncommon, no matter how significant the learning problem, for young children from prekindergarten through 3rd and 4th grade to demonstrate variability in IQ and achievement testing due to a wide range of expectations in the early grades. This developmentally appropriate variability does not allow for a statistical discrepancy between IQ and achievement to be demonstrated (e.g., Dombrowski, Kamphaus, &

Reynolds, 2004; Mather & Roberts, 1994). It is only after age 9, when achievement test content becomes increasingly more sophisticated, relies more heavily on information acquired through reading, and places demands on higher-order cognition, that children with significant learning difficulties begin to flounder (e.g., Vaughn et al., 2003).

Often, educators have found themselves frustrated by this wait-to-fail model, with their hands tied, unable to offer early intervention and remediation through special education (e.g., Vaughn & Fuchs, 2003), even though this time period is critical for remediation of basic skills (e.g., Fletcher et al., 1998; Stage, Abbott, Jenkins, & Berninger, 2003; Vellutino, Scanlon, & Lyon, 2000). A student's achievement scores have to deteriorate significantly to be large enough to suggest "disability," making identification of SLD in young children rare (e.g., Mather & Roberts).

Problem 6: Ability-achievement discrepancy becomes a "test and place" system that takes valuable time and resources away from intervention designed to improve achievement.
Instead of prereferral intervention, the discrepancy model relies heavily on administration of IQ and achievement tests, and determining eligibility based on scores from these batteries, rather than interpretation of specific underlying psychological processes that have led to the SLD. As a result, the multidisciplinary team process places focus on eligibility rather than instruction and remediation (Lyon et al., 2001; Reschly & Hosp, 2004; VanDerHeyden et al., 2007). After a multidisciplinary team determines that a child is eligible for SLD services, he or she is *placed* in a special education system that supposedly provides an individualized education program. However, the link between actual summative test data and real-world remediation strategies is often unarticulated and generic at best, unrelated to the achievement deficit or curriculum the child is expected to learn (Reschly, 2005; Peterson & Shinn, 2002).

There is a resounding absence of a direct link between assessment and eligibility procedures and subsequent intervention, and standard achievement measures generally have poor instructional utility (Bocian, Beebe, MacMillan, & Gresham, 1999). This has led to few empirical studies that link cognitive assessment to intervention, with many opponents of standardized assessment suggesting there is no such thing as "aptitude-treatment interaction," based on research from the 1970s (e.g., Reschly & Ysseldyke, 2002). In addition, children who are placed in special education often receive

≋ *Rapid Reference 8.2*
....

Ability-Achievement Discrepancy Is Invalid for SLD Identification

Ability-achievement discrepancy is not a valid approach for identifying and serving children with SLD because:

- It does not discriminate between children who have SLD and those who are low achievers.
- It has been applied inconsistently across states, districts, and schools, making SLD identification arbitrary and capricious.
- It leads to overidentification of minority students.
- Rigid cutoff scores are meaningless and potentially discriminatory.
- Early intervention is critical, yet young children are seldom discrepant, so they must "wait to fail" before getting needed services.
- Intelligence test results are seldom related to intervention because the focus has been on "test and place" decision making, not intervention.

"life sentences," where they are seldom declassified, with only minimal achievement gains documented (Donovan & Cross, 2002; Lyon et al., 2001), suggesting special education has not really been special in meeting the needs of children with disabilities (e.g., Detterman & Thompson, 1997; Reynolds, 1988). Rapid Reference 8.2 summarizes why the traditional ability-achievement discrepancy method is invalid for SLD identification.

RESPONSE TO INTERVENTION FOR SERVING CHILDREN WITH SLD: PANACEA OR PREVENTION?

Given the inadequacy of discrepancy methods in identifying SLD and serving the educational needs of these children (Stanovich, 2005), many have called for the abandonment of summative intelligence testing (e.g., Siegel, 1989) in favor of ongoing formative evaluation using curriculum-based measurement (Hosp, Hosp, & Howell, 2007) and interventions that appear to have classroom relevance or ecological validity (Reschly & Ysseldyke, 2002), in a model called RTI.

Rooted in behavioral psychology (e.g., Gresham, 2004) and beliefs that disability is merely a socially constructed phenomenon (e.g., Ysseldyke, 2009), this approach tends to view learning problems as external to the child. Based on the assumption that learning problems are environmentally influenced, this position suggests that SLD might not even exist (e.g., Ysseldyke & Marston, 2000). Furthermore, proponents of this approach believe SLD should be transformed into a generic "learning difficulty" category (Fletcher, Coulter, Reschly, & Vaughn, 2004; Stanovich, 1994), with individual cognitive or neuropsychological differences in learning or behavior considered irrelevant, inconsequential, or even unscientific (e.g., Fletcher, Francis, Morris, & Lyon, 2005; Reschly, 2005; Stanovich, 2005).

Although there is some debate over whether a standard-protocol RTI approach (e.g., O'Connor, 2000; Vaughn et al., 2003; Vellutino et al., 1996) or problem-solving RTI approach (e.g., Ikeda & Gustafson, 2002; Tilly, 2008) should be used (Fuchs & Fuchs, 2006), with the former leading to external validity, and the latter to internal validity in decision making (Fiorello et al., 2009; Hale, Fiorello et al., 2008), most advocates argue for a multitier approach, with increasing intervention intensity used to establish response (Barnett, Daly, Jones, & Lentz, 2004). The focus of most RTI advocates is on primary intervention, or preventing learning problems in children, not on remediating their problems (e.g., Shapiro, 2006). Regardless of the method used, an RTI method offers several advantages over the wait-and-fail methods that epitomized ability-achievement discrepancy (Brown-Chidsey & Steege, 2005), as suggested in Rapid Reference 8.3.

Certainly, if practitioners had to choose between testing to determine discrepancy and providing ongoing progress monitoring and intervention through an RTI approach, RTI would appear to be the (much) better choice. In fact, we have no problems with RTI as a model for serving children's learning and behavioral needs, and some of us argue it should be mandated (Hale, 2006). Given the problems with discrepancy, why not use an RTI approach to identify SLD? Despite its promise for serving the needs of many children, we must conclude RTI *can never be a valid method for SLD identification* because it is scientifically flawed as a method of disability determination (see Fiorello et al., 2009; Hale, Flanagan et al., 2008; Hale et al., 2010; Rapid Reference 8.4).

Although we wrote one of the first articles to challenge the validity of RTI for SLD identification (Hale et al., 2004), there have been numerous authors who have since concurred with our arguments, and we have all concluded that best-practice models should include a comprehensive evaluation of cognitive and/or neuropsychological processes in the identification of SLD, even if RTI is utilized first (e.g., Berninger & Holdnack, 2008; Fiorello et al., 2009; Flanagan, Ortiz, Alfonso, & Dynda, 2006; Fletcher-Janzen & Reynolds, 2008; Kaufman, 2008; Kavale et al., 2005; Kavale, Kauffman, Bachmeier, & LeFever, 2008; Machek &

≡ Rapid Reference 8.3

Advantages of Using an RTI Approach

Child Need	Discrepancy Disadvantage	RTI Advantage
Early identification of learning problem critical for intervention efficacy	Discrepancy and SLD identification unlikely in young children	Regular progress monitoring allows earlier recognition of problem
Identification of learning delay versus learning deficit	Rigid cutoff criteria established for identification; higher-functioning children more likely identified as SLD	No need to recognize delay versus deficit, all treated under the same generic learning problem instructional umbrella
Specific learning objectives tied to curriculum	Psychologists not taught to link assessment data to intervention	Curriculum-based measurement tied to school-based competencies
Rights without labels	Services provided only to children identified with SLD	Identification not necessary for service delivery
Nondiscriminatory evaluation and service delivery in Least Restrictive Environment	Minorities more likely to be identified; special education became *life sentence* whereby few children were reintegrated into general education	Children not segregated because of "intelligence," but served in diverse general education environment accepting of all learners
Determining learning characteristics and needs	Team resources spent on testing and identification; psychologist as gatekeeper	Team resources spent on early intervention and identification
SLD children require individualized instruction	Special education overwhelmed with poorly identified students, and generally not effective	Differentiation and increasingly intensive instruction possible

Nelson, 2007; Mather & Gregg, 2006; Mastropieri & Scruggs, 2005; Miller & Hale, 2008; Ofiesh, 2006; Schrank, Miller, Caterino, & Desrochers, 2006; Reynolds & Shaywitz, 2009; Semrud-Clikeman, 2005; Willis & Dumont, 2006; Wodrich, Spencer, & Daley, 2006).

≡ *Rapid Reference 8.4*

....

Reasons RTI Alone Cannot Be Used for SLD Identification

RTI alone cannot be used for SLD identification because:

- RTI advocates cannot agree whether a standard protocol or a problem-solving RTI approach should be used.
- There is no agreed-upon curriculum, instructional methods, or measurement tools with adequate technical quality for use in an RTI model.
- RTI research has primarily focused on word reading, and methods across grades and different content areas have not been examined sufficiently.
- There is no consensus on what constitutes an empirically based approach, and whether using a single-subject design is sufficient to make any approach "empirical."
- There is no consensus on how to determine response, or lack of response, with different methods, resulting in different children being labeled as responders or nonresponders.
- There is no consensus on establishing appropriate achievement benchmarks or intervention timelines to determine the aim line slope (a critical component of determining individual responsiveness).
- There are no agreed-upon methods for teacher training or supervision methods to ensure interventions are carried out with integrity.
- There is no possible way to determine whether a child who is nonresponsive to intervention meets SLD statutory requirements.
- Failure to respond to intervention can happen for multiple reasons, only one of which is SLD.

Although problems with implementation of RTI are significant from a measurement perspective, hindering RTI's utility for SLD identification (Fuchs & Deshler, 2007; Gerber, 2005; Kavale et al., 2008; McKenzie, 2009), probably the most *catastrophic* problems are the last two points listed in Rapid Reference 8.4; that is, we can only know that a nonresponsive child did not respond to our best attempts at intervention; and we don't know *why* the child did not respond (Fiorello et al., 2009; Hale et al., 2006; Hale, Fiorello et al., 2008).

In the standard RTI protocol, all things are held constant, with regular empirically based instruction provided to all children. We know that the decision of response and nonresponse has external validity—any child who does not respond is different from a majority of the children in the classroom who do (Fiorello et al., 2009; Hale, Fiorello, & Thompson, in press; Hale & Morley, 2009)—a fact that makes this standard protocol RTI approach preferred among many researchers (Fuchs & Fuchs, 2006). In contrast, the focus of the problem-solving approach should be internal validity (Fiorello et al., 2009; Hale et al., 2010; Hale & Morley, 2009), as the curricula, instructional methods, measurement, and contingencies may be manipulated, either in isolation or in combination, in an attempt to achieve a child's response.

CAUTION

Despite its promise for serving the needs of many children, we must conclude that RTI can never be a valid method for SLD identification because it is scientifically flawed as a method of disability determination.

Although internal validity in a problem-solving approach is enhanced when several variables are manipulated over time in an attempt to obtain a response (which *is* effective practice), these multiple manipulations effectively eliminate the problem-solving RTI method for determining SLD, because there is no way to determine whether it was the child or one of the changes that led to nonresponse. In single-subject designs, only *one* independent variable can be manipulated; all others must be held constant if causation is to be considered (Fiorello et al., 2009; Hale, Fiorello et al., 2008; Hale & Morley, 2009). Even if one variable is manipulated, there is still no real way to determine whether the decision of response and nonresponse has any external validity, because the design is individualized for each student (e.g., Fuchs & Fuchs, 2006), thereby precluding its use for SLD and other disorder determination.

CAUTION

To suggest that any child who does not respond to our best attempts at intervention is SLD by default is just bad science and practice, especially if the problem-solving approach is used, because it violates the basic tenets of establishing causation in single-subject design (i.e., manipulates multiple independent variables).

Why is the lack of external validity in problem solving so problematic for SLD identification? One of the realities about science and disability determination is that we have to know what a disability *is*, not what it *isn't*. In the science of disability determination, we call this a "true positive." Once a true positive is identified, we can then determine the number of children who are correctly identified (i.e., true positives and true negatives) and those who are not correctly identified (i.e., false positives and false negatives), which helps define the sensitivity and specificity of the measures used in a diagnostic model (Reynolds, 1997).

CAUTION

RTI is a flawed method for SLD identification because there is no true positive in an RTI model. We know only that a child didn't respond; we do not know why he or she didn't respond.

Without definition of a true positive for a disorder, there is no way to determine the sensitivity and specificity of the measures, so any method for determining disability will be hopelessly flawed (see Reynolds, 1997; Spitzer & Wakefield, 1999). Acknowledging this problem, Gerber (2005) noted that the RTI approach suffers from the same circularity problems that discrepancy advocates had when they confused construct measurement with the actual construct itself.

These definition and measurement problems explain, in part, why studies that have tried to use RTI methods to determine SLD (e.g., responder/nonresponder status) have been unsuccessful: that different methods for determining response result in different subsets of children classified as responders or nonresponders (Barth et al., 2008; Fuchs, Fuchs, & Compton, 2004; Speece, 2005). As Fuchs and Fuchs (2006) noted, "This [unreliability of RTI diagnosis] is important because a major criticism of IQ-achievement discrepancy as a method of SLD identification has been unreliability of the diagnosis (p. 99)." In other words, using RTI for SLD classification is *unreliable* and, therefore, *invalid* because there is no *true positive* in an RTI model (Hale, Fiorello et al., 2008).

> **DON'T FORGET**
> ....
> RTI offers considerable advantages over past practices in serving the learning needs of many children, but it is equally clear that those who are chronically nonresponsive to increasingly intensive interventions need something different (Fuchs & Deshler, 2007), and a comprehensive evaluation should lead to more targeted interventions based on individual needs.

Obviously, there are numerous plausible explanations for nonresponse to intervention, only one of which may be SLD (Fuchs & Deshler, 2007; Hale et al., 2006; Mather & Gregg, 2006; Schrank et al., 2006). As a result, the final regulations (34 C.F.R. Parts 300 and 301; 2006) were clear in stating that "RTI is only one component of the process to identify children in need of special education and related services. Determining why a child has not responded to research-based interventions requires a comprehensive evaluation. . . . An RTI process does not replace the need for a comprehensive evaluation." We argue here that cognitive and neuropsychological assessment can provide that additional information for more accurate identification of SLD and for ultimately establishing responsiveness in those children who do not respond in an RTI model.

ADDRESSING IDEA SLD STATUTORY AND REGULATORY REQUIREMENTS USING THE THIRD METHOD APPROACH

Discrepancy and RTI are not the only approaches for SLD identification, according to the OSERS (34 C.F.R. Parts 300 and 301; Federal Register,

2006) final IDEA regulations, as there are *three* methods for determining SLD. We will argue here that the *only* plausible approach is the third method (often referred to as a *pattern of strengths and deficits*), because it is the only one that can address the SLD statutory (i.e., definition) and regulatory (i.e., method) IDEA requirements (Hale et al., 2006).

When IDEA (2004) was passed, ability-achievement discrepancy was no longer required, and an RTI approach could be used to identify SLD, but the third method of SLD identification was presented in the final Federal Regulations (34 C.F.R. Parts 300 and 301; Federal Register, 2006), which indicates schools: "(3) May permit the use of other alternative research-based procedures for determining whether a child has a specific learning disability, as defined in §300.8(c)(10)" (p. 46786).

Although this third method language is necessarily vague and nonspecific to allow autonomy in implementation, it is commonly associated with a pattern of strengths and deficits model of SLD identification, an approach that has gained traction as a viable alternative to discrepancy and RTI approaches by several state boards of education (see Zirkel & Thomas, 2009).

Of the leading candidates for a pattern of strengths and deficits approach, Hale, Flanagan et al. (2008) highlight similarities among their third method approaches for identification of SLD and other disorders. Unlike discrepancy and RTI approaches, these empirical methods address the statutory and regulatory IDEA SLD identification requirements through careful evaluation of cognitive and/or neuropsychological process-ing patterns, and the academic achievement deficits associated with these patterns (Fiorello, Hale et al., 2008; Hale, Flanagan et al., 2008; Kavale et al., 2005). As a result, they are entirely consistent with IDEA requirements for indentifying a child with SLD (34 C.F.R. Parts 300 and 301; Federal Register, 2006), but they also help determine whether the child has another disorder interfering with academic achievement, some-thing that cannot be accomplished using discrepancy or RTI methods.

DON'T FORGET

The Learning Disabilities Roundtable for the U.S. Department of Education noted, "The identification of a core cognitive deficit, or a disorder in one or more psychological processes, that is predictive of an imperfect ability to learn, is a marker for a specific learning disability." Children with SLDs process information *differently* than other children, and as school practitioners, is it incumbent upon us to articulate that in meaningful ways, both for assessment and intervention purposes.

Third method pattern approaches that include formal cognitive and neuro-psychological assessment make sense given the conclusions drawn by 14 professional organizations that composed the Learning Disabilities Roundtable (LDR; 2002, 2004) advisory panel. They concluded, "[t]he identification of a core cognitive deficit, or a disorder in one or more of the basic psychological processes, predictive of an imperfect ability to learn, is a marker for an SLD" (p. 5; LDR, 2002) and ". . . also acknowledges intra-individual differences as a fundamental concept of SLD" (p. 13; LDR, 2004).

Third method approaches also make empirical sense given children with brain-based disorders such as SLD and ADHD experience developmental *deficits* (see Berninger & Richards, 2002; Castellanos et al., 2002; Collins & Rourke, 2003; Fiez & Petersen, 1998; Filipek, 1999; Fine, Semrud-Clikeman, Keith, Stapleton, & Hynd, 2007; Francis et al., 1996; Geary, Hoard, & Hamsom, 1999; Hale & Fiorello, 2004; Naglieri & Bornstein, 2003; Nicholson & Fawcett, 2001; Pugh et al., 2000; Shaywitz, Lyon, & Shaywitz, 2006; Simos et al., 2005; Stein & Chowdbury, 2006; Tallal, 2006), not simply learning *delays* as RTI advocates suggest (e.g., Barnett et al., 2004). Not only is the pattern of strengths and deficits approach recommended by many SLD researchers and stakeholders, but it is also consistent with the views of representative samples of school-based practitioners (Caterino et al., 2008; Machek & Nelson, 2010) and professional organizations such as the National Association of School Psychologists (NASP; 2007) and American Academy of School Psychology (Schrank et al., 2006; Hale et al., 2010).

DON'T FORGET
....
Neuropsychological research clearly shows that children with SLD and other high-incidence disorders have learning deficits, *not* learning delays; therefore, interventions cannot just be more intensive, they must be individualized.

Of the third method approaches, our C-DM (see Figure 8.1; Hale & Fiorello, 2004), as part of a comprehensive evaluation that includes nonresponse to intervention and other data sources (Hale, 2006), can be used to determine whether a child has SLD, other disability, or some other cause for his or her learning and behavior difficulties. Using individual assessments of standardized cognitive and achievement measures, practitioners identify cognitive strength(s), cognitive deficit(s), and an achievement deficit(s), in addition to other data sources in the C-DM approach (Hale & Fiorello). The null hypothesis that there is no difference between the cognitive strength and cognitive deficit, or the cognitive strength and achievement deficit, is tested using the relatively straightforward standard error of difference formula (SED; Anastasi & Urbina, 1997).

The C-DM approach has been advocated for use in school psychology and neuropsychology research and practice (Elliott et al., in press; Hain et al., 2009;

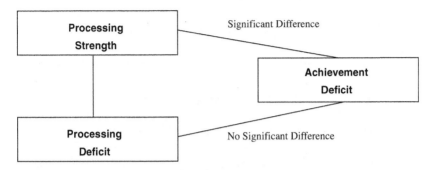

Figure 8.1. The Concordance-Discordance Model of SLD Identification

Source: After Hale & Fiorello, 2004.

Fiorello et al., 2009; Hale & Fiorello, 2004; Hale et al., 2006; Miller, Getz, & Leffard, 2006), and has been adopted in principle in modern achievement measures (e.g., WIAT-III; Wechsler, 2009). Hale, Fiorello et al. (2008) found that fewer children were identified with SLD using C-DM than the traditional discrepancy approach (25% who met discrepancy criteria did not show significant C-DM), so it has the potential to reduce overidentification of SLD, a concern of many in the field (e.g., Kavale et al., 2005).

> **CAUTION**
> ···
> The C-DM approach for SLD identification requires careful evaluation of cognitive strengths, deficits, and associated achievement deficits to ensure ecological validity of findings. It is inappropriate to just choose the highest cognitive score, the lowest cognitive score, and the lowest achievement score, and then see if they are significantly different, as this strictly numerical approach will lead to poor diagnostic and intervention decisions.

Despite the promise of a C-DM approach for advancing practice, Hale and Fiorello (2004) admonish practitioners to avoid just using the highest cognitive score, the lowest cognitive score, and the lowest achievement score, and then determine whether they are significantly different. They argue that clinical significance and ecological validity of findings must accompany statistical significance in SLD identification. It is important to examine the literature to ensure that the cognitive strength is often not related to the academic deficit in question (e.g., fluid reasoning and word reading); and the cognitive deficit should be empirically associated with the academic deficit (e.g., working memory and reading comprehension).

The eight-step C-DM process provided in Rapid Reference 8.5 is designed to ensure that any child classified with SLD meets the IDEA statutory and regulatory SLD requirements (Hale, 2006). C-DM computation using the standard error of the difference formula is relatively straightforward because standard scores (SS) and reliability coefficients (often referred to as "internal consistency" or "coefficient alpha") for age level are reported in the respective cognitive and achievement manuals; and on the WIAT-III, the discordant computations are actually computed by the software.

≡ Rapid Reference 8.5

Steps in the Concordance-Discordance Model of SLD Identification

Step	Clinical Objective	Clinical Question/Decision Rules
I	Score standardized cognitive test and determine whether global composite score (e.g., IQ), factor scores, or subtest scores should be interpreted.	Ia. Are all subtest scores consistent enough to interpret global composite score (e.g., IQ)? →YES, C-DM unlikely, probably not SLD; discontinue or consider other possible measure of processing deficits. →NO, C-DM possible; go to Step Ib. Ib. If not consistent across the entire test, are the subtest scores consistent within factors to interpret factor scores? →YES, C-DM possible; go to Step 2. →NO, consider subtest combinations to form new factor score within cognitive measure; go to Step Ic. Ic. If no subtest combinations appear to represent a new factor, can other standardized measures be added to cognitive measure to create new factor score? →YES, new subtest combination appropriate for use in C-DM model; go to Step 2. →NO, consider combining subsets from additional measure of at least two subtests to create new factor score for use in C-DM analyses; go to Step 2.

Step	Clinical Objective	Clinical Question/Decision Rules
2	Score standardized achievement test and examine to see if composites or subsets indicate achievement deficit.	2a. Do standardized achievement scores indicate an academic deficit that is consistent with prior evaluation (e.g., nonresponse to intervention), classroom permanent products, and teacher-reported achievement deficits?
		→YES, C-DM possible; go to Step 3.
		→NO, explore other possible causes for poor test performance, or explanations for poor performance in the classroom, and consider achievement retesting to verify/refute achievement deficit; return to Step 2 or discontinue.
3	Review cognitive (e.g., CHC) and/or neuropsychological literature to ensure obtained cognitive deficit(s) is associated with achievement deficit(s).	3a. Could obtained cognitive deficits interfere with deficient academic achievement area?
		→YES, cognitive and/or neuropsychological deficits have been found to be related to deficit achievement area in the literature; go to Step 4.
		→NO, C-DM unlikely unless research not conducted; check for ecological validity of cognitive and achievement deficits; return to Step 2 or discontinue.
4	Obtain reliability coefficients for cognitive strengths, cognitive deficit(s), and achievement deficit(s).	4a. Are factor/subtest reliability coefficients (e.g., coefficient alpha) available in the cognitive and achievement technical manuals?
		→YES, factor strengths and deficits; and achievement score reliabilities are in the manuals; go to Step 5.
		→NO, new factor scores and reliability coefficients must be computed; average factor scores and reliability coefficients for new factors (use Fisher's z-transformation for reliabilities; see Hale, Fiorello et al., 2008); go to Step 5.
5	Calculate standard error of the difference (SED) formula to establish discordance between cognitive strength and cognitive deficit.	5a. Enter reliability coefficients for cognitive strength and deficit into SED formula, and solve for SED:
		$SED = SD\sqrt{2 - rxx - ryy}$
		5b. Multiply obtained SED value by 1.96 for $p < .05$, or 2.58 for $p < .01$.
		5c. Is obtained difference between cognitive strength and deficit greater than SED critical value?

(continued)

Step	Clinical Objective	Clinical Question/Decision Rules
		→YES, there is a significant difference between cognitive strength and deficit, so child likely has a deficit in the basic psychological processes that is interfering with academic achievement; go to Step 6.
		→NO, consider other possible cognitive deficit responsible for achievement deficit; go to Step 1. Or the child may have another disability interfering with achievement; consider further evaluation. Or the child does not have a SLD; try to serve in intensive response-to-intervention model.
6	Calculate SED formula to establish discordance between cognitive strength and achievement deficit.	6a. Enter reliability coefficients for cognitive strength and academic deficit into SED formula, and solve for SED: $$SED = SD\sqrt{2 - rxx - ryy}$$ 5b. Multiply obtained SED value by 1.96 for $p < .05$, or 2.58 for $p < .01$. 5c. Is obtained difference between cognitive strength and academic deficit greater than SED critical value? →YES, there is a significant difference between cognitive strength and deficit, so child likely has unexpected underachievement consistent with a specific learning disability; go to Step 7. →NO, consider other possible cognitive deficit and/or achievement deficit; go to Step 1. Or the child may have another disability interfering with achievement; consider further evaluation. Or discontinue; the child does not have an SLD, so try to serve in intensive RTI model.
7	Calculate SED formula to establish concordance between cognitive deficit and achievement deficit.	6a. Enter reliability coefficients for cognitive deficit and academic deficit into SED formula, and solve for SED: $$SED = SD\sqrt{2 - rxx - ryy}$$ 5b. Multiply obtained SED value by 1.96 for $p < .05$, or 2.58 for $p < .01$. 5c. Is obtained difference between cognitive strength and academic deficit less than SED critical value? →YES, there is no significant difference between cognitive deficit and the achievement

Step	Clinical Objective	Clinical Question/Decision Rules
		deficit, thus cognitive deficit plausible cause for achievement deficit; consider team determination of specific learning disability classification; begin individualized instruction in inclusive or more restrictive environment as necessary; go to Step 8.
		→NO, is the achievement deficit significantly below the cognitive deficit? If so, this could mean other factors are causing additional impairment; consider for specific learning disability classification and individualized service delivery, and additional evaluation to determine why achievement deficit is substantial; go to Step 8.
		→NO, is the achievement deficit significantly above the cognitive deficit? If so, this could mean the child is using a compensatory strategy to score better on the academic measure, determine if results still warrant specific learning disability classification and/or individualized service delivery; go to Step 8.
8	Determine whether C-DM findings have ecological validity and achieve team consensus for SLD or other disorder determination.	Reexamine empirical literature, RTI data, teacher reports, classroom permanent products, classroom observations, and other evaluation data (including C-DM results) to determine whether child meets IDEA statutory and regulatory requirements of SLD or other disorder warranting special education services; consider within the context of other team evaluation data; consider SLD classification and service delivery in least restrictive environment.

In many cases, the factors reported in the manual may not adequately reflect the child's cognitive profile of strengths and deficits, so new factor scores must be created using at least two subtests that measure the same construct. For instance, a child with a reading disability may show the Arithmetic, Coding, Information, Digit Span (ACID) profile, a finding common in several of our reading disability subtypes (Fiorello et al., 2006). In this case, an ACID factor score and reliability coefficient would be calculated for use in C-DM. Another possibility is a child with poor fluid reasoning (Gf), as measured by the WISC-IV Matrix Reasoning and Picture Concepts subtests (see Flanagan & Kaufman, 2009, for actual norms for Gf, based on the aforementioned subtests; Keith, Fine, Taub, Reynolds, &

Kranzler, 2006) that leads to a math word problems/reasoning achievement deficit. In this case, the new *Gf* factor score and reliability coefficient would be needed for use in the C-DM.

A case example that clearly illustrates the problems with using only the published factor scores in C-DM can be found in Hale et al. (2006). They reported the evaluation results and interventions for a child who performed within the average range on all WISC-IV Indexes, but had a significant SLD in math and written language. Although cognitive and neuropsychological testing revealed the child had a significant right hemisphere "nonverbal" LD, the factor scores were comparable because the child had a very low score on the Comprehension subtest, thereby depressing the Verbal Comprehension Index, and a very high score on Picture Concepts, thereby inflating Perceptual Reasoning, with both global scores ending up in the average range. If only the reported factor scores were analyzed using C-DM, this child's SLD would have gone undetected. To accomplish computation of these new factor scores and reliability coefficients for use in the C-DM, please see Hale, Fiorello et al. (2008).

ENSURING DIAGNOSTIC, ECOLOGICAL, AND TREATMENT VALIDITY: THE COGNITIVE HYPOTHESIS TESTING APPROACH

Comprehensive evaluations of cognitive and neuropsychological processes are essential practice in determining whether a child has an SLD or other disorder affecting academic and behavioral functioning in the classroom (Fiorello et al., 2009; Hale, Fiorello et al., 2008), a position advocated by many accomplished scholars in the field (Berninger & Holdnack, 2008; Fiorello et al., 2009; Flanagan et al., 2006; Fletcher-Janzen & Reynolds, 2008; Kaufman, 2008; Kavale et al., 2008; Machek & Nelson, 2007; Mastropieri & Scruggs, 2005; Mather & Gregg, 2006; Miller & Hale, 2008; Ofiesh, 2006; Reynolds & Shaywitz, 2009; Schrank et al., 2006; Semrud-Clikeman, 2005; Willis & Dumont, 2006; Wodrich et al., 2006). Although comprehensive evaluations are essential practice, we realize they are costly, both in time and money, so we need to do *fewer* evaluations, but do a more thorough job when we do them. To accomplish this, Hale and Fiorello (2004) argue schools must *intervene*

CAUTION

When assessing any disability or disorder, finding a true positive is the only way to ensure meaningful intervention. Not only does a comprehensive evaluation ensure any child classified with SLD meets statutory and regulatory requirements, but it also ensures that a true positive can be ascertained, from which empirically based decisions can be made.

to *assess*. If RTI is done well (intervene), only those children who are non-responders in a RTI model will need a comprehensive evaluation (assess) for SLD and other disorder determination (Fiorello et al., 2009).

Only nonresponders at Tiers 1 and 2 would be referred for comprehensive evaluations for SLD and other disorder consideration, and possible Tier 3 special education services. Standard protocol and problem-solving protocol RTI approaches are necessary (Hale, 2006), because they take into account both external and internal validity, respectively, in the decision-making process. Some RTI advocates suggest poor achievement and nonresponse is sufficient for SLD classification in an RTI model (e.g., Fletcher et al., 2005; Reschly, 2005), but a comprehensive evaluation of cognitive and neuro-psychological processes is necessary, both for identification and intervention purposes at Tier 3 (e.g., Berninger & Holdnack, 2008; Fiorello et al., 2009; Flanagan et al., 2006; Fletcher-Janzen & Reynolds, 2008; Hale, Fiorello et al., 2008; Kaufman, 2008; Kavale et al., 2008; Mather & Gregg, 2006; Miller & Hale, 2008; Reynolds & Shaywitz, 2009; Schrank et al., 2006; Semrud-Clikeman, 2005; Willis & Dumont, 2006; Wodrich et al., 2006).

DON'T FORGET

Hale's (2006) three-tier Balanced Practice Model includes a Tier I standard protocol RTI approach (serving approximately 85% of children), and for nonresponders, a Tier 2 individualized problem-solving RTI (serving approximately 10% of children), both of which can happen in general education settings (Fiorello et al., 2009; Hale, 2006). Tier 3 would also include problem-solving and single-subject interventions through special education, but the comprehensive evaluation would be used to ensure accurate SLD diagnoses and targeted interventions.

The CHT model (Hale & Fiorello, 2004; see Figure 8.2) uses a scientist-practitioner approach for integrating cognitive and neuropsychological assessment and intervention for children who do not respond to standard interventions. The CHT approach and RTI share similar characteristics in that each requires ongoing data-based decision making over time, which is a problem with traditional one-time evaluations and decisions based on them (Fletcher et al., 2005). CHT uses the scientific method (theory, hypothesis testing, data collection, data interpretation) not only to establish the concurrent and ecological validity of results, but also to link this information to subsequent intervention to establish treatment efficacy. Although profile analysis is encouraged when subcomponent scores are significantly different within factors, as is the case with C-DM, the CHT model overcomes traditional profile analyses by using the intellectual/

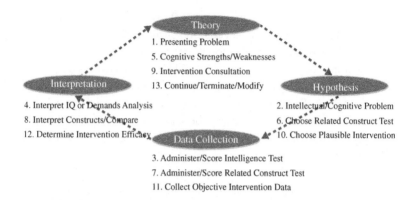

Figure 8.2. The Cognitive Hypothesis Testing Model

Source: Hale, J.B., & Fiorello, C.A. (2004). *School Neuropsychology: A Practitioner's Handbook*. New York: Guilford.

cognitive tests only as *screening* tools. Any hypotheses derived from these screening tools and other data sources (e.g., RTI, history, ratings) must be tested using other cognitive or neuropsychological measures with greater specificity, and then evaluated to ensure they have concurrent, ecological, and ultimately treatment validity (Hale & Fiorello, 2004).

Although some advocates still support a global factor/IQ interpretation (e.g., Watkins et al., 2007), which may be relevant in some cases, evidence has emerged that idiographic analysis of cognitive and neuropsychological sub-components leads to more accurate diagnostic decision making and treatment recommendations (e.g., Hale et al., 2007; Hale, Fiorello et al. 2008). The majority of measures available today are designed to measure multiple constructs, not IQ or a single *g* factor (Elliott et al., in press; Fiorello et al., 2001, 2007; Flanagan, Ortiz, & Alfonso, 2007; Hale et al., 2006, 2007, Hale, Fiorello et al. 2008, Hale, Flanagan et al., 2008; McGrew & Wendling, 2010). Large-scale factor-analytic studies have provided us with Cattell-Horn-Carroll (CHC) theory, with these factors specifically linked to educational outcomes (Flanagan et al.; McGrew & Wendling).

Paralleling validation of CHC empirical findings has been a veritable explosion of neuropsychological research in reading, math, or writing disabilities, and other high-incidence disorders such as attention-deficit/hyperactivity disorder and depression (see D'Amato, Fletcher-Janzen, & Reynolds, 2005; Denckla, 2007; Feifer & Rattan, 2009; Hale & Fiorello, 2004; Miller, 2009). These neuro-psychological studies are paving a fascinating empirical path that demonstrates a convergence of neuropsychological (e.g., Lurian) and cognitive-psychometric (e.g., CHC) theories, thereby providing crucial validity evidence for a synthesis of both approaches (Fiorello, Hale et al., 2008, Fiorello et al., 2009). As researchers demonstrate the neurobiological correlates of cognitive functions (e.g., Alarcon, Pennington, Filipek, & Defries, 2000), we can use CHT methods not only to gain a greater understanding of child strengths and deficits, but also to establish a crucial foundation for ecological and treatment validity evidence of findings (Hale, Fiorello et al., 2008), something that cannot be ascertained through global IQ interpretation or nonresponse to more intensive intervention (Fiorello et al., 2009; Hale, Fiorello et al.).

One of the most egregious errors clinicians have made for decades is assuming that cognitive and neuropsychological data interpretation requires an assumption that we are measuring a stable underlying *trait* (e.g., intelligence), when in fact we are only measuring the child's *state* at the time of evaluation. Multifactorial intellectual/cognitive subtest performance varies for multiple reasons not easily identified in large group studies (Baron, 2005), but individual administration and careful clinical interpretation can identify the child's cognitive, neuropsychological, academic, and behavioral state at the time of evaluation. This is why CHT requires that any hypotheses derived from these findings be confirmed or refuted using multiple data sources, to ensure effective differential diagnoses that can lead to individualized interventions sensitive to the child's needs (Hale & Fiorello, 2004). These interventions are then developed, monitored, evaluated, and recycled until treatment efficacy is obtained (Hale & Fiorello), and single-subject case study data support the utility of such approaches (e.g., Fiorello et al., 2006; Hale et al., 2006; Reddy & Hale, 2007).

LINKING ASSESSMENT TO INTERVENTION: MAKING CHT ASSESSMENT RESULTS RELEVANT FOR CHT INTERVENTIONS

In its infancy, neuropsychological research was primarily focused on disorder identification, and this will continue to be an important facet of research on SLD and other high-incidence disorders, especially for children who do not respond to intervention (Berninger, 2006; Hale et al., 2006; Hale, Flanagan et al., 2008; Kavale et al., 2005; Semrud-Clikeman, 2005; Willis & Dumont, 2006). However, neuropsychological research must also focus on developing effective interventions that have demonstrated ecological and treatment validity, which is the critical second half of the CHT approach to assessment and intervention (Hale & Fiorello, 2004).

CHT is designed to help practitioners address the valid criticism that cognitive and neuropsychological assessment is seldom related to intervention (e.g., Reschly, 2005), by helping practitioners use the problem-solving approach advocated by NASP (Thomas & Grimes, 2008), to develop, implement, monitor, evaluate, and recycle interventions until treatment efficacy is achieved (Hale & Fiorello, 2004). The CHT approach has been used to document brain-behavior-intervention relationships in children with reading (Fiorello et al., 2006), math (Hale et al., 2006), and attention (Reddy & Hale, 2007) disorders, and has been advocated for use in both educational (Elliott et al., in press; Hale, Fiorello et al., 2008) and neuropsychological (Fletcher-Janzen, 2005; Miller et al., 2006) settings.

CHT intervention methods are advanced by recent neuroimaging and neuropsychological evidence that demonstrate children with SLD, attention disorders, and other psychopathologies have brain-based deficits that respond to intervention (e.g., Berninger et al., 2000; Chenault, Thomson, Abbott, & Berninger, 2006; Fiorello et al., 2006; Gustafson, Ferreira, & Ronnberg, 2007; Hale, Fiorello, & Brown, 2005; Hale et al., 2006; Helland, 2007; Lovett, Steinbach, & Frijters, 2000; Naglieri & Johnson, 2000; Shaywitz et al., 2003; Simos et al., 2005; Smit-Glaude, Van Strien, Licht, & Bakker, 2005). These neuroimaging and neuropsychological findings show that children use multiple brain areas simultaneously to complete cognitive and academic tasks (see Fiorello et al., 2009).

The deficit (not delay) model is supported by findings that suggest the brain areas typical children use to solve a task are different for those with SLD and other disabilities (see Hale, Fiorello et al., 2008); and for those with disabilities who respond to intervention, their brain functions normalize on neuro-psychological and neuroimaging measures (Coch, Dawson, & Fischer, 2007; Hale et al., 2005; Richards et al., 2006; Simos et al., 2005). For a comprehensive review of the relationship between cognitive and neuropsychological processes related to reading, math, and writing, and their relevance for intervention, please see Hale, Fiorello et al. (2008) and McGrew and Wendling (2010).

CONCLUSION

The proof is in the pudding. This chapter has documented the relevance of cognitive and neuropsychological assessment for SLD identification and intervention, but much work needs to be done to ensure these types of data are used to improve the lives of children in a meaningful way. Educating teachers and practitioners about the value of cognitive and neuropsychological assessment is one important step, but the real value added from such approaches is that these data influence intervention and result in better outcomes for children with SLD and other disabilities.

Systematic group and single-subject studies documenting treatment efficacy of cognitive and neuropsychological findings are greatly needed, and it is up to each practitioner to document the concurrent, ecological, and treatment validity of his or her assessment results with the children he or she serves. In this way, children identified with SLD will truly get the individualized services they deserve, and indeed a free, appropriate public education designed to meet their needs.

TEST YOURSELF

....

1. **Children with SLD have learning delays, not learning deficits. True or False?**

2. **Intelligence tests measure only a stable underlying ability trait, not a state at the time of testing. True or False?**

3. **Neither ability-achievement discrepancy nor RTI is sufficient for determining whether a child has a specific learning disability. True or False?**

4. **There is a true positive in an RTI model, so we clearly know that a child who is nonresponsive in an RTI model is SLD. True or False?**

5. **According to the authors, the next paradigm shift will be application of neuropsychological principles and practices in the schools, often referred to as *school neuropsychology*. True or False?**

6. **Cognitive hypothesis testing is only useful for differential diagnosis of SLD and other disorders; it has nothing to do with intervention. True or False?**

7. **In cognitive hypothesis testing, the intelligence test is used as a screening tool of cognitive processes, with hypotheses derived from subtest profiles verified or refuted using additional measures. True or False?**

8. **The concordance-discordance model establishes a cognitive strength, a cognitive weakness, and an associated achievement deficit using the standard error of the difference formula. True or False?**

9. **There is no evidence that cognitive and neuropsychological processes are related to intervention. True or False?**

10. **There are studies that show changes in brain activity are associated with RTI. True or False?**

Answers: 1. False; 2. False; 3. True; 4. False; 5. True; 6. False; 7. True; 8. True; 9. False; 10. True.

Nine

EVIDENCE-BASED DIFFERENTIAL DIAGNOSIS AND TREATMENT OF READING DISABILITIES WITH AND WITHOUT COMORBIDITIES IN ORAL LANGUAGE, WRITING, AND MATH

Prevention, Problem-Solving Consultation, and Specialized Instruction

Virginia W. Berninger

I n this chapter a case is made for the importance of evidence-based, treatment-relevant differential diagnosis for two kinds of reading disability: *dyslexia*, which affects word-level reading and spelling; and *oral and written language learning disability* (OWL LD) which is also referred to as specific language impairment (SLI) or language learning disability (LLD) and affects syntax- and text-level as well as word-level reading and writing. Also discussed are research findings that explain (a) which targeted reading skills and related impaired hallmark phenotypes (behavioral expression of underlying genotypes and neural signatures) should be assessed; and (b) why the hallmark phenotypes are best assessed within a working memory architecture that accounts for the accuracy and fluency problems observed in individuals with reading disabilities. In addition, the same topics are covered for dysgraphia and dyscalculia, which may also be identified in some individuals with dyslexia or OWL LD.

Practical information for diagnosing the specific reading disabilities with or without comorbid specific learning disabilities affecting writing and/or math are offered, along with discussion of other factors to consider in educational planning, including bilingual/dialect, family and home, socioeconomic, and medical/health issues. For example, not all reading problems are due to *learning disabilities* (LDs); some are related to those other factors or to *developmental disabilities* (DDs), which should be diagnosed on the basis of development outside the normal range in one or all five developmental domains.

ISSUES IN DEFINING SPECIFIC READING DISABILITIES

Evidence-Based Diagnoses Versus Eligibility Decisions

A source of misunderstanding and frustration for parents (Berninger, 2008d) and professionals (Berninger & Holdnack, 2008) is that federally mandated, state-implemented criteria for special education eligibility under the category of learning disabilities are not the same as evidence-based differential diagnoses. A diagnosis identifies the nature of a specific learning disability and has implications for its probable etiology, instructional requirements, and prognosis. Ironically, in an era when educational practitioners are encouraged to use evidence-based instructional practices, they are not encouraged to use evidence-based differential diagnoses of specific learning disabilities.

Because eligibility criteria vary widely across and within states in the United States, considerable confusion has arisen about what a specific learning disability is. The confusion may have been heightened rather than dampened by the recent reauthorization of the Individuals with Disabilities Education Improvement Act (IDEA; 2004). For example, comprehensive evaluation that may include IQ-achievement discrepancy and response to intervention (instruction) beg the central issue of defining what a specific learning disability is. Ironically, civil rights for an educationally disabling condition during the K–12 school years are guaranteed only for those who are eligible for special education services, based on eligibility criteria which are not consistent across and within states. Civil rights are not guaranteed based on research-supported criteria for diagnosing specific learning disabilities that are defined consistently across states and schools.

To define evidence-based, treatment-relevant diagnoses consistently across states and schools would require a cross-disciplinary diagnostic manual for developmental and learning disabilities, written by qualified professionals in the multiple disciplines with relevant research and clinical training and experience within their disciplines in *both* DDs *and* LDs. Decisions about whether to address the instructional needs through differentiated instruction in general and/or special education (Berninger & Wolf, 2009a) could be left to local schools and parents, as long as evidence-based diagnoses were used to generate evidence-based treatment plans that were implemented artfully and evaluated for effectiveness based on student response to the instruction

Five Developmental Domains

A major factor contributing to the definitional confusion is that the initial arbitrary approach of defining specific learning disabilities on the basis of discrepancy from Full Scale IQ was flawed on many grounds (see Berninger, 2007c, 2008b, 2008d for further discussion of the ideas in the summary that follows). To begin, there is no evidence that size of discrepancy alone defines a specific learning disability—the amount of discrepancy may depend on the amount of appropriate instruction an individual student has received. Although IQ, which is not really a quotient as in division, is not a comprehensive assessment of all kinds of human intelligence, it does have construct validity as a measure of scholastic aptitude, accounting for a sizable percent, but not all the variance, in academic achievement. The *most notable flaw*, however, is that the Full Scale IQ is *not* a substitute for a careful assessment of each of the five domains of development—*cognition/memory, receptive and expressive language, gross and fine motor, attention and executive functions,* and *social emotional*—to determine whether the child demonstrates a reliable profile of *developmental disability (DD)* in which all domains or selected ones remain outside the normal range (below −2 standard deviations from the mean) for age, or of a *specific learning disability* (SLD) in which all domains of development remain within the normal range and only a few selected skills related to reading, writing, and/or math acquisition do not (see Berninger, 2007c).

Moreover, the publishers of the most widely used IQ test do not advocate for use of the Full Scale IQ in eligibility decisions. They base this recommendation on research showing that (a) the Verbal Comprehension, Perceptual Organization (Nonverbal Reasoning), Working Memory, and Processing Speed Indices load on different factors; and (b) the first two are known to be a strength and the last two a weakness in individuals with learning disabilities (Prifitera, Saklofske, & Weiss, 2005). Thus, measures of reasoning alone provide a better indicator for gauging prognosis of what achievement might be if an individual could overcome his or her learning disability.

It does not follow, however, that cognitive assessment is not relevant to diagnosis of specific learning disabilities. It is relevant to determining whether an individual has a developmental disability (with all or selected domains of development outside the normal range) or a specific learning disability (all five domains of development within the normal range). These distinctions, which are too often ignored, are important for many reasons. Of these reasons, four are specific to DDs and three to SLDs, as discussed next.

Developmental Disabilities (DDs)

First, many parents of children with DDs are confused because they think that the evidence-based instructional research on reading conducted with children without DDs also generalizes to their children. Practitioners cannot with professional honesty suggest to parents of children with DDs affecting each of the five developmental domains that it is realistic that their child will achieve at grade level or pass tests of high-stakes standards.

Second, more research is needed on effective reading, writing, and math instruction for students with specific DDs, neurogenetic disorders, fetal alcohol syndrome or effect, and head or spinal cord injury due to physical violence or accident; results should be generalized only to students with the same condition.

Third, some children may have undiagnosed DDs because formal assessment of each of the five developmental domains has not been conducted. Clinical experience has shown that some children who were previously not responsive to instruction at grade level became responsive after appropriate assessment and diagnosis of DDs when instruction was introduced at the assessed mental age level.

Fourth, a thorough assessment of each of the five developmental domains in individuals with DDs is relevant to (a) rendering decisions about independent living at and after transition from schooling, and (b) helping parents to plan for the adult years.

Specific Learning Disabilities (SLDs)

Fifth, SLDs may mask cognitive strengths that are not identified without formal cognitive assessment, especially in those who are twice exceptional, and may be gifted and learning disabled at the same time (Gilger, 2008; Yates, Berninger, & Abbott, 1994).

Sixth, the nature of the cognitive ability from which reading and writing achievement are discrepant may contribute to the differential diagnosis. For example, in the case of dyslexia, individuals tend to be discrepant from Verbal IQ; but those who have oral and written language learning disability that affects learning language (OWL LD or SLI) during the preschool years, and using language to learn during the school-age years, are more likely to be discrepant from nonverbal than verbal reasoning or to have nonverbal reasoning within the normal range (Berninger, 2007c, 2008b; Berninger, O'Donnell, & Holdnack, 2008).

Seventh, many students who struggle with SLDs harbor nagging doubts that they are not smart. Providing feedback, based on appropriate cognitive assessment with age norms, can be used to provide honest feedback to the students with SLD(s) and their parents that their thinking ability falls within the normal range, and, as may be the case for some individuals, in the above-average, superior, or very-superior range.

Key Academic Skills in Reading, Writing, and Math Domains

Based on programmatic research from 1980 to 2009, with the reading and writing research funded by the Eunice Kennedy Shriver National Institute of Child Health and Human Development, and the math research funded by the United States Department of Education, we concluded that assessment of SLDs should focus on target academic skills and related phenotypes. In the mildly impaired, only one or a few of the academic and phenotype skills tend to be affected, whereas in the more severely affected all or most of the academic skills and phenotypes are impaired (Berninger, Abbott, Thomson, & Raskind, 2001). An overview of these target academic skills and phenotypes follows. Although the focus is on target reading skills and related phenotypes relevant to diagnosing specific reading disabilities, target writing and math skills and phenotypes are also presented because some children with SLD in reading also have comorbid SLD in writing and/or math.

The *target academic skills,* which research showed are separable within profiles of intraindividual differences *and* are also instructionally relevant, are as follows by academic domain (e.g., Berninger, 2007a, 2007b, 2007c; Berninger & Richards, 2002; Berninger, Raskind, Richards, Abbott, & Stock, 2008):

Reading: Oral reading—accuracy and rate of reading pronounceable, nonmeaningful pseudowords (phonological decoding), single real words, and passages; and accuracy and rate of silent reading comprehension

Writing: Automatic legible letter writing; phonological, orthographic, and morphological spelling; fluency and quality of written composing of narrative and expository text

Math: Counting, math fact retrieval, place value, part-whole relationships, multistep computational operations with whole numbers, fractions, and mixed numbers, and problem solving (not only single-step and multistep story problems yoked to the basic computational operations but also measurement, geometry, algebra, and other areas of specialization within mathematics)

HALLMARK PHENOTYPES

Through a multidisciplinary learning center funded by the National Institutes of Health, we had an opportunity to collaborate with geneticists who requested that we assess skills that are related to reading or writing but are not reading or writing. Based on a review of the research literature available at the time, we developed a test battery of these reading- and writing-related skills. Through subsequent genetic analyses it was shown that some of these are *phenotypes*, that is, behavioral markers of gene expression. Through this center, we also participated in brain-imaging studies and also identified *endophenotypes* (neural signatures of the brain that are associated with the behavioral phenotypes) for target reading or writing skills. Based on this interdisciplinary research (e.g., Altemeier, Abbott, & Berninger, 2008; Amtmann, Abbott, & Berninger, 2007; Berninger et al., 2006; Berninger, Abbott, Nagy, & Carlisle, 2009; Berninger et al., 2010; Berninger et al., 2008; Garcia, Abbott, & Berninger, 2010; Richards, Aylward, Raskind et al., 2006), we identified *hallmark phenotypes* that are valid for diagnosing these SLDs or that replicated relevant findings of others. This multidisciplinary research included structural and functional imaging of brain, assessments of phenotypes, aggregation (heritability), segregation (genetic transmission mechanisms), chromosome linkage, and gene candidates (alleles or variations in gene sequences) in genetics studies with families having multigenerational histories of specific learning disabilities, and instructional-assessment studies that evaluated effects of treatments at the brain and behavioral levels of analysis.

Furthermore, we gathered evidence that these hallmark phenotypes are best understood within a *working memory architecture* (Berninger, Abbott et al., 2009; Berninger et al., 2008), which serves as the language-learning mechanism supporting oral and written language acquisition (Berninger et al., in press). Neural correlates have been identified for many of the phenotypes for the working memory components (Richards, Aylward, Berninger et al., 2006; Richards, Aylward, Raskind et al., 2006; Richards, Berninger, Winn et al., 2007; Richards, Berninger, Stock et al., 2009; Richards, Berninger, & Fayol, 2009; Richards, Berninger, Winn et al, 2009), which explain the accuracy problems (due to impairments in specific components) and fluency problems (due to impairments in temporal coordination of the components) in learning to read, write, and do math (e.g., Berninger, 2007c; Berninger et al., 2006).

Figure 9.1 illustrates the components of the working memory architecture that support normal reading and writing acquisition, but which, if they are not developing normally, may result in specific learning disabilities. These components include (a) three word forms for storage and processing of spoken words

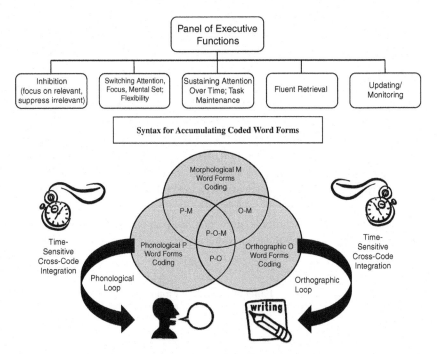

Figure 9.1. Working Memory Architecture Supporting Language Learning Within Which Dyslexia and Oral and Written Language Learning Disability (OWL LD) Can Be Defined and Differentiated

Source: Berninger, 2007c; Berninger et al., in press.

and their sound units (phonological), written words and their letter units (orthographic), and word parts such as base words and affixes that signal meaning or grammar (morphological) and a syntactic unit for storing and processing accumulating words; (b) two loops for connecting these word forms and syntax with the end organs that have direct contact with the external world— the mouth (phonological loop) and the hand (orthographic loop); and (c) a panel of executive functions for self-regulation, that is, mental self-government. The overlapping of the three word forms indicates that learning to read and spell requires learning to coordinate the interrelationships among the word forms, two at a time (phonological-orthographic, P-O; orthographic-morphological, O-M; and phonological-morphological, P-M) and three at a time (phonological-orthographic-morphological, P-O-M).

Depending on which component(s) are impaired, an individual may exhibit *dysgraphia* (impaired handwriting related to impaired orthographic word-form storage and processing and/or orthographic loop, plus any of the executive functions) (Berninger, 2008a); *dyslexia* (impaired word-level decoding, word reading, and spelling related to impaired phonological and/or orthographic word form storage and processing and phonological loop, plus any of the executive functions) (Berninger et al., 2001, 2006); or *OWL LD* (impairments in morphological word form and syntactic storage and processing, plus any of the loops or executive functions), (Berninger, 2007a, 2007b, 2007c; Berninger, 2008b).

Figure 9.2 illustrates a working memory architecture that supports arithmetic calculation, which shares some components with the working memory architecture supporting written language learning. For example, the phonological word form and the phonological loop are involved in naming oral and written numbers and oral counting; and the orthographic word form and orthographic loop are involved in writing visual symbols (numerals) for number concepts expressed as integers and decimals using the place value concept or as fractions. Likewise, the

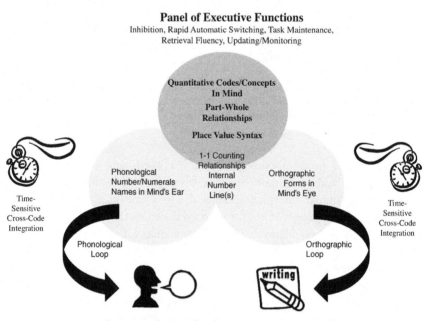

Loops externalize internal number concepts/quantitative codes by naming or writing numerals that stand for them (cross-code integration).

Figure 9.2. Constellation of Impaired Hallmark Phenotypes in Dyscalculia Within a Working Memory Architecture

Source: Berninger, 2007b, 2007c; Berninger & Richards, 2002.

same panel of executive functions used for reading and writing may also contribute to the self-regulation of processes related to working memory coding, naming, recognizing, or writing of symbols for quantitative concepts (e.g., the internal number line, multiplace numbers, and part-whole relationships). If any working memory components are impaired, the child may have problems in (a) oral counting (using phonological word-form name and phonological loop via mouth); (b) written counting (using orthographic coding of numerals and orthographic loop via hand); (c) math fact retrieval (using phonological or orthographic codes for accessing stored summaries of relationships between three values along the number line for one of four arithmetic operations, and possibly communicating the summary through loops for mouth or hand); and/or (d) calculation, based on applying the sequential steps for the four operations (addition, subtraction, multiplication, and division algorithms).

Comorbidities

The working memory architecture model provides a conceptual framework for organizing a constellation of behavioral markers of underlying processes (phenotypes) that are related to specific academic skills. As such, it can be used for differential diagnosis (how SLDs are the same and different) and identification of *comorbidities* (co-occurrence of more than one SLD in some individuals). That is, even though many individuals show hallmark phenotypes for only one SLD, some individuals may show signs of more than one SLD, for example, dyslexia plus dysgraphia or OWL LD plus dysgraphia (see Rapid References 9.1 to 9.4). The goal of this chapter is to focus on the two most common SLDs affecting reading: dyslexia and OWL LD (Rapid References 9.1 and 9.2). These specific reading disabilities may occur alone or in combination with dysgraphia and/or dyscalculia in some individuals (see Rapid References 9.3, 9.4, and 9.5).

Language(s) Spoken in Home, and Other Home and Family Issues Related to Literacy Learning

Near the end of the first decade of the 21st century, most schools in North America and Europe and elsewhere faced challenges in educating students who do not speak the same language at home as they do at school, or are not equally facile in speaking the language of home and the language of school. In the United States, these students are often referred to as English Language Learners (ELLs). However, please see Rapid Reference 9.6 for five important

≡ *Rapid Reference 9.1*

Hallmark Impaired Phenotypes in Dyslexia

Includes any of the following or set of the following in Figure 9.1, plus Pseudoword Reading and Spelling:

Working Memory Components

- *Executive functions:*
  - Inhibition (on Delis-Kaplan Executive Function System [D-KEFS; Delis, Kaplan, & Kramer, 2001] Stroop Color Word Form)
  - Rapid Automatic Switching (RAS) (Wolf & Denckla, 2005; RAS based on total time score); Process Assessment of the Learner-Second Edition [PAL-II; Berninger, 2007a] RAS based on total time score)
  - Sustained RAS over rows (PAL-II RAS based on rate change across rows)
  - Verbal Fluency (D-KEFS Verbal Fluency)
  - Updating and monitoring working memory (Repetition score on D-KEFS Verbal Fluency)
- *Phonological Word Form Coding* (grade-appropriate phonological coding task: rhyming, syllables, phonemes, and/or rimes; age-appropriate Comprehensive Test of Phonological Processing [CTOPP; Wagner, Torgesen, & Rashotte, 1999] Nonword Repetition)
- *Orthographic Word Form Coding* (grade appropriate receptive orthographic coding task)
- *Phonological Loop* Rapid Automatic Naming (RAN) (Wolf & Denckla, 2005; RAN based on total time score); PAL-II RAN based on total time score
- *Orthographic Loop* (legible, automatic letter writing on PAL-II alphabet task at 15 seconds; grade-appropriate PAL-II expressive orthographic coding task; Wechsler Intelligence Scale for Children–Fourth Edition [WISC-IV; Wechsler, 2003] Coding)

Word-Level Written Language Components

- *Phonological Decoding* (oral pseudoword reading):
  - Accuracy (Woodcock-Johnson III Tests of Achievement [WJ III ACH; Woodcock, McGrew, & Mather, 2001] Word Attack; Wechsler Individual Achievement Test–Third Edition [WIAT-III; Pearson, 2009] Pseudoword Decoding; PAL-II Pseudoword Reading accuracy; Kaufman Test of Educational Achievement–Second Edition [KTEA-II; Kaufman, & Kaufman, 2004] Nonsense Word Decoding)
  - Automaticity (Test of Word Reading Efficiency [TOWRE; Torgesen et al., 1999] Phonemic Reading Efficiency, Pseudoword Rate; PAL-II Pseudoword Reading Fluency; KTEA-II Decoding Fluency)
- *Written Spelling*
  - (WJ III ACH Spelling of Sounds; WIAT-III Spelling; PAL-II Word Choice accuracy and fluency)

≡ *Rapid Reference 9.2*

Hallmark Impaired Phenotypes in Oral and Written Language Learning Disability (OWL LD)

Includes any of the following or set of the following in Figure 9.1, which correspond to those for Dyslexia in Rapid Reference 9.1, plus Morphological Word Form Coding and Syntax Coding and Oral Real Word and Passage Reading and Reading Comprehension.

Working Memory Components

- *Executive functions*
  - Inhibition (on D-KEFS Stroop Color Word Form)
  - RAS (Wolf & Denckla, 2005; RAS based on total time score; PAL-II RAS based on total time score)
  - Sustained RAS over rows (PAL-II RAS based on rate change across rows)
  - Verbal Fluency (D-KEFS Verbal Fluency)
  - Updating and monitoring working memory (Repetition score on D-KEFS Verbal Fluency)
- *Syntax Coding* (Clinical Evaluation of Language Fundamentals–Fourth Edition [CELF-IV; Semel, Wiig, & Secord, 2003] Sentence Formulation; PAL- II: Does It Fit? Sentence Structure Coding)
- *Morphological Word Form Coding* (PAL-II: Are They Related?)
- *Phonological Word Form Coding* (grade-appropriate phonological coding task: rhyming, syllables, phonemes, and/or rimes; age-appropriate CTOPP Nonword Repetition)
- *Orthographic Word Form Coding* (grade-appropriate PAL-II receptive orthographic coding task)
- *Phonological Loop* RAN (Wolf & Denckla, 2005; RAN based on total time score; PAL-II RAN based on total time score)
- *Orthographic Loop* (legible, automatic letter writing on alphabet task at 15 seconds; grade-appropriate expressive orthographic coding task; WISC- IV Coding)

Word-Level Written Language

- *Orally Reading Real Words* (Access to Words in Semantic Memory, that is, Word Retrieval, as in Oral and Written Verbal Fluency, TOWRE Sight Word Efficiency)
  - Accuracy (WJ III ACH Letter-Word Identification; WIAT-III Word Reading; PAL-II Morphological Decoding accuracy; KTEA-II Letter and Word Recognition
  - Automaticity (TOWRE Sight Word Reading Efficiency; PAL- II Morphological Decoding fluency; KTEA-II Word Recognition Fluency) Orally Reading Passages—Gray Oral Reading Test–Fourth Edition (GORT-4; Wiederholt & Bryant, 2001) accuracy and fluency (time)

(continued)

Text-Level Written Language
- *Reading Comprehension:*
  - Cloze procedures (WJ III ACH Passage Comprehension)
  - Answering factual and inferential questions about text (WIAT-III Reading Comprehension)
  - PAL-II Sentence Sense (integrating word identification and sentence meaning—accuracy and fluency)

≡ *Rapid Reference 9.3*

Hallmark Impaired Phenotypes

- *Dyslexia plus Dysgraphia:* Includes any in Rapid Reference 9.1 for Dyslexia, plus any of the following for Dysgraphia, or;
- *OWL LD plus Dysgraphia:* Includes any in Rapid Reference 9.2 for OWL LD, plus any of the following for dysgraphia (also see Figure 9.1).

Letter and Word Form Coding
Orthographic Coding (Richards, Berninger, & Fayol, 2009) (PAL-II grade-appropriate Receptive Orthographic Coding)

Grapho-Motor Function
- Finger Sequencing (Richards, Berninger, Stock et al., 2009) (PAL-II Finger Succession)

Loop from Mind to Environment Through Hand
Orthographic Loop (Berninger, Nielsen, Abbott, Wijsman, & Raskind, 2008a) (legible, automatic letter writing on PAL-II alphabet task at 15 seconds; grade-appropriate PAL-II expressive orthographic coding task; WISC-IV Coding)

Handwriting
- *Handwriting Automaticity* (legible, in order, and fast)
  - PAL-II Alphabet Writing Automatic Legible Letters Writing (at 15 seconds)
  - PAL-II Handwriting Summary Score for Total Automatic Letter Legibility Composite for Alphabet Writing from memory and Copy Sentence Task
- *Handwriting Legibility*
  - PAL-II Total Legible Letter Writing on Alphabet Task
  - PAL-II Handwriting Summary Score for Total Legibility Composite for Alphabet Writing from memory and Copy Sentence Task
- *Handwriting Speed*
  - PAL-II Alphabet Writing Total Time
  - PAL-II Handwriting Summary Score for Total Time Composite for Alphabet Writing from memory and Copy

- *Sustained Handwriting Over Time*
  - Decline in Total Legible Letter Writing across the Copy Paragraph Task, from 30 seconds to 60 seconds to 90 seconds

Written Composition of Text

- *Compositional Fluency* PAL-II Narrative Compositional Fluency Total Number of Words
- *Letter Legibility* during Composing:
  - PAL-II Expository Note Taking Letter Legibility
  - PAL-II Expository Report Writing Letter Legibility
  - Also complete the process observations for handwriting rating scales and handwriting errors.

≣ *Rapid Reference 9.4*

Hallmark Impaired Phenotypes (see Figures 9.1 and 9.2)

- *Dyslexia plus Dyscalculia*: Include any impaired phenotypes for Dyslexia in Rapid Reference 9.1 and for Dyscalculia below, or;
- *OWL LD plus Dyscalculia*: Include any impaired phenotypes for OWL LD in Rapid Reference 9.2 and for Dyscalculia below)

Working Memory Architecture

- *Executive functions*
  - Inhibition (on D-KEFS Stroop Color Word Form)
  - RAS (Wolf & Denckla, 2005; RAS Letters and Numerals based on total time score; PAL-II RAS Words and Double Digits based on total time score; PAL-II switching Mixed Addition and Subtraction and switching Mixed Multiplication and Division on Math Fact Retrieval)
  - Sustained RAS over rows (PAL-II RAS based on changing rate across rows)
  - Monitoring (PAL-II Finding the Bug)
- *Storage and Processing* of Quantitative Codes in Oral and Written Formats (PAL II Quantitative Working Memory and Visual-Spatial Working Memory)
- *Phonological Loop* RAN (Wolf & Denckla, 2005; RAN Numerals based on total time score; PAL-II RAN Single Numerals and Double Digits based on total time score)
- *Orthographic Loop* (PAL-II automatic, legible numeral writing at 15 seconds; PAL-II written responses on multidigit Numeric Coding; WISC-IV Coding B; PAL-II Look and Write Fact Retrieval, which use the orthographic loop and can be compared to PAL-II Listen and Say Fact Retrieval, which uses the phonological loop)

(continued)

Numeric Concepts Underlying Calculation
- *Counting* (externalizing number line with oral naming code; math fact fluency is forward or backward counting by increment of 1 or more; PAL-II Counting and Fact Retrieval)
- *Place Value* (syntax for representing an infinite number of numbers with 10 digits) PAL-II Place Value (compare oral and written responses)
- *Part-Whole Relationships* (increasing quantity of parts in the whole lowers the magnitude of a number—a higher counting number is not always greater in magnitude—quantitative relationships can be relative; PAL-II Part-Whole Concepts, Fractions, and Mixed Numbers)
- *Telling Time* (multiple, circular, embedded internal number lines; PAL-II Telling Time)

Math Fact Retrieval
- PAL-II Input-Output Combination Modalities for Each of Four Basic Operations (time for accurate retrieval, that is, fluency)
  - Addition
  - Subtraction
  - Multiplication
  - Division

Computational Operations
- *PAL-II Visual Spatial Alignment*: Representation of multiplace numerals horizontally and vertically for calculation
- *PAL-II Oral Verbal*: Explanation of the steps of calculation algorithms (addition, subtraction, multiplication, and division)
- *PAL-II Paper and Pencil*: Execution of multistep addition, subtraction, multiplication, and division operations, and retrieval of related math facts (accuracy and time)

guidelines for determining whether these bilingual, and possibly multilingual children, are necessarily at a disadvantage. Indeed research also points to advantages for some bilingual learners (Petitto, 2009). In addition, for children who are learning the dominant language at school, their conversational skills and mastery of academic language for abstract learning purposes may not be equally developed.

Language learning issues span dialects within the mainstream language (Washington & Thomas-Tate, 2009) and other languages brought to the school by immigrant families. Language learning issues also interact with parental educational levels and socioeconomic backgrounds, and challenges children may face regarding parents' unemployment, health issues of a parent or family member, or other family issues that may affect children's school learning, whether or not they have SLD(s) or DD(s).

Thus, not all reading disabilities may have the same etiology or developmental path: Reading problems can be due to DDs in each of five or selected domains of development; SLDs such as dyslexia or OWL LD in children whose development is otherwise in the normal range across the five domains of development; language issues related to second language learning, a variety of home, family, or school factors; or some combination of these factors with SLD(s) or DD(s). Of greatest relevance to the volume in which this chapter appears, although all educational professionals should be committed to optimizing the educational opportunities and achievement of *all* students (free and appropriate public education—FAPE—for all) (Berninger, 1998; Berninger & O'Malley, in press; Berninger & Wolf, 2009a), it does not follow that all students with reading problems have exactly the same instructional needs. However, they may have common, as well as unique instructional needs, and so it is often possible to accommodate the instructional needs of all students through differentiated instruction (see Berninger & Wolf, 2009a for practical suggestions for this goal).

CAUTION

Not all students with reading problems have the same instructional needs.

As we have found in our programmatic research, children from different countries, races, and cultural and language groups may have biologically based specific learning disabilities, which do not only occur in white children whose parents are affluent. Just because children whose parents are affluent and white may have been politically active, visible, and articulate in calling attention to the unmet needs of students with specific learning disabilities in obtaining evidence-based, treatment-relevant diagnoses and related instruction, it does not follow that SLDs affect only affluent white children or other children of privilege. Nor is that view supported by research.

≡ *Rapid Reference 9.5*

Hallmark Impaired Phenotypes (see Figures 9.1 and 9.2)

- *Dyslexia plus Dysgraphia and Dyscalculia*: Include any impaired phenotypes for Dyslexia in Rapid Reference 9.1 and Dyscalculia in Rapid Reference 9.4, or;
- *OWL LD plus Dysgraphia and Dyscalculia*: Include any impaired phenotypes for OWL LD in Rapid Reference 9.2 and Dyscalculia in Rapid Reference 9.4.

Instructional Issues

Without doubt, teachers show as much variation in their preparation and ability to teach reading, writing, and math as individual students show in the ease with which they learn to read, write, and do math. However, we have worked with many students with severe SLDs in reading who came from classrooms where teachers used evidence-based instruction, and many other students were reading very well. We have found it best to adopt a no-fault policy. We do not blame the teachers for struggling in teaching students who are more challenging to teach, or the affected students themselves who struggle more than their classmates to learn. Moreover, we know of no evidence that there is a single, one-size-fits-all instructional program for all students with SLDs. Such a program does not exist because students with SLDs differ not only in their learning profiles, defined on the basis of target academic skills and associated hallmark phenotypes, but also in their developmental profiles (even if all five domains are in the normal range, they show variation in relative strengths and weaknesses), and the systems variables affecting their learning at school and home and in the community.

Despite the research showing the value of phonological awareness and phonics instruction for beginning reading, many students with dyslexia and OWL LD in our studies had not responded adequately to that instruction, especially if it was delivered as declarative knowledge with much emphasis on verbalization of rules, which they have difficulty in applying to reading real words and text. The multidisciplinary research (family genetics, brain imaging, and instruction-assessment links) helped us to understand that the underlying learning disability is related to selective impairment in a multicomponent working memory architecture that interferes with word-level or syntax-/text-level language learning accuracy and fluency (temporal coordination).

The students with dyslexia and dysgraphia responded to specialized instruction designed to overcome their diagnosed SLD in reading related to impaired components in a working memory architecture or its inefficiency in coordinating the components in time. This instruction emphasized procedural learning (exercising the phonological and orthographic loops in Figure 9.1) to create internal-external connections and coordination of phonological, orthographic, and morphological word forms and their parts (see Figure 9.1). Also, each lesson was structured to teach to all levels of language (subword, word, and text) close in time, to facilitate efficiency of the temporal coordination of the working memory architecture that supports the language-learning mechanism (Berninger, 2008b, 2008c; Berninger et al., in press).

Unlike other instructional approaches that emphasize intensity (more of the same), the instructional approach we have found to be effective for students in our intervention studies was designed—as recommended by George Ojemann, the pioneering neurosurgeon at the University of Washington who studied language functions prior to brain surgery—to avoid habituation (tending to tune out when stimulus input or task requirements are unchanging). That is, when asked to keep performing the same task over and over, the learner may fail to respond. Dr. Ojemann shared the valuable insight, for which I am grateful, that the brain habituates quickly to language. To avoid habituation, we frequently varied the nature and duration of the language-based instructional activities (e.g., warm up to create automatic associations between spelling units and corresponding sound units, followed by practice in transferring this procedural knowledge to real words or pseudowords in isolation, and then oral reading and rereading of text for fluency and comprehension). When the target task does not last long, the brain continues to stay "on task," but when the task changes, the brain, which seeks novelty, redirects attention to the new task. Thus, the net effect is that the learner stays on task when tasks do not last longer than the learner's ability to focus on a particular task. Also, the tasks included all the levels of language so the learner had practice in coordinating the different levels of language close in time in working memory so that all the levels could function in concert, like an orchestra in which all the instruments are in synchrony.

≡ Rapid Reference 9.6

Guidelines for Working With Linguistically Diverse Students

1. Do not assume that because a student does not speak the dominant mainstream language of the school at home that the student is necessarily disadvantaged or has a language-learning disability. Multidisciplinary research has shown that bilingualism can convey advantages in language development (Petitto, 2009). Celebrate language diversity. Ask children to share vocabulary from the language spoken in the home with classmates.

2. Do not make assumptions about which language or languages are spoken at home just by the language a child uses in the classroom. Ask the parents. Many times in our research we found that other languages (sometimes more than one) were spoken at home, and schools had not always been informed that the child was being exposed to more than one language. Find out who is speaking which languages and in which context and for which purposes with the child.

(continued)

3. Do not assume that a student is more proficient in the language(s) spoken in the home than the language spoken at school. Children in immigrant families may hear spoken language that is a mix of both languages, and not a mainstream version of either one, because their parents and siblings, who are learning the new language, may not have completed many years of formal education in schools using the first language.

4. Parents' educational backgrounds may affect the bilingual child's language learning as much as the languages spoken at home. Some immigrant parents have had very little formal education in the country of origin, whereas others may have had substantial formal schooling.

5. Dialect differences within the mainstream language pose as many challenges for some students as learning a second language (Washington & Thomas-Tate, 2009). Seek consultation from a professional with expertise in the dialects spoken in a school.

Understanding the Value of Differential Diagnosis Within a Broader Assessment Context

In addition to assessing target academic skills and hallmark phenotypes, as discussed earlier, it is important to consider other variables that may affect a student's response to reading, writing, and math instruction. (See Rapid Reference 9.7 for reminders to reach out to parents to obtain developmental and family history and other information that is relevant to facilitating home-school relationships and planning educational programs that meet student's instructional needs; also see Berninger, 2007c, for a questionnaire to assist in this process). In all aspects of the artful translation of scientific research into educational practice (Rosenfield & Berninger, 2009), including planning, evaluating, and implementing evidence-based assessment and instruction, it is essential to consider all systems variables (e.g., classroom, school, community, family, cultural), as well as the assessed learning profile of the individual student. For example, in separate studies, two Native American students were transformed from treatment nonresponders to treatment responders by moving them from a

DON'T FORGET

In all aspects of the artful translation of scientific research into educational practice (Rosenfield & Berninger, 2009), including planning, evaluating, and implementing evidence-based assessment and instruction, it is essential to consider all systems variables (e.g., classroom, school, community, family, cultural), as well as the assessed learning profile of the individual student.

pull-out group of two to a large group within the general education class-room (unpublished observations). Finally, it is important to find out which medical or health conditions may be relevant for educational planning (Wodrich, 2008).

Practical Significance of Genetic-Based Specific Learning Disabilities

Some believe that the research showing normalization of specific brain regions or timing patterns (e.g., Richards, Aylward, Berninger et al., 2006) following specialized instruction for students with specific reading disabilities means that instruction alone can overcome biologically based SLDs. Such a conclusion may be premature until it can be shown that one-time intervention that normalizes brain function in the short run normalizes it in the long run across schooling on all relevant neural substrates. Also, in our family genetics study, from which we recruited children for the instructional studies combined with brain imaging, we included only families with a multigenerational history of specific learning disabilities affecting written language (Berninger et al., 2001, 2006); so results may not generalize to an unselected population of poor readers in general.

We also studied the adults in that family genetics study who varied in whether they compensated (i.e., overcame the earlier struggles in schools). Some did, but some did not; and many showed residual impairments in the related hallmark phenotypes even if the reading or writing skills reached normal levels (e.g., Berninger et al., 2001; Berninger et al., 2006).

Of significance, many who appeared to compensate on the basis of age-normed, psychometric tests reported substantial difficulty in sustaining mental effort to complete reading (and writing) assignments. Amtmann, Abbott, and Berninger (2007) reported evidence supporting a reason for this self-reported difficulty. When compared to individuals without dyslexia, who tended to start out fast and stay fast in sustaining timed, cross-code integration (RAN for phonological loop function) and flexible executive functions (RAS for switching attention) in working memory over time (the rate change across the rows on RAN and RAS) (see Figure 9.1), individuals with dyslexia were classified in one of two groups, based on growth mixture modeling: (1) slow and slower or (2) steady slow. This invisible disability in sustaining mental effort over time, which others cannot observe and experience, especially when multiple codes or component processes have to be integrated in real time, may be a fundamental core deficit shared by many of the SLDs. An fMRI study using the n-back working memory paradigm also showed a difference between children with and without dyslexia in tracking stimuli over time (2 trials back) compared to processing current stimuli (0 trials back) (Richards, Berninger, Winn et al., 2009). Although brain differences on language tasks were normalized in response to language-based interventions, this working memory-related brain difference was not, suggesting that language intervention may be necessary but not sufficient for overcoming the working-memory impairments in dyslexia, which all require interventions to normalize temporal coordination of components of working memory.

Moreover, dyslexia (Berninger et al., 2008a, 2008b) and OWL LD (Silliman & Scott, 2009) are reading and writing disabilities—not just reading disabilities. Among those with earlier reading problems, spelling problems tended to persist through the adult years, especially in males (Berninger et al., 2008a, 2008b). Also, many who learn to read with explicit code instruction continue to experience extreme difficulty with the writing requirements of the curriculum, which increase in volume and complexity in the upper grades (e.g., Berninger et al., 2008a). This developmental phenomenon—responding to earlier evidence-based instruction, but facing ongoing learning challenges as the curriculum and requirements change across schooling from upper elementary to middle school to high school to higher education—serves as reminder that instruction may alter the epigenetics (Cassiday, 2009) of the brain but not the gene sequences created at conception. Epigenetics alters the behavioral expression of genes, but not their underlying constraints, which may cause learners who overcame earlier reading (and possible writing and/or math) problems to become vulnerable again as learning tasks change across schooling and development.

DON'T FORGET

Children who respond to early evidence-based instruction may face challenges in later grades as the curriculum requirements change.

EVIDENCE-BASED, THEORY-GUIDED DIFFERENTIAL DIAGNOSIS OF SLDs

Role of Cognitive Assessment

Research supports use of Full Scale IQ during assessment of all five developmental domains to assess the cognitive domain in determining whether an individual age 6 years or above has DD. Research also supports (a) use of the Verbal Reasoning Factor/Index/Composite (e.g., Wechsler, 2003) for diagnosing dyslexia (selective impairment in reading and spelling that is unexpected based on level of verbal intelligence, which research shows is average or better (Berninger et al., 2001; Berninger et al., 2006); and (b) use of Nonverbal Reasoning Factor/ Index/Composite (e.g., Wechsler, 2003) for diagnosing OWL LD, because language impairments in morphology, syntax, and text may interfere with development or expression of verbal reasoning, but nonverbal reasoning is at least within the limits of the normal range (see Berninger, O'Donnell, & Holdnack, 2008; Silliman & Scott, 2009).

Common Working Memory Architecture That Supports Language Learning

The working memory architecture shown in Figure 9.1 can be orchestrated to perform a variety of language tasks (listening, speaking, reading, and writing), as well as the language-related processes in math calculations (see Figure 9.2). Dyslexia and OWL LD share impairments within the working memory architecture—for example, in phonological loop and/or orthographic loop, and any of the executive functions (see Figures 9.1 and 9.2, and Berninger et al., 2006; Berninger et al., 2008). The loops forge the connections between the internal mental representations of spoken and written words, and the communication with the external world outside the mind, which can be achieved only through the primary motor (mouth or hand) and sensory systems, which send feedback to the motor system. Examples of this feedback include tactile sensations from mouth movements during articulation or from sequential finger movements during writing, auditory sensations for the words spoken by mouth, and visual sensations for words written by hand. That is why it is important to have a child's hearing and vision and somatosensory systems evaluated to determine whether they are functioning in the normal range (see Rapid Reference 9.7).

≣ *Rapid Reference 9.7*

Guidelines for Determining Students' Hearing, Vision, and Somatosensory Functioning

1. Through parent questionnaire or interview (Berninger, 2007c), find out if (a) the parent had any concerns about his or her child during infancy or the preschool years related to development (cognitive, language, motor, social emotional, attention and self-regulation of behavior); (b) any professional has diagnosed a medical, developmental, or other kind of disorder in the child;

(continued)

and (c) anyone in the family (this generation or past generations) had difficulty learning to read, write, and/or do math.

2. Ask what languages are spoken in the home. If more than one language is spoken, ask who speaks which language to the student, and why and for what purpose. If appropriate, explore whether another dialect of the mainstream language might be spoken at home than at school (see Washington & Thomas-Tate, 2009).

3. If through review of information provided by the parent or teacher or observation of the child, there is any reason to suspect that development of cognition, language, motor, social emotional, and attention and self-regulation of behavior may not be solidly within the normal range, administer standardized tests with sound psychometric properties to assess each of the five developmental domains to describe the student's developmental profile across the five relevant domains. Determine whether the student may have Pervasive Developmental Disability across the five domains of development or a Primary Area of Developmental Disability (e.g., primary language or primary motor) or Multiple Areas of Developmental Disability (two or more but not all five domains in the Developmental Disability range). Then note all other factors to take into account in educational planning the following: (a) language(s) spoken at home, (b) for students who are bilingual or multilingual, degree of competency in conversational and academic language for the dominant language at school, (c) past and current family and cultural issues that are relevant to educational functioning and planning, (d) approaches that might foster positive home-school relationships.

4. If there is no reason, based on parent and teacher interview and classroom observations during instruction or formal assessment, to document developmental disability in one or more of the five developmental domains (cognitive, language, motor, social emotional, attention, and self-regulation of behavior), then assess the following to determine whether the student has dyslexia or OWL LD, with or without dysgraphia or dyscalculia: (a) the target academic skills for each domain (reading, writing, and/or math), for which the teacher, parent, or other professional reports or observes difficulty (see text); and (b) the related phenotypes (see Figures 9.1 and 9.2).

5. If evidence-based differential diagnostic criteria are met for dyslexia or OWL LD, with or without comorbid dysgraphia or dyscalculia, consult resources for instructional approaches and resources for evidence-based instruction for each of these specific learning disabilities (e.g., Berninger, 2007c). Plan instructional intervention relevant to the diagnosis within a grade-appropriate instructional format and a progress-monitoring plan to evaluate whether the student improves on the target reading, writing, and/or math skills and related phenotypes that were impaired prior to the instructional intervention (see Berninger & Abbott, 2003; Berninger & Wolf, 2009a, 2009b). If not, problem solve additional intervention; if so, plan progress monitoring at subsequent grade levels to evaluate whether progress continues when nature of curriculum requirements change and increase in volume and complexity (see Berninger, 2007c, for guidance). Evaluate progress not only on the basis of whether the student improves on normed tests relative to age peers or high-stakes tests relative to criterion-based standards, but also whether the

student engages in reading (and writing and math) for pleasure, and spontaneously, and shows signs of improved self-efficacy and hope that academic success is within his or her reach (see Berninger & Hidi, 2006).

6. Based on parent questionnaire, school screenings, and classroom observations during instruction, determine whether there is reason to suspect any of the following and, if so, take the related action:

   a. Vision problems? If yes, refer for near-point and far-point evaluation by a qualified physician or optometrist.

   b. Hearing problems? If yes, refer for complete audiology exam by qualified audiologist.

   c. Somatosensory problems? If yes, assess tactile touch (PAL-II Finger Localization), kinesthesia (sensing movement through touch) (PAL-II Finger Tip Writing), and sensory-symbol integration (PAL-II Finger Recognition and Finger Tip Writing). Also, refer to a neurologist who can also assess the vestibular sense, cranial nerves, and markers of neural anomalies (e.g., choreiform twitch or dysdiadokinesis).

The executive functions help the reading, writing, and math brain self-regulate the learning process in response to teacher-guided instruction or during student self-guided learning activities. Flexibility (switching attention) in executive management (self-regulation) of learning is as important as automaticity of the loops during cross-code integration (e.g., Altemeier et al., 2008; Berninger & Nagy, 2008).

DON'T FORGET
....

Children learn to read by cross-code integration of orthographic codes for written language, and phonological codes for oral language through the phonological loop during oral reading. They learn to write by cross-code integration of phonological codes for spoken words, and orthographic codes for written language through the orthographic loop during handwriting, spelling, and composing (see Figure 9.1).

Hallmark Features of Dyslexia Versus OWL LD

Signs of dyslexia often are not observed until kindergarten, when parents and teachers notice that a child has unusual difficulty in naming letters and associating sounds with letters (i.e., cross-code integration of letters and spoken names or sounds) (Berninger, 2008a). Signs of OWL LD, in contrast, are typically observed during the preschool years, when affected children have unusual difficulty learning language (especially with word retrieval and morphological skills, which can affect vocabulary acquisition, and syntax and/or text inferencing, which requires understanding what is implied but not stated and can affect listening comprehension). Then, during the school years, individuals with OWL LD have difficulty using language to learn written language, for example, using language to self-regulate their learning, understand teachers' instructional language, and learn vocabulary specific to different subjects in the curriculum (e.g., math or science). The same skills that were impaired during the preschool years—word retrieval, morphology, syntax, and/or text inferencing—may still be impaired and affect real word reading, reading comprehension, spelling, and written composition (see Silliman & Scott, 2009).

Thus, during the school years, individuals with dyslexia and OWL LD differ in whether they are impaired only at the word-level in reading (pseudoword and real word reading) and writing (spelling) (dyslexia) or also at the syntactic level (and typically the text level) (OWL LD). However, children with dyslexia and OWL LD exhibit intraindividual differences in whether they are impaired in all the components of the working memory architecture (all executive functions, both loops, and three word forms) or only a subset of them. Those with dyslexia tend not to be impaired in morphological word form or syntax for storing and processing accumulating words in working memory, whereas those with OWL LD tend to be impaired in morphological word form and syntax (Berninger, 2008b; Berninger, Raskind et al., 2008).

Individuals with dyslexia have different instructional needs than those with OWL LD (Berninger & O'Malley, in press); for example, whether instruction should emphasize all three word forms and syntax but with special emphasis on phonological awareness (dyslexia) or special emphasis on phonological, morphological, and syntactic awareness (OWL LD). Each SLD benefits from orthographic awareness instruction (e.g., Berninger, Winn, et al., 2008; Richards, Aylward, Berninger, et al., 2006; Berninger & O'Malley, 2009). In addition, the bidirectional relationship between oral reading fluency and reading comprehension (Berninger, Abbott, Trivedi, et al., 2009) is relevant to planning instruction to improve oral reading fluency. Individuals with OWL LD may benefit from instruction to facilitate their word retrieval from semantic memory and listening comprehension. The word retrieval treatment may improve their automatic reading of real words, and in turn their oral reading fluency. The listening comprehension treatment may improve their reading comprehension and in turn their oral reading fluency.

Hallmark Features of Possible Comorbid Dysgraphia

If the individuals with either dyslexia or OWL LD are especially impaired in orthographic coding, finger sequencing, and/or the orthographic loop that

integrates the internal orthographic codes with external wr
words, they are likely to have dysgraphia (Berninger, 2008a),
specific reading disability, and possibly dyscalculia due to their
numerals, math facts, and written calculations (Berninger, in
9.1 and 9.2 and Rapid Reference 9.1. Early in schooling a ch
may have difficulty learning to form legible letters. However, once the child does
form letters that are reasonably legible, it is also important to assess with
appropriate tests whether the letters are accessed in and retrieved from memory
in order and produced automatically (effortlessly and quickly); if not, then the
efficiency of working memory during writing may be compromised. It is also
important to assess handwriting speed and ability to sustain letter production in
working memory over time (see Berninger, 2008a).

Hallmark Features of Possible Comorbid Dyscalculia

An individual with dyslexia or OWL LD may have dyscalculia related to impaired
math concepts in counting, place value, or part-whole relationships (see Figure
9.2). In such cases, the individual may or may not also have dysgraphia, which can
also affect the written processes involved in math fact retrieval and written
calculation in dyscalculia (see Rapid References 9.4 and 9.5).

APPLICATIONS OF DIFFERENTIAL DIAGNOSIS TO PREVENTION

One of the contributions of the response to intervention (RTI) approach is that
schools are providing more early intervention than in the past. However, that
alone may not be adequate to identify SLDs in reading that require more
specialized instruction than that provided in many general education classrooms
for reading problems. For example, if the child has OWL LD, he or she will need
explicit instruction to facilitate word retrieval, morphological and syntactic
awareness, and inferential thinking, and not only phonological awareness.
Also, without early diagnostic assessment, comorbid dysgraphia and/or
dyscalculia may not be identified and treated during an early sensitive period
when children are more likely to respond to the writing instruction and
instruction related to the reading and writing aspects of math. If,

CAUTION

Without early diagnostic assessment, comorbid dysgraphia and/or dyscalculia may not be identified and treated during an early sensitive period when children are more likely to respond to the writing instruction and instruction related to the reading and writing aspects of math.

ad, the nature of the reading disability (dyslexia or OWL LD and possible additional LDs in writing and math) could be diagnosed early in schooling, and relevant, evidence-based, early intervention implemented, children with biologically based dyslexia or OWL LD, plus or minus writing and/or math SLDs, might have more optimal academic achievement outcomes in the long run.

Just because an SLD has a genetic or brain basis does not mean that it cannot be prevented or its severity greatly reduced. One key to prevention is to ensure that schoolwide prevention programs are in place that (a) include universal screening for a few target skills that are grade-appropriate, (b) take into account preschool developmental and family history (see Rapid Reference 9.7), and (c) link screening results and preschool history to implementing evidence-based instruction and progress monitoring. Based on assessment and instructional research, evidence-based, grade-specific prevention programs can prevent failure to respond to early literacy instruction (Berninger, 2007c; Pearson Education, Inc., 2009). (See also instructional resources and strategies that can be implemented as a supplement to any curriculum a school has adopted: Berninger, 1998, Phonological and Orthographic Lessons; Handwriting Lessons; and Talking Letters, Berninger & Abbott, 2003; five lessons in Tier 1 and Lessons 6, 7, and 8 in Tier 2, Berninger, 2008c; and Berninger & Fayol, 2008.)

Another key to prevention is to monitor progress throughout schooling. As previously explained, if because of the biological vulnerability, a student cannot keep up with the changing curriculum requirements, then appropriate, specialized instruction can be implemented at any time during schooling, especially if evidence-based differential diagnosis has been carefully documented in the child's school records.

APPLICATIONS OF DIFFERENTIAL DIAGNOSIS TO PROBLEM-SOLVING CONSULTATION

Even if schoolwide prevention programs are in place, the need for problem-solving consultation to help teachers assist any student who struggles with reading (or comorbid oral language, writing, and/or math problems) is needed, for many reasons. First, as explained earlier, children with biologically based SLDs may respond to early interventions (changes at the epigenetic level, behavioral expression of genes), but because of remaining biological vulnerability (gene sequences set at conception) may encounter new struggles when faced with curriculum requirements that change in nature, volume, and complexity. Second, as also discussed in this chapter, not all struggles with reading (or comorbid oral language, writing, and/or math) are due to biologically based SLDs. Educational professionals must also try to optimize the academic achievement of students with DDs or neurogenetic disorders other than SLDs or brain injuries, students living in low-literacy homes or with families that speak another language or dialect than the one used at school, students who are homeless, students whose parents have low incomes and/or little formal education, and students whose families are confronting financial or health crises. Third, professionals also have to help struggling students who have moved into the school after the schoolwide prevention program, or who have moved frequently during their schooling.

See Berninger (2007c) for guidance in problem-solving consultation, which includes teacher questionnaires and interviews geared to reason for referral (in reading or other areas of the curriculum); classroom observation during reading instruction (or instruction in other areas of difficulty); a parent questionnaire about developmental, educational, and family history; and a matrix for linking all of the preceding to evidence-based assessment for problem identification, instructional modification, and monitoring response to instruction. In the process of problem-solving consultation, some students may show indicators of dyslexia or OWL LD, with or without comorbid SLDs, and require evidence-based interventions for their specific SLDs. However, many students who do not benefit from evidence-based intervention can benefit from the problem-solving consultation process, which draws on the interdisciplinary expertise of many professionals partnering to improve educational outcomes for any student in need of help.

Problem-solving consultation is more flexible than the prescriptive procedures of special education, but does not violate the letter or spirit of special education legal code. In fact, many practitioners who engage in problem-solving consultation on a regular basis have shared their high degree of professional satisfaction, whereas those in situations where all they can do is assess for eligibility decisions for special education sometimes have expressed frustration at not being able to do more to help teachers help students overcome their academic struggles. With experience and commitment on the part of professionals, and support from special education administrators, the psychologists, speech and language specialists, and physical and occupational therapists have often found ways to combine assessment and problem-solving consultation in ways that enhance their partnerships with teachers and ability to help more students improve learning outcomes. For one inspiring story that involved a systemwide partnership between psychologists and teachers, see Dunn and Miller (2009).

APPLICATIONS OF DIFFERENTIAL DIAGNOSIS TO SPECIALIZED INSTRUCTION: PRACTICAL RESOURCES

Many of our instructional studies evaluated alternative approaches for teaching 4th to 9th grade students recruited from families with multigenerational histories of SLDs in the family genetics studies. The effectiveness of the instruction was often evaluated on the basis of both behavioral and brain response to the instruction. These lessons can be found in Berninger and Abbott (2003, Lesson Sets 8, 11, 12, 13, 14, and 15) and Berninger and Wolf (2009b). Earlier in this chapter it was explained how these lessons were designed to overcome impairments in the working memory architecture supporting oral and written language learning.

Another common, research-supported feature of the lessons was instructional activities that develop linguistic awareness of phonological, orthographic, and morphological word forms and their parts and interrelationships (e.g., Berninger & Fayol, 2008; Berninger, Raskind et al, 2008). For instructional resources for developing such linguistic awareness, see Berninger and Abbott (2003, Lesson Sets 11, 12, and 15); and Berninger and Wolf (2009b).

The lessons also provided hope themes to convince the struggling learners that they could become successful learners and that their teachers could help them do so (see Berninger & Hidi, 2006; Berninger & Wolf, 2009b). Thus, effective instruction for overcoming specific reading disabilities addresses the impaired target academic skills and related phenotypes within a learning environment designed to overcome the impairments and inefficiencies in working memory; but it should also meet the learner's needs in all five domains of development: social, emotional, and motivational (see Berninger & Hidi, 2006), attention and self-regulation (executive functions), language (oral and written), motor (response modes), and cognitive (high intellectual engagement).

🐟 TEST YOURSELF 🐟

1a. What are the defining reading and writing skills that are likely to be impaired in dyslexia?

Answer: Accuracy and/or rate of oral reading of real words and pseudowords on a list or real words in a passage; and spelling.

1b. Which reading-related phenotypes differentiate dyslexia and OWL LD? Which of these phenotypes may be shared across the two LDs?

Answer: Differentiating phenotypes: OWL LD is more likely to have impaired syntactic and morphological skills (especially with inflectional and derivational suffixes) than dyslexia. Dyslexia and OWL LD are likely to have impaired phonological and/or orthographic coding, rapid automatic naming (RAN) and switching (RAS), and rapid automatic alphabet writing (or combination of these).

1c. How do children with dyslexia and OWL LD differ in their instructional needs?
Answer: Children with OWL LD need additional instruction in (a) morphological and syntactic awareness and how these linguistic awareness skills are related to reading comprehension and written expression of ideas, and (b) explicit cueing following text reading to ensure they are developing vocabulary meaning, sentence interpretation, and factual recall and inferential reasoning, all of which contribute to reading comprehension.

1d. Which instructional needs do children with dyslexia and OWL LD have in common?
Answer: Children with dyslexia and OWL LD need explicit instruction in (a) automatic correspondences between one- and two-letter spelling units and phonemes (alphabetic principle); (b) reflection on the interrelationships among phonological, orthographic, and morphological units in written words (e.g., word sorts); (c) transfer of (a) and (b) to oral reading of single words in context; (d) repeated reading of single words and words in context; and (e) explicit comprehension instruction.

2a. What are the defining writing skills that are likely to be impaired in dysgraphia?
Answer: Handwriting: automatic legible letter writing of alphabet from memory and on copy tasks; overall handwriting legibility; and overall handwriting speed especially on sustained writing tasks.
What are the writing-related phenotypes that are likely to be impaired in dysgraphia?
Answer: Receptive and expressive orthographic coding and planning and executive sequential finger movements (finger succession) (orthographical loop function).

2b. What additional instructional needs does a student with dyslexia plus dysgraphia or OWL LD plus dysgraphia have?
Answer: Explicit instruction in (a) looking games, to develop orthographic coding (holding written words in working memory while analyzing letters in them that do not have corresponding phonemes or that correspond to alternative phonemes); and (b) plan for letter formation (numbered arrow cues), translation of the plan (covering the letter while seeing it in the mind's eye and then writing it from memory), and review and revision if necessary to make sure the written letter looks like the model letter with the numbered arrow cues. It is also important to name the letter at each step of the strategy because verbal names are retrieval cues that facilitate letter learning.

3a. What are the defining math skills that are likely to be impaired in dyscalculia?
Answer: (a) Lack of one-to-one correspondence in counting; (b) impaired accuracy and/or rate of retrieving basic math facts for addition, subtraction, multiplication, and/or division; (c) impaired knowledge or application of knowledge of the sequential steps of the four arithmetic operations (addition, subtraction, multiplication, and/or division) or placement of the numerals correctly in two-dimensional rows and columns.
What are the math-related phenotypes that may be impaired in dyscalculia?
Answer: (a) Counting along a number line in working memory; (b) understanding and applying place value (generation of infinite number of numbers from 10 digits);

(*continued*)

(c) understanding and applying part-whole relationships to fractions, decimals, mixed numbers, and telling time; (d) automatic, legible numeral writing or overall legibility or speed of writing numerals; (e) coding multiplace numerals in working memory; (f) rapid automatic naming of numerals; and (g) integration of kinesthetic information from fingers with numeric symbols (fingertip writing).

3b. What additional instructional needs does a student with dyslexia plus dyscalculia or OWL LD plus dyscalculia have?

Answer: Explicit instruction in automatic, legible numeral writing; coding multiplace numerals in working memory; understanding the relationship of counting along a number line to learn basic math facts for addition, subtraction, multiplication, and division; explicit strategies related to the temporal sequence of steps of calculation and placement of numerals on paper during the written calculation; strategies and practice in solving math word problems and calculations in working memory and with paper and pencil, and self-checking strategies.

4a. Is there anything in federal special education law that says that educational professionals cannot proactively use evidence-based diagnosis and implement evidence-based, treatment-relevant instruction for specific LD diagnoses in general education?

Answer: No, the law does not prevent best practices in diagnosis and treatment.

4b. Is the purpose of federal special education law (or state implemented legal code) to define day-to-day professional operating procedures in schools or to ensure that the civil rights of students with educationally handicapping conditions are protected?

Answer: The federal law protects civil rights of those with educationally disabling conditions, but does not specify day-to-day procedures for teaching reading, writing, and math and assessing response to instruction to determine whether instruction should be modified, and if so, how.

5. Which is probably more professionally gratifying?

(a) To test children solely to decide if they are eligible for Tier 2 supplementary instruction or Tier 3 special education using RTI data or comprehensive psychometric test data.

(b) To partner with teachers to implement a schoolwide prevention program based on target reading, writing, and math skills, which, if underdeveloped for grade, can be taught to enhance the probability of responding to the instructional program in general education classrooms (prevent failure before it happens).

(c) To provide problem-solving consultation for teachers as they observe individual students struggling with reading (with or without writing or math problems) so that the nature of the learning problems can be identified (including but not restricted to LDs and DDs), and plan instructional modifications to improve learning and progress monitoring to evaluate whether learning does improve.

(d) b and c

Answer: d

Ten

A CHC-BASED OPERATIONAL DEFINITION OF SLD

Integrating Multiple Data Sources and Multiple Data Gathering Methods

Dawn P. Flanagan
Vincent C. Alfonso
Jennifer T. Mascolo

> The field needs a definition that reflects its best understanding of the SLD construct.
>
> —Kavale, Spaulding, and Beam, 2009, p. 46

Despite several decades of inquiry into the nature of specific learning disability (SLD), the federal definition of SLD (IDEA, 2004) has remained the same for 30 years. As such, the federal definition of SLD does not reflect the best thinking about the SLD construct (Kavale et al., 2009). In recognition of this fact, numerous proposals to modify the definition were proffered over the years. For example, the National Joint Committee on Learning Disabilities (NJCLD), a group of organizations that share a common concern about SLD, articulated several points of contention with the federal definition and, in 1981, put forth their own definition of SLD (Kavale et al.).

Although the NJCLD definition was well received and endorsed by the Inter-agency Committee on Learning Disabilities (ICLD), for example, it had little influence on the federal definition. If the field of SLD is to recapture its status as a reliable entity in special education and psychology, then more attention must be paid to updating and operationalizing the federal definition (Kavale & Forness, 2000). Accordingly, Kavale and colleagues proposed a "richer" description of SLD that indicates the boundaries of the term and the class of things to which it belongs. In addition, their definition delineates what SLD is and what it is not. Although not a radical departure from the federal definition, their definition, by comparison, provides a more comprehensive description of the nature of SLD. Kavale and colleagues' definition is as follows:

> Specific learning disability refers to heterogeneous clusters of disorders that significantly impede the normal progress of academic achievement. . . . The lack of progress is exhibited in school performance that remains below expectation for chronological and mental ages, even when provided with high-quality instruction. The primary manifestation of the failure to progress is significant underachievement in a basic skill area (i.e., reading, math, writing) that is not associated with insufficient educational, cultural/familial, and/or sociolinguistic experiences. The primary severe ability-achievement discrepancy is coincident with deficits in linguistic competence (receptive and/or expressive), cognitive functioning (e.g., problem solving, thinking abilities, maturation), neuropsychological processes (e.g., perception, attention, memory), or any combination of such contributing deficits that are presumed to originate from central nervous system dysfunction. The specific learning disability is a discrete condition differentiated from generalized learning failure by average or above (>90) cognitive ability and a learning skill profile exhibiting significant scatter, indicating areas of strength and weakness. The major specific learning disability may be accompanied by secondary learning difficulties that also may be considered when planning the more intensive, individualized special education instruction directed at the primary problem. (p. 46)

Kavale and colleagues (2009) further stated that their richer description of SLD "can be readily translated into an operational definition providing more confidence in the validity of a diagnosis of SLD" (p. 46). The purpose of this chapter is to describe such an operational definition. First, the chapter explains why operational definitions are important and necessary for SLD identification. Second, an operational definition of SLD that captures the nature of SLD, as reflected in the federal definition and in Kavale and colleagues' definition, is described. Third, because an operational definition of SLD does not prescribe approaches to or methods of instruction and intervention, this chapter demonstrates how to link assessment findings to educational recommendations.

THE NEED FOR AN OPERATIONAL DEFINITION OF SLD

With no change in the federal definition of SLD, attention was placed on articulating ways to operationalize it with the intent of improving the practice of SLD identification (Flanagan, Ortiz, Alfonso, & Mascolo, 2002, 2006; Kavale & Flanagan, 2007; Kavale & Forness, 2000; Kavale et al., 2009). For more than three decades, the main operational definition of SLD has been the "discrepancy criterion." Discrepancy was first introduced in Bateman's (1965) definition of LD and was later formalized in the Federal Regulations as follows:

> (1) The child does not achieve commensurate with his or her age and ability when provided with appropriate educational experiences, and (2) the child has a *severe discrepancy between achievement and intellectual ability* in one or more areas relating to communication skills and mathematics abilities. (U.S. Office of Education [USOE], 1977, p. 65083; emphasis added)

Several problems with the traditional ability-achievement discrepancy approach to SLD identification have been discussed extensively in the literature and are highlighted in other chapters in this book (e.g., Rapid Reference 8.2 in Hale, Wycoff, & Fiorello, this volume) and, therefore, will not be repeated here. With the reauthorization of IDEA in 2004, and the corresponding deemphasis on the traditional ability-achievement discrepancy criterion for SLD identification, there have been a number of attempts to operationalize the federal definition, many of which are presented in this book (see Rapid Reference 10.1 for examples).

Perhaps the most comprehensive operational definition of SLD was described over a decade ago by Kavale and Forness (2000). These

DON'T FORGET
....
An operational definition provides a process for the identification and classification of concepts that have been defined formally.

CAUTION
....
There are no rules for converting concepts to operational definitions. Therefore, "operational definitions are judged by significance (i.e., is it an authoritative marker of the concept?) and meaningfulness (i.e., is it a rational and logical marker of the concept?)" (Kavale et al., 2009, p. 41).

≡ *Rapid Reference 10.1*

Examples of How the 2004 Federal Definition of SLD Has Been Operationally Defined

- Absolute Low Achievement (see Lichtenstein & Klotz, 2007, for a discussion)
- Ability-achievement Discrepancy (see Zirkel & Thomas, 2010, for a discussion)
- Dual Discrepancy (e.g., Fuchs & Fuchs, 1998)
- Failure to Respond to Scientifically-Based Intervention (e.g., Fletcher, Barth, & Steubing, this volume; Fletcher, Lyon, Fuchs, & Barnes, 2007)
- Pattern of Academic and Cognitive Strengths and Weaknesses (also called Alternative Research-Based Approaches or "Third Method" Approaches; e.g., Hale et al., this volume; Hale, Flanagan, & Naglieri, 2008; Naglieri, this volume)

Note. All examples include a consideration of exclusionary factors as specified in the federal definition of SLD.

researchers reviewed critically the available definitions of LD and methods for their operationalization and found them to be largely inadequate. Therefore, they proposed a modest, hierarchical operational definition that reflected current research on the nature of learning disability. This operational definition is illustrated in Figure 10.1.

In their definition, Kavale and Forness (2000) attempted to incorporate the complex and multivariate nature of LD. Figure 10.1 shows that LD is determined through evaluation of performance at several "levels," each of which specifies particular diagnostic conditions. Furthermore, each level of the evaluation hierarchy depicted in Figure 10.1 represents a necessary, but not sufficient condition for LD determination. Kavale and Forness contended that it is only when the specified criteria are met at all five levels of their operational definition that LD can be established as a "discrete and independent condition" (p. 251). Through their operational definition, Kavale and Forness provided a much more rational and defensible approach to the practice of LD identification than that which had been offered previously. In short, their operationalization of LD used "foundation principles in guiding the selection of elements that explicate the nature of LD" (p. 251), which represented both a departure from and an important new direction for current practice.

Flanagan and colleagues (2002) identified some aspects of Kavale and Forness's operational definition that they believed needed to be modified. For

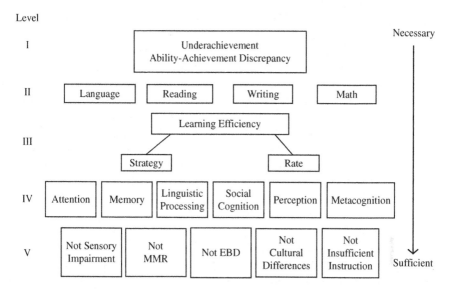

Figure 10.1. Kavale and Forness's (2000) Operational Definition of SLD

Source: Kavale, K. A., & Forness, S. R. (2000). What definitions of learning disability say and don't say: A critical analysis. *Journal of Learning Disabilities, 33, 3*, 239–256.

example, although Kavale and Forness's operational definition captured the complex and multivariate nature of LD, it was not predicated on any particular theoretical model and it did not specify what methods might be used to satisfy criteria at each level. In addition, the hierarchical structure depicted in Figure 10.1 implies somewhat of a linear approach to LD identification, whereas the process is typically more recursive and iterative. Consequently, Flanagan and colleagues proposed a similar operational definition of SLD, but based their definition primarily on the Cattell-Horn-Carroll (CHC) theory and its research base. In addition, these researchers provided greater specification of methods and criteria that may be used to identify SLD (Flanagan et al., 2002; Flanagan, Ortiz Alfonso, & Dynda 2006; Flanagan, Ortiz, & Alfonso, 2007).

Because operational definitions represent only temporary assumptions about a concept, they are subject to change (Kavale et al., 2009). Flanagan and colleagues have modified their operational definition over the last decade to ensure that it reflects the most current theory, research, and thinking with regard to (a) the nature of SLD; (b) the methods of evaluating various elements and concepts inherent in SLD definitions (viz., the federal definition); and (c) criteria for establishing SLD as a discrete condition separate from undifferentiated low

DON'T FORGET

The operational definition of SLD presented in Rapid Reference 10.2 is based primarily on CHC theory, but encourages a continuum of data-gathering methods, beginning with curriculum-based measures (CBM) and progress monitoring and culminating in norm-referenced tests of cognitive abilities and neuropsychological processes for students who demonstrate an inadequate response to intervention.

DON'T FORGET

An operational definition of SLD is needed to provide more confidence in the validity of the SLD diagnosis.

achievement. The most recent iteration of Flanagan and colleagues' operational definition of SLD is presented in Rapid Reference 10.2. Because this definition is primarily grounded in CHC theory, it is referred to herein as "the CHC-based operational definition of SLD."

Rapid Reference 10.2 shows that the CHC-based operational definition of SLD is arranged according to levels, similar to Kavale and Forness's (2000) definition. At each level, the definition includes (a) defining characteristics regarding the nature of SLD (e.g., child has difficulties in one or more areas of academic achievement); (b) the focus of evaluation for each characteristic (e.g., academic achievement, cognitive processing, exclusionary factors); (c) examples of evaluation methods and relevant data sources (e.g., standardized, norm-referenced tests and educational records, respectively); and (d) the criteria that need to be met to establish that an individual possesses a particular characteristic of SLD (e.g., below-average performance in an academic area, such as basic reading skill). As may be seen in Rapid Reference 10.2, the "Nature of SLD" column includes a description of what SLD is and what it is not. Overall, the levels represent an adaptation and extension of the recommendations offered by Kavale and colleagues (e.g., Kavale & Forness, 2000, Kavale et al., 2009), but also include concepts from a variety of other researchers (e.g., Berninger, this volume; Fletcher-Janzen & Reynolds, 2008; Geary, Hoard, & Bailey, this volume; Hale & Fiorello, 2004; Hale et al., in press; Naglieri, this volume; Reynolds & Shaywitz, 2009a, 2009b; Siegel, 1999; Stanovich, 1999; Vellutino, Scanlon, & Lyon, 2000).

The CHC-based operational definition of SLD presented in Rapid Reference 10.2 differs from the one offered by Kavale and Forness (2000) (Figure 10.1) in four important ways. First, it is grounded in a well-validated contemporary theory on the structure of abilities (i.e., CHC theory). Second, in lieu of the traditional ability-achievement discrepancy method, a specific pattern of cognitive and academic ability and neuropsychological processing strengths and

An Operational Definition of Specific Learning Disability

Level	Nature of SLD[1]	Focus of Evaluation	Examples of Evaluation Methods and Data Sources	Criteria for SLD	SLD Classification and Eligibility
I	Difficulties in one or more areas of academic achievement, including (but not limited to)[2] Basic Reading Skill, Reading Comprehension, Reading Fluency, Oral Expression, Listening Comprehension, Written Expression, Math Calculation, Math Problem Solving.	**Academic Achievement:** Performance in specific academic skills (e.g., Grw, Gq, Gc); may also include performance on measures of phonological and orthographic processing.	Response to quality instruction and intervention via progress monitoring, performance on norm-referenced, standardized achievement tests, evaluation of work samples, observations of academic performance, teacher/parent/ child interview, history of academic performance, data from other members of multidisciplinary team (MDT) (e.g., speech-language pathologist, interventionist, reading specialist).	Performance in one or more academic areas is weak or deficient[3] (despite attempts at delivering quality instruction) as evidenced by converging data sources.	**Necessary**
II	SLD does not include a learning problem that is the result of visual, hearing, or motor disabilities; of intellectual disability; of social or emotional disturbance; or of environmental, educational, cultural, or economic disadvantage.	**Exclusionary Factors:** Identification of potential primary causes of academic skill weaknesses or deficits, including intellectual disability, cultural or linguistic difference, sensory impairment, insufficient instruction or opportunity to learn.	Data from the methods and sources listed at Levels I and III; behavior rating scales; attendance records; social/ developmental history, family history; vision/hearing[4]; medical records; prior evaluations; interviews with current or past counselors, psychiatrists, etc.	Performance is not *primarily* attributed to these exclusionary factors, although one or more of them may *contribute* to learning difficulties.	

(continued)

Level	Nature of SLD[1]	Focus of Evaluation	Examples of Evaluation Methods and Data Sources	Criteria for SLD	SLD Classification and Eligibility
III	A disorder in one or more of the basic psychological/neuro-psychological processes involved in understanding or in using language, spoken or written; such disorders are presumed to originate from central nervous system dysfunction.	organic or physical health factors, social/emotional or psychological disturbance. **Cognitive Abilities and Processes:** Performance in cognitive abilities (e.g., Gc, Gf, Gv, Ga, Glr, Gsm, Gs), neuropsychological processes (e.g., attention, executive functioning, and learning efficiency).	Performance on norm-referenced tests, evaluation of work samples, observations of cognitive performance, task analysis/testing limits, teacher/parent/child interview, history of academic performance, records review.	Performance in one or more cognitive abilities and/or neuropsychological processes (related to academic skill deficiency) is weak or deficient as evidenced by converging data sources.	
IV	Unexpected Underachievement: The specific learning disability is a discrete condition differentiated from generalized learning failure by average or better cognitive ability and a learning skill profile exhibiting significant variability, indicating processing areas of strength and weakness.	**Data Integration— Analysis of a Pattern of Strengths and Weaknesses Consistent with SLD:** Determination of whether academic skill weaknesses or deficits are related to specific cognitive area(s) of	Data gathered at all previous levels, as well as any additional data, following a review of initial evaluation results (e.g., hypothesis testing, demand analysis).	No statistically significant or clinically meaningful difference between cognitive and academic deficits (e.g., *circumscribed aptitude-achievement consistency*); statistically significant or clinically meaningful difference between (cognitive and academic) deficits and (cognitive and academic) strengths (e.g., *circumscribed ability-achievement discrepancy with cognitive areas of strength represented by standard scores*	

≥90). Clinical judgment supports the impression that the child's overall ability to think and reason will enable him or her to benefit from tailored or specialized instruction/intervention, compensatory strategies, and accommodations, such that his or her performance rate and level will likely approximate more typically achieving, nondisabled peers.

weakness or deficit; pattern of data reflects a below-average aptitude-achievement consistency with otherwise average or better ability to think and reason.

V	Specific learning disability has an adverse impact on educational performance.		
	Special Education Eligibility:[5] Determination of least restrictive environment (LRE) for delivery of instruction and educational resources.	Data from all previous levels and MDT meeting, including parents.	Child demonstrates significant difficulties in daily academic activities that cannot be remediated, accommodated, or otherwise compensated for, without the assistance of individualized special education services.

[1]This column includes concepts inherent in the federal definition (IDEA, 2004) and in Kavale, Spaulding, and Beam's (2009) definition of *specific learning disability*.

[2]Poor spelling with adequate ability to express ideas in writing is often typical of dyslexia and/or dysgraphia. Even though IDEA 2004 includes only the broad category of written expression, poor spelling and handwriting are often symptomatic of a specific writing disability and should not be ignored (Wendling & Mather, 2010).

[3]Weak or deficient performance (also called, *normative weakness*) is defined typically by standard score performances that are low average (i.e., ≤89) or significantly below average (i.e., ≤84), respectively, and that have ecological validity (e.g., standardized test performance is consistent with performance observed in the child's everyday classroom or educational environment).

[4]In cases where there is an established history of vision and/or hearing difficulties, the impact of those difficulties on present learning. As such, a more comprehensive review of data (e.g., audiology and optometry/ophthalmology evaluations) and consideration of specific factors related to early vision/hearing difficulties (e.g., length of problem, severity and impact of problem, age of onset) in relation to the student's learning experiences (i.e., what was being taught at that time) should be undertaken where possible.

[5]The major specific learning disability may be accompanied by secondary learning difficulties, which also may be considered when planning the more intensive, individualized special-education instruction directed at the primary problem. For information on linking assessment data to intervention, see Rapid Reference 10.11.

weaknesses is used as a defining characteristic or marker for SLD. (It is important to understand that any pattern used for SLD determination should be supported by research on the relations between CHC abilities, processes, and academic outcomes, as well as evidence on the neurobiological correlates of learning disorders in reading, math, writing, and language.) Third, the evaluation of exclusionary factors occurs earlier in the SLD identification process in the current operational definition to prevent individuals from having to undergo needless testing. Fourth, the CHC-based operational definition emphasizes that SLD assessment is a recursive process (rather than a linear one) and that information generated and evaluated at one level may inform decisions made at other levels. The recursive nature of the SLD identification process is reflected by the arrows in Rapid Reference 10.2. Each level of the CHC-based operational definition of SLD is described in more detail in the next section.

CAUTION

Most individuals have statistically significant strengths and weaknesses in their cognitive ability and processing profiles. Intraindividual differences in cognitive abilities and processes are commonplace in the general population (McGrew & Knopik, 1996; Oakley, 2006). Therefore, statistically significant variation in cognitive and neuropsychological functioning in and of itself must not be used as de facto evidence of SLD. Instead, the pattern must reflect what is known about the nature of SLD (see Rapid Reference 10.2).

THE CHC-BASED OPERATIONAL DEFINITION OF SLD

It is assumed that the levels of evaluation depicted in Rapid Reference 10.2 are undertaken after prereferral intervention activities (consistent with Tiers 1 and 2 of a response to intervention [RTI] approach) have been conducted with little or no success and, therefore, a focused evaluation of specific abilities and processes through standardized testing is deemed necessary (Flanagan, Fiorello, & Ortiz, 2010). Moreover, prior to beginning an SLD assessment, other data from multiple sources should have already been collected within the context of intervention implementation. These data may include results obtained from informal testing, direct observation of behaviors, work samples, reports from people familiar with the child's difficulties (e.g., teachers, parents), and perhaps information provided by the child him- or herself. In principle, Level I assessment should begin only after the nature of a child's learning difficulties has been fully investigated and documented.

It is beyond the scope of this chapter to provide a detailed discussion of assessment- and interpretation-related activities for each level of the operational definition. Therefore, only a brief summary of each level follows (see Flanagan, Ortiz, & Alfonso, 2011, and Flanagan, Ortiz et al., 2006, for a more comprehensive description of the operational definition included in Rapid Reference 10.2).

Level I: Difficulties in One or More Areas of Academic Achievement

By definition, SLD is marked by dysfunction in learning. That is, learning is somehow disrupted from its normal course on the basis of some type of internal disorder or dysfunction. Although the specific mechanism that inhibits learning is not directly observable, one can proceed on the assumption that it manifests in observable phenomena, particularly academic achievement. Thus, Level I of the operational definition involves documenting that some type of *learning difficulty* exists. Accordingly, the process at Level I involves comprehensive measurement of the major areas of academic achievement (e.g., reading, writing, math, and language).

> ### CAUTION
> ....
> The finding of low academic achievement is not sufficient for SLD identification because this condition alone may be present for a variety of reasons, only one of which is SLD.

The academic areas that are generally assessed at this level in the operational definition include the eight areas of achievement specified in the federal definition of SLD (IDEA, 2004). These eight areas are math calculation, math problem solving, basic reading skill, reading fluency, reading comprehension, written expression, listening comprehension, and oral expression. Most of the skills and abilities measured at Level I represent an individual's stores of acquired knowledge. These specific knowledge bases (e.g., Quantitative Knowledge [*Gq*], Reading and Writing Ability [*Grw*]), Vocabulary Knowledge [*Gc*-VL]) develop largely as a function of formal instruction, schooling, and educationally related experiences (Carroll, 1993). Typically, the eight areas of academic achievement are measured using standardized, norm-referenced tests. In fact, many comprehensive achievement batteries measure all eight areas, such as the Wechsler Individual Achievement Test–Third Edition (WIAT-III; Pearson, 2010; see Rapid Reference 10.3). It is important to realize that data on academic performance should come from multiple sources (see Rapid Reference 10.2, Level I, column 4). Following the collection of data on academic performance, it is necessary to determine whether the child has a weakness or deficit in one or more specific academic skills.

Rapid Reference 10.3

Correspondence Between Eight Areas of SLD and WIAT-III Subtests and Composites

Areas in Which SLD May Manifest (Listed in IDEA 2004)	WIAT–III Subtests	WIAT–III Composites
Oral Expression	Oral Expression	Oral Language
Listening Comprehension	Listening Comprehension	Oral Language
Written Expression	Alphabet Writing Fluency	Written Expression
	Sentence Composition	
	Essay Composition	
	Spelling	
Basic Reading Skill	Early Reading Skills	Basic Reading
	Word Reading	
	Pseudoword Decoding	
Reading Fluency Skills	Oral Reading Fluency	Reading Comprehension and Fluency
Reading Comprehension	Reading Comprehension	Reading Comprehension and Fluency
Mathematics Calculation	Numerical Operations	Mathematics
Mathematics Problem Solving	Math Problem Solving	Mathematics
Mathematics Calculation	Math Fluency—Addition	Math Fluency
	Math Fluency—Subtraction	
	Math Fluency—Multiplication	

Adapted from Table 2.1 (p. 21) in Lichtenberger, E. O., and Breaux, K. C. (2010). *Essentials of WIAT-III and KTEA-II Assessment.* Hoboken, NJ: Wiley.

Determining whether a child has a weakness or deficit usually involves making normative-based comparisons of the child's performance against a representative sample of same-age or same-grade peers from the general population. If weaknesses or deficits in the child's academic achievement profile are not identified, then the issue of SLD may be moot because such weaknesses are a necessary component of the definition.

DON'T FORGET

A weakness is typically defined as performance on standardized, norm-referenced tests that falls below average (where average is defined as standard scores between 90 and 110, inclusive, based on a scale having a mean of 100 and standard deviation of 15). A deficit is often defined as performance on norm-referenced tests that falls greater than one standard deviation below the mean (i.e., standard scores <85).

CAUTION

Some children who struggle academically may not demonstrate academic weaknesses or deficits on standardized, norm-referenced tests of achievement, particularly very bright students, for a variety of reasons. For example, some children may have figured out how to compensate for their processing deficit(s) (e.g., through the use of executive functions). Therefore, it is important not to assume that a child with a standard score of 90 on a "broad reading" composite is "okay," particularly when a parent, teacher, or the student him- or herself expresses concern. Under these circumstances, a more focused assessment of the CHC abilities and neuropsychological processes related to reading should be conducted. Error and demand analysis may also prove helpful in such situations.

The presence of a normative weakness or deficit established through standardized testing, and corroborated by other data sources, such as CBM, clinical observations of academic performance, work samples, and so forth, is a necessary (but insufficient) condition for SLD determination. Therefore, when weaknesses or deficits in academic performance are found (irrespective of the particular methods by which they are identified), the process advances to Level II.

Level II: Exclusionary Factors—Identification of Potential Primary Causes of Academic Skill Weaknesses or Deficits

Level II involves evaluating whether any documented weaknesses or deficits found through Level I evaluation are or are not *primarily* the result of factors that may be, for example, largely external to the child, or noncognitive in nature.

Because there can be many reasons for weak or deficient academic performance, causal links to SLD should not be ascribed prematurely. Instead, reasonable hypotheses related to other potential causes should be developed. For example, cultural and linguistic differences are two common factors that can affect both test performance and academic skill acquisition adversely and result in achievement data that appear to suggest SLD (see Ortiz, this volume). In addition, lack of motivation, social/emotional disturbance, performance anxiety, psychiatric disorders, sensory impairments, and medical conditions (e.g., hearing or vision problems) also need to be ruled out as potential explanatory correlates to any weaknesses or deficits identified at Level I. At Level II, the practitioners must judge the extent to which any factors other than cognitive impairment can be considered the *primary* reason for the academic performance difficulties. If performance cannot be attributed primarily to other factors, then the second criterion necessary for establishing SLD according to the operational definition is met, and assessment may continue to the next level.

> **DON'T FORGET**
> ....
> Because the process of SLD determination does not necessarily occur in a strict linear fashion, evaluations at Levels I and II often take place concurrently, as data from Level II is often necessary to understand performance at Level I. The circular arrows between Levels I and II in Rapid Reference 10.2 are meant to illustrate the fact that interpretations and decisions that are based on data gathered at Level I may need to be informed by data gathered at Level II.

It is important to recognize that although factors such as having English as a second language may be present and may affect performance adversely, SLD may also be present. Certainly, children who may have vision problems, chronic illnesses, limited English proficiency, and so forth, may also have SLD. Therefore, when these or other factors at Level II are present, or even when they are determined to be *contributing* to poor performance, SLD should not be ruled out. Rather, only when such factors are determined to be *primarily* responsible for weaknesses in learning and academic performance, not merely contributing to them, should SLD, as an explanation for dysfunction in performance, be discounted. Examination of exclusionary factors is necessary to ensure a fair and equitable interpretation of the data collected for SLD determination and, as such, is not intended to *rule in* SLD. Rather, careful examination of exclusionary factors is intended to rule out other possible explanations for deficient academic performance.

One of the major reasons for placing the evaluation of exclusionary factors at this (early) point in the SLD assessment process is to provide a mechanism that is efficient in both time and effort and that may prevent the unnecessary administration of additional tests. However, noteworthy is the fact that it may not be possible to completely and convincingly rule out all of the numerous potential exclusionary factors at this stage in the assessment process. For example, the data gathered at Levels I and II may be insufficient to draw conclusions about such conditions as intellectual disability (ID; formally called mental retardation), which often requires more thorough and direct assessment (e.g., assessment of cognitive ability and adaptive behavior). When exclusionary factors have been evaluated carefully and eliminated as possible *primary* explanations for poor academic performance—at least those that can be evaluated at this level—the process may advance to the next level.

Level III: Performance in Cognitive Abilities and Neuropsychological Processes

The criterion at this level is similar to the one specified in Level I except that it is evaluated with data from an assessment of cognitive abilities, neuropsychological processes, and learning efficiency. Analysis of data generated from the administration of standardized tests represents the most common method available by which cognitive and neuropsycholological functioning in children is evaluated. However, other types of information and data are relevant to cognitive performance (see Rapid Reference 10.2, Level III, column 4). Practitioners should actively seek out and gather data from other sources as a means of providing corroborating evidence for standardized test findings. For example, when test findings are found to be consistent with the child's performance in the classroom, a greater degree of confidence may be placed on test performance because interpretations of cognitive deficiency have ecological validity—an important condition for any diagnostic process (Hale & Fiorello, 2004). Rapid Reference 10.4 provides an example of the cognitive abilities and neuropsychological processes measured by the Wechsler Intelligence Scale for Children–Fourth Edition (WISC–IV; Wechsler, 2003). For similar information on all major intelligence tests and selected neuropsychological instruments, see Flanagan et al. (2011) and Flanagan, Alfonso, Ortiz, and Dynda (2010).

A particularly salient aspect of the CHC-based operational definition of SLD is the concept that a weakness or deficit in a cognitive ability or process underlies difficulties in academic performance or skill development. Because research demonstrates that the relationship between the cognitive dysfunction and the manifest learning problems are causal in nature (e.g., Fletcher, Taylor, Levin, & Satz, 1995; Hale & Fiorello, 2004), data analysis at this level should seek to ensure

Rapid Reference 10.4

Cognitive Abilities and Neuropsychological Processes Measured by the Wechsler Intelligence Scale for Children–Fourth Edition (WISC-IV) Subtests

Subtest	CHC Broad and Narrow Abilities					Neuropsychological Domains							
	Gf	Gc	Gsm	Gv	Gs	Sensory-Motor	Speed and Efficiency	Attention	Visual-Spatial	Auditory-Verbal	Memory and/or Learning	Executive	Language
Arithmetic[1]	√ (RQ)		√ (MW)					√		√	√	√	√R
Block Design				√ (SR, Vz)		√			√			√	
Cancellation					√ (P, R9)	√	√	√	√			√	
Coding					√ (R9)	√	√	√	√		√	√	
Comprehension		√ (K0, LD)								√	√		√E/R
Digit Span			√ (MS, MW)					√		√	√	√	

	Gf	Gc	Gsm	Gv	Gs						Exec
Information		√ (K0)					√	√	√		√E
Letter-Number Sequencing			√ (MW)				√	√	√		
Matrix Reasoning	√ (I,RG)					√	√				
Picture Completion		√ (K0)		√ (CF)		√	√	√			
Picture Concepts	√ (I)	√ (K0)				√	√	√			
Similarities	√ (I)	√ (VL,LD)				√	√	√	√		√E
Symbol Search					√ (P,R9)	√	√	√	√		
Vocabulary		√ (VL)				√	√	√			√E
Word Reasoning	√ (I)	√ (VL)				√	√	√			√E/R

Note. Gf = Fluid Intelligence; Gc = Crystallized Intelligence; Gsm = Short-Term Memory; Gv = Visual Processing; Gs = Processing Speed; RQ = Quantitative Reasoning; MW = Working Memory; SR = Spatial Relations; Vz = Visualization; P = Perceptual Speed; R9 = Rate-of-Test-Taking; K0 = General (verbal) Knowledge; LD = Language Development; MS = Memory Span; I = Induction; RG = General Sequential Reasoning; CF = Flexibility of Closure; VL = Lexical Knowledge. The following Cattell-Horn-Carroll (CHC) broad abilities are omitted from this table because none is a primary ability measured by the WISC-IV: Glr (Long-Term Storage and Retrieval); Ga (Auditory Processing); Gt (Decision/Reaction Time or Speed); and Grw (Reading and Writing Ability). Most CHC test classifications are from *Essentials of Cross-Battery Assessment, Second Edition* (Flanagan, Ortiz, & Alfonso, 2007). Classifications according to neuropsychological domains were based on the authors' readings of neuropsychological texts (eg, Fletcher-Janzen & Reynolds, 2008; Hale & Fiorello, 2004; Lezak, 1995; Miller, 2007, 2010), and are also found in Flanagan, Alfonso, Mascolo, and Hale (in press).

[1]Cognitive ability classifications for the Arithmetic subtest are based on the analyses conducted by Keith, Fine, Taub, Reynolds, and Kranzler (2006). It is important to note that the Keith et al. analyses did not include any other measures of math achievement, and, therefore, Gq was not represented adequately in their study. Arithmetic has been identified in many other studies as a measure of Gq, particularly Math Achievement (A3) (see Flanagan & Kaufman, 2009, for a discussion).

that identified weaknesses or deficits on cognitive tests bear an empirical relationship to those weaknesses or deficits in academic skills identified previously. It is this very notion that makes it necessary to draw upon cognitive and neuropsychological theory and research to inform operational definitions of SLD and increase the reliability and validity of the SLD identification process. Theory and its related research base not only specify the relevant constructs that ought to be measured at Levels I and III, but predict the manner in which they are related. Furthermore, application of current theory and research provides a substantive empirical foundation from which interpretations and conclusions may be drawn. Rapid References 10.5 and 10.6 provide a summary of the relations between CHC cognitive abilities and processes and reading and math achievement, respectively.

Rapid References 10.5 and 10.6 provide two sets of findings from two different literature reviews (i.e., Flanagan, Ortiz et al., 2006, and McGrew & Wendling, 2010). Because the literature reviews yielded some differences with regard to which abilities and processes are most relevant to academic achievement, these rapid references include a "Comments" section that offers some possible explanations for the differences. A more extensive discussion of the implications of the findings reported in these rapid references may be found in McGrew and Wendling and Flanagan et al. (2011). Likewise, Rapid Reference 10.7 provides a summary of the literature on the relations between CHC cognitive abilities and writing achievement (Flanagan, Oritz et al., 2006).

The information contained in Rapid References 10.5 to 10.7 may be used to guide how practitioners organize their assessments at this level. That is, prior to selecting cognitive and neuropsychological tests, the practitioner should have knowledge of those cognitive abilities and processes that are most important for understanding academic

DON'T FORGET

If no weaknesses or deficits in cognitive abilities or processes are found, then an essential criterion for SLD determination is not met.

DON'T FORGET

Because new data are gathered at Level III, reevaluation or further consideration of exclusionary factors should be undertaken. The circular arrows between Levels II and III in Rapid Reference 10.2 are meant to illustrate the fact that interpretations and decisions that are based on data gathered at Level III may need to be informed by data gathered at Level II. Likewise, data gathered at Level III is often necessary to rule out (or in) one or more exclusionary factors listed at Level II in Rapid Reference 10.2. Reliable and valid identification of SLD depends in part on being able to understand academic performance (Level I), cognitive performance (Level III), and the many factors that may facilitate or inhibit such performances (Level II).

Summary of the Literature on Relations Between CHC Abilities and Reading Achievement

CHC Ability	Flanagan, Ortiz, Alfonso, and Mascolo (2006) General Reading Review[1] (116 independent studies)	McGrew and Wendling (2010) Basic Reading Skills and Reading Comprehension Findings[2] (19 CHC/WJ studies)	Comments
Gf	Inductive (I) and General Sequential Reasoning (RG) abilities play a moderate role in reading comprehension.	Quantitative Reasoning (RQ) is tentative/speculative at ages 6–8 and 14–19 years for Basic Reading Skills (BRS).[3] Broad Gf is tentative/speculative at ages 14–19 years for Reading Comprehension (RC).	The lack of a consistent relationship between Gf abilities and reading in the McGrew and Wendling summary may be related to the nature of the dependent measures. For example, RC was represented by the WJ Passage Comprehension and Reading Vocabulary tests, both of which draw minimally on reasoning (e.g., they do not require an individual to draw inferences or make predictions).
Gc	Language Development (LD), Lexical Knowledge (VL), and Listening Abilities (LS) are important. These abilities become increasingly important with age.	LS is moderately consistent at ages 6–8 years for BRS. LS is highly consistent at ages 6–19 years for RC. General Fund of Information (K0) is consistent at ages 6–8 and	The findings across the Flanagan et al. and McGrew and Wendling summaries are quite similar given that Broad Gc in the McGrew and Wendling summary is defined primarily by the narrow abilities *(continued)*

CHC Ability	Flanagan, Ortiz, Alfonso, and Mascolo (2006) General Reading Review[1] (116 independent studies)	McGrew and Wendling (2010) Basic Reading Skills and Reading Comprehension Findings[2] (19 CHC/WJ studies)	Comments
		moderately consistent at ages 9–19 years for BRS.	of LD and VL. However, Flanagan et al. did not find a consistent relationship between the narrow ability of K0 and reading, as K0 was not well represented in the studies they reviewed.
		K0 is highly consistent at ages 6–19 years for RC.	
		Broad Gc is moderately consistent at ages 6–13 and highly consistent at ages 14–19 years for BRS.	
		Broad Gc is highly consistent at ages 6–19 years for RC.	
Gsm	Memory Span (MS) is important especially when evaluated **within the context of working memory.**	Working Memory (MW) is moderately consistent at ages 6–19 years for BRS and highly consistent for RC at ages 6–19 years.	Both the Flanagan et al. and McGrew and Wendling summaries highlight the importance of Gsm for reading.
		MS is tentative/speculative at ages 6–8 and moderately consistent at ages 9–19 years for BRS.	
		MS is consistent at ages 6–13 and moderately consistent at ages 14–19 years for RC.	
		Broad Gsm is consistent at ages 6–8 and highly consistent at ages 9–19 years for BRS.	
		Broad Gsm is consistent at ages 6–8 and 14–19 years for RC.	

Gv	Orthographic processing	Visual Memory (MV) is moderately consistent at ages 14–19 years for RC. Broad Gv is not consistently related to BRS or RC.	One possible explanation for the lack of a Gv relationship with BRS in the McGrew and Wendling summary is that the types of tasks used to measure visual processing in the studies they reviewed (e.g., spatial relations) do not measure the visual aspects of reading (e.g., orthographic processing). Orthographic processing or awareness (the ability to rapidly map graphemes to phonemes) may be more closely related to the perceptual speed tasks found on cognitive tests (e.g., Symbol Search on the Wechsler Scales).
Ga	**Phonetic Coding (PC), or phonological awareness/ processing, is very important during the elementary school years.**	PC is moderately consistent at ages 6–13 and consistent at ages 14–19 years for BRS. PC is consistent at ages 6–8 and 14–19 years, and tentative/ speculative at ages 9–13 years, for RC. Speech Sound Discrimination and Resistance to Auditory Stimulus Distortion (US/UR) are consistent at ages 9–19 years for BRS. Broad Ga is not consistently related to BRS.	Interestingly, and in contrast to Flanagan et al.'s summary, McGrew and Wendling's summary does not show a strong relation between PC/phonological processing and reading at any age level. Given the wealth of research on the relations between PC/phonological processing and reading, coupled with the neuroimaging research showing normalization of brain function in response to effective interventions for PC/phonological processing deficits, a reasonable

(continued)

CHC Ability	Flanagan, Ortiz, Alfonso, and Mascolo (2006) General Reading Review[1] (116 independent studies)	McGrew and Wendling (2010) Basic Reading Skills and Reading Comprehension Findings[2] (19 CHC/W studies)	Comments
		Broad *Ga* is moderately related at ages 6–8 years for RC.	assumption is that PC/phonological processing plays an important role in reading development during the early elementary school years. The relationship between PC/phonological processing and reading may be more prominent in students with reading difficulties, a population not included in the McGrew and Wendling samples.
Glr	Naming Facility (NA), or rapid automatic naming, is very important during the elementary school years. Associative Memory (MA) was also found to be related to reading at young ages (e.g., age 6 years).	MA is consistent at ages 6– 8 years for BRS. Meaningful Memory (MM) is highly consistent at ages 9–19 years for RC. NA is consistent at ages 14–19 and moderately consistent at ages 9–13 years for RC. Broad *Glr* is consistent at ages 6–8 years for BRS. Broad *Glr* is consistent at ages 9–13 years for RC.	The lack of a significant relation between NA and BRS in the early elementary school years (ages 6–8 years) in the McGrew and Wendling summary is surprising, as rapid automatized naming or rate has always been implicated in young children who struggle with reading achievement, particularly reading fluency. However, the outcome measures in the studies reviewed by McGrew and

| Gs | **Perceptual Speed (P) is important during all school years, particularly the elementary school years.** | P is consistent at ages 6–8 and 14–19 years and moderately consistent at ages 9–13 years for BRS. P is consistent at ages 14–19 and moderately consistent at ages 6–13 years for RC. Broad Gs is moderately consistent at ages 6–13 years for BRS. Broad Gs is tentative/speculative at ages 6–13 years for RC. | Wendling may not have measured reading fluency well, or at all. Flanagan et al.'s summary shows a stronger relation between Gs and reading than McGrew and Wending's summary. Nevertheless, the findings of both investigations show that Gs and P, in particular, are important for reading. |

Note. Information in the third column of this table is from the present authors' interpretation of a complete set of tables obtained from Kevin McGrew. For a discussion of the limitations of the findings reported in this table, see McGrew and Wending (2010).

[1]The absence of comments for a particular CHC ability and achievement area in the Flanagan et al. review indicates that the research reviewed either did not report any significant relations between the respective CHC ability and the achievement area, or, if significant findings were reported, they were only for a limited number of studies. Comments in bold represent the CHC abilities that demonstrated the strongest and most consistent relationship to mathematics achievement.

[2]Qualitative descriptors of consistency for McGrew and Wending (2010) analyses were coded as follows: The label "highly consistent" means that a significant finding was noted in 80% or more of the studies reviewed; "moderately consistent" means that a significant finding was noted in 50% to 79% of the studies reviewed; and "consistent" means that a significant finding was noted in 30% to 49% of the studies reviewed. *Tentative/speculative* results were those that were: (a) between 20% and 29% in consistency, (b) based on a very small number of analyses (e.g., *n* = 2), and/or (c) based only on McGrew's (2007) exploratory multiple regression analysis of manifest WJ III variables at the individual IV test level (McGrew & Wending, 2010).

Summary of the Literature on Relations Between CHC Abilities and Mathematics Achievement

CHC Ability	Flanagan, Ortiz, Alfonso and Mascolo (2006). General Math Review[1] (32 independent studies)	McGrew and Wendling (2010) Basic Math Skills and Math Reasoning Findings[2] (10 CHC/WJ studies)	Comments
Gf	Inductive (I) and General Sequential (RG) reasoning abilities are consistently related to math achievement at all ages.	Quantitative Reasoning (RQ) is highly consistent at ages 6–19 years. RG is highly consistent at ages 14–19 years for Math Reasoning (MR) and consistent at ages 6–19 years for Basic Math Skills (BMS).	Broad Gf is highly consistent at ages 6–13 and moderately consistent at ages 14–19 years for MR, and moderately consistent at ages 6–19 years for BMS. In McGrew and Wendling's analyses, Induction was part of the RQ tasks and was subsumed by Gf.
Gc	Language development (LD), Lexical Knowledge (VL), and Listening Abilities (LS) are important. These abilities become increasingly important with age.	LD and VL are consistent at ages 9–13 and highly consistent at ages 14–19 years for BMS. LD and VL are consistent at ages 6–8 years, moderately consistent at ages 9–13, and highly consistent at ages 14–19 years for MR.	The lack of a relationship between LD/VL and BMS at ages 6–8 years in McGrew and Wendling is surprising, as elementary math contains several language concepts (e.g., less than, greater than, sum, in all, together). This finding is likely related to the

		LS is consistent at ages 6–8 and highly consistent at ages 9–19 years for MR. LS is highly consistent for BMS at ages 6–19 years. KO is moderately consistent up to age 13 and highly consistent at ages 14–19 years for MR only.	nature of the math tasks used in the studies reviewed. General Fund of Information (KO) was either not represented or did not demonstrate a consistent relationship with math achievement in the Flanagan et al. review. Broad Gc is moderately consistent at ages 9–19 years for BMS. Broad Gc is consistent at ages 6–8 years, moderately consistent at ages 9–13, and highly consistent at ages 14–19 years for MR. Broad Gsm is consistent at ages 14–19 years for MR only.
Gsm	Memory Span (MS) is important especially when evaluated **within the context of working memory.**	Working Memory (MW) is highly consistent at ages 6–19 years for BMS and MR. MS is consistent at ages 6–8 years for MR only.	
Gv	May be important primarily for higher-level or advanced mathematics (e.g., geometry, calculus).	Spatial Scanning (SS) is consistent at ages 6–8 years for BMS only.	Gv abilities related to math achievement are either not measured or not measured adequately by current intelligence batteries. Alternatively, the importance of an adequately measured Gv ability may be masked by the presence of other important variables

(continued)

CHC Ability	Flanagan, Ortiz, Alfonso and Mascolo (2006). General Math Review[1] (32 independent studies)	McGrew and Wendling (2010) Basic Math Skills and Math Reasoning Findings[2] (10 CHC/ WJ studies)	Comments
			Wendling).
Ga		Phonetic Coding (PC) is consistent at ages 6–13 years for BMS, BMS is moderately consistent at ages 6–8 and consistent at ages 9–19 years for MR.	The relationship in the McGrew and Wendling study between PC and BMS reflects the use of Sound Blending as the PC indicator. Memory Span is necessary for optimal performance on Sound Blending, which may account for the presence of the relationship.
		Speech Sound Discrimination and Resistance to Auditory Stimulus Distortion (US/UR) are moderately consistent at ages 9–13 years for MR only.	
Glr		Meaningful Memory (MM) is moderately consistent at ages 14–19 years for MR.	MM and MA were either not represented or did not demonstrate a consistent relationship with math achievement in the Flanagan et al. review.
		MM is moderately consistent at ages 9–13 years for BMS.	
		Associative Memory (MA) is consistent at ages 6–8 years.	The relationship between Naming Facility (NA) and BMS would likely be more robust if the cognitive task stimuli involved the rapid
		NA is consistent at ages 6–19 years for BMS only.	

Gs	**Speed of Processing (Gs) and, more specifically, Perceptual Speed (P) is important during all school years, particularly during elementary school.**	Broad Gs is moderately consistent at ages 6–13 and consistent at ages 14–19 years for BMS.	naming of numbers rather than pictures.
		Broad Gs is consistent at ages 6–8 and moderately consistent at ages 9–13 years for MR.	In McGrew and Wendling's summary of the relations between Gs and math, P is also described as Attention-Concentration/Executive Functioning (AC/EF).
		AC/EF is consistent at ages 6–8 years for BMS.	
		AC/EF is highly consistent for ages 9–13 and consistent for ages 14–19 years for BMS.	
		P is highly consistent at ages 6–19 years for BMS and moderately consistent at ages 6–19 years for MR.	

Note. Information in the third column of this table is from the present authors' interpretation of a complete set of tables obtained from Kevin McGrew. For a discussion of the limitations of the findings reported in this table, see McGrew and Wendling (2010).

[1] The absence of comments for a particular CHC ability and achievement area (e.g., *Ga* and mathematics) in the Flanagan et al. review indicates that the research reviewed either did not report any significant relations between the respective CHC ability and the achievement area, or, if significant findings were reported, they were only for a limited number of studies. Comments in bold indicate the CHC abilities that demonstrated the strongest and most consistent relationship to mathematics achievement.

[2] Qualitative descriptors of consistency for McGrew & Wendling (2010) analyses were coded as follows: The label "highly consistent" denotes that a significant finding was noted in 80% or more of the studies reviewed; "moderately consistent" denotes that a significant finding was noted in 50% to 79% of the studies reviewed; "consistent" denotes that a significant finding was noted in 30% to 49% of the studies reviewed.

≡ Rapid Reference 10.7

Summary of the Literature on Relations Between CHC Abilities and Writing Achievement

CHC Ability	Writing Achievement
Gf	Inductive (I) and General Sequential Reasoning (RG) abilities are related to basic writing skills, primarily during the elementary school years (e.g., 6–13) and consistently related to written expression at all ages.
Gc	**Language Development (LD), Lexical Knowledge (VL), and General Information (K0) are important primarily after age 7. These abilities become increasingly important with age.**
Gsm	**Memory Span (MS) is important to writing, especially spelling skills, whereas Working Memory has shown relations with advanced writing skills (e.g., written expression).**
Gv	
Ga	Phonetic Coding (PC), or phonological awareness/processing, is very important during the elementary school years for both basic writing skills and written expression (primarily before age 11).
Glr	Naming Facility (NA), or rapid automatic naming, has demonstrated relations with written expression, primarily the fluency aspect of writing.
Gs	**Perceptual Speed (P) is important during all school years for basic writing, and is related to all ages for written expression.**

Note. The absence of comments for a particular CHC ability (e.g., Gv) indicates that the research reviewed either did not report any significant relations between the respective CHC ability and writing achievement, or, if significant findings were reported, they were for only a limited number of studies. Comments in bold represent the CHC abilities that showed the strongest and most consistent relation to writing achievement. Information in this table was reproduced from Flanagan, Ortiz, Alfonso, and Mascolo (2006) with permission from the publisher, John Wiley & Sons, Inc. All rights reserved.

performance in the area(s) in question (i.e., the area(s) identified as weak or deficient at Level I). Evaluation of cognitive performance should be comprehensive in the areas of suspected dysfunction. Evidence of a cognitive weakness or deficit is a necessary condition for SLD determination.

Level IV: Data Integration—Analysis of a Pattern of Strengths and Weaknesses Consistent with SLD

This level of evaluation revolves around a theory- and research-guided examination of performance across academic skills, cognitive abilities, and neuropsychological processes to determine whether the child's underachievement (as identified at Level I) is indeed *unexpected*. When the process of SLD identification has reached this level, three necessary criteria for SLD identification have already been met: (1) one or more weaknesses or deficits in academic performance; (2) one or more weaknesses or deficits in cognitive abilities and/or neuropsychological processes; and (3) exclusionary factors determined not to be the primary causes of the academic and cognitive weaknesses or deficits. What has not been determined, however, is whether the pattern of results supports the notion of unexpected underachievement in a manner that suggests SLD. The nature of unexpected underachievement, within the context of the CHC-based operational definition suggests that not only does a child possess specific, circumscribed, and related academic and cognitive weaknesses or deficits—referred to as a *below-average aptitude-achievement consistency*—but that these weaknesses exist along with average or better overall intelligence.

It is important to understand that discovery of consistencies among cognitive abilities and/or processes and academic skills in the below-average (or lower) range could result from intellectual disability or generally below-average cognitive ability. Therefore, identification of SLD cannot rest on below-average aptitude-achievement consistency alone. A child must also demonstrate evidence of average or better functioning (i.e., standard scores generally ≥90) in cognitive and neuropsychological domains that are not as highly correlated with the presenting problem. For example, in the case of a child with reading decoding difficulties, it would be necessary to determine that performance in areas less related to this skill (e.g., *Gf*, math ability) are average or better. Such a finding would suggest that the related weaknesses in cognitive and academic domains are not due to a more pervasive form of cognitive dysfunction, thus supporting the notion of *unexpected underachievement*—that the child could in all likelihood perform within normal limits (e.g., at or close to grade level) in whatever achievement skill he or she was found to be deficient if not for *specific* cognitive ability or processing weaknesses or deficits. Moreover, because the child has generally average or better overall cognitive ability, the academic skill deficiency is indeed unexpected. In sum, the finding of a pattern of circumscribed and related deficits (i.e., below-average aptitude-achievement consistency) within a generally average or better ability profile is convincing evidence of SLD, particularly when the student who demonstrates this pattern does not respond well to evidence-based instruction, and exclusionary factors have been ruled out as the primary causes of the deficits.

DON'T FORGET

The term *aptitude* within the context of the CHC-based operational definition of SLD represents the specific cognitive ability or neuropsychological processing deficits that are empirically related to the academic skill deficiency. For example, if a child's basic reading skill deficit is related to cognitive deficits in phonological processing (a *Ga* ability) and rapid automatic naming (a *Glr* ability), then the combination of below-average *Ga* and *Glr* performances represent his or her aptitude for basic reading. Moreover, the finding of below-average performance on measures of phonological processing, rapid automatic naming, and basic reading skill represents a *below-average aptitude-achievement consistency* or, more specifically, a *below-average reading aptitude-reading achievement consistency*. The concept of aptitude-achievement consistency reflects the notion that there are well-documented relationships between specific academic skills and specific cognitive abilities and processes (see Rapid References 10.5 to 10.7). Therefore, the finding of below-average performance in related academic and cognitive areas is an important marker for SLD.

Determining an otherwise average (or better) ability profile for a child who has a below-average aptitude-achievement consistency is not a straightforward task, and there is no agreed-upon method for determining this condition. Nevertheless, there is increasing agreement that a child who meets criteria for SLD has at least some cognitive capabilities that are indeed average or better (e.g., Berninger, this volume; Flanagan, Kaufman, Kaufman, & Lichtenberger, 2008; Flanagan et al., 2010; Geary et al., this volume; Hale & Fiorello, 2004; Hale et al., this volume; Kaufman, 2008; Kavale & Forness, 2000; Kavale & Flanagan, 2007; Kavale et al., 2009; Naglieri, this volume). In fact, the earliest recorded definitions of learning disability were developed by clinicians based on their observations of individuals who experienced considerable difficulties with the acquisition of basic academic skills, despite their average or above-average general intelligence (Kaufman, 2008). Indeed, "all historical approaches to SLD emphasize the spared or intact abilities that stand in stark contrast to the deficient abilities" (Kaufman, pp. 7–8). By failing to differentially diagnose SLD from other conditions that impede learning, such as intellectual disability and low average ability (e.g., a "slow learner"), the SLD construct loses its meaning and there is a tendency (albeit well intentioned) to accept anyone under the SLD rubric who has learning difficulties for reasons other than *specific* cognitive dysfunction.

CAUTION

When a student does not meet criteria specified in the CHC-based operational definition of SLD, it is possible that the student is a "slow learner" (SL; i.e., a student with below-average cognitive ability). According to Kavale, Kauffman, Bachmeier, and LeFever (2008), "About 14% of the school population may be deemed SL, but this group does not demonstrate unexpected learning failure, but rather an achievement level consonant with IQ level. . . . [S]low learner has never been a special education category, and 'What should not happen is that a designation of SLD be given to a slow learner' (Kavale, 2005, p. 555)" (p. 145).

While it may be some time before consensus is reached on what constitutes "average or better ability" for the purpose of SLD identification, a child who has SLD ought to be able to perform academically at a level that approximates that of his or her more typically achieving peers *when provided with individualized instruction as well as appropriate accommodations, curricular modifications, and the like.* In addition, in order for a child with SLD to reach performances (in terms of both rate of learning and level of achievement) that approximate his or her nondisabled age mates, he or she must possess the ability to learn compensatory strategies and apply them independently, which often requires higher-level thinking and reasoning, including intact executive functioning (McCloskey, Perkins, & Van Divner, 2009). Individuals with SLD can overcome or bypass the effects of their disability under certain circumstances. Special education provides the mechanism to assist the child with SLD in bypassing his or her processing deficits through individualized instruction and intervention and through the provision of appropriate adaptations, accommodations, and compensatory strategies. However, to succeed in bypassing or minimizing the effects of an individual's SLD in the educational setting to the point of achieving at or close to grade level, overall average cognitive or intellectual ability is very likely requisite (see Fuchs and Young, 2006, for a discussion of the mediating effects of IQ on response to intervention).

CAUTION

While at least average overall cognitive ability is likely necessary for a child with SLD to be successful at overcoming or bypassing his or her cognitive processing deficits, many other factors may facilitate or inhibit academic performance, including intact executive functioning, motivation, determination, perseverance, familial support, quality of individualized instruction, student-teacher relationship, existence of comorbid conditions, and so forth.

In an attempt to determine whether a child who demonstrates a below-average aptitude-achievement consistency also has average or better overall cognitive ability, Flanagan and colleagues (2007) developed a program called the SLD Assistant, which is a means of parceling out cognitive deficits from global functioning and judging the robustness of the spared abilities or cognitive integrities. The SLD Assistant is not meant to replace clinical judgment, but rather to support it. Others have also developed methods and suggested formulae for determining whether individuals have cognitive strengths that are in stark contrast to their cognitive weaknesses (see Hale et al., this volume; Naglieri, this volume). Ultimately, the determination regarding whether or not a child with a below-average aptitude-achievement consistency is SLD (and not SL or ID, for example), or exhibits unexpected (not expected) underachievement, must rely to some extent on clinical judgment. Such judgment, however, is bolstered by converging data sources that were gathered via multiple methods and clinical tools.

CAUTION

Overall average (or better) cognitive ability is difficult to determine in students with SLDs because their specific cognitive deficits often attenuate total test scores (e.g., IQ). Therefore, such decisions should be based on multiple data sources and data-gathering methods. For example, a student with an SLD in mathematics may have a below-average WISC–IV Full Scale IQ due to weaknesses in processing speed and working memory. However, if the student has an average or better WISC–IV GAI and average or better reading and writing ability, for example, then it is reasonable to assume that this student is of at least average ability. Of course, the more converging data sources available to support this conclusion, the more confidence one can place in such a judgment.

It is also important to realize that overall average (or better) cognitive ability (as measured by most current intelligence tests) can be present in an individual who has executive functioning difficulties. In other words, an individual's executive control capacities *are not assessed* by traditional measures of intelligence and cognitive abilities. This is because the examiner serves as "the executive control board" during the administration of norm-referenced, standardized tests of intelligence (Feifer & Della Tofallo, 2007, p. 18). For example, the examiner tells the individual exactly what to do, motivates the individual, provides (and repeats) directions, monitors progress, and so forth, as dictated by standardized administration procedures. By contrast, on tests of executive functioning, the individual's performance processes are evaluated (i.e., approach to task, problem solving and planning ability, organization, speed and efficiency, flexibility in shifting cognitive resources, etc.). As such, an individual may have high intelligence, despite marked difficulties in executive functioning.

Level V: SLD Adversely Impacts Educational Performance

When a child meets criteria for an SLD diagnosis, it is typically obvious that the child has difficulties in daily academic activities that need to be addressed. The purpose of this level of evaluation is to determine whether the identified condition (i.e., SLD) impairs academic functioning to such an extent that special education services are warranted.

Children with SLD require individualized instruction, accommodations, and curricular modifications to varying degrees, based on such factors as the nature of the academic setting, the severity of the learning disability, the developmental level of the child, the extent to which the child is able to compensate for specific weaknesses, the manner in which instruction is delivered, the content being taught, and so forth. As such, some children with SLD may not require special education services, such as when their academic needs can be met through classroom-based accommodations (e.g., use of a word bank during writing tasks, extended time on tests) and differentiated instruction (e.g., allowing a student with a writing deficit to record reflections on a reading passage and transcribe them outside of the classroom prior to submitting a written product). Other children with SLD may require both classroom-based accommodations *and* special education services. And in cases where a child with SLD is substantially impaired in the general education setting, a self-contained special education classroom may be required to meet his or her academic needs adequately.

In sum, there are two possible questions at this level that must be answered by the multidisciplinary team (MDT). First, can the child's academic difficulties be remediated, accommodated, or otherwise compensated for without the assistance of individualized special education services? If the answer is yes, then services (e.g., accommodations, curricular modifications) may be provided, and their effectiveness monitored, in the general education setting. If the answer is no, then the MDT must answer the question, "What is the nature and extent of special education services that will be provided to the child?" In answering this question, the MDT must ensure that individualized instruction and educational resources are provided to the child in the least restrictive environment (LRE).

Summary of the CHC-Based Operational Definition of SLD

The preceding sections provided a brief summary of the major components of the CHC-based operational definition of SLD. This definition provides a common foundation for the practice of SLD identification, and will likely be most effective when it is informed by cognitive and neuropsychological theory and research that supports (a) the identification and measurement of constructs associated with SLD,

(b) the relationship between academic skills and cognitive abilities and processes, and (c) a defensible method of interpreting results. Of the many important components of the definition, the central focus revolved around specification of criteria at the various levels of evaluation that should be met to establish the presence of SLD. These criteria included identification of empirically related academic and cognitive abilities and processes in the below-average range, as compared to same-age peers from the general population; determination that exclusionary factors are not the primary cause of the identified academic and cognitive deficits; and identification of a pattern of performance consistent with unexpected underachievement, including identification of at least average overall cognitive ability.

When the criteria specified at each level of the operational definition are met, it may be concluded that the data gathered are sufficient to support a diagnosis of SLD in a manner consistent with IDEA (2004) and its attendant regulations, and Kavale et al.'s (2009) definition of SLD. Because the conditions outlined in Rapid Reference 10.2 are based on current SLD research, the CHC-based operational definition presented here represents progress toward a more complete and defensible approach to the process of evaluating SLD than previous methods (see also Flanagan et al. 2011; Hale et al., 2008; Kavale, Kaufman, Naglieri, & Hale, 2005; Kavale et al., 2008). We believe that an operational definition of this type has the potential to increase agreement among professionals with respect to who does and does not have SLD. Moreover, because of its foundation in CHC theory and research, the operational definition presented here identifies specific targets for remediation, thereby increasing significantly the possibilities for truly individualized intervention (Kavale et al., 2005).

BEYOND SLD IDENTIFICATION: LINKING CHC ASSESSMENT DATA TO INSTRUCTION AND INTERVENTION

Although targets for remediation are identified, the CHC-based operational definition of SLD does not prescribe how a student's unique pattern of cognitive strengths and weaknesses leads to instructional and intervention planning. Therefore, this section provides practitioners with information that demonstrates how to use cognitive assessment data, in particular, for that purpose. A brief case of a student with reading difficulties is presented here to illustrate how practitioners can use cognitive assessment data to inform instruction and intervention planning.

A Reading Case Example

Billy is a 4th grader who has substantial reading difficulties. While he appears to decode text accurately, his ability to read fluently and comprehend text is limited.

These difficulties persisted despite the implementation of prereferral interventions. Specifically, Billy received afterschool reading help and weekend tutoring since the spring of 3rd grade and participated in a school-based reading lab twice a week for 30 minutes for the past 6 months. Billy's afterschool reading help and weekend tutoring are similar in that they focus on providing homework support. In both the afterschool and weekend settings, Billy's stated needs drive instruction; that is, his tutors help him in areas that he identifies as problematic or challenging. A needs-based structure such as this is geared toward making Billy responsible for his learning, and helping him advocate for himself when he requires assistance. Although he reportedly requests help after school and from his tutor, similar requests for assistance are rare in the classroom, presumably for social reasons (e.g., Billy is embarrassed to ask for help in front of his friends).

Billy's school-based reading lab is more structured and teacher-driven than his tutoring setting. Specifically, Billy's reading lab teacher works with a small group of students and engages them in independent reading activities. She makes her way around the small group and asks each student to read aloud from an appropriately leveled reader. She offers corrective feedback during the individual read-alouds and teaches her students to use context to decode unknown words.

Though Billy reportedly enjoys his reading lab and tutoring sessions, and is an active participant, he has made minimal gains relative to other students in his reading lab group. Moreover, he remains far behind the rest of his class in terms of his reading performance, particularly with regard to automaticity and comprehension. Because there is a strong comprehension component on his weekly language arts tests, Billy fails most of them and is beginning to demonstrate avoidance behaviors during reading lessons (e.g., complaining of physical ailments, asks for frequent bathroom breaks). Moreover, Billy has recently experienced social repercussions, as other students have become increasingly impatient with him when he is reading text or attempting to answer questions about what he has read.

To better understand the factors underlying his reading difficulties and why he is not responding to intervention at an expected rate and level, Billy was evaluated using standardized academic, cognitive, and social-emotional measures (see Rapid References 10.8 through 10.10). Specifically, Billy was administered subtests from the WIAT-III, WISC-IV, Woodcock-Johnson III Tests of Cognitive Abilities (WJ III COG; Woodcock, McGrew, & Mather, 2001), and the Behavior Assessment System for Children–Second Edition, Teacher and Parent Rating Scales and Self-Report of Personality (BASC2; Reynolds & Kamphaus, 2004). In addition, data were gathered via observations, work samples, and teacher/parent interviews.

Academic results from the WIAT-III indicate that although Billy performed in the Average range in reading decoding, he demonstrated normative weaknesses in reading comprehension and reading fluency (see Rapid Reference 10.8). An error analysis of his reading comprehension performance revealed that Billy primarily had difficulties with inferential comprehension questions. Test record notes stated that Billy focused during the administration of academic tasks, but often read dysfluently and seemed unsure when answering questions about what he had read. Moreover, although Billy was allowed and encouraged to refer back to the text to respond to comprehension questions, he did not do this prior to offering a response and, therefore, answered several literal, fact-based questions incorrectly. Billy frequently asked for comprehension questions to be repeated by the examiner. Following a relatively lengthy reading passage, Billy responded rather haphazardly and paid little attention to the examiner's questions. On a reading fluency task, Billy took a long time to finish the passage and had difficulty answering the comprehension questions at the end of each passage.

DON'T FORGET

Billy displays difficulties with reading comprehension that are consistent with poor executive functioning skills (e.g., difficulty focusing attentional processes; lacks strategies to reflect upon information being read).

Beyond reading comprehension and fluency issues, Billy's performance on speeded math tasks involving simple single-digit computations was also weak. Billy's low performance primarily reflected issues with speed, as nearly all of his responses were accurate.

Notwithstanding the aforementioned weaknesses, Billy's overall math performance, when considering basic computational skills and math problem-solving skills in untimed conditions, was Average. However, Billy's performance on the Oral and Written Expression Composites, as well as the Basic Reading Composite, was in the Low Average range, but still within the normal limits of functioning. It is noteworthy that although Billy's performance on a single oral expression task was a normative weakness, it was determined that this performance was contrary to his classroom functioning and, therefore, not reflective of his actual expressive language skills.

In terms of cognitive performance (see Rapid Reference 10.9), Billy's WISC-IV Full Scale IQ was not interpretable due to substantial variability across the indexes comprising this global ability score. However, because Billy's Verbal

Rapid Reference 10.8

Billy's Academic Test Performance on the Wechsler Individual Achievement Test–Third Edition (WIAT-III)

BATTERY Academic Test Composite	Score	Performance	General Impressions	Link to Classroom Performance
WIAT-III			Decoding skills are adequately developed; however, Billy's reading speed and reading comprehension are weak. A WIAT-III Skills Analysis revealed particular difficulty with inferential reading comprehension questions. Difficulties with literal comprehension questions were also noted but likely attributable to behavioral issues (e.g., not referencing the text when answering questions, despite being encouraged to do so).	Billy decodes well during read-aloud activities. He participates minimally during discussion of independently read text, particularly when students are asked to make predictions regarding the direction of the story line or the thoughts and feelings of the characters. Billy will often try to keep up with the class during independent reading assignments and will frequently reference where his classmates are in the passage (e.g., asking, "What page are you on?"). As such, Billy often skips text to catch up, which further impedes his comprehension.
Reading Comprehension	80	Normative Weakness		
Oral Reading Fluency				
Word Reading	82	Normative Weakness		
Pseudoword Decoding	90	Average/WNL		
	92	Average/WNL		
Total Reading Composite		**Normative Weakness**		
Basic Reading Composite	**82**	**Average/WNL**		
Reading Comp and Fluency	**91**	**Normative**		
	77	**Weakness**		
WIAT-III			Billy's writing skills in terms of mechanics and idea generation	Billy's writing ability in the classroom is described by his
Spelling	92	Average/WNL		
Sentence Composition	90	Average/WNL		

(continued)

BATTERY Academic Test Composite	Score	Performance	General Impressions	Link to Classroom Performance
Essay Composition	88	Low Average/WNL	are adequately developed. While Billy's performance was within normal limits across writing measures, the impact of his long-term retrieval weaknesses was evident on the WIAT-III essay task. Specifically, Billy had difficulty generating supporting reasons for his topic statement and recalling specific facts relating to his essay topic. Moreover, Billy was still writing when the time limit expired. Although any additional statements were not included in scoring, he continually stated, "I didn't finish," and asked for additional time.	teacher as "average." He performs best on writing homework where time restrictions are not an issue. During in-class writing tasks, Billy does not always finish his work, but the work completed is generally of good quality. At times, Billy's writing is verbose, as he uses many words to explain a simple concept, which is likely due to his long-term retrieval weaknesses.
Written Expression	**87**	**Low Average/ WNL**		
WIAT-III				
Math Problem Solving	88	Low Average/WNL	Billy's math skills are generally in the lower end of the average range. He exhibited the most difficulty with speeded tasks, which is likely the result of his overall weakness in processing speed.	Billy's math performance in the classroom is stronger than his reading performance. Although Billy struggles with reading word problems, which extends the time he requires to complete math tasks, once he understands the problem, his
Numerical Operations	95	Average/WNL		
Math Fluency—Addition	88	Low Average/WNL		
Math Fluency—Subtraction	86	Low Average/WNL		
Math Fluency—Multiplication	84	Normative Weakness		

Math Fluency Composite	84	Normative Weakness
Mathematics Composite	90	Average/WNL

computations are typically accurate. Billy tends to have the most difficulty on math word problems that require abstraction or higher-level thinking (e.g., math logic problems). These difficulties are consistent with his identified weaknesses in fluid reasoning and the difficulties described by his teacher (e.g., difficulty generalizing or abstracting). However, his reasoning difficulties do not exert a functional impact on his overall math performance at this time, as math reasoning comprises just one part of his general math curriculum. That is, Billy's curriculum focuses heavily on computation.

WIAT-III

Listening Comprehension	95	Average/WNL
Oral Expression	82	Normative Weakness
Oral Language Composite	87	Low Average/WNL

However, Billy demonstrated variability on the WIAT-III Oral Word Fluency task, which comprises the Oral Expression Composite. His performance on this task reflected a normative weakness and was related to the tasks demands

Billy's teacher estimated his expressive and receptive language abilities to be age- and grade-appropriate. Notwithstanding, she noted that Billy sometimes requires "time to collect his thoughts," prior to offering an oral

(continued)

BATTERY Academic Test Composite	Score	Performance	General Impressions	Link to Classroom Performance
			(i.e., the ability to quickly retrieve specific words within narrow parameters, such as words sharing a similar beginning sound). Billy's deficits in processing speed and long-term retrieval, specifically naming facility, made this task difficult for him. Notwithstanding, Billy's score on the Expressive Vocabulary task that comprises this cluster was within normal limits.	response. Despite the time he requires, the quality of his oral response is similar to that of most same-age and grade peers in his class.

Note. Scores are based on a scale having a mean of 100 and a standard deviation of 15. WNL = Within Normal Limits (standard scores of 85–115, inclusive). Normative Weakness = standard scores <85; Low Average = standard scores of 85–89, inclusive; Average = standard scores of 90–110, inclusive.

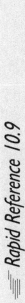

Billy's Cognitive Test Performance on the WISC-IV and Selected Tests from the WJ III

BATTERY Cognitive Test Composite	Score	Performance	General Impressions	Link to Classroom Performance
WISC-IV				
Similarities	6	Normative Weakness	Word knowledge and ability to answer questions involving social judgment is similar to that of most children his age from the general population; reasoning with verbal information is weak.	Often misinterprets meaning of words spoken by teacher, and experiences difficulty making inferences and predictions on reading tasks.
Vocabulary	9	Average/WNL		
Comprehension	8	Average/WNL		
VCI (*Gc*)	**87**	**Low Average/WNL**		
WISC-IV				
Block Design	14	Normative Strength	Billy's difficulty with higher-level reasoning on Similarities is further supported by his Gf Clinical Cluster. Although Billy performed in the High Average range on a task of Spatial Relations and Visualization, he demonstrated difficulty on visual tasks requiring him to reason inductively and deductively.	Difficulty generalizing or abstracting.
Picture Completion	11	Average/WNL		
Picture Concepts	6	Normative Weakness		
Matrix Reasoning	6	Normative Weakness		
PRI (*Gf/Gv*)	**92**	**Average/WNL**		
Gv Clinical Cluster	**114**	**High Average/WNL**		
Gf Clinical Cluster	**77**	**Normative Weakness**		

(continued)

BATTERY Cognitive Test Composite	Score	Performance	General Impressions	Link to Classroom Performance
WISC-IV				
Digit Span	10	Average/WNL	Billy demonstrated average memory ability compared to same-age peers from the general population.	Teacher reported some difficulties with memory, as evidenced by having to reexplain concepts taught in class on the same day.
Letter-Number Sequencing	9	Average/WNL		
WMI (Gsm)	**97**	**Average/WNL**		
WISC-IV				
Coding	5	Normative Weakness	Billy's difficulties with timed tasks are supported by his low Processing Speed Index on the WISC-IV. Billy consistently had difficulty completing items within the time allotted. On a speeded task where he was required to quickly match similar numbers, he became very confused and would physically try to cover up those numbers that did not match, in an attempt to see what was left that did match. On another task that required him to copy a series of symbols that were paired with numbers according to a key, Billy took care in writing the symbols, and	Billy's rate of work completion is slow in general, especially during reading tasks. He is consistently the last person to still be reading instructions, reading his leveled reader, or reading test questions. He is described as the student who always raises his hand when asked, "Who needs more time?"
Symbol Search	6	Normative Weakness		
PSI (Gs)	**75**	**Normative Weakness**		

WJ III			
Visual-Auditory Learning	82	Normative Weakness	continually referenced his work against the key to ensure that it was accurate. In both instances, Billy's responses were accurate; however, he completed a minimal number of items on each task.
Retrieval Fluency	80	Normative Weakness	
Long-Term Retrieval (Glr) Factor	**78**	**Normative Weakness**	Billy has a deficit in long-term retrieval. He experiences difficulty with both associative memory (connecting known information to new information) and retrieving known information quickly.
Rapid Picture Naming	83	Normative Weakness	Billy's teacher describes him as a student who is inconsistent in his performance. She reported that Billy seems to remember things in class when they are taught, but then requires a detailed re-explanation of concepts to understand and complete his homework. Billy does better on tasks after they are reviewed more than once. When given cumulative tests, Billy often performs most poorly on the information that was taught earlier in the year.
WJ III			
Sound Blending	105	Average/WNL	Billy's auditory processing skills are average, suggesting that his present difficulties with fluent decoding are not the result of an underlying deficit in
Auditory Attention	109	Average/WNL	Billy can decode text accurately, and demonstrates good listening skills during individual and group instruction.

(continued)

BATTERY Cognitive Test Composite	Score	Performance	General Impressions	Link to Classroom Performance
Auditory Processing (*Ga*) Factor	107	Average/WNL	phonemic awareness. His deficit on a rapid automatic naming task suggests that the speed at which he retrieves those phonological representations is slow.	

Note. WISC-IV = Wechsler Intelligence Scale for Children–Fourth Edition; WJ III = Woodcock-Johnson III Tests of Cognitive Abilities. Scores on WISC-IV Indexes and WJ III tests are based on a scale having a mean of 100 and a standard deviation of 15. Scores on WISC-IV subtests are based on a scale having a mean of 10 and standard deviation of 3. WNL = Within Normal Limits (standard scores of 85–115 and scaled scores of 7–10, inclusive). Normative Weakness = standard scores < 85 and scaled scores < 7; Low Average = standard scores of 85–89, inclusive; Average = standard scores of 90–110 and scaled scores of 8–12, inclusive; High Average = standard scores of 111–115, inclusive; Normative Strength = standard scores >115 and scaled scores >13. *Gc* = Crystallized Intelligence; *Gf* = Fluid Intelligence; *Gv* = Visual Processing; *Ga* = Auditory Processing; *Gsm* = Short-Term Memory; *Glr* = Long-Term Retrieval; *Gs* = Processing Speed; VCI = Verbal Comprehension Index; PRI = Perceptual Reasoning Index; WMI = Working Memory Index; PSI = Processing Speed Index.

Comprehension Index (VCI; standard score = 87) and Perceptual Reasoning Index (PRI; standard score = 92) performances were similar, a General Ability Index (GAI), which removes the influence of Working Memory (standard score = 97) and Processing Speed (standard score = 75), was calculated. Billy obtained a GAI of 89 (90% confidence interval = 84–95), which is ranked at the 23rd percentile and classified as Low Average/Within Normal Limits. It is noteworthy that although Billy's VCI and PRI were within normal limits (i.e., standard score ≥ 85), Billy demonstrated normative weaknesses on specific subtests within these domains. Moreover, Billy's performances on PRI tasks varied substantially, rendering this index uninterpretable. As such, separate WISC-IV clinical clusters for Fluid Reasoning (*Gf*-nonverbal) and Visual Processing (*Gv*) were calculated based on the recommendation of Flanagan and Kaufman (2009). While the *Gv* clinical cluster was High Average (standard score = 114), the *Gf*-nonverbal clinical cluster was a normative weakness (standard score = 77). Billy's Processing Speed Index was in the normative weakness range, as well (i.e., standard score < 85). Supplemental measures from the WJ III indicated that Billy's Auditory Processing (*Ga*) was Average (standard score = 107) while his Long-term Retrieval (*Glr*) fell in the normative weakness range (standard score = 78).

Billy Meets Criteria for SLD Following the CHC-Based Operational Definition

While examining Billy's cognitive and academic data from a normative perspective (i.e., relative to same-age peers from the general population), it is also feasible to determine whether Billy meets criteria for SLD following the operational definition described in this chapter. A review of Billy's academic data revealed a normative weakness in math fluency, which was consistent with teacher reports regarding a generally slow rate of work completion. Noteworthy is the fact that Billy's slow speed did not appear to be due to a lack of basic skill acquisition in terms of math computations, but rather a general slowness in the retrieval of known math facts. Billy also demonstrated normative weaknesses in reading fluency and reading comprehension that were consistent with classroom performance, parent and teacher reports, work samples, data from prereferral interventions, and general observations. Based on these findings, Billy meets criteria at Level I of the operational definition. That is, he exhibits weaknesses or deficits on standardized norm-referenced tests in one or more areas of academic achievement, and these weaknesses are corroborated by multiple data sources.

Billy also meets criteria at Level II of the operational definition because his poor academic performance is not primarily attributable to any of the exclusionary factors listed in the operational definition. Specifically, Billy's hearing and vision are normal; his attendance is good; his health history is unremarkable; and his teacher implemented prereferral interventions in an attempt to address his academic weaknesses. Additionally, although Billy demonstrates anxiety, which contributes to his difficulties and sometimes has a negative effect on his achievement, it is not judged to be the primary cause of his academic skill deficiencies (see Rapid Reference 10.10 for additional information on Billy's current social/emotional functioning).

Billy meets Level III criteria of the operational definition because his performance in one or more cognitive abilities and/or processes that are related to his academic skill deficiencies is weak or deficient. That is, Billy demonstrated normative weaknesses in *Gf*, *Glr*, and Processing Speed (*Gs*). These weaknesses are related directly to his documented difficulties with reading and math fluency and reading comprehension, specifically comprehension tasks requiring Billy to make inferences or predictions about what he has read. A reevaluation of exclusionary criteria following cognitive testing suggested that his performance on cognitive tasks cannot be primarily attributed to exclusionary factors.

Billy meets criteria at Level IV of the operational definition because his pattern of academic and cognitive strengths and weaknesses is consistent with SLD. Specifically, Billy demonstrates a below-average aptitude-achievement consistency within an otherwise average or normal ability profile. Billy's aptitude (for reading) is composed of weaknesses or deficits in *Gf*, *Glr*, and *Gs*. His performances in these cognitive areas, as well as in reading (comprehension and fluency), were below average (demonstrating aptitude-achievement consistency). In contrast, his functioning within the domains of Crystallized Intelligence (*Gc*), Short-Term Memory (*Gsm*), *Gv*, and *Ga* were generally Average; his WISC-IV GAI was within normal limits; and the SLD Assistant (Flanagan et al., 2007) supported an otherwise average or normal ability profile for Billy, despite his specific cognitive weaknesses. Furthermore, there are no statistically significant or clinically meaningful differences between Billy's cognitive and academic deficits, but there are statistically significant differences between his cognitive strengths and his cognitive and academic deficits. Finally, it is believed that Billy's overall cognitive ability (along with his generally positive attitude toward school and his desire to learn and achieve) will enable him to benefit substantially from tailored instruction, as well as compensatory strategies and accommodations.

Because criteria were met across Levels I through IV of the operational definition, Billy was identified as SLD (in the areas of Reading Comprehension and Reading Fluency). Finally, Billy meets Level V criteria because the MDT determined that his skill deficits in reading cannot be properly remediated, accommodated, or otherwise compensated for without the assistance of individualized special education services.

Billy's Functioning on the Behavior Assessment System for Children, 2nd Edition (BASC-2)

Measure/Procedure	Performance	General Impressions	Link to Classroom Performance
BASC-2 TRS Attention	Clinically Significant	Billy's teacher endorsed issues with attention to a significant degree in the classroom. Although difficulties with attention were likewise endorsed in the home environment, not to the same degree as in the school setting. Other issues endorsed by Billy's teacher included difficulty keeping up with the rest of the class during lessons and failure to complete assignments within the allotted time. Billy's parents also endorsed difficulty with completing homework assignments. Although Billy regularly turns in homework, his parents noted that it requires much effort, time, and assistance. Beyond issues with attention and learning, Billy's teacher and parents reported that Billy often complains of stomachaches and other physical ailments (headaches), noting that such complaints largely occur when Billy is feeling particularly vulnerable	Billy's teacher describes him as a student who can initiate a task but who gradually "loses focus." The difficulties described in the classroom setting were observed during testing sessions, and tended to occur when Billy perceived a task as difficult or when the task was lengthy. At these times, Billy stayed engaged in the task but began responding haphazardly. Billy's teacher also reported difficulties with his rate of work completion. He is often the last student to complete work and regularly asks for "more time." Finally, Billy's teacher noted that he often requires a review of information before he can begin working on an independent assignment. This is especially true if some time has passed between the initial presentation of a concept and the assignment of independent work
BASC-2 PRS Attention	Average		
BASC-2 SRP Attention	Average		
BASC-2 TRS Learning Problems	Clinically Significant		
BASC-2 (TRS, PRS) Somatization	Clinically Significant		
BASC-2 (TRS, PRS, SRP) Anxiety	Clinically Significant		

(continued)

Measure/Procedure	Performance	General Impressions	Link to Classroom Performance
		(e.g., during a test, when he is running out of time; during lengthy homework assignments).	intended to reinforce the concept. Although Billy's teacher noted that he becomes inattentive during tasks, she explained that his need for a review of information is not usually related to a lack of attention. In light of his cognitive data, this latter weakness is most likely explained by Billy's deficits in long-term retrieval.
Parent and Teacher Interview	Significant	Consistent with BASC-2 results, teacher and parent interviews suggest that Billy is anxious and that his anxiety surrounds his academic performance. Specifically, Billy is often afraid to offer a response in class for "fear of being wrong," as explained by his teacher. Billy's mother reported that his anxiety is compounded by his own awareness of his academic difficulties and limitations, as well as the social repercussions of such difficulties (e.g., kids becoming impatient with the time it takes him to read aloud).	In the classroom, Billy's anxiety sometimes manifests as disengagement from a task. This disengagement typically occurs once Billy perceives a task as overwhelming, or when he becomes aware of the social repercussions of failure. Finally, Billy's rate of work completion is further slowed by his anxiety, as he will work in a slow and deliberate manner on tasks that bring about anxiety (e.g., reading comprehension). Billy's mother was quick to note that even when he isn't anxious, he works slowly, though the anxiety certainly adds to the time he takes.

The scales reported in this table reflect either clinically significant findings or discrepant results (i.e., parent versus teacher ratings of attention). All other BASC-2 scales (not reported in this table) were within normal limits. TRS = Teacher Rating Scales; PRS = Parent Rating Scales; SRP = Self-Report of Personality.

Tailoring Interventions Based on the Results of a Comprehensive Evaluation

Tailoring instruction and intervention to address Billy's academic weaknesses warrants careful consideration of his cognitive assessment results. This is accomplished by using Rapid References 10.9 and 10.11. Rapid Reference 10.9 describes Billy's cognitive strengths and weaknesses and how his weaknesses manifest in the classroom. Rapid Reference 10.11 includes information about (a) the major cognitive domains of functioning in CHC theory, (b) how deficits in these domains manifest in general as well as in specific academic areas, and (c) interventions and recommendations that can be tailored to the unique learning needs of the individual. In addition to understanding an individual's cognitive strengths and weaknesses, tailoring interventions involves a consideration of factors such as curricular demands, the student's interests and level of motivation, availability of resources, an understanding of the student's home environment and level of parental support, and so forth.

The information in Rapid Reference 10.9 shows that Billy demonstrates a deficit in reasoning (WISC-IV Matrix Reasoning, Picture Concepts) and that this weakness also impacts his reasoning on language-based tasks (WISC-IV Similarities). Rapid Reference 10.5 documents a relationship between Inductive (I) and General Sequential Reasoning (RG) and reading comprehension. Given that Billy demonstrated low fluid reasoning and low reading comprehension, with noted difficulties in inferencing, we can begin to look at how to intervene with his reading comprehension difficulty. A review of recommendations in Rapid Reference 10.11 for intervening with fluid reasoning deficits reveals several suggestions beyond the interventions Billy has already received. For example, the use of graphic organizers to arrange information Billy has read in a visual format seems appropriate, particularly because Billy has strength in the area of *Gv*. As such, Billy can be taught how to use a story map to identify the main idea in a text (see Rapid Reference 10.12). Additionally, to address Billy's fluid reasoning deficit, a recommendation might be made to move Billy to a cooperative reading group that consists of students with strong inferencing skills. In this way, students can be asked to "think aloud" and engage in brainstorming when answering reading questions. Finally, the use of a reciprocal teaching strategy may assist in further exposing Billy to "think aloud" activities, specifically with the "predicting" aspect of this method (see Rapid Reference 10.13).

Beyond reasoning, it is essential to address Billy's weaknesses in *Glr* (i.e., associative memory and naming facility). Specifically, Billy's associative

Rapid Reference 10.11

Manifestations of CHC Broad Ability Weaknesses and Suggested Recommendations and Interventions

CHC Broad Ability	CHC Broad Ability Definition	General Manifestations of the CHC Broad Ability	Manifestations of the CHC Broad Ability in Academic Areas	Recommendations/ Interventions
Fluid Reasoning (Gf)	• Novel reasoning and problem solving • Processes are minimally dependent on learning and acculturation • Involves manipulating rules, abstracting, generalizing, and identifying logical relationships	**Difficulties with:** *Higher-level thinking* • Transferring or generalizing learning • Deriving solutions for novel problems • Extending knowledge through critical thinking • Perceiving and applying underlying rules or process(es) to solve problems	**Reading Difficulties:** • Inferential reading comprehension • Abstracting main idea (s) **Math Difficulties:** • Math reasoning (word problems) • Internalizing procedures and processes used to solve problems • Apprehending relationships between numbers **Writing Difficulties:** • Essay writing and generalizing concepts • Developing a theme	• Develop student's skill in categorizing objects and drawing conclusions. • Use demonstrations to externalize the reasoning process. • Gradually offer guided practice (e.g, guided questions list) to promote internalization of procedures or process(es). • Offer targeted feedback. • Use cooperative learning. • Implement reciprocal teaching.

		• Comparing and contrasting ideas	• Use graphic organizers to arrange information in visual format. • Institute metacognitive strategies. • Compare new concepts to previously learned (same versus different) • Make use of analogies, similes, and metaphors when presenting tasks.
Crystallized Intelligence (Gc)	• Breadth and depth and knowledge of a culture • Developed through formal education and general learning experiences • Stores of information and declarative and procedural knowledge • Ability to verbally communicate and reason with previously learned procedures	*Difficulties with:* • Vocabulary acquisition • Knowledge acquisition • Comprehending language • Fact-based/informational questions • Using prior knowledge to support learning	***Reading Difficulties:*** • Decoding and comprehension ***Math Difficulties:*** • Understanding math concepts and the "vocabulary of math" ***Writing Difficulties:*** • Grammar (syntax) • Bland writing with limited descriptors • Verbose writing • Inappropriate word usage	• Provide an environment rich in language and experiences. • Ensure frequent practice with and exposure to words. • Read aloud to children. • Vary reading purpose (leisure, information). • Work on vocabulary building. • Teach morphology. • Use text talks.

(continued)

CHC Broad Ability	CHC Broad Ability Definition	General Manifestations of the CHC Broad Ability	Manifestations of the CHC Broad Ability in Academic Areas	Recommendations/ Interventions
Auditory Processing (*Ga*)	• Ability to analyze and synthesize auditory information	*Difficulties with:* • Hearing information presented orally; initially processing oral information • Paying attention, especially in the presence of background noise • Discerning the direction from which auditory information is coming • Foreign language acquisition • Acquiring receptive vocabulary	***Language Difficulties:*** • Understanding class lessons • Expressive language—"poverty of thought" ***Reading Difficulties:*** • Acquiring phonics skills • Decoding and comprehension • Using phonetic strategies ***Math Difficulties:*** • Word problems ***Writing Difficulties:*** • Spelling • Note taking • Poor quality of writing	• Implement phonemic awareness activities. • Emphasize sight-word reading. • Teach comprehension monitoring (e.g., Does the word I heard/read make sense in context?). • Annunciate sounds in words in an emphatic manner when teaching new words for reading or spelling. • Use work preview/ text preview to clarify unknown words.

				• Provide guided notes during note-taking activities. • Build in time for clarification questions related to items "missed" or "misheard" during lecture. • Supplement oral instructions with written instructions. • Shorten instructions. • Arrange preferential seating. • Localize sound source for student • Minimize background noise.
Long-Term Retrieval (*Glr*)	• Ability to store information (e.g., concepts, words, facts) and fluently retrieve it later through association	*Difficulties with:* • Learning new concepts • Retrieving or recalling information by using association • Performing consistently across different task formats (e.g., recognition versus recall formats)	***Reading Difficulties:*** • Accessing background knowledge to support new learning while reading (Associative Memory deficit) • Slow to access phonological representations during decoding (RAN deficit)	• Repeated practice with and review of newly presented information • Teach memory strategies (verbal rehearsal to support encoding, use of mnemonic devices)

(*continued*)

CHC Broad Ability	CHC Broad Ability Definition	General Manifestations of the CHC Broad Ability	Manifestations of the CHC Broad Ability in Academic Areas	Recommendations/ Interventions
		• Speed with which information is retrieved and/or learned • Paired learning (visual-auditory) • Recalling specific information (words, facts)	**Math Difficulties:** • Recalling procedures to use for math problems • Memorizing and recalling math facts **Writing Difficulties:** • Accessing words to use during essay writing • Specific writing tasks (compare and contrast; persuasive writing) • Note-taking **Language Difficulties:** • Expressive—circumlocutions, speech fillers, "interrupted" thought, pauses • Receptive—making connections throughout oral presentations (e.g., class lecture)	• Use multiple modalities when teaching new concepts (pair written with verbal information)* • Limit the amount of new material to be learned; introduce new concepts gradually and with a lot of context • Be mindful of when new concepts are presented • Make explicit the associations between newly learned and prior information • Use lists to facilitate recall (prompts) • Expand vocabulary to minimize impact of word retrieval deficits

Processing Speed (Gs)	• Speed of processing, particularly when pressured to pay focused attention	*Difficulties with:*	***Reading Difficulties:***	• Build in wait-time for student when fluency of retrieval is an issue
		• Efficient processing of information	• Slow reading speed	
			• Impaired comprehension	• Provide background knowledge first before asking a question to "prime" student for retrieval
	• Usually measured by tasks that require rapid processing, but are relatively easy	• Quickly perceiving relationships (similarities and differences between stimuli or information)	• Need to reread for understanding	
			Math Difficulties:	• Provide opportunities for repeated practice.
		• Working within time parameters	• Automatic computations	• Conduct speed drills.
			• Computational speed is slow though accurate	• Introduce computer activities that require quick, simple decisions.
		• Completing simple, rote tasks quickly	• Slow speed can result in reduced accuracy due to memory decay	• Extend time for work
				• Reduce the quantity of work required.
			Writing Difficulties:	• Increase "wait" times, both after questions are asked and after responses are given.
			• Limited output due to time factors	
			• Labored process results in reduced motivation to produce	

(continued)

CHC Broad Ability	CHC Broad Ability Definition	General Manifestations of the CHC Broad Ability	Manifestations of the CHC Broad Ability in Academic Areas	Recommendations/ Interventions
			Language Difficulties: • Cannot retrieve information quickly—slow, disrupted speech because cannot get out thoughts quickly enough • Is slow to process incoming information; puts demands on memory store, which can result in information overload and loss of meaning	
Visual Processing (Gv)	• Ability to analyze and visualize information	Difficulties with: • Recognizing patterns • Reading maps, graphs, charts • Attending to fine visual detail • Recalling visual information • Appreciation of spatial characteristics of objects (e.g., size, length)	**Reading Difficulties:** • Orthographic coding (using visual features of letters to decode) • Sight-word acquisition • Using charts and graphs within a text in conjunction with reading • Comprehension of text involving spatial	• Capitalize on student's phonemic skills for decoding tasks. • Teach orthographic strategies for decoding (e.g., word length, shape of word). • Overlay graphs and charts with visual labels.

Ability	Characteristics	Academic Difficulties	Instructional Strategies
	• Recognition of spatial orientation of objects	concepts (e.g., social studies text describing physical boundaries, movement of troops along a specified route) ***Math Difficulties:*** • Number alignment during computations • Reading and interpreting graphs, tables, and charts ***Writing Difficulties:*** • Spelling sight-words • Spatial planning during writing tasks (e.g., no attention to margins, words that overhang a line) • Inconsistent size, spacing, position, and slant of letters	• Provide oral explanation for visual concepts. • Review spatial concepts and support comprehension through use of hands-on activities and manipulatives (e.g., using models to demonstrate the moon's orbital path). • Highlight margins during writing tasks. • Provide direct handwriting practice. • Use graph paper to assist with number alignment.
Short-Term Memory (Gsm)	• Ability to hold information in immediate awareness and use or transform it within a few seconds	*Difficulties with:* • Following oral and written instructions • Remembering information long enough to apply it • Remembering the sequence of information • Rote memorization ***Reading Difficulties:*** • Reading comprehension • Decoding multisyllabic words • Orally retelling or paraphrasing what one has read	• Provide opportunities for repeated practice and review. • Provide supports (e.g., lecture notes, study guides, written directions) to supplement oral instruction.

(continued)

CHC Broad Ability	CHC Broad Ability Definition	General Manifestations of the CHC Broad Ability	Manifestations of the CHC Broad Ability in Academic Areas	Recommendations/ Interventions
			Math Difficulties: • Rote memorization of facts • Remembering mathematical procedures • Multistep problems and regrouping • Extracting information to be used in word problems ***Writing Difficulties:*** • Spelling multisyllabic words • Redundancy in writing (word and conceptual levels) • Note taking	• Break down instructional steps for student. • Provide visual support (e.g., times table) to support acquisition of basic math facts. • Outline math procedures for student and provide procedural guides or flashcards for the student to use when approaching problems. • Highlight important information within a word problem. • Have student write all steps and show all work for math computations.

≡ Rapid Reference 10.12

Story Map 1

Write notes in each section.

Setting:	Time:	Place:

↓

Characters:

↓

Problem:

↓ ↔ **Plot/Events:**

Resolution:

≡ Rapid Reference 10.13

Name:_____

Chapter or Book title: _____

Reciprocal Teaching Worksheet

http://www.itre.uef.edu/forpd/

Prediction: Before you begin to read the selection, look at the title or cover, scan the pages to read the major headings, and look at any illustrations. Write down your prediction(s).	
Prediction:	**Support:**
Main Ideas: As you finish reading each paragraph or key section of text, identify the main idea of that paragraph or section.	**Questions:** For each main idea listed, write down at least one question.
Main Idea 1: _____	Question 1: _____
Main Idea 2: _____	Question 2: _____
Main Idea 3: _____	Question 3: _____
Main Idea 4: _____	Question 4: _____
Main Idea 5: _____	Question 5: _____
Summarize: Write a brief summary of what you read.	
Clarify: Copy down words, pharases, or sentences in the passage that are unclear. Then explain how you clarified your understanding.	
Word of Pharase:	**Clarify:**

memory deficit limits his ability to access background knowledge and to see how new information relates to already known information. To address this weakness, Billy should be given text previews. For instance, a resource room teacher could review a reading selection with him and engage him in conversation that would "prime" his knowledge (e.g., "This story is about hockey; let's think about all the things we already know about hockey."). In addition, Billy's general classroom teacher should make explicit associations between new and prior information, whenever possible (e.g., "Today we are going to do a science experiment similar to the one we did last week, in that we will be generating a hypothesis, making predictions, and testing the hypothesis").

Billy's rapid automatic naming (RAN) deficit impacts the speed with which he accesses phonological representations of words during reading. While Billy's decoding appears automatic at this time, as his content area curriculum progresses (e.g., science, social studies) and he is faced with unfamiliar or technical terms, he may need to rely on his phonetic skills to decode such words. It is likely that his deficit in RAN will interfere with both fluency and comprehension. Therefore, the text preview method should continue to be used so that Billy can identify and practice with unknown words prior to reading. A recommendation could also be made to his general education teacher to shorten the amount of text he is required to read and/or extend the time that he has for reading, to help compensate for his deficit in RAN, especially in content area texts (e.g., science, social studies) where Billy is likely to encounter several unknown words.

Finally, to accommodate Billy's weakness in *Gs*, a recommendation for extended time during independent reading should be considered. A home-based recommendation to engage in paired-reading activities using grade-level text might also be offered to Billy's mother, as it would allow Billy *repeated practice* with grade-appropriate, high-frequency words.

In all, systematically reviewing Rapid Reference 10.11 and Billy's specific cognitive and academic ability profile within the context of the entire case allowed for tailored recommendations. Unlike the remedial instruction Billy received that focused on a *manifest academic difficulty* in global reading via direct instruction in the use of context cues and immediate feedback for decoding errors, the recommendations detailed previously also addressed the *cognitive deficits* that underlie the academic difficulties. Practitioners are encouraged to review the resources included in Rapid Reference 10.14 for further information regarding the interventions and recommendations presented in this chapter.

DON'T FORGET
....

It is critical to continue to monitor progress following any change in a student's intervention. Regardless of where interventions take place (e.g., the general education setting at Tier 3 or the special education setting), it is the responsibility of the scientist-practitioner (e.g., school psychologist) to evaluate current practice (tailored interventions) to guide future practice (maintain intervention, change intervention). In other words, we must engage in practice and research simultaneously to effect positive change in the students with whom we work (Della Toffalo, 2010).

≡ Rapid Reference 10.14
....

Recommendations for Further Reading on Linking Assessment Data to Intervention

Mather, N., & Jaffe, L. (2002). *Woodcock-Johnson III: Reports, recommendations, and strategies.* Hoboken, NJ: Wiley.

McCarney, S. B., & Cummins-Wunderlich, K. (2006). *Prereferral intervention manual, third edition.* Columbia, MO: Hawthorne Educational Services, Inc.

Wendling, B., & Mather, N. (2009). *Essentials of evidence-based academic interventions.* Hoboken, NJ: Wiley.

CONCLUSION

The operational definition of SLD presented in this chapter is grounded in CHC theory and research, which assists in (a) determining whether specific cognitive ability or processing deficits are the probable cause of a student's academic difficulties; (b) distinguishing between SLD and other conditions and disorders (e.g., ID, SL), through both inclusionary and exclusionary criteria; and (c) identifying targets for remediation, compensation, accommodation, and/or curriculum modification (see also Flanagan et al., 2010). Because the operational definition is informed by the network of validity evidence in support of CHC theory in particular, it has the potential to increase the reliability and validity of SLD classification in the schools. Notwithstanding, the CHC-based operational definition, like other alternative research-based methods or third method approaches to SLD identification, must be studied to determine its reliability and validity.

≡ Rapid Reference 10.15.

Criteria for Determining the Adequacy and Utility of Diagnostic Systems (Keogh, 2005)

- *Homogeneity.* Do category members resemble one another?[1]
- *Reliability.* Is there agreement about who should be included in the category?
- *Validity.* Does category membership provide consistent information?

[1]Because individuals with SLDs are a *heterogeneous* group, it seems unreasonable to expect that this criterion of an SLD diagnostic system can be met. However, individuals with SLDs share a common set of features, as outlined in Rapid Reference 10.2 (e.g., academic skill deficit, cognitive ability or processing weakness(es), cognitive integrities or overall average intellectual ability, statistically significant differences between cognitive strengths and cognitive and academic weaknesses, etc.). Thus, category members may possess a common set of characteristics (thereby meeting the homogeneity criterion) but still be heterogeneous in nature (e.g., some have academic deficits in reading, others in math; some have cognitive deficits in phonological processing, others in memory).

Keogh (2005) discussed criteria for determining the adequacy and utility of diagnostic systems, such as the ability-achievement discrepancy, RTI, and third method approaches. These criteria are included in Rapid Reference 10.15.

Keogh (2005) suggested that, "LD is real and that it describes problems that are distinct from other conditions subsumed under the broad category of problems in learning and achievement" (p. 101). The question is how to best capture the distinctiveness of SLD. Therefore, we offered the CHC-based operational definition for SLD identification. Future directions in SLD identification should focus on evaluating this and other third method approaches following Keogh's criteria. Until such research is made available, the operational definition presented here remains a viable and inherently practical alternative to the traditional ability-achievement discrepancy method and the RTI-only approach, and it certainly rests on a bed of evidence (derived primarily from the CHC, neuropsychology, assessment, and SLD literature). Indeed, when speaking about his own approach to identifying and intervening with students who have SLD, Della Toffalo (2010) stated,

> Make no mistake . . . integrated models of identifying (and serving) students with LDs do not arrive prepackaged along with dozens of studies touting their 'scientific validation.' However, they are evidence-based

because they emanate from the marriage of a collective body of knowledge that has been acquired through research in the fields of neuroscience, pedagogy, assessment, and intervention. (pp. 180–181)

Like most alternatives to the discrepancy and RTI-only approaches, the CHC-based operational definition *expands* the methods of assessment that are available to the practitioner, and culminates in a comprehensive understanding of the child that is clear and of value to all (Flanagan et al., 2010). When commenting on their own operational definition, as well as that of Flanagan and colleagues (2002), Kavale and colleagues (2005) stated,

> Even if a student never enters the special education system, the general education teacher, the student's parents, and the student him- or herself would receive valuable information regarding *why* there was such a struggle in acquiring academic content, to the point of possibly needing special education. (p. 12; emphasis added)

Not surprisingly, understanding *why* often leads to determining *how*—how to remediate, compensate, and accommodate weaknesses. Thus, it makes practical and clinical sense to gather data from a variety of assessment tools, including cognitive and neuropsychological tests, when students demonstrate an inadequate response to intervention. The developers and supporters of such comprehensive assessment approaches agree on this point (see Hale et al., in press).

In sum, SLD identification is complex and requires a great deal of empirical and clinical knowledge on the part of practitioners. Although many children's academic needs can be well served in the absence of information garnered from comprehensive evaluations, there continue to be children whose difficulties are neurologically based and who require specially designed instruction to overcome or compensate for their weaknesses, or to make appreciable gains academically. Obscuring the differences between individuals with general cognitive deficiencies (e.g., ID), slow learners, and those with SLD by adopting simpler methods of identification (e.g., absolute low achievement; RTI-only) interferes with our ability to study these groups and intervene with them more effectively. A greater correspondence between diagnosis and treatment may be achieved when SLD is defined more discretely via an operational definition.

🐟 TEST YOURSELF 🐟

1. An operational definition provides a process for the identification and classification of concepts that have been defined formally. True or False?

2. The CHC-based operational definition of SLD is arranged according to levels. At each level, the definition includes
   (a) defining characteristics regarding the nature of SLD.
   (b) the focus of evaluation for each characteristic.
   (c) examples of evaluation methods and relevant data sources.
   (d) the criteria that need to be met to establish that an individual possesses a particular characteristic of SLD.
   (e) all of the above.

3. Low academic achievement and a consideration of exclusionary factors are all that are necessary for a diagnosis of SLD. True or False?

4. According to IDEA (2004) a student may have an SLD in all of the following academic areas except
   (a) math calculation.
   (b) basic reading skill.
   (c) spelling.
   (d) listening comprehension.

5. Potential explanatory reasons for academic underachievement include
   (a) lack of motivation.
   (b) social/emotional disturbance.
   (c) performance anxiety.
   (d) psychiatric disorders.
   (e) all of the above.

6. A *below-average aptitude-achievement consistency* is a criterion for SLD identification in the CHC-based operational definition of SLD. True or False?

7. Children with SLD may require one or more of the following except
   (a) individualized instruction.
   (b) grade retention.
   (c) accommodations.
   (d) curricular modifications.

8. The term *aptitude* within the context of the CHC-based operational definition of SLD represents the specific cognitive ability or neuropsychological processing deficits that are empirically related to the academic skill deficiency. True or False?

9. Basic psychological processes include all of the following except

(a) auditory working memory.

(b) processing speed.

(c) perseverence.

(d) visual discrimination.

10. Flanagan and colleagues (2007) developed a program called the SLD Assistant, which is a means of parceling out cognitive deficits from global functioning and judging the robustness of the spared abilities or cognitive strengths. The SLD Assistant replaces clinical judgment because clinical judgment is often incorrect or inaccurate. True or False?

Answers: 1. True; 2. e; 3. False; 4. c; 5. e; 6. True; 7. b; 8. True; 9. c; 10. False.

Eleven

SEPARATING CULTURAL AND LINGUISTIC DIFFERENCES (CLD) FROM SPECIFIC LEARNING DISABILITY (SLD) IN THE EVALUATION OF DIVERSE STUDENTS

Difference or Disorder?

Samuel O. Ortiz

Following his translation of the Binet Scales into English in the early 1900s, and excited about this new tool that was about to revolutionize psychology and mental measurement, Henry Herbert Goddard quickly set about testing individuals to explore the nature of intelligence. He found a rather captive audience for his testing endeavors in the long lines of immigrants who had landed at Ellis Island in New York Harbor, waiting to be processed into the United States. After his assistants identified individuals likely to be "feeble-minded," based solely on appearance, Goddard proceeded to administer his test (which had now been translated from French to English) to scores of individuals who had just landed on the American shore for the very first time. Goddard (1913) described the scene as follows:

> We picked out one young man whom we suspected was defective, and, through the interpreter, proceeded to give him the test. The boy tested 8 by the Binet scale. The interpreter said, "I could not have done that when I came to this country," and seemed to think the test unfair. We convinced him that the boy was defective. (p. 105)

The question is and remains a relatively simple one: Do the results from testing indicate difference or disorder? But even when the answer was proposed to him directly, Goddard failed to discern or appreciate the significant impact that unfamiliarity with the culture upon which he had adapted his test (i.e., the United States), might be having on test performance and measurement of intelligence. Undeterred, and on the basis of such evidence and additional testing of four specific groups of immigrants from Europe, Goddard ultimately concluded, much to his horror, that on average, 80% of all Jewish, Hungarian, Italian, and Russian immigrants were, in the special word he coined for the purpose, *morons* or mentally defective (Goddard, 1917). Although the more likely explanation for his findings had been revealed by the interpreter, Goddard offered a mixed rationale that attributed poor performance to deficiency in both intelligence and personal qualities. Providing a harbinger of conclusions offered later by others, Goddard (1917) stated, "We cannot escape the general conclusion that these immigrants were of surprisingly low intelligence" (p. 251) and "it should be noted that the immigration of recent years is of a decidedly different character from the early immigration" (p. 266).

The issue arose again when the United States entered World War I. In 1918, Goddard joined other leading psychologists of the day, including Lewis Terman, David Wechsler, and Carl Brigham, to create a formidable team led by Robert M. Yerkes, under contract by the Department of the Army, to find a way to identify and differentiate men who should give orders (i.e., officers) from those who should take them (i.e., enlisted men). Under Yerkes's direction, the group developed the Army Mental Test, but they quickly recognized that among the 1.75 million men they would eventually test, many did not speak English, or speak it well. In addition, many did not read English and thus could not comprehend the instructions to the tests, let alone answer written multiple-choice items. The result was the development of two versions of the test: the Alpha (for those who could read American newspapers) and the Beta (for those who could not). The Beta was administered via verbal instructions in English; in addition, there was a formal demonstration that served as a model for what was expected of the examinee. Yerkes and his staff believed strongly in the innate quality of intelligence such that these minor accommodations were thought sufficient to obviate the effect of language proficiency or literacy on test results. Yerkes noted, however, that the average raw score on the Beta for native English speakers (those who had scored at the lowest level of the Alpha and were retested with the Beta) was 101.6 (classified as Very Superior, Grade A). The average raw score for nonnative English speakers who took the Beta only because they could not read in English or did not speak it was 77.8 (classified as Average, Grade C). In his

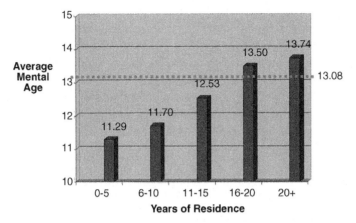

Figure 11.1. Mean Mental Age on Binet Scales in a Nonnative English-Speaking Sample From Yerkes's Data, as Analyzed by C. C. Brigham (1921)

*Note: The value of 13.08 represents the average mental age for all men evaluated with the Army Mental tests who were also given the Binet Scales.

1921 report to the Army, Yerkes admitted that "there are indications to the effect that individuals handicapped by language difficulty and illiteracy are penalized to an appreciable degree in Beta as compared with men not so handicapped" (p. 395). This thought appeared to trouble Yerkes, and he was later saved by the creative thinking of one of his lieutenants, Carl C. Brigham, who provided an alternative explanation for performance, which effectively eliminated language or literacy as a cause. During the course of the war, the group had collected data on the performance of nonnative English speakers using the Binet Scales. The results, presented in Figure 11.1, proved to be quite similar to the findings from the Beta, in that the longer an individual had lived in the United States, the higher that individual's mental age on the Binet Scales. Brigham reported these data in his 1923 treatise, *A Study of American Intelligence*, and offered the following conclusion:

> Instead of considering that our curve indicates a growth of intelligence with increasing length of residence, we are forced to take the reverse of the picture and accept the hypothesis that the curve indicates a gradual deterioration in the class of immigrants examined in the army, who came to this country in each succeeding 5 year period since 1902. (pp. 110–111) . . . The average intelligence of succeeding waves of immigration has become progressively lower. (p. 155)

It is not difficult to understand why early psychologists rejected outright or minimized performance differences that occurred as a function of cultural or linguistic differences. Not only did they have complete faith in the idea that intelligence was completely innately driven, but they were unapologetically "patriotic" in their world views. For example, Brigham (1923) noted that whereas the Alpha test may be affected by education, "examination Beta involves no English, and the tests cannot be considered as educational measures in any sense" (p. 100). His personal attitudes in this regard are evident in his other comments, to wit:

> If the tests used included some mysterious type of situation that was "typically American," we are indeed fortunate, for this is America, and the purpose of our inquiry is that of obtaining a measure of the character of our immigration. Inability to respond to a "typically American" situation is obviously an undesirable trait. (p. 96)

Although it is truly unfortunate that the passage of nearly nine decades of psychological research has done little to clarify the issue for practitioners, it is important to recognize that the attitudes and beliefs of a century ago have not necessarily faded from the mainstream fabric of the United States. For example, one need but mention the terms *black-white achievement gap* or *bilingual education* and a heated debate ensues quickly, with arguments that would sound very familiar to the people of Brigham's time. Thus, when we turn our attention to evaluate a construct as complex as specific learning disability (SLD) in culturally and linguistically diverse individuals, we must recognize that the methods, tools, and procedures we use bring with them a legacy that continues to favor notions that minimize or discount entirely environmental correlates of performance. This is not to say that the tests available to practitioners today are "biased" on the basis of their legacy. Rather, it means that it must be recognized that tests are products of the people who develop them and the culture from which they emanate. They must necessarily reflect those values in the content, design, and structure, and in this way they will always be "culture bound" (Sattler, 1992).

EVALUATION OF SLD IN CULTURALLY AND LINGUISTICALLY DIVERSE INDIVIDUALS

As may be evident in the other chapters in this volume, evaluation of SLD in monolingual English-speaking individuals is complex and wide-ranging with respect to methods, tools, procedures, and theory. When cultural and linguistic factors are considered—including first- and second-language acquisition processes, language proficiency, dominance, and development; native-language versus English-only instruction; level of acculturation; parental education and socioeconomic status; and opportunity for learning—it becomes clear that the complexity has increased exponentially (Harris & Llorente, 2005; Ortiz, 2008; Rhodes, Ochoa, & Ortiz, 2005).

Conversely, the fact that the nature of all of these influences is extraneous (they have no bearing on intrinsic ability per se) means that the basic issue is one of validity, as reflected in the simple question proposed at the outset. In formal terms, the question is whether the results obtained from testing are trustworthy and valid estimates of the individual's true or actual abilities (or lack thereof), or instead invalid measures reflecting more the individual's degree of English language proficiency or level of acculturation. Therefore, in practical terms, evaluation of SLD in culturally and linguistically diverse individuals must first attend to ensuring that measurement of the intended ability constructs was accomplished in a valid and defensible manner. If such validity cannot be established, then there is no point in going any further, because the results cannot be ascribed any meaning relative to the existence of SLD. In other words, if a practitioner engages in the process of identifying SLD in a diverse individual, it will not matter which theory, method, or definition is employed if the test results cannot be trusted. Consequently, the purpose of this chapter is to present an approach that is designed to assist practitioners in determining whether their test results (if such data were gathered) are valid and may be defensibly interpreted, or whether the results are invalid and primarily indicators of cultural and linguistic factors. The specific manner in which SLD is identified is a choice that remains in the purview of the practitioner's professional judgment and is not altered simply because the examinee comes from a diverse background. Any of the approaches described in the other chapters of this book, which utilize standardized tests, will serve well the purpose for guiding practitioners in making a determination of SLD. None of those approaches, however, will be defensible unless the practitioner has first determined the extent to which any obtained test results were potentially influenced by cultural and linguistic factors.

DON'T FORGET

Evaluation of SLD in culturally and linguistically diverse individuals must first attend to ensuring that measurement of the intended ability constructs was accomplished in a valid and defensible manner.

ENHANCING VALIDITY IN TESTING OF CULTURALLY AND LINGUISTICALLY DIVERSE INDIVIDUALS

Serious attention to the potential for inequitable evaluation and lack of fairness in testing emerged in concert with the civil rights movement that characterized the

1950s and 1960s. In the early 1970s, some researchers had turned their attention to the issue of unbiased evaluation and the pursuit of nondiscriminatory assessment (Oakland, 1976, Oakland & Laosa, 1976). The nexus of the problem was outlined clearly at that time to the extent that "it is recognized that nondiscriminatory assessment may be considered one dimension of the more general problem of valid assessment of any child" (Oakland, p. 1). Examination of such assessment practices has resulted in the creation of various ethical guidelines (American Psychological Association, 1990, 2002) and professional standards (American Education Research Association, American Psychological Association, & National Council on Measurement in Education, 1999), which require psychologists to adhere to various principles in establishing adequate reliability, validity, and fairness in testing. Whereas the prescriptions for fairness and bias reduction in testing are relatively clear, exactly how such adequacy is actually achieved in practice, and how it bears upon the validity of the obtained results, is rarely spelled out.

As noted in the previous section, little clinical significance can be ascribed to test results if the primary reason for the levels of obtained performance was due to external factors, namely cultural or linguistic variables. Even a reliably constructed and theoretically based composite cannot be said to be a valid measure of, say, short-term memory, unless it can be demonstrated convincingly that the result was not attenuated by extraneous factors, particularly cultural and linguistic variables. Good reliability is a necessary, but not sufficient condition for ensuring validity. And invalidity effectively precludes interpretation. It is not clear whether traditional methods of evaluation were derived specifically in response to the issue of validity, but it is clear that the approaches pay attention to it to one degree or another. There have been four general approaches offered in the literature as viable methods for addressing cultural and linguistic differences. Each one attempts to increase "fairness," in the hope that by doing so validity may be established. The relative advantages and disadvantages of these approaches are discussed in the following section.

Modified or Adapted Testing

Perhaps some of the first attempts to address the various problems involved in the evaluation of English learners with standardized tests involved modifications or adaptations of the test itself or its administration. Among the various adaptations that have been suggested, the most common include eliminating or not administering certain test items with presumed culturally biased content, mediating culturally based task concepts prior to administration, repeating verbal instructions to ensure full comprehension, accepting responses in either the native language or language of the test, administering only the subtests that do not rely on oral expression, and eliminating or modifying time constraints. Such procedures are extensions of what is often referred to as "testing the limits" and represent a clinical approach to evaluating diverse individuals. These procedures are designed to aid examinees in performing to the extent of their true ability by reducing aspects of the testing process that might attenuate the scores. Unfortunately, any time a test is administered with such alterations, it no longer remains standardized, and unknown amounts of error are introduced into the testing situation, resulting in a loss of confidence in the test's reliability and validity. Despite the benevolent intent of such procedures, any results derived from their application are rendered suspect and will preclude valid and defensible interpretation.

Another common testing adaptation involves attempts to overcome the language barrier via use of a translator/interpreter. The presumption that testing will be valid as long as the individual comprehends what is being said or asked continues to neglect the culturally based aspects of the testing process itself, as well as the fact that the test remains culturally bound. More importantly, and ignoring the significant problems in translating tests on the fly with or without the aid of trained and untrained interpreters, tests have yet to be standardized in this manner. That is, the use of a translator/interpreter in the testing process represents another violation of standardized procedures, which again undermines the reliability and validity of the results and continues to prevent interpretation.

Beyond issues related to test administration, another significant problem with tests given in English to culturally and linguistically diverse individuals rests with norm sample representation. Test developers often attempt to control for cultural or linguistic differences by including individuals from diverse racial and ethnic backgrounds. But race and ethnicity are not the same as culture or cultural difference. According to Salvia and Ysseldyke (1991),

> When we test students using a standardized device and compare them to a set of norms to gain an index of their relative standing, we assume that the students we test are similar to those on whom the test was standardized; that is, we assume their acculturation [and linguistic history] is comparable, but not necessarily identical, to that of the students who made up the normative sample for the test. . . . When a child's general background experiences differ from those of the children on whom a test was standardized, then the use of the norms of that test as an index for

evaluating that child's current performance or for predicting future performances may be inappropriate. (p. 7)

Representation within a norm sample on the basis of racial or ethnic categories is simply not a sufficient proxy for the degree to which an individual is or is not familiar with the culture of the test. Likewise, neither race nor ethnicity provides specific information on whether an individual is or is not proficient in English, and to what degree. Despite demonstration of high-quality technical characteristics and the use of sophisticated sampling techniques, norm samples that are stratified on the basis of race, ethnicity, country of origin, and that consist of individuals who are predominantly or exclusively monolingual English speakers, are unlikely to meet standards for adequate representation of a bilingual-bicultural individual. This problem plagues both test development and research, where it has been noted that

> most studies compare the performance of students from different ethnic groups. . .rather than ELL and non-ELL children within those ethnic groups. . . . A major difficulty with all of these studies is that the category Hispanic includes students from diverse cultural backgrounds with markedly different English-language skills. . . . This reinforces the need to separate the influences of ethnicity and ELL status on observed score differences. (Lohman, Korb, & Lakin, 2008, pp. 276–278)

Because the alteration of the standardized requirements of the testing process in any manner effectively precludes the assignment of meaning to the collected data, modifications or adaptations in testing are of limited utility. Even if such adaptations could be seen as valid, the significant problems with norm sample adequacy would still preclude validity of any conclusions regarding comparative differences. In practice, such procedures may be most useful in allowing practitioners to derive qualitative information—that is, in observing behavior, evaluating learning propensity, evaluating developmental capabilities, analyzing errors, and so forth. Perhaps the best recommendation for the use of this type of method would be to administer tests in a standardized manner first and then retest with any modifications or adaptations that might help illuminate the actual or true level of the individual's ability.

Nonverbal Testing

Much like development of the Beta version of the Army examination (Yerkes, 1921), the use of nonverbal methods and tests in the evaluation of English learners has been predicated on a simple notion: Eliminate the language barrier and testing can proceed as usual. Nonverbal tests have in fact become quite popular in psychological practice, to the present day, and a variety of tools has been published expressly for this purpose. Similar to the claims originally put forth by Brigham (1923), these tests offer the promise of validity based on the idea that language has been effectively removed from the testing equation. For example, according to Weiss and colleagues (2006), administration of a nonverbal cognitive assessment is still promoted as "an acceptable answer to this problem" (p. 49). This appears, however, to be an overly optimistic view. First, *nonverbal testing* is rather a misnomer; it is probably better characterized as *language-reduced assessment*. This is because no matter the test, its use in any evaluation requires that the examiner and examinee be able to communicate with each other. Even tests that claim that they can be administered in a completely nonverbal manner (i.e., using gestures or pantomime) first require that the examinee understand and comprehend the meaning of the gestures. How such meaning—which must necessarily include instructions on when to start, when to stop, what is a right answer, when to work quickly, as well as other testing issues including establishing rapport or explaining the purpose of testing and so forth—is conveyed to the examinee in the absence of any verbal interaction is not clear. Even if it is possible to do so, the fact remains that the teaching of gestures is akin to the teaching of a new, albeit very brief and limited "language." Thus, whether spoken language is used or not, administration of a test always requires some type of communication between examinee and examiner.

Nonverbal testing may reduce the language barrier, but it clearly does not eliminate it. Likewise, claims regarding cultural fairness do not eliminate cultural content. Given the emphasis on abilities that are less verbal, there might be some reduction in cultural content, unless the use of visual stimuli includes pictures of actual objects and artifacts, which continue to embed culture even with the reduction in language. In addition, nonverbal tests are often used to derive a score that will serve as an indicator of an individual's general intelligence. Such practice, especially in the context of SLD evaluation, is problematic for several reasons. First, it has been demonstrated that nonverbal estimates of intelligence may be no more fair or valid than those that include verbal abilities (Figueroa, 1989). Second, the range of abilities measured by a nonverbal composite is by definition likely to be narrower than that measured by verbal batteries, despite correlations with broader measures of intelligence (Flanagan, Ortiz, & Alfonso, 2007; Ortiz, 2008). Third, the majority of referrals for SLD evaluation are based on problems in language arts, particularly reading. This means that in terms of evaluating the cognitive deficits most likely responsible for reading difficulties, an assessment for SLD would need to include testing for those abilities most related to reading, including auditory processing (*Ga*) and crystallized knowledge (*Gc*) (Flanagan et al., 2007; Flanagan, Ortiz, Alfonso, & Mascolo, 2006). These abilities cannot be easily measured, or measured at all, with nonverbal tests, and would therefore not be useful for evaluation of SLD. And last, nonverbal tests are also subject to the same problems with norm sample representation that exist for verbal tests, as noted in the previous section—that is, neither type of tests has norm samples that systematically and adequately control for differences in acculturative experiences or language development that characterize bilingual and bicultural individuals. In sum, language-reduced tests are not as helpful in the evaluation of the abilities of individuals from diverse cultural and linguistic backgrounds as they are often stated to be. Although they may provide better estimates of true functioning in certain areas, they do not represent a satisfactory solution with respect to validity and fairness in testing, and in some cases will be inadequate to serve the purpose of SLD identification.

Native-Language Testing

With the recent development of standardized tests in languages other than English, coupled with a slight increase in the number of psychologists with sufficient competency in evaluations conducted in languages other than English, there has been some growth in the area of native-language evaluation. Such practice has become identified with the unfortunate and inaccurate label of "bilingual assessment." Bilingual assessment implies evaluation that is to be conducted bilingually, that is, with the use of two languages simultaneously, as is the custom when bilinguals speak to each other. Native-language tests, however, are not standardized using two languages (it would be impossible to standardize this anyway), but only one. Except on some tests where responses are accepted when given in either language, code-switching (into or out of English) is not specified or standardized. Thus, bilingual assessment is better described as *monolingual testing* even in those situations where a test is given in one language followed by retesting in another language.

However it may be characterized best, use of a native-language test requires that the psychologist speak that language (i.e., will likely be bilingual). The ability to communicate with the examinee directly is an important and significant benefit to this approach, and places the psychologist in a position to conduct assessment activities in a manner (i.e., bilingually) that is not available to the monolingual psychologist, even with the aid of translator/interpreter. This notion may partly explain why the simple hiring of a bilingual practitioner is often seen as a definitive solution to the problem of evaluating diverse individuals. However, "mere possession of the capacity to communicate in an individual's native language does not ensure appropriate, nondiscriminatory assessment of that individual. Traditional assessment practices and their inherent biases can be easily replicated in any number of languages" (Flanagan, McGrew, & Ortiz, 2000, p. 291). In addition, not only are there no truly "bilingual" tests or assessment protocols, but very little is currently known about the performance of bilinguals on monolingual tests administered in the primary language.

Compared to the body of research on the use of tests administered in English, testing in the native language is a relatively new research tradition, with little empirical evidence upon which to guide appropriate activities or base standards of practice. The basic question regarding how a bilingual individual in the United States would be expected to perform on a test administered in the native language has yet to be answered. Such a question is bound to be complicated by factors such as the individual's age, level and type of prior education, current language of instruction, and type of instructional program (Goldenberg, 2008). In addition, when native-language testing is accomplished in the United States, the examinee cannot rightly be viewed as a monolingual speaker or from a monocultural background. Because the norms of native-language tests often utilize monolingual speakers from other countries who are being raised by parents who speak the language and who are being educated in the native language, they do not form an adequately representative norm sample for comparison of performance to individuals now residing in the United States. As noted by Harris and Llorente (2005), "these children indeed represent a proportion of U.S. school children who are ELLs. Realistically, however, little is known about the language abilities of these learners and the degree to which they are bilingual" (pp. 392–393). Even when test developers attempt to include bilinguals, they are not sampled systematically with respect to the two major variables (current proficiency in both languages and level of acculturation) that would be necessary to create representative groups. For example, despite inclusion of bilinguals in the developmental sample of the Wechsler Intelligence Scale for Children, Fourth Edition (WISC-IV) Spanish (Wechsler, 2005), they are arranged primarily by country of origin, length of time in the United States, or length of schooling in the United States, all of which fail to account for the influence of cultural and linguistic *differences* (Harris & Llorente). In addition, it should be noted that the actual WISC-IV Spanish norms are equated to the WISC-IV norms, and thus the Spanish version does not have actual, separate norms (Braden & Iribarren, 2005).

English Language Testing

Given the increasingly large numbers of culturally and linguistically diverse individuals in the U.S. population, coupled with the fraction of professionals with sufficient competency to conduct evaluations in the native language, it is not likely that all such individuals will be evaluated in the native language or by bilingual professionals. The reality is that the majority of diverse individuals will be evaluated by a monolingual English-speaking practitioner, and that the evaluation will be conducted primarily, if not exclusively, in English. As compared to the three prior methods, such an approach would seem to be the most biased. In many ways, it echoes Brigham's comments about handling a "typically American situation" because it makes no concessions to the fact that the child is not a native English speaker, does not alter the content or administration of the test, and does not investigate the abilities the child may have, which can be accomplished in the native language but not in English. On the other hand, if we dispense with Brigham's mistaken notions about personal character, we can in fact recognize that this is also the only approach where there exists a great deal of scientific research regarding how culturally and linguistically diverse individuals actually perform on tests—tests given to them in English, of course.

Although not likely intentional, the field of psychometrics has nonetheless provided perhaps the most reasonable basis for evaluating the test performance of bilinguals. The development of standardized procedures, coupled with repeated evaluation of individuals proficient enough in English to reasonably comprehend test instructions, has established a rather extensive and cohesive database regarding the manner in which bilinguals perform tests administered in English (Brigham, 1923; Cummins, 1984; Figueroa, 1989; Goddard, 1917; Jensen, 1974, 1976; Mercer, 1979; Sanchez, 1934; Valdes & Figueroa, 1994; Vukovich & Figueroa, 1982; Yerkes, 1921). A review of this research indicates that nonnative English speakers consistently perform more poorly (about one full standard deviation below average) compared to native English speakers on tasks that rely on English language development, skills, or proficiency, and that they perform comparably to them (at or near the normative mean) on tasks that do not require such verbal or language-based development or skill (Cummins; Figueroa; Valdes & Figueroa). If this research is viewed from the perspective of understanding the degree to which factors such as differences in language and acculturative development affect test performance, it can be used effectively as an empirically based method for gauging the degree of attenuation that may have occurred in testing as a function of the presence of the main operating variables, namely English language proficiency and acculturative knowledge. Ideally, individuals

≡ *Rapid Reference 11.1*

Approaches to Address Cultural and Linguistic Differences

Four general approaches are offered in the literature as viable methods for addressing cultural and linguistic differences.

1. Modified or Adapted Testing
2. Nonverbal Testing
3. Native-Language Testing
4. English-Language Testing

from diverse cultural and linguistic backgrounds should rightly be evaluated by qualified, competent professionals with specific expertise in nondiscriminatory assessment and knowledge of the manner in which such differences influence test performance (Ortiz, 2008). There is nothing, however, that prevents such professionals from evaluating in both the native language and in English. And when there is no other option available but to evaluate in English, the same type of expertise and knowledge may be applied to assist in determining whether the results were in fact due to difference or disorder (see Rapid Reference 11.1).

DIFFERENCE VERSUS DISORDER

It should be evident at this point that there is no simple solution in determining whether, and to what extent, obtained test data were primarily influenced by cultural or linguistic factors. But as has been noted in the previous sections there does not exist any single "best" instrument or procedure that will produce incontrovertibly valid results. Completely unbiased assessment is an illusion, and it will likely not prove possible to eliminate either the language or the culture that is embedded in the test from which it emanated. In efforts to identify SLD, practitioners will need to adopt a more reasonable goal—one that seeks first to establish the validity of the test results. If successful in this endeavor, it will allow application of whichever method for SLD identification the practitioner may prefer. When it can be determined whether experiential differences in culture or language were the main influences on performance (rather than actual ability), and when those differences are deemed only to be contributory at best, a practitioner will be able to defend the validity of any conclusions and support inferences drawn from the obtained data irrespective of the method used to arrive at a diagnosis of SLD. In this way, there is considerable value in any approach that is designed specifically to examine the fundamental question in evaluating culturally and linguistically diverse individuals regarding the extent to which the obtained results are a reflection of cultural or linguistic differences or actual measured ability.

The Culture-Language Test Classifications

The process of systematically evaluating the impact and extent of cultural and linguistic influences in testing has been formalized via a research-based approach developed precisely in response to the issue of validity. In general, the approach rests on two interrelated components: the Culture-Language Test Classifications (C-LTC) and the Culture-Language Interpretive Matrix (C-LIM) (Flanagan & Ortiz, 2001; Flanagan et al., 2007; Mpofu & Ortiz, 2010; Ortiz & Dynda, 2010; Rhodes et al., 2005).

As Brigham (1923) and Yerkes (1921) noted in their data from Army Mental tests, the longer an individual had lived in the United States, the better the individual scored on the Binet Scales. Likewise, native English speakers out-performed nonnative English speakers. This relationship, however, has often been oversimplified into a verbal-nonverbal dichotomy, which is perhaps part of the reason for the popularity of nonverbal approaches in the evaluation of culturally and linguistically diverse individuals (Figueroa, 1990). In addition, the relationship has been the subject of considerable research on the topic of "test bias," but it has been well established that the performance difference cannot be entirely attributed to the inherent psychometric qualities of tests, and the notion of *psychometric* bias in testing is not well supported (Figueroa; Jensen, 1980; Reynolds, 2000; Sandoval, Frisby, Geisinger, Scheuneman, & Grenier, 1998). Whereas it may be accurate to say that tests are not psychometrically biased per se, this does not mean that measurement of performance is automatically valid. Most researchers acknowledge that language and cultural differences appear to attenuate performance, but the focus on test bias has been the reason why the attenuation remains poorly understood (Figueroa & Hernandez, 2000; Jensen, 1976, 1980; Lohman et al., 2008; Sandoval, 1979; Sandoval et al.).

From the very inception of intelligence testing to the present day, research has consistently indicated that an individual's familiarity with the content of the test (acculturation) and the degree to which he or she comprehends the language in which the test is based (proficiency) are directly related to test performance (Valdes & Figueroa, 1994). It was on the basis of this research, and recognition that subtests appear to vary on these dimensions, that the C-LTC was derived. By using both empirical studies (where data were available) and logic (based on expert consensus), classifications of tests of intelligence and cognitive abilities were established along the two important dimensions: (1) the degree to which a particular test or subtest contains or requires familiarity, specific knowledge, or an understanding of U.S. mainstream culture; and (2) the degree to which a particular test or subtest requires expressive or receptive language skills, because the ability being measured is language based, the correct response requires verbal competency, or appropriate administration rests upon adequate verbal comprehension by the examinee. Through the application of a simple, three-level (Low, Moderate, and High) system, tests were thus classified in a matrix according to the degree of cultural loading and degree of linguistic demand. Figure 11.2 provides an example of the C-LTC specifically for the subtests drawn from the Woodcock-Johnson III Tests of Cognitive Abilities (WJ III COG; Woodcock, McGrew, & Mather, 2001).

The initial intent of the C-LTC was similar to those underlying nonverbal approaches in that it was thought practitioners could select tests classified as "low" in both cultural loading and linguistic demand and thereby perform evaluations that would be valid and produce the best estimates of true ability. This proved problematic, however, in that there are some abilities (e.g., *Gc* and *Ga*) that

	LOW	MODERATE	HIGH
LOW	Spatial Relations (*Gv*-Vz, SR)	Visual Matching (*Gs*-P, R9) Numbers Reversed (*Gsm*-MW)	Concept Formation (*Gf*-I) Analysis Synthesis (*Gf*-RG) Auditory Working Memory (*Gsm*-MW)
MODERATE	Picture Recognition (*Gv*-MV) Planning (*Gv*-SS) Pair Cancellation (*Gs*-R9)	Visual-Auditory Learning (*Glr*-MA) Delayed Recall—Visual Auditory Learning (*Glr*-MA) Retrieval Fluency (*Glr*-FI) Rapid Picture Naming (*Glr*-NA)	Memory for Words (*Gsm*-MS) Incomplete Words (*Ga*-PC) Sound Blending (*Ga*-PC) Auditory Attention (*Ga*-US/U3) Decision Speed (*Gs*-R4)
HIGH			Verbal Comprehension (*Gc*-VL, LD) General Knowledge (*Gc*-K0)

Figure 11.2. Culture-Language Test Classifications of the WJ III COG

Note. Figure adapted from *Essentials of Cross-Battery Assessment, 2nd Edition,* Copyright © 2007, John Wiley & Sons, Inc. Used with permission.

cannot be measured in a "low culture/low language" way, and to measure a broad range of abilities might necessitate the use of several batteries rather than just one or two. A more useful approach evolved later from the C-LTC when it was recognized that the arrangement of the test classifications, if administered to a culturally and linguistically diverse individual, would produce a pattern of decline in test performance just as had been observed historically (Cummins, 1984; Mercer, 1979; Valdes & Figueroa, 1994). This observation is illustrated in Figure 11.3 and differs slightly from prior observations of test performance in that it does not view the pattern as a simple dichotomous one (i.e., verbal versus nonverbal), but instead viewed the decline as a continuum from least attenuated (low culture/low language cells) to most attenuated (high culture/high language cells). This observation has been borne out by prior research that showed comparable scores for ELLs on the WISC-IV, as compared to the largely monolingual English-speaking norm sample, were not achieved until individuals reach the 25th percentile rank (Standard Score [SS] > 90) on a standardized test of English language proficiency (Cathers-Schiffman & Thompson, 2007). Current research continues to demonstrate that although language proficiency and

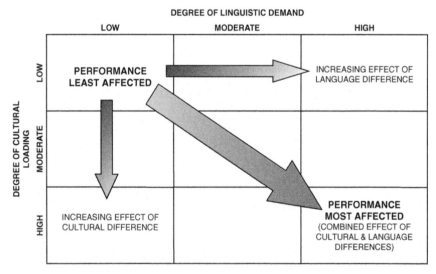

Figure 11.3. Pattern of Expected Performance for Culturally and Linguistically Diverse Individuals Showing Attenuation Due to Increasing Cultural and Linguistic Characteristics of Tests

Source: Adapted from *Essentials of Cross-Battery Assessment, 2nd Edition,* Copyright © 2007, John Wiley & Sons, Inc. Used with permission.

level of acculturative knowledge play a role in test performance, the impact is actually related to the degree that the test itself requires language or acculturative development (Aguera, 2006; Dynda, 2008; Nieves-Brull, 2006; Sotelo-Dynega, 2007; Tychanska, 2009). That is, the more a test has linguistic demands, and the more a test relies on cultural content, the greater the decline in performance for culturally and linguistically diverse individuals.

The Culture-Language Interpretive Matrix

The C-LIM is essentially an extension of the C-LTC that examines test performance directly and the degree to which this performance may have been influenced by cultural and linguistic differences. (Readers interested in the specific procedures for using and evaluating results with the C-LIM are referred to the original source (Flanagan et al., 2007), as such detail is not practical in this chapter, and only a general procedural and conceptual discussion can be offered.) Because of the arrangement of the tests within the matrix, a de facto test of validity is created, which allows examination of the extent to which test performance may or may not be ascribed primarily to such differences. Specifically, when test scores are entered into the matrix, aggregates for each cell are calculated among any tests that share the same classification. If the resulting pattern of performance follows that which has been demonstrated by the historical and current literature (i.e., higher performance on tests classified in the low culture/low language cell, and lower performance on tests classified in the high culture/high language cell), then in such an arrangement the tests must necessarily reflect the primary and significant impact of cultural and linguistic factors, and are thus invalid and not interpretable. This does not mean, however, that the data are entirely useless, because it can be inferred that if an individual's test scores evidence the expected pattern of decline and are within the expected range across the cells of the matrix, then performance is similar if not equal to other culturally and linguistically diverse individuals who do not have an educationally disabling condition.

The research upon which this pattern of decline has been observed is based on measurement of "normal" individuals, not those with a particular type of disability. Thus, performance that compares favorably to the obtained research values strongly suggests the absence of cognitive dysfunction, and would likely rule out the possibility of SLD or any other neurocognitively-based disorder. Conversely, when the results do not decline systematically, as would be expected, and where values are obtained that are not similar to the values reported in the literature for the type of test given, it can be assumed that cultural and linguistic factors were at best contributory factors and that the obtained results were not primarily due to experiential differences. In this manner, a practitioner can be confident that the obtained results can be defended as valid, and interpretation may proceed as desired. The results can be rearranged back to the theoretical factor structure upon which the test was built; and in cases where deficient performance is noted, valid conclusions about possible SLD or other dysfunction may well be drawn. It is cautioned, however, that scores that remain in the expected range (SS = 80–85) for crystallized intelligence (Gc) not be viewed as definitive evidence of deficient functioning, given that the attenuating effect of cultural and linguistic differences is not likely to disappear completely, even in cases where there may be a learning disability present in other areas of functioning.

Current research on the performance of English learners with speech-language impairment (also called, specific language impairment) (SLI) suggests that language-based disabilities (those most likely to be reflected in measures of Gc) result in a steeper rate of decline and values that are substantially below those expected for individuals with no such impairment (Tychanska, 2009). In addition, care must be taken not to assume that the lack of a declining pattern or values below expectation automatically implies the presence of a learning disability. The C-LIM is neither designed nor intended as a diagnostic tool. Rather, its only purpose is to assist practitioners in systematically evaluating the impact of cultural and linguistic factors so that a decision regarding validity can be made. In keeping with best practices in testing, it is incumbent upon the practitioner to ensure that noncognitive factors have not encroached upon the testing situation and influenced the pattern of results (e.g., fatigue, inattention, lack of effort or motivation, uncooperative test behavior, improper administration, etc.) (Oakland & Harris, 2009).

> ## CAUTION
> ....
> The C-LIM should not be used as a diagnostic tool for SLD in culturally and linguistically diverse individuals.

Figures 11.4 and 11.5 provide a WJ III COG example of the typical pattern of decline that would be expected of an individual with average ability who comes from a culturally and linguistically diverse background in both matrix and graph form. Despite representation as typical, there is no implication that individuals will have patterns that are identical to the one portrayed in the matrix and graph. Although the same relative pattern of decline from top left to bottom right remains the hallmark of the systematic influence of cultural and linguistic variables on test performance, differences in individual levels of acculturation and English-language proficiency can alter the resulting averages. That is, as an

Name ___Maria___   Grade ___3___   Evaluator ___Dr. Psychologist___
Age ___8.4___   Date ___1/6/2010___

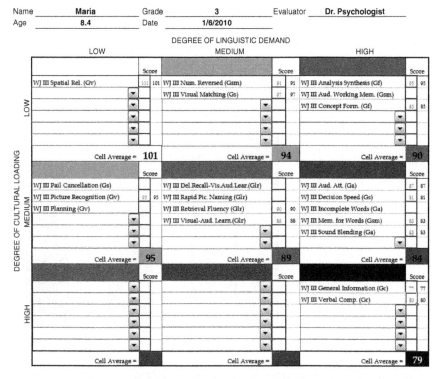

Figure 11.4. Culture-Language Interpretive Matrix Using Hypothetical WJ III COG Data Indicating Primary Effect of Cultural and Linguistic Factor (Results not valid; suggest normal functioning.)

Source: Captured from the Automated Culture-Language Interpretive Matrix included on the CD-ROM in *Essentials of Cross-Battery Assessment, 2nd Edition,* Copyright © 2007, John Wiley & Sons, Inc. Used with permission.

individual's levels of English proficiency and acculturative knowledge differ from those of the individuals on whom the test was normed, the resulting values should show corresponding differences relative to level of performance and degree of score attenuation. In other words, individuals who are markedly different (i.e., very limited English proficiency, significant lack of acculturative knowledge or development) will have lower scores, particularly on tests with increasing cultural and linguistic demands, than individuals who are less different (i.e., possess better English proficiency and more acculturative knowledge).

Thus, it is important to evaluate and apprehend an individual's language proficiency and level of acculturative knowledge to create the appropriately fair

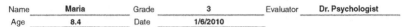

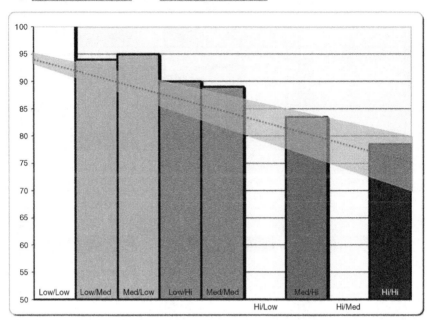

Figure 11.5. Culture-Language Interpretive Matrix Graph Using Hypothetical WJ III COG Data Indicating Primary Effect of Cultural and Linguistic Factors (Results not valid; suggest normal functioning.)

Source: Captured from the Automated Culture-Language Interpretive Matrix included on the CD-ROM in *Essentials of Cross-Battery Assessment, 2nd Edition,* Copyright © 2007, John Wiley & Sons, Inc. Used with permission.

context in which the scores should be compared and examined. To facilitate this process, the C-LIM provides a guide to expected performance via the use of a dashed line with a gray-colored band around it. This shaded area represents the range that would be expected for individuals who are "moderately" different from the mainstream rather than those who are characterized as only "slightly" or "markedly" different. The middle designation is used in the C-LIM primarily because it better represents the scores that would be expected given the background, development, and experience of typical ELLs presently enrolled in U.S. public schools. Such children, with their rather limited levels of English language proficiency and acculturation, are not those on whom research is generally conducted or those for whom tests administered in English are considered appropriate. Thus, their performance is expected to be slightly lower

Name	Stanislaw	Grade	2	Evaluator	Dr. Psychologist
Age	7.2	Date	11/23/2009		

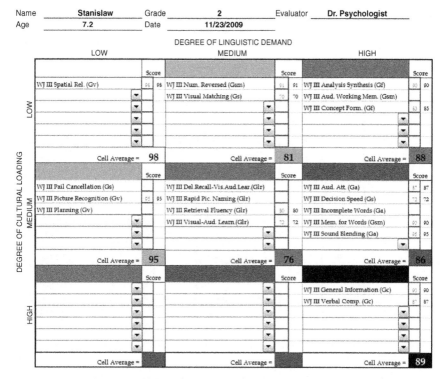

Figure 11.6. Culture-Language Interpretive Matrix Using Hypothetical WJ III COG Data Indicating Only Contributory Effect of Cultural and Linguistic Factors (Results valid; may support SLD.)

Source: Captured from the Automated Culture-Language Interpretive Matrix included on the CD-ROM in *Essentials of Cross-Battery Assessment, 2nd Edition,* Copyright © 2007, John Wiley & Sons, Inc. Used with permission.

(but consistent in terms of decline) than the estimates culled from research. Once again, interested readers are referred to Flanagan and colleagues (2007) for a more in-depth discussion regarding complete guidelines and detailed instructions for interpretation.

In contrast to the preceding illustrations, Figures 11.6 and 11.7 provide an example of test results that do not follow the expected pattern of decline for an individual from a diverse cultural and linguistic background. In this case, there is some indication of decline, but it is neither a clear nor systematic drop in performance relative to increasing cultural and linguistic demands. In addition, there are cells in which the aggregate score simply does not fall within the range that would be expected given the degree of cultural loading and linguistic demand

Name	**Stanislaw**	Grade	**2**	Evaluator	**Dr. Psychologist**
Age	7.2	Date	11/23/2009		

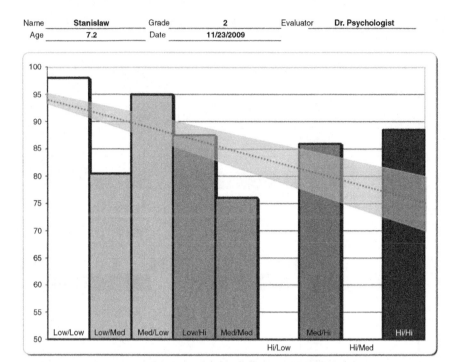

Figure 11.7. Culture-Language Interpretive Matrix Graph Using Hypothetical WJ III COG Data Indicating Only Contributory Effect of Cultural and Linguistic Factors (Results valid; may support SLD.)

Source: Captured from the Automated Culture-Language Interpretive Matrix included on the CD-ROM in *Essentials of Cross-Battery Assessment, 2nd Edition,* Copyright © 2007, John Wiley & Sons, Inc. Used with permission.

of the respective tests. On the basis of the issues discussed previously, this pattern cannot be said to indicate the presence of the primary influence of cultural and linguistic differences. The obtained values simply do not stand in accord with what would be expected, and the areas in which performance was quite low cannot be explained by or attributed to cultural or linguistic factors.

In short, this means that the results are likely to be valid because they cannot be said to have been systematically confounded by extraneous variables (i.e., cultural and linguistic). And with the confirmation of validity comes the defense for interpretation, which might proceed in the following manner. Were all the scores within the average range, and no normative deficiencies noted, the question of disability, particularly SLD would be somewhat moot since the identification of a cognitive deficit as the presumptive cause of manifest academic difficulties is often a part of the identification process. But in this case, there are performances that are significantly lower than what might be reasonably explained by cultural or linguistic factors; this indicates that some variable other than cultural or linguistic difference was present and served to depress the performance. With sufficiently compelling and converging evidence, these data could be examined from their usual theoretical and structural framework to provide an indication of what type of cognitive deficit may be present, and inform conclusions regarding the possible presence of SLD using whatever definition or method selected by the practitioner. Despite the intentionally narrow utility of the C-LIM, its value is clearly evident in that it allows the process of SLD (or other disability) identification to move forward when it is defensible, and effectively precludes it when it is not.

Although the C-LIM was designed to evaluate scores drawn from tests administered in English, some practitioners have wondered whether the C-LTC and C-LIM might be used with native-language tests, as well, such as the WISC-IV Spanish (Wechsler, 2005) and Bateria-III (Munoz-Sandoval, Woodcock, McGrew, & Mather, 2005). In principle, given the problems with adequate norm sample representation discussed previously, the classifications of the tests are likely to be quite similar, because the issues are identical (Esparza-Brown, 2007). For example, a native Spanish-speaking student in the United States may not be receiving native-language instruction (i.e., bilingual education) and thus may show relatively poorer performance in Spanish against a norm group composed of monolingual Spanish speakers being educated in Spanish. The decline in performance would be the result of a process known as *language attrition*, which is due to limited use and development as a function of lack of formal education (Bialystok, 1991; Hakuta, 1991). Unfortunately, due to the fact that there is very little research on how bilinguals of varying proficiency perform on tests given to them in the native language, no definitive recommendations can be offered regarding expectations of performance, and use of the C-LTC and C-LIM in this regard cannot be recommended or endorsed.

CONCLUSION

Whichever method or process a practitioner chooses to adopt for the identification of SLD, fair or equitable assessment will not occur if the results from the use of standardized tests cannot be defended as valid indications of ability or disability. For this reason, this chapter did not address a particular method for identifying SLD in culturally and linguistically diverse individuals, but instead discussed the manner in which validity of test results could be examined directly, and whether or not subsequent interpretation could be defended. At the present time there is no one best or preferred method for identifying SLD in diverse individuals, and the decision regarding which one is most appropriate for a given referral rests with the practitioner. Irrespective of the approach chosen, however, if the use of standardized tests is a part of the process, there will be a need to address the issue of validity, or they may be of little or no value to the assessment.

In sum, the C-LTC and C-LIM are designed only to address issues of validity and are not intended to be used in isolation or promoted as a complete solution to the problems inherent in evaluating individuals from diverse cultural and linguistic backgrounds. True fairness and equity in evaluation is achieved via the application of a broad and systematic framework for nondiscriminatory assessment that seeks to reduce all forms of potential bias to the maximum extent possible (Ortiz, 2008). The C-LTC and C-LIM represent a systematic approach to the issue of validity and are based on the application of both prior and current empirical research. Their application is rather limited, in that currently they are intended for use with tests administered in English; but in doing so they offer practitioners a formal way to address the validity of obtained results that is in keeping with the literature on the known performance of culturally and linguistically diverse individuals when evaluated in English. Although application of other approaches—including modified/adapted, nonverbal, or native-language testing—offer intuitive appeal, they are insufficient to ensure fairness, and continue to be problematic in a variety of ways.

Consequently, there is no single approach, tool, procedure, or method that can be recommended as best practice for the identification of SLD in culturally and linguistically diverse individuals, nor should there be. In most cases, the determination as to whether an individual has SLD will ultimately rest with the clinical judgment of the practitioner. In making that judgment, however, practitioners must be confident in the validity of the obtained results; and in this regard, the   C-LTC and C-LIM will prove very helpful, especially to those who are not bilingual and must resort to the administration of tests in English. By assisting practitioners in effectively addressing the difference versus disorder question, practitioners now have at their disposal a systematic method, supported by modern cognitive theory and scientific research, that is defensible within the context of a broader assessment, fully meets ethical guidelines, and is consistent with prevailing standards and guidelines for nondiscriminatory practice (Oakland, 1976, Ortiz, 2008). Future research will certainly alter some of the test classifications, and perhaps even some of the expected values for culturally and linguistically diverse learners, especially as considerations regarding current age, grade, and instructional program are integrated into the methodology.

When used in conjunction with other information relevant to nondiscriminatory assessment, including level of acculturation, language development and proficiency, socioeconomic status, academic history, familial history, developmental data, work samples, curriculum-based data, intervention results, and so forth, the C-LIM and the classifications upon which it is based (C-LTC) hold promise for assisting practitioners in dealing directly with the issue of validity, upon which any determination of SLD must stand.

TEST YOURSELF

1. **When immigrants to the United States were evaluated with the early translations of the Binet Scales,**
   (a) results did not show any difference in their performance compared to monolinguals.
   (b) they performed poorly compared to monolinguals, but it was believed that this was an inherent flaw in the character and intellect of immigrants.
   (c) they performed better compared to monolinguals, which indicated a flaw in the test.
   (d) they were always excluded from participation in the U.S. armed services.

2. **When data from the Army Beta and intelligence testing of immigrants indicated that length of residence was related to test performance,**
   (a) it was reasoned that the intelligence of immigrants coming to the United States was declining.
   (b) the test was modified to control for this variable.
   (c) a conclusion was drawn regarding the fact that the test was not valid for use with immigrants.
   (d) a search for a better theoretical framework for the Army Mental Tests was conducted.

3. **When bias is defined traditionally with respect to the psychometric properties of a test, research has provided strong evidence of bias in which of the following areas?**
   (a) Reliability
   (b) Factor structure
   (c) Prediction
   (d) None of the above

4. **The main obstacle in the evaluation of SLD (or other disabilities) in individuals from culturally and linguistically diverse backgrounds is**
   (a) selecting the most appropriate test.
   (b) distinguishing difference from disorder.

(continued)

    (c) finding a trained translator/interpreter.

    (d) ensuring standardized administration.

5. **When using standardized tests in the evaluation of SLD (or other disabilities) in individuals from culturally and linguistically diverse backgrounds, the main concern revolves around questions of**

    (a) reliability.

    (b) specificity.

    (c) validity.

    (d) prediction.

6. **Some of the major problems in modifying/adapting tests or using native-language tests in evaluating diverse individuals include**

    (a) lack of appropriate norm samples that control for language proficiency and acculturative knowledge development.

    (b) violation of standardized administration procedures.

    (c) violations in the assumption of comparability.

    (d) all of the above

7. **Although they are helpful in reducing the oral language requirements, it is often mistakenly believed that nonverbal tests**

    (a) can be administered without any communication between the examiner and examinee.

    (b) control the cultural influences that can affect test performance.

    (c) have norm samples that are appropriate for bilinguals.

    (d) all of the above

8. **Testing culturally and linguistically diverse individuals in English seems counterintuitive but is defensible in large part because**

    (a) there is nearly a century's worth of research on how bilinguals perform on tests when evaluated in English.

    (b) loopholes in the law permit it.

    (c) there are just too many culturally and linguistically diverse children who need evaluation.

    (d) it is significantly less expensive to do so.

9. **When using the Culture-Language Interpretive Matrix, which of the following general interpretive statements is incorrect?**

    (a) When test performance increases diagonally across the cells from the upper left to the bottom right, scores should be deemed to be invalid and should not be interpreted.

    (b) When test performance increases diagonally across the cells from the lower left to the top right, scores should be deemed to be invalid and should not be interpreted.

    (c) When test performance decreases diagonally across the cells from the upper left to the bottom right, scores should be deemed to be invalid and should not be interpreted.

(d) When test performance decreases diagonally across the cells from the lower left to the top right, scores should be deemed to be invalid and should not be interpreted.

10. The primary purpose of the Culture-Language Interpretive Matrix is to

(a) reduce the psychometric bias found in tests.

(b) evaluate the impact of cultural and linguistic differences on test performance so that a decision regarding the validity of the test results can be made systematically.

(c) assist bilingual psychologists in performing evaluations in the native language.

(d) eliminate the need for clinical judgment or collection of data regarding cultural, linguistic, and educational background.

Answers: 1. b; 2. a; 3. d; 4. b; 5. c; 6. d; 7. d; 8. a; 9. c; 10. b.

References

CHAPTER I

Aaron P. G. (1997). The impending demise of the discrepancy formula. *Review of Educational Research, 67*, 461–50.

American Psychiatric Association. (2000). *Diagnostic and statistical manual of mental disorders* (4th ed., text rev.). Washington, DC: Author.

Bradley, R., Danielson, L. C., & Hallahan, D. P. (2002). *Identification of learning disabilities: Research to practice*. Mahwah, NJ: Erlbaum.

Ceci, S. J. (1990). *On intelligence—more or less: A bio-ecological treatise on intellectual development.* Englewood Cliffs, NJ: Prentice Hall.

Cortiella, C. (2009). *The State of Learning Disabilities 2009*. New York: National Center for Learning Disabilities.

Della Toffalo, D. (2010). Linking school neuropsychology with response-to-intervention models. In D. C. Miller (Ed.), *Best practices in school neuropsychology: Guidelines for effective practice, assessment, and evidence-based interventions* (pp. 159–184). New York: Guilford.

Flanagan, D. P., Fiorello, C., & Ortiz, S. O. (2010). Enhancing practice through application of Cattell-Horn-Carroll theory and research: A "third method" approach to specific learning disability identification. *Psychology in the Schools, 47*, 739–760.

Fuchs, L. S., & Fuchs, D. (1998). Treatment validity: A unifying concept for reconceptualizing the identification of learning disabilities. *Learning Disabilities Research and Practice, 13*, 204–219.

Gresham, F., Restori, A., & Cook, C. (2008). To test or not to test: Issues pertaining to response to intervention and cognitive testing. *Communiqué, 37*, 5–7.

Hale, J., Alfonso, V., Berninger, V., Bracken, B., Christo, C., Clark, E., et al. (2010). Critical issues in response-to-intervention, comprehensive evaluation, and specific learning disabilities identification and intervention: An expert white paper consensus. *Learning Disability Quarterly.*

Hale, J. B., & Fiorello, C. A. (2004). *School neuropsychology: A practitioner's handbook.* New York: Guilford.

Hale, J. B., Fiorello, C. A., Dumont, R., Willis, J. O., Rackley, C., & Elliott, C. (2008). Differential ability scales—second edition (neuro)psychological predictors of math performance for typical children and children with math disabilities. *Psychology in the Schools, 45*, 838–858.

Hale, J. B., Flanagan, D. P., & Naglieri, J. A. (2008). Alternative research-based methods for IDEA (2004) identification of children with specific learning disabilities. *Communiqué, 36*(8), 1, 14–17.

Hammill, D. D. (1990). On defining learning disabilities: An emerging consensus. *Journal of Learning Disabilities, 23*, 74–84.

Kaufman, A. S. (2008). Neuropsychology and specific learning disabilities: Lessons from the past, as a guide to present controversies and future clinical practice. In E. Fletcher-Janzen and C.R. Reynolds (Eds.), *Neuropsychological perspectives on learning disabilities in the era of RTI: Recommendations for diagnosis and intervention* (pp. 1–13). Hoboken, NJ: Wiley.

Kavale, K. A., & Flanagan, D. P. (2007). Ability-achievement discrepancy, RTI, and assessment of cognitive abilities/processes in SLD identification: Toward a contemporary operational definition (pp. 130–147). In S. Jimerson, M. Burns, & A. Van Der Heyden (Eds.), *Handbook of response to intervention: The science and practice of assessment and intervention.* New York: Springer Science.

Kavale, K. A., & Forness, S. R. (1995). Social skill deficits and training: A meta-analysis. In T. E. Scruggs & M. A. Mastropieri (Eds.), *Advances in learning and behavioral disabilities* (Vol. 9, pp. 119–160). Greenwich, CT: JAI Press.

Kavale, K. A., & Forness, S. R. (2000). What definitions of learning disability say and don't say: A critical analysis. *Journal of Learning Disabilities, 33*(3), 239–256.

Kavale, K. A., & Forness, S. R. (2006). Learning disability as a discipline. In H.L. Swanson, K. R. Harris, & S. Graham (Eds.), *Handbook of learning disabilities* (pp. 76–93). New York: Guilford.

Kavale, K. A., Kauffman, J. M., Bachmeier, R. J., & LeFever, G. B. (2008). Response-to-intervention: Separating the rhetoric of self-congratulation from the reality of specific learning disability identification. *Learning Disability Quarterly, 31*, 135–150.

Kavale, K. A., Spaulding, L. S., & Beam, A. P. (2009). A time to define: Making the specific learning disability definition prescribe specific learning disability. *Learning Disability Quarterly, 32*, 39–48.

Kirk, S. A. (1962). *Educating exceptional children.* Boston: Houghton Mifflin.

Learning Disabilities Roundtable. (2005). 2004 learning disabilities roundtable: Comments and recommendations on regulatory issues under the Individuals Education Improvement Act of 2004, Public Law 108–446. Available from www.nasponline.org/advocacy/2004LDRoundtableRecsTransmittal.pdf

Learning Disability Association of America (n.d.). *History of LDA.* Available from www.ldanatl.org/about/print_history.asp.

Lyon, G. R., Fletcher, J. M., Shaywitz, S. E., Shaywitz, B. A., Torgesen, J. K., Wood, F. B., Schulte, A., & Olson, R. (2001). *Rethinking learning disabilities.* Washington, DC: Thomas Fordham Foundation. Available from www.ppionline.org/documents/SpecialEd_ch12.pdf.

Mather, N., & Goldstein, S. (2008). *Learning disabilities and challenging behaviors: A guide to intervention and classroom management* (2nd ed.). Baltimore, MD: Brookes.

President's Commission on Excellence in Special Education Report. (2002). *A new era: Revitalizing special education for children and their families.* Jessup, MD: ED Pubs, Education Publications Center, U.S. Department of Education. Available from www2.ed.gov/inits/commissionsboards/whspecialeducation/reports/info.html.

Reschly, D. J. (2004). Paradigm shift, outcomes criteria, and behavioral interventions: Foundations for the future of school psychology. *School Psychology Review, 33*, 408–416.

Reschly, D. J., Hosp, J. L., & Schmied, C. M. (2003). And miles to go . . . : State SLD requirements and authoritative recommendations. Nashville, TN: National Research Center on Learning Disabilities. Available from www.nrcld.org/about/research/states.

Reynolds, C. R., & Shaywitz, S. E. (2009a). Response to intervention: Prevention and remediation, perhaps. Diagnosis, no, *Child Development Perspectives, 3*(1), 44–47.

Reynolds, C. R., & Shaywitz, S. E. (2009b). Response to intervention: Ready or not? Or, from wait-to-fail to watch-them-fail. *School Psychology Quarterly, 24*(2), 130–145.

Siegel, L. S. (1999). Issues in the definition and diagnosis of learning disabilities: A perspective on Guckenberger v. Boston University. *Journal of Learning Disabilities, 32*(4), 304–319.

Stanovich, K. E. (1988). Explaining the differences between the dyslexic and the garden-variety poor reader: The phonological-core variable-difference model. *Journal of Experimental Child Psychology, 38*, 175–190.

Sternberg, R. J., & Grigorenko, E. L. (2002). *Our labeled children: What every parent and teacher needs to know about learning disabilities.* Cambridge, MA: Perseus.

Stuebing, K. K., Fletcher, J. M., LeDoux, J. M., Lyon, G. R., Shaywitz, S. E., & Shaywitz, B. A. (2002). Validity of IQ-discrepancy classifications of reading disabilities: A meta-analysis. *American Educational Research Journal, 39,* 469–518.

United States Department of Education. (2006). *28th annual report to Congress on the implementation of the Individuals with Disabilities Education Act, 2006,* Volume 1. Washington, DC: USDOE.

United States Department of Education. (2008). *Data analysis system.* Washington, DC: IES National Center for Educational Statistics. Available from http://nces.ed.gov/das.

Wiederholt, J. L. (1974). Historical perspectives on the education of the learning disabled. In L. Mann & D. Sabatino (Eds.), *The second review of special education* (pp. 103–152). Philadelphia: JSE Press.

World Health Organization. (2006). International Classification of Diseases—10th Revision. Geneva, Switzerland: WHO Publications.

Ysseldyke, J. E. (2005). Assessment and decision making for students with learning disabilities: What if this is as good as it gets? *Learning Disability Quarterly, 28,* 125–128.

Zirkel, P. A., & Thomas, L. B. (2010). State laws for RTI: An updated snapshot. *Teaching Exceptional Children, 42*(3), 56–63.

CHAPTER 2

Adams, M. (1990). *Beginning to read: Thinking and learning about print.* Cambridge, MA: MIT Press.

Arns, M., Peters, S., Breteler, R., & Verhoeven, L. (2007). Different brain activation patterns in dyslexic children: Evidence from the EEG power and coherence patterns for the double-deficit theory of dyslexia. *Journal of Integrated Neuroscience, 6*(1), 175–190.

Backes, W., Vuurman, E., Wennekes, R., Spronk, P., Wuisman, M., van Engelshoven, J., & Jolles, J. (2002). Atypical brain activation of reading processes in children with developmental dyslexia. *Journal of Child Neurology, 17*(12), 867–871.

Barton, S. (1998) Teaching methods that work. Retrieved from Bright Solutions for Dyslexia, Inc., www.dys-add.com/teach.html, November 12, 2009.

Berninger, V. W., & Richards, T. L. (2002). *Brain literacy for educators and psychologists.* London: Academic Press.

Bremner, J.D. (2005). *Brain imaging handbook.* New York: W.W. Norton.

Canter, A. (2006, February). Problem solving and RTI: New roles for school psychologists. *Communiqué, 34*(5), insert. Available from www.nasponline.org/advocacy/rtifactsheets .aspx.

Cao, F., Bitan, T., & Booth, J. R. (2008). Effective brain connectivity in children with reading difficulties during phonological processing. *Brain and Language, 107*(2), 91–101.

Catts, H. W., Adlof, S. M., & Weismer, S. E. (2006). Language deficits in poor comprehenders: A case for the simple view of reading. *Journal of Speech, Language, and Hearing Research, 49,* 278–293.

Cutting, L. E., Materek, A., Cole, C. A. S., Levine, T. M., & Mahone, E. M. (2009). Effects of fluency, oral language, and executive function on reading comprehension performance. *Annals of Dyslexia, 59*(1), 34–54.

Deford, D. E., Lyons, C. A., & Pinnell, G. S. (1991). *Bridges to literacy: Learning from reading recovery.* Portsmouth, NH: Heinemann.

Demos, J. N. (2005). *Getting started with neurofeedback.* New York: W.W. Norton.

Feifer, S. G., & DeFina, P. D. (2000). *The neuropsychology of reading disorders: Diagnosis and intervention.* Middletown, MD: School Neuropsych Press.

Feifer, S. G., & Della Toffalo, D. (2007). *Integrating RTI with cognitive neuropsychology: A scientific approach to reading.* Middletown, MD: School Neuropsych Press.

Fletcher, J. M., Lyon, G. R., Fuchs, L. S., & Barnes, M.A. (2007). *Learning disabilities: From identification to intervention*. New York: Guilford.

Goldberg, E. (2001). *The executive brain: Frontal lobes and the civilized mind*. New York: Oxford University Press.

Goswami, U. (2007). Typical reading development and developmental dyslexia across languages. In D. Coch, G. Dawson, & K. W. Fischer (Eds.), *Human behavior, learning, and the developing brain* (pp. 145–167). New York: Guilford.

Grigorenko, E. L. (2007). Triangulating developmental dyslexia. In D. Coch, G. Dawson, & K. W. Fischer (Eds.), *Human behavior, learning, and the developing brain* (p. 117–144). New York: Guilford.

Hale, J. B., & Fiorello, C.A. (2004). *School neuropsychology: A practitioner's handbook*. New York: Guilford.

Harm, M. W., & Seidenberg, M. S. (2004). Computing the meanings of words in reading: Cooperative division of labor between visual and phonological processes. *Psychological Review, 111*, 662–720.

Heim, S., Tschierse, J., Amunts, K., Wilms, M., Vossel, S., Willmes, K., Grabowska, A., & Huber, W. (2008). Cognitive subtypes of dyslexia. *Acta Neurobiologiae Experimentalis, 68*, 73–82.

Ho, C. S., Chan, D. W., Lee, S. H., Tsang, S. M., & Luan, V. H. (2004). Cognitive profiling and preliminary subtyping in Chinese developmental dyslexia. *Cognition, 91*, 43–75.

Kavale, K.A., & Forness, S. R. (2000). What definitions of learning disability say and don't say. *Journal of Learning Disabilities, 33*(3), 239–256.

King, W. M., Giess, S. A., & Lombardina, L. J. (2007). Subtyping children with developmental dyslexia via bootstrap aggregated clustering and the gap statistic: Comparison with the double-deficit hypothesis. *International Journal of Language and Communication Disorders, 42*, 77–95.

Lachmann, T., Berti, S., Kujala, T., & Schroger, E. (2005). Diagnostic subgroups of developmental dyslexia have different deficits in neural processing of tones and phonemes. *International Journal of Psychophysiology, 56*, 105–120.

McCandliss, B. D., & Noble, K. G. (2003). The development of reading impairment: A cognitive neuroscience model. *Mental Retardation and Developmental Disabilities, 9*, 196–205.

Moats, L. (2004). Relevance of neuroscience to effective education for students with reading and other learning disabilities. *Journal of Child Neurology, 19*(10), 840–845.

Morris, R. D., Stuebing, K. K., Fletcher, J. M., Shaywitz, S. E., Lyon, G. R., Shankweiler, D. P., Katz, L., Francis, D. J., & Shaywitz, B. A. (1998). Subtypes of reading disability: Variability around a phonological core. *Journal of Educational Psychology, 90*, 347–373.

Nation, K., Clarke, P., Marshall, C. M., & Durand, M. (2004). Hidden language impairments in children: Parallels between poor reading comprehension and specific language impairments? *Journal of Speech, Language, and Hearing Research, 47*, 199–211.

Nation, K., & Snowling, M. (1997). Assessing reading difficulties: The validity and utility of current measures of reading skill. *British Journal of Educational Psychology, 67*, 359–370.

National Joint Committee on Learning Disabilities (2005). Responsiveness to intervention and learning disabilities. Retrieved from www.ldonline.org/njcld, August 30, 2008.

National Reading Panel (2000). *Teaching children to read: An evidenced based assessment of the scientific research literature on reading and its implications for reading instruction*. Washington, DC: National Institutes of Child Health and Human Development.

Noble, K. G., & McCandliss. (2005). Reading development impairment: Behavioral, social and neurobiological factors. *Journal of Developmental and Behavioral Pediatrics, 26*, 370–378.

Pernet, C. R., Poline, J. B., Demonet, J. F., & Rousselet, G. A. (2009). Brain classification reveals the right cerebellum as the best biomarker of dyslexia. *BMC Neuroscience, 10*, 67.

Posner, M. I., & Rothbart, M. K. (2007). *Educating the human brain*. Washington, DC: American Psychological Association.

Pugh, K. R., Mencl, W. E., Jenner, A. R., Katz, L., Frost, S. J., Lee, J. R., Shaywitz, S. E., & Shaywitz, B. A. (2000). Functional neuroimaging studies of reading and reading disability (developmental dyslexia). *Mental Retardation and Developmental Disabilities Research Reviews, 6,* 207–213.

Ramus, F. (2003). Developmental dyslexia: Specific phonological deficit or general sensorimotor dysfunction? *Current Opinion in Neurobiology, 13,* 212–218.

Ramus, F. (2004). Neurobiology of dyslexia: A reinterpretation of the data. *Trends in Neurosciences, 27,* 720–726.

Reiter, A., Tucha, O., & Lange, K. W. (2004). Executive functions in children with dyslexia. *Dyslexia, 11,* 116–131.

Reynolds, C. R. (2007). RTI, neuroscience, and sense: Chaos in the diagnosis and treatment of learning disabilities. In E. Fletcher-Janzen, & C.R. Reynolds (Eds.), *Neuropsychological perspectives on learning disabilities in the era of RTI* (pp. 14–27). Hoboken, NJ: Wiley.

Sandak, R., Mencl, W. E., Frost, S., Rueckl, J. G., Katz, L., Moore, D. L., Mason, S. A., Fulbright, R. K., Constable, R. T., & Pugh, K. R., (2004). The neurobiology of adaptive learning in reading: A contrast of different training conditions. *Cognitive, Affective, & Behavioral Neuroscience, 4*(1), 67–88.

Schatschneider, C., & Torgeson, J. K. (2004). Using our current understanding of dyslexia to support early identification and intervention. *Journal of Child Neurology, 19,* 759–765.

Shaywitz, S. (2004). *Overcoming dyslexia.* New York: Random House.

Shaywitz, S., & Shaywitz, B. (2005). Dyslexia: Specific reading disability. *Biological Psychiatry, 57,* 1301–1309.

Snow, C. E., Burns, M. S., & Griffin, P., Eds. (1998). *Preventing reading difficulties in young children.* Washington DC: National Academy Press.

Stein, J. (2000). The neurobiology of reading. *Prostaglandins, Leukotrienes and Essential Fatty Acids, 63*(1/2), 109–116.

Suldo, S. M., Olson, A., & Evans, J. R. (2001). Quantitative EEG evidence of increased alpha peak frequency in children with precocious reading ability. *Journal of Neurotherapy, 5,* 39–50.

Swingle, P. G. (2008). *Biofeedback for the brain.* New Brunswick, NJ: Rutgers University Press.

Temple, E. (2002). Brain mechanisms in normal and dyslexic readers. *Current Opinion in Neurobiology, 12,* 178–193.

Uhry, J. K., & Clark, D. B. (2005). *Dyslexia: Theory and practice of instruction.* Baltimore, MD: York.

U.S. Department of Education, Office of Special Education and Rehabilitative Services (2006). Twenty-sixth annual report to Congress on the implementation of the Individuals with Disabilities Education Act. Washington, DC: Author.

Vargo, F. E., Grosser, G. S., & Spafford, C. S. (1995). Digit span and other WISC-R scores in the diagnosis of dyslexia in children. *Perceptual and Motor Skills, 80,* 1219–1229.

Willcutt, E. G., Olson, R. K., Pennington, B. F., Boada, R., Ogline, J. S., Tunick, R. A., & Chabildas, N. A. (2001). Comparison of the cognitive deficits in reading disability and attention deficit hyperactivity disorder. *Journal of Abnormal Psychology, 110,* 157–172.

CHAPTER 3

Antell, S. E., & Keating, D. P. (1983). Perception of numerical invariance in neonates. *Child Development, 54,* 695–701.

Ashcraft, M. H. (1982). The development of mental arithmetic: A chronometric approach. *Developmental Review, 2,* 213–236.

Baddeley, A. D. (1986). *Working memory.* Oxford, UK: Oxford University Press.

Barbaresi, W. J., Katusic, S. K., Colligan, R. C., Weaver, A. L., & Jacobsen, S. J. (2005). Math learning disorder: Incidence in a population-based birth cohort, 1976–82, Rochester, Minn. *Ambulatory Pediatrics, 5,* 281–289.

Barrouillet, P., Fayol, M., & Lathuliére, E. (1997). Selecting between competitors in multiplication tasks: An explanation of the errors produced by adolescents with learning disabilities. *International Journal of Behavioral Development, 21,* 253–275.

Berch, D. B., & Mazzocco, M. M. M. (Eds.) (2007). *Why is math so hard for some children? The nature and origins of mathematical learning difficulties and disabilities.* Baltimore, MD: Brookes.

Blackwell, L., Trzesniewski, K., & Dweck, C.S. (2007). Implicit theories of intelligence predict achievement across an adolescent transition: A longitudinal study and an intervention. *Child Development, 78,* 246–263.

Brannon, E. M. (2002). The development of ordinal numerical knowledge in infancy. *Cognition, 83,* 223–240.

Briars, D., & Siegler, R. S. (1984). A featural analysis of preschoolers' counting knowledge. *Developmental Psychology, 20,* 607–618.

Bull, R., & Johnston, R. S. (1997). Children's arithmetical difficulties: Contributions from processing speed, item identification, and short-term memory. *Journal of Experimental Child Psychology, 65,* 1–24.

Bull, R., Johnston, R. S., & Roy, J. A. (1999). Exploring the roles of the visual-spatial sketch pad and central executive in children's arithmetical skills: Views from cognition and developmental neuropsychology. *Developmental Neuropsychology 15,* 421–442.

Butterworth, B. (2005). The development of arithmetical abilities. *Journal of Child Psychology and Psychiatry, 46,* 3–18.

Butterworth, B., & Reigosa, V. (2007). Information processing deficits in dyscalculia. In D. B. Berch & M. M. M. Mazzocco (Eds.), *Why is math so hard for some children? The nature and origins of mathematical learning difficulties and disabilities* (pp. 65–81). Baltimore, MD: Brookes.

Carpenter, T. P., & Moser, J. M. (1984). The acquisition of addition and subtraction concepts in grades one through three. *Journal for Research in Mathematics Education, 15,* 179–202.

Case, R & Okamoto (1996). The role of central conceptual structures in children's thought. *Monographs of Society in Research and Child Development,* 61.

Conway, A. R. A., & Engle, R. W. (1994). Working memory and retrieval: A resource-dependent inhibition model. *Journal of Experimental Psychology: General, 123,* 354–373.

Dehaene, S. (1997). *The number sense: How the mind creates mathematics.* New York: Oxford University Press.

Dehaene, S., Piazza, M., Pinel, P., & Cohen, L. (2003). Three parietal circuits for number processing. *Cognitive Neuropsychology, 20,* 487–506.

Engle, R. W., Tuholski, S. W., Laughlin, J. E., & Conway, A. R. A. (1999). Working memory, short-term memory, and general fluid intelligence: A latent-variable approach. *Journal of Experimental Psychology: General, 128,* 309–331.

Feigenson, L., Dehaene, S., & Spelke, E. (2004). Core systems of number. *Trends in Cognitive Sciences, 8,* 307–314.

Fuchs, L. S., & Fuchs, D. (2002). Mathematical problem-solving profiles of students with mathematics disabilities with and without comorbid reading disabilities. *Journal of Learning Disabilities, 35,* 573–573.

Fuchs, L. S., Fuchs, D., Hamlett, C. L., Powell, S. R., Capizzi, A. M., & Seethaler, P. M. (2006). The effects of computer-assisted instruction on number combination skill in at-risk first graders. *Journal of Learning Disabilities, 39,* 467–475.

Fuchs, L. S., Powell, S. R., Seethaler, P. M., Cirino, P. T., Fletcher, J. M., Fuchs, D., & Hamlett, C. L. (in press). The effects of strategic counting instruction, with and without deliberate practice, on number combination skill among students with mathematics difficulties. *Learning and Individual Differences.*

Fuson, K. C. (1982). An analysis of the counting-on solution procedure in addition. In T. P. Carpenter, J. M. Moser, & T. A. Romberg (Eds.), *Addition and subtraction: A cognitive perspective* (pp. 67–81). Hillsdale, NJ: Erlbaum.

Fuson, K. C. (1988). Children's counting and concepts of number. New York: Springer-Verlag.

Gallistel, C. R., & Gelman, R. (1992). Preverbal and verbal counting and computation. *Cognition, 44*, 43–74.

Geary, D. C. (1990). A componential analysis of an early learning deficit in mathematics. *Journal of Experimental Child Psychology, 49*, 363–383.

Geary, D. C. (1993). Mathematical disabilities: Cognitive, neuropsychological, and genetic components. *Psychological Bulletin, 114*, 345–362.

Geary, D. C. (1995). Reflections of evolution and culture in children's cognition: Implications for mathematical development and instruction. *American Psychologist, 50*, 24–37.

Geary, D. C. (2006). Development of mathematical understanding. In D. Kuhl & R. S. Siegler (Vol. Eds.), *Cognition, perception, and language*, Vol 2 (pp. 777–810). W. Damon (Gen. Ed.), *Handbook of child psychology* (6th Ed.). Hoboken, NJ: Wiley.

Geary, D. C. (2007). An evolutionary perspective on learning disability in mathematics. *Developmental Neuropsychology, 32*, 471–519.

Geary, D. C. (2010). Missouri longitudinal study of mathematical development and disability. In R. Cowan, M. Saxton, & A. Tolmie (Eds.), *Understanding number development and number difficulties (No. 7, British Journal of Educational Psychology*, Monograph Series II: Psychological Aspects of Education—Current Trends). Leicester, UK: British Psychological Society.

Geary, D. C., Bailey, D. H., & Hoard, M. K. (2009). Predicting mathematical achievement and mathematical learning disability with a simple screening tool: The Number Sets Test. *Journal of Psychoeducational Assessment, 27*, 265–279.

Geary, D. C., Bow-Thomas, C. C., & Yao, Y. (1992). Counting knowledge and skill in cognitive addition: A comparison of normal and mathematically disabled children. *Journal of Experimental Child Psychology, 54*, 372–391.

Geary, D. C., Boykin, A. W., Embretson, S., Reyna, V., Siegler, R., Berch, D. B., & Graban, J. (2008). Report of the task group on learning processes. In National Mathematics Advisory Panel, *Reports of the task groups and subcommittees* (pp. 4-i–4-221). Washington, DC: United States Department of Education.

Geary, D. C., & Brown, S. C. (1991). Cognitive addition: Strategy choice and speed-of-processing differences in gifted, normal, and mathematically disabled children. *Developmental Psychology, 27*, 398–406.

Geary, D. C., Hamson, C. O., & Hoard, M. K. (2000). Numerical and arithmetical cognition: A longitudinal study of process and concept deficits in children with learning disability. *Journal of Experimental Child Psychology, 77*, 236–263.

Geary, D. C., Hoard, M. K., & Bailey, D. H. *Fact retrieval deficits in low achieving children and children with mathematical learning disability.* Under editorial review.

Geary, D. C., Hoard, M. K., Byrd-Craven, J., & DeSoto, C. M. (2004). Strategy choices in simple and complex addition: Contributions of working memory and counting knowledge for children with mathematical disability. *Journal of Experimental Child Psychology, 74*, 213–239.

Geary, D. C., Hoard, M. K., Byrd-Craven, J., Nugent, L., & Numtee, C. (2007). Cognitive mechanisms underlying achievement deficits in children with mathematical learning disability. *Child Development, 78*, 1343–1359.

Geary, D. C., Hoard, M. K., Nugent, L., & Byrd-Craven, J. (2008). Development of number line representations in children with mathematical learning disability. *Developmental Neuropsychology*, *33*, 277–299.

Geary, D. C., & Lin, J. (1998). Numerical cognition: Age-related differences in the speed of executing biologically-primary and biologically-secondary processes. *Experimental Aging Research*, *24*, 101–137.

Gelman, R., & Gallistel, C. R. (1978). *The child's understanding of number*. Cambridge, MA: Harvard University Press.

Gelman, R., & Meck, E. (1983). Preschooler's counting: Principles before skill. *Cognition*, *13*, 343–359.

Gersten, R., Clarke, B., & Mazzocco, M. M. M. (2007). Historical and contemporary perspectives on mathematical learning disabilities. In D. B. Berch & M. M. M. Mazzocco (Eds.), *Why is math so hard for some children? The nature and origins of mathematical learning difficulties and disabilities* (pp. 7–28). Baltimore, MD: Brookes.

Gersten, R., Ferrini-Mundy, J., Benbow, C., Clements, D. H., Loveless, T., Williams, V., & Arispe, I. (2008). Report of the task group on instructional practices. In National Mathematics Advisory Panel, *Reports of the task groups and subcommittees* (pp. 606–624). Washington, DC: United States Department of Education.

Gersten, R., Jordan, N. C., & Flojo, J. R. (2005). Early identification and interventions for students with mathematics difficulties. *Journal of Learning Disabilities*, *38*, 293–304.

Goldman, S. R., Pellegrino, J. W., & Mertz, D. L. (1988). Extended practice of basic addition facts: Strategy changes in learning disabled students. *Cognition and Instruction*, *5*, 223–265.

Groen, G. J., & Parkman, J. M. (1972). A chronometric analysis of simple addition. *Psychological Review*, *79*, 329–343.

Groen, G., & Resnick, L. B. (1977). Can preschool children invent addition algorithms? *Journal of Educational Psychology*, *69*, 645–652.

Halberda, J., & Feigenson, L. (2008). Developmental change in the acuity of the "number sense": The approximate number system in 3-, 4-, 5-, and 6-year-olds and adults. *Developmental Psychology*, *44*, 1457–1465.

Halberda, J., Mazzocco, M. M. M., & Feigenson, L. (2008, October 2). Individual differences in non-verbal number acuity correlate with maths achievement. *Nature*, *455*, 665–669.

Hanich, L. B., Jordan, N. C., Kaplan, D., & Dick, J. (2001). Performance across different areas of mathematical cognition in children with learning difficulties. *Journal of Educational Psychology*, *93*, 615–626.

Hoard, M. K., Geary, D. C., & Hamson, C. O. (1999). Numerical and arithmetical cognition: Performance of low- and average-IQ children. *Mathematical Cognition*, *5*, 65–91.

Jordan, N.C., Glutting, J., & Ramineni, C. (in press). The importance of number sense to mathematics achievement in first and third grades. *Learning and Individual Differences*.

Jordan, N. C., & Hanich, L. (2000). Mathematical thinking in second grade children with different forms of LD. *Journal of Learning Disabilities*, *33*, 567–578.

Jordan, N. C., Hanich, L. B., & Kaplan, D. (2003a). Arithmetic fact mastery in young children: A longitudinal investigation. *Journal of Experimental Child Psychology*, *85*, 103–119.

Jordan, N. C., Hanich, L. B., & Kaplan, D. (2003b). A longitudinal study of mathematical competencies in children with specific mathematics difficulties versus children with comorbid mathematics and reading difficulties. *Child Development*, *74*, 834–850.

Jordan, N. C., & Montani, T. O. (1997). Cognitive arithmetic and problem solving: A comparison of children with specific and general mathematics difficulties. *Journal of Learning Disabilities*, *30*, 624–634.

Kail, R. (1991). Developmental change in speed of processing during childhood and adolescence. *Psychological Bulletin*, *109*, 490–501.

Koontz, K. L., & Berch, D. B. (1996). Identifying simple numerical stimuli: Processing inefficiencies exhibited by arithmetic learning disabled children. *Mathematical Cognition, 2*, 1–23.

Kovas, Y., Haworth, C. M. A., Dale, P. S., & Plomin, R. (2007). The genetic and environmental origins of learning abilities and disabilities in the early school years. *Monographs of the Society for Research in Child Development, 72* (3, Serial No. 288).

Landerl, K., Bevan, A., & Butterworth, B. (2003). Developmental dyscalculia and basic numerical capacities: A study of 8–9-year-old students. *Cognition, 93*, 99–125.

LeFevre, J.-A., Smith-Chant, B. L., Fast, L., Skwarchuk, S.-L., Sargla, E., Arnup, J. S., et al. (2006). What counts as knowing? The development of conceptual and procedural knowledge of counting from kindergarten through grade 2. *Journal of Experimental Child Psychology, 93*, 285–303.

Levine, S. C., Jordan, N. C., & Huttenlocher, J. (1992). Development of calculation abilities in young children. *Journal of Experimental Child Psychology, 53*, 72–103.

Lewis, C., Hitch, G. J., & Walker, P. (1994). The prevalence of specific arithmetic difficulties and specific reading difficulties in 9-year-old to 10-year-old boys and girls. *Journal of Child Psychology and Psychiatry, 35*, 283–292.

Light, J. G., & DeFries, J. C. (1995). Comorbidity of reading and mathematics disabilities: Genetic and environmental etiologies. *Journal of Learning Disabilities, 28*, 96–106.

Locuniak, M. N., & Jordan, N. C. (2008). Using kindergarten number sense to predict calculation fluency in second grade. *Journal of Learning Disabilities, 41*, 451–459.

MacMillan, N. A. (2002). Signal detection theory. In J. Wixted & H. Pashler, *H. Stevens' Handbook of Experimental Psychology (3rd ed.), Vol. 4: Methodology in Experimental Psychology* (pp. 43–90). Hoboken, NJ: Wiley.

Mandler, G., & Shebo, B. J. (1982). Subitizing: An analysis of its component processes. *Journal of Experimental Psychology: General, 111*, 1–22.

Mazzocco, M. M. M. (2007). Defining and differentiating mathematical learning disabilities and difficulties. In D. B. Berch & M. M. M. Mazzocco (Eds.), *Why is math so hard for some children? The nature and origins of mathematical learning difficulties and disabilities* (pp. 29–48). Baltimore, MD: Brookes.

McLean, J. F., & Hitch, G. J. (1999). Working memory impairments in children with specific arithmetic learning difficulties. *Journal of Experimental Child Psychology, 74*, 240–260.

Murphy, M. M., Mazzocco, M. M. M., Hanich, L. B., & Early, M. C. (2007). Cognitive characteristics of children with mathematics learning disability (MLD) vary as a function of the cutoff criterion used to define MLD. *Journal of Learning Disabilities, 40*, 458–478.

National Mathematics Advisory Panel. (2008). *Foundations for success: Final report of the National Mathematics Advisory Panel*. Washington, DC: United States Department of Education. Available from www.ed.gov/about/bdscomm/list/mathpanel/report/final-report.pdf.

Ohlsson, S., & Rees, E. (1991). The function of conceptual understanding in the learning of arithmetic procedures. *Cognition and Instruction, 8*, 103–179.

Oliver, B., Harlaar, N., Hayiou-Thomas, M. E., Kovas, Y., Walker, S. O., Petrill, S. A., et al. (2004). A twin study of teacher-reported mathematics performance and low performance in 7-year-olds. *Journal of Educational Psychology, 96*, 504–517.

Ostad, S. A. (1997). Developmental differences in addition strategies: A comparison of mathematically disabled and mathematically normal children. *British Journal of Educational Psychology, 67*, 345–357.

Ostad, S. A. (1998). Developmental differences in solving simple arithmetic word problems and simple number-fact problems: A comparison of mathematically normal and mathematically disabled children. *Mathematical Cognition, 4*, 1–19.

Posner, M. I., Boies, S. J., Eichelman, W. H., & Taylor, R. L. (1969). Retention of visual and name codes of single letters. *Journal of Experimental Psychology Monograph, 79*, 1–16.

Raghubar, K., Cirino, P., Barnes, M., Ewing-Cobbs, L., Fletcher, J., & Fuchs, L. (2009). Errors in multi-digit arithmetic and behavioral inattention in children with math difficulties. *Journal of Learning Disabilities, 42*, 356–371.

Raghubar, K. P., Barnes, M., & Hecht, S. A. (in press). Working memory and mathematics: A review of developmental, individual difference, and cognitive approaches. *Learning and Individual Differences.*

Russell, R. L., & Ginsburg, H. P. (1984). Cognitive analysis of children's mathematical difficulties. *Cognition and Instruction, 1*, 217–244.

Shalev, R. S., Manor, O., & Gross-Tsur, V. (2005). Developmental dyscalculia: A prospective six-year follow-up. *Developmental Medicine & Child Neurology, 47*, 121–125.

Shalev, R. S., Manor, O., Kerem, B., Ayali, M., Badichi, N., Friedlander, Y., & Gross-Tsur, V. (2001). Developmental dyscalculia is a familial learning disability. *Journal of Learning Disabilities, 34*, 59–65.

Siegler, R. S. (1996). *Emerging minds: The process of change in children's thinking.* New York: Oxford University Press.

Siegler, R. S, & Booth, J. L. (2004). Development of numerical estimation in young children. *Child Development, 75*, 428–444.

Siegler, R. S., & Jenkins, E. (1989). *How children discover new strategies.* Hillsdale, NJ: Erlbaum.

Siegler, R. S., & Shrager, J. (1984). Strategy choice in addition and subtraction: How do children know what to do? In C. Sophian (Ed.), *Origins of cognitive skills* (pp. 229–293). Hillsdale, NJ: Erlbaum.

Spinath, B., Spinath, F. M., Harlaar, N., & Plomin, R. (2006). Predicting school achievement from general cognitive ability, self-perceived ability, and intrinsic value. *Intelligence, 34*, 363–374.

Starkey, P. (1992). The early development of numerical reasoning. *Cognition, 43*, 93–126.

Starkey, P., & Cooper, R. G., Jr. (1980). Perception of numbers by human infants. *Science, 210*, 1033–1035.

Strauss, M. S., & Curtis, L. E. (1984). Development of numerical concepts in infancy. In C. Sophian (Ed.), *Origins of cognitive skills: The eighteenth annual Carnegie symposium on cognition* (pp. 131–155). Hillsdale, NJ: Erlbaum.

Swanson, H. L. (1993). Working memory in learning disability subgroups. *Journal of Experimental Child Psychology, 56*, 87–114.

Swanson, H. L., & Sachse-Lee, C. (2001). Mathematical problem solving and working memory in children with learning disabilities: Both executive and phonological processes are important. *Journal of Experimental Child Psychology, 79*, 294–321.

Walberg, H. J. (1984). Improving the productivity of America's schools. *Educational Leadership, 41*, 19–27.

Wechsler, D. (2001). *Wechsler Individual Achievement Test–Second Edition–Abbreviated (WIAT–II–A).* San Antonio, TX: The Psychological Corporation, Harcourt Brace & Co.

Wynn, K., Bloom, P., & Chiang, W.-C. (2002). Enumeration of collective entities by 5-month-old infants. *Cognition, 83*, B55–B62.

Xu, F., & Spelke, E. S. (2000). Large number discrimination in 6-month-old infants. *Cognition, 74*, B1–B11.

CHAPTER 4

American Psychiatric Association. (2000). *Diagnostic and statistical manual of mental disorders* (4th ed. text rev.). Washington, DC: Author.

Bailet, L. L. (1991). Beginning spelling. In A. M. Bain, L. L. Bailet, & L. C. Moats (Eds.), *Written language disorders: Theory into practice* (pp. 1–21). Austin, TX: PRO-ED.

Baumann, J. F., & Kame'enui, E. J. (2004). *Vocabulary instruction: Research to practice.* New York: Guilford.

Bear, D. R., Invernizzi, M., Templeton, S., & Johnston, F. (2008). *Words their way: Word study for phonics, vocabulary, and spelling instruction.* Upper Saddle River, NJ: Prentice Hall.

Berninger, V. W. (1996). *Reading and writing acquisition: A developmental neuropsychological perspective.* Boulder, CO: Westview Press.

Berninger, V. W. (2004). Understanding the graphia in dysgraphia. In D. Dewey & D. Tupper (Eds.), *Developmental motor disorders: A neuropsychological perspective* (pp. 328–350). New York: Guilford.

Berninger, V. W. (2009). Highlights of programmatic, interdisciplinary research on writing. *Learning Disabilities Research & Practice, 24,* 69–80.

Berninger, V. W., & Richards, T. (2002). *Brain literacy for educators and psychologists.* San Diego, CA: Academic Press.

Berninger, V. W., & Wolf, B. J. (2009a). *Helping students with dyslexia and dysgraphia make connections: Differentiated instruction lesson plans in reading and writing.* Baltimore, MD: Brookes.

Berninger, V. W., & Wolf, B. J. (2009b). *Teaching students with dyslexia and dysgraphia: Lessons from teaching and science.* Baltimore, MD: Brookes.

Bernstein, B. E. (2008). *Learning disorder: Written expression.* Retrieved from http://emedicine.medscape.com/article/918389-overview, October 20, 2009.

Blachman, B. A. (1994). Early literacy acquisition: The role of phonological awareness. In G. P. Wallach & K. G. Butler (Eds.), *Language learning disabilities in school-age children and adolescents* (pp. 253–274). New York: Merrill.

Bruck, M. (1993). Component spelling skills of college students with childhood diagnoses of dyslexia. *Learning Disability Quarterly, 16,* 171–184.

Connelly, V., Campbell, S., MacLean, M., & Barnes, J. (2006). Contribution of lower-order skills to the written composition of college students with and without dyslexia. *Developmental Neuropsychology, 29,* 175–196.

Cutler, L., & Graham, S. (2008). Primary grade writing instruction. A national survey. *Journal of Educational Psychology, 100,* 907–919.

Dehn, M. J. (2008). *Working memory and academic learning: Assessment and intervention.* Hoboken, NJ: Wiley.

Deno, S. L., Fuchs, L. S., Marston, D., & Shin, J. (2001). Using curriculum-based measurement to establish growth standards for students with learning disabilities. *School Psychology Review, 30,* 507–524.

Deuel, R. K. (1992). Motor skill disorder. In S. R. Hooper, G. W. Hynd, & R. E. Mattison (Eds.), *Developmental disorders: Diagnostic criteria and clinical assessment* (pp. 239–282). Hillsdale, NJ: Erlbaum.

Deuel, R. K. (1994). Developmental dysgraphia and motor skill disorders. *Journal of Child Neurology, 10,* 6–8.

Ehri, L. C. (2000). Learning to read and learning to spell: Two sides of a coin. *Topics in Language Disorders, 20*(3), 19–36.

Ehri, L. C. (2006). Alphabetics instruction helps students learn to read. In R. M. Joshi & P. G. Aaron (Eds.), *Handbook of orthography and literacy* (pp. 649–677). Mahwah, NJ: Erlbaum.

Englert, C. S. (2009). Connecting the dots in a research program to develop, implement, and evaluate strategic literacy interventions for struggling readers and writers. *Learning Disabilities Research & Practice, 24,* 104–120.

Englert, C. S., & Raphael, T. E. (1988). Constructing well-formed prose: Process, structure and metacognitive knowledge. *Exceptional Children, 54,* 18–25.

Englert, C. S., Raphael, T. E., Anderson, L., Anthony, H., & Stevens, D. (1991). Exposition: Reading, writing, and the metacognitive knowledge of learning disabled students. *Learning Disabilities Research, 5,* 5–24.

Fletcher, J. M., Lyon, G. R., Fuchs, L. S., & Barnes, M. A. (2007). *Learning disabilities: From identification to intervention.* New York: Guilford.

Floyd, R. G., McGrew, K. S., & Evans, J. J. (2008). The relative contribution of the Cattell-Horn-Carroll cognitive abilities in explaining writing achievement during childhood and adolescence. *Psychology in the Schools, 45*(2), 132–144.

Gentry, J. R. (1982). An analysis of developmental spelling in GYNS AT WRK. *Reading Teacher, 36,* 192–200.

Goswami, U. (2006). Orthography, phonology, and reading development: A cross-linguistic perspective. In R. M. Joshi & P. G. Aaron (Eds.), *Handbook of orthography and literacy* (pp. 463–480). Mahwah, NJ: Erlbaum.

Graham, S., Berninger, V. W., Abbott, R. D., Abbott, S. P., & Whitaker, D. (1997). Role of mechanics in composing of elementary school students: A new methodological approach. *Journal of Educational Psychology, 89,* 170–182.

Graham, S., & Harris, K. R. (2005). *Writing better: Effective strategies for teaching students with learning difficulties.* Baltimore, MD: Brookes.

Graham, S., & Harris, K. R. (2009). Almost 30 years of writing research: Making sense of it all with the Wrath of Khan. *Learning Disabilities Research & Practice, 24,* 58–68.

Graham, S., MacArthur, C. A., & Fitzgerald, J. (Eds.) (2007). *Best practices in writing instruction.* New York: Guilford.

Graham, S., & Perin, D. (2007). *Writing next: Effective strategies to improve writing of adolescents in middle and high schools.* A report to the Carnegie Corporation of New York. Washington, DC: Alliance for Excellent Education.

Gregg, N. (1995). *Written expression disorders.* The Netherlands: Kluwer Academic Publishers.

Gregg, N. (2009). *Adolescents and adults with learning disabilities and ADHD: Assessment and accommodation.* New York: Guilford.

Gregg, N., & Mather, N. (2002). School is fun at recess: Informal analyses of written language for students with learning disabilities. *Journal of Learning Disabilities, 35,* 7–22.

Hale, J. B., & Fiorello, C. A. (2004). *School neuropsychology: A practitioner's handbook.* New York: Guilford.

Hamstra-Bletz, L., & Blote, A. W. (1993). A longitudinal study on dysgraphic handwriting in primary school. *Journal of Learning Disabilities, 26,* 689–699.

Harris, K. R., & Graham, S. (1992). *Helping young writers master the craft: Strategy instruction and self-regulation in the writing process.* Cambridge, MA: Brookline Books.

Harris, K. R., Graham, S., Mason, L.H., & Friedlander, B. (2008). *Powerful writing strategies for all students.* Baltimore, MD: Brookes.

Henderson, E. H. (1990). *Teaching spelling* (2nd ed.). Boston: Houghton Mifflin.

Hochman, J. C. (2009). *Teaching basic writing skills: Strategies for effective expository writing instruction.* Longmont, CO: Sopris West.

Hooper, S. R., Montgomery, J., Swartz, C., Reed, M. S., Sandler, A. D., Levine, M. D., Watson, T. E., & Wasileski, T. (1994). Measurement of written language expression. In G. R. Lyon (Ed.), *Frames of reference for the assessment of learning disabilities: New views on measurement issues* (pp. 375–417). Baltimore, MD: Brookes.

Individuals with Disabilities Education Improvement Act (IDEIA) of 2004, PL 108-446.

Isaacson, S. L. (1989). Role of secretary vs. author: Resolving the conflict in writing instruction. *Learning Disability Quarterly, 12,* 209–217.

Jones, D. (2004, December). *Automaticity of the transcription process in the production of written text.* Doctor of Philosophy Thesis, Graduate School of Education, University of Queensland, Australia.

Joshi, R. M., Hoien, T., Feng, X., Chengappa, R., & Boulware-Gooden, R. (2006). Learning to spell by ear and by eye: A cross-linguistic comparison. In R. M. Joshi & P. G. Aaron (Eds.), *Handbook of orthography and literacy* (pp. 569–577). Mahwah, NJ: Erlbaum.

Katusic, S. K., Colligan, R. C., Weaver, A. L., & Barbaresi, W. J. (2009). The forgotten learning disability: Epidemiology of written-language disorder in a population-based birth cohort (1976–1982), Rochester, Minnesota. *Pediatrics, 123,* 1306–1313.

Kaufman, A. S., & Kaufman, N. L. (2004). *Kaufman Test of Educational Assessment–Second Edition.* Circle Pines, MN: AGS Publishing.

Kemp, N., Parrila, R. K., & Kirby J. R. (2009). Phonological and orthographic spelling in high-functioning adult dyslexics. *Dyslexia: The Journal of the British Dyslexia Association. 15,* 105–128.

Kronenberger, W. G., & Dunn, D. W. (2003). Learning disorders. *Neurologic Clinics, 21,* 941–952.

Levine, M. (1987). *Developmental variations and learning disorders.* Cambridge, MA: Educators Publishing Service.

MacArthur, C., & Graham, S. (1993). Integrating strategy instruction and word processing into a process approach to writing instruction. *School Psychology Review, 22,* 671–682.

MacArthur, C., Graham, S., & Fitzgerald, J. (Eds.) (2006). *Handbook of writing research.* New York: Guilford.

Mather, N., Roberts, R., Hammill, D. & Allen, E. (2008). *Test of Orthographic Competence.* Austin, TX: PRO-ED.

Mather, N., Wendling, B. J., & Roberts, R. (2009). *Writing assessment and instruction for students with learning disabilities.* San Francisco: Jossey-Bass.

Mayes, S. D., & Calhoun, S. L. (2006). WISC-IV and WISC-III profiles in children with ADHD. *Journal of Attention Disorders, 9,* 486–493

Mayes, S. D., & Calhoun, S. L. (2007). Challenging the assumptions about the frequency and coexistence of learning disability types. *School Psychology International, 28,* 437–448.

McCloskey, G., Perkins, L. A., & Van Divner, B. (2009). *Assessment and intervention of executive function difficulties.* New York: Routledge.

Miceli, G., & Capasso, R. (2006). Spelling and dysgrapia. *Cognitive Neuropsychology, 23,* 110–134.

Moats, L. C. (1995). *Spelling: Development, disability, and instruction.* Timonium, MD: York Press.

National Center for Education Statistics (2009). *Digest of Education Statistics, 2008* (NCES 2009-020), Chapter 2: U.S. Department of Education.

National Commission on Writing in America's Schools and Colleges (2003; 2004). *Neglected R: The need for a writing revolution.* Princeton, NJ: College Entrance Examination Board.

National Institute for Neurological Disorders and Stroke (NINDS), 2009 Dysgraphia information page. Retrieved from www.ninds.nih.gov/disorders/dysgraphia/dysgraphia.htm, October 20, 2009.

Persky, H. R., Daane, M. C., & Jin, Y. (2003). *The nation's report card: Writing 2002.* (NCES 2003–529). U. S. Department of Education. Institute of Education Sciences. National Center for Education Statistics. Washington, DC: Government Printing Office.

Raskind, W. H. (2001). Current understanding of the genetic basis of reading and spelling disability. *Learning Disability Quarterly, 24,* 144–157.

Rosenblum, S., Weiss, P. L., & Parush, S. (2004). Handwriting evaluation for developmental dysgraphia: Process versus product. *Reading and Writing, 17,* 433–458.

Salahu-Din, D., Persky, H., and Miller, J. (2008). *The nation's report card: Writing 2007* (NCES 2008–468). National Center for Education Statistics, Institute of Education Sciences, U.S. Department of Education. Washington, DC: Government Printing Office.

Schumaker, J. B., & Deshler, D. D. (2009). Adolescents with learning disabilities as writers: Are we selling them short? *Learning Disabilities Research & Practice, 24*, 81–92.

Smith, C. R. (1997, February). *A hierarchy for assessing and remediating phonemic segmentation difficulties.* Paper presented at the Learning Disabilities Association International Conference, Chicago, IL.

Stecker, P. M., Fuchs, L. S., & Fuchs, D. (2005). Using curriculum-based measurement to improve student achievement: Review of research. *Psychology in the Schools, 42*, 795–819.

Swanson, H. L., & Siegel, L. (2001). Learning disabilities as a working memory deficit. *Issues in Education: Contributions from Educational Psychology, 7*, 1–48.

Weintraub, N., & Graham, S. (1998). Writing legibly and quickly: A study of children's ability to adjust their handwriting to meet common classroom demands. *Learning Disabilities Research & Practice, 13*, 146–152.

Wiznitzer, M., & Scheffel, D. L. (2009). Learning disabilities. In R. B. David, J. B. Bodensteiner, D. E. Mandelbaum, & B. Olson (Eds.), *Clinical pediatric neurology* (pp. 479–492). New York: Demos Medical Publishing.

Woodcock, R. W., McGrew, K. S., Schrank, F. A., & Mather, N. (2001, 2007). *Woodcock-Johnson III Tests of Cognitive Abilities.* Rolling Meadows, IL: Riverside Publishing.

Woodcock, R. W., McGrew, K. S., Schrank, F. A., & Mather, N. (2001, 2007). *Woodcock-Johnson III Tests of Achievement.* Rolling Meadows, IL: Riverside Publishing.

CHAPTER 5

Adams, A. M., & Gathercole, S. E. (1995). Phonological working memory and speech production in preschool children. *Journal of Speech and Hearing Research, 38*, 403–414.

Adams, A. M., & Gathercole, S. E. (2000). Limitations in working memory: Implications for language development. *International Journal of Language and Communication Disorders, 35*, 95–116.

American Psychiatric Association. (2000). *Diagnostic and statistical manual of mental disorders* (4th ed., text rev.), Washington, DC: American Psychiatric Association.

American Speech-Language-Hearing Association, (2005). *Evidence-based practice in communication disorders.* [Position Statement]. Available from www.asha.org/policy.

Anderson, V., Anderson, D., & Anderson, P. (2006). Comparing attentional skills in children with acquired and developmental nervous system disorders. *Journal of the International Neuropsychological Society, 12*, 519–531.

Awh, E., Barton, B., & Vogel, E. K. (2007). Visual working memory represents a fixed number of items regardless of complexity. *Psychological Science, 18*, 622–628.

Baddeley, A. D. (1986). *Working memory.* Oxford, UK: Clarendon Press.

Baddeley, A. D. (1996). Working memory. *Science, 255*, 556–559.

Barkley, R. A. (1997). *ADHD and the nature of self-control.* New York: Guilford.

Beck, I. L., Perfetti, C. A., & McKeown, M. G. (1982). Effects of long-term vocabulary instruction on lexical access and reading comprehension. *Journal of Educational Psychology, 74*, 506–521.

Bedore, L., & Leonard, L. (1998). Specific language impairment and grammatical morphology: A discriminant function analysis. *Journal of Speech, Language, and Hearing, Research, 41*, 1185–1192.

Botting, N., & Conti-Ramsden, G. (2004). Characteristics of children with specific language impairment. In L. Verhoeven and H. van Balkom (Eds.), *Classification of developmental language disorders: Theoretical issues and clinical implications* (pp. 23–28). Mahwah, NJ: Erlbaum.

Bracken, B. A. (2006a). *Bracken Basic Concept Scale–Third Edition: Receptive (BBCS-3:R)*. San Antonio, TX: Pearson.

Bracken, B. A. (2006b). *Bracken Basic Concept Scale–Expressive (BBCS: E)*. San Antonio, TX: Pearson.

Breslau, N., Chilcoat, H., DelDotto, J., Andreski, P., & Brown, G. (1996). Low birth weight and neurocognitive status at six years of age. *Biological Psychiatry, 40*, 389–397.

Brown, C. M., & Hagoort, P. (1999). *The neurocognition of language*. Oxford, UK: Oxford University Press.

Brown, T. R. (2000). *Attention-deficit disorders and comorbidities in children, adolescents, and adults*. Washington, DC: American Psychiatric Press.

Colombo, J. (2004). Visual attention in infancy: Process and product in early cognitive development. In M. I. Posner (Ed.), *Cognitive neuroscience of attention* (pp. 329–341). New York: Guilford.

Conti-Ramsden, G., & Botting, N. (1999). Classification of children with specific language impairment: Longitudinal considerations. *Journal of Speech, Language, and Hearing Research, 42*, 1195–1204.

Cowan, N. (1996). Short-term memory, working memory and their importance in language processing. *Topics in Language Disorders, 17*, 1–18.

Cowan, N., Day, L., Saults, J. S., Keller, T. A., Johnson, T., & Flores, L. (1992). The role of verbal output time and the effects of word length on immediate memory. *Journal of Memory and Language, 31*, 1–17.

Culatta, B., & Wiig, E. H. (2002). Language disabilities in school-age children and youth. In G. H. Shames & N. B. Anderson (Eds.) *Human communication disorders: An introduction*, 6th ed. (pp. 218–257). Boston: Allyn & Bacon.

Deevy, P., & Leonard, L. (2004). The comprehension of wh-questions in children with specific language impairment. *Journal of Speech, Language, and Hearing Research, 47*, 802–815.

Delis, D. C., Kaplan, E., & Kramer, J. (2001). *Delis-Kaplan Executive Function Scale*. San Antonio, TX: Pearson/PsychCorp.

Dornbush, M. P., & Pruitt, S. K. (1995). *Teaching the tiger: A handbook for individuals in the education of students with attention deficit disorders, Tourette syndrome, or obsessive-compulsive disorders*. Duarte, CA: Hope Press.

Dunn, L. M., & Dunn, D. M. (2006). *Peabody Picture Vocabulary Test–IV* (PPVT-IV). Eagan, MN: Pearson.

Entringer, S., Buss, C., Kumsta, R., Hellhammer, D. H., Wadhwa, P. D., & Wüst, S. (2009). Prenatal psychological stress exposure is associated with subsequent working memory performance in young women. *Behavioral Neuroscience, 123*, 886–893.

Fields, R. D. (2008, March). White matter matters. *Scientific American.* 54–61.

Fuchs, D., Mock, D., Morgan, P. L., & Young, C. L. (2003). Responsiveness-to-intervention: Definitions, evidence and implications for the learning disabilities construct. *Learning Disabilities Research & Practice, 18*, 157–171.

Gentner, D., & Namy, L. L. (2006). Analogical processes in language learning. *Current Directions in Psychological Science, 15*, 297–301.

German, D. J., & Newman, R. S. (2004). The impact of lexical factors on children's word-finding errors. *Journal of Speech, Language, and Hearing Research, 47*, 624–636.

German, D., & Simon, E. (1991). Analysis of children's word-finding skills in discourse. *Journal of Speech and Hearing Research, 34*, 309–316.

Gilger, J. W., & Wise, S. E. (2004). Genetic correlates of language and literacy impairments. In C. A. Stone, E. R. Silliman, B. J. Ehren, & K. Appel (Eds.) *Handbook of language and literacy: development and disorders* (pp. 25–48). New York: Guilford.

Haskill, A. M., & Tyler, A. A. (2007). A comparison of linguistic profiles in subgroups of children with specific language impairment. *American Journal of Speech-Language Pathology, 16*, 209–221.

Ho, H-Z., Baker, L. A., & Decker, S. N. (2005). Covariation between intelligence and speed of cognitive processing: genetic and environmental influences. *Behavior Genetics, 18*, 247–261.

Hresko, W. P., Reid, D. K., & Hammill, D. D. (1999). *Test of Early Language Development–3*. Austin, TX: PRO-ED.

Joanisse, M. F. (2004). Specific language impairments in children: Phonology, semantics, and the English past tense. *Current Directions in Psychological Science, 13*, 156–160.

Johnson, C. J. (2006). Getting started in evidence-based practice for childhood speech-language disorders. *American Journal of Speech-Language Pathology, 15*, 20–35.

Kail, R. V. (2007). Longitudinal evidence that increases in processing speed and working memory enhance children's reasoning. *Psychological Science, 18*, 312–313.

Kuhl, P. K. (2004). Early language acquisition: Cracking the speech code. *Neuroscience, 5*, 831–843.

Larson, V. L., & McKinley, N. L. (2003) *Communication solutions for older students: Assessment and intervention strategies*. Greenville, NC: Thinking Publications/Super Duper.

Leonard, C. M., Eckert, M. A., Given, B., Virginia, B., & Eden, G. (2006). Individual differences in anatomy predict reading and oral language impairments in children. *Brain, 129*, 3329–3342.

Leonard, C. M., Eckert, M. A., & Kuldau, J. M. (2006). Exploiting human anatomical variability as a link between genome and cognome. *Genes, Brain and Behavior, 5*, 64–77.

Leonard, C. M., Eckert, M. A., Lombardino, L. J., Oakland, T., Kranzler, J., Mohr, C. M., et al. (2001). Anatomical risk factors for phonological dyslexia. *Cerebral Cortex, 11*, 148–157.

Leonard, C. M., Kuldau, J. M., Maron, L., Ricciuti, N., Mahoney, B., Bengtson, M., & DeBose, C. (2008). Identical neural risk factors predict cognitive deficit in dyslexia and schizophrenia. *Neuropsychology, 22*, 147–158.

Leonard, C. M., Lombardino, L. J., Walsh, K., Eckert, M. A., Mockler, J. L., Rowe, L. A., et al. (2002). Anatomical risk factors that distinguish dyslexia from SLI predict reading skill in normal children. *Journal of Communication Disorders, 35*, 501–531.

Leonard, L. B. (1998). *Children with specific language impairment*. Cambridge, MA: MIT Press.

Leonard, L. B. (2009). Is expressive language disorder an accurate diagnostic category? *American Journal of Speech-Language Pathology, 18*, 115–123.

Leonard, L. B., Weismer, S. E., Miller, C. A., Francis, D. J., Tomblin, J. B., & Kail, R. V. (2007). Speed of processing, working memory, and language impairment in children. *Journal of Speech, Language, and Hearing Research, 50*, 408–428.

Lezak, M. D., Howieson, D. B., & Loring, D. W. (2004). *Neuropsychological assessment* (4th ed.). Oxford, UK: Oxford University Press.

Manly, T., Anderson, V., Nimmo-Smith, I., Turner, A., Watson, P., & Robertson, I. (2001). The differential assessment of children's attention: The Test of Everyday Attention for Children (TEA-Ch), normative sample and ADHD performance. *Journal of Child Psychology and Psychiatry, 42*, 1065–1081.

McGregor, K. K., Newman, R. M., Reilly, R., & Capone, N. C. (2002). Semantic representation and naming in children with specific language impairment. *Journal of Speech, Language and Hearing Research, 45*, 998–1014.

Miller, C. J., Miller, S. R., Bloom, J. S., Jones, L., Lindstrom, W., Craggs, J., et al. (2006). Testing the double-deficit hypothesis in an adult sample. *Annals of Dyslexia, 56*, 83–102.

Miller, G. A. (1956). The magical number seven plus or minus two: Some limits in our capacity for processing information. *Psychological Review, 63*, 81–97.

National Joint Committee on Learning Disabilities (NJCLD) (1994). [Position paper.] *Reprinted in Topics in Language Disorders,* 16 (1996), 69–73.

Nippold, M. A., Hesketh, L. J., Duthie, J. K., & Mansfield, T. C. (2005). Conversational versus expository discourse: A study of syntactic development in children, adolescents, and adults. *Journal of Speech, Language, and Hearing Research, 40*, 1048–1064.

Nippold, M. A., Mansfield, R. C., & Billow, J. L. (2007). Peer conflict explanations in children, adolescents, and adults: Examining the development of complex syntax. *American Journal of Speech-Language Pathology, 16*, 179–188.

Nippold, M. A., Mansfield, R. C., Billow, J. L., & Tomblin, J. B. (2008). Expository discourse in adolescents with language impairments: Examining syntactic development. *American Journal of Speech-Language Pathology, 17*, 256–366.

Nippold, M. A., Mansfield, R. C., Billow, J. L., & Tomblin, J. B. (2009). Syntactic development in adolescents with a history of language impairments: A follow-up investigation. *American Journal of Speech-Language Pathology, 18*, 241–251.

Ottinger, B. (2003). *Dictionary: A reference guide to the world of Tourette syndrome, Asperger syndrome, attention deficit hyperactivity disorders and obsessive compulsive disorder for parents and professionals.* Shawnee Mission, KS: Autism Asperger Publishing Co.

Paul, R. (2000). *Language disorders from infancy through adolescence* (2nd ed.). St. Louis, MO: Mosby.

Pinborough-Zimmerman, J., Satterfield, R., Miller, J., Bilder, D., Hossain, S., & McMahon, W. (2007). Communication disorders and comorbid intellectual disability, autism, and emotional/behavioral disorders. *American Journal of Speech-Language Pathology, 16*, 359–367.

Prestia, K. (2003). Tourette's syndrome: Characteristics and interventions. *Intervention in Schools and Clinics, 39*, 67–71.

Rice, M. L., & Wexler, K. (2001). *Rice/Wexler Test of Early Grammatical Impairment.* San Antonio, TX: Pearson Assessment/PsychCorp.

Rice, M., Taylor, C., & Zubrick, S. (2008). Language outcomes of 7-year-old children with and without a history of late language emergence at 24 months. *Journal of Speech, Language, and Hearing Research, 51*, 394–407.

Roid, G. H. (2003). *Stanford-Binet Intelligence Scales* (5th ed.). Itasca, IL: Riverside.

Roncadin, C., Pascual-Leone, J., Rich, J. B., & Dennis, M. (2007). Developmental relations between working memory and inhibitory control. *Journal of the International Neuropsychological Society, 13*, 59–67.

Rose, S. A., Feldman, J. F., & Jankowski, J. J. (2002). Processing speed in the 1st year of life: A longitudinal study of preterm and full-term infants. *Developmental Psychology, 38*, 895–902.

Semel, E., Wiig, E. H., & Secord, W. A. (2004). *CELF-Preschool–2.* San Antonio, TX: Pearson Assessment/PsychCorp.

Semrud-Clikeman, M., Steingard, R., Filipek, P., Biederman, J., Bekken, K., & Renshaw, P. (2000). Using MRI to examine brain-behavior relationships in males with attention deficit disorder with hyperactivity. *Journal of the American Academy of Child and Adolescent Psychiatry, 39*, 477–484.

Tallal, P. (2003). Language disabilities: Integrating research approaches. *Current Directions in Psychological Science, 12*, 206–211.

Tomblin, J. B., Mainela-Arnold, E., & Zhang, X. (2007). Procedural learning in adolescents with and without specific language impairments. *Language Learning Development, 3*, 269–293.

Tomblin, J. B., & Zhang, X. (2006). The dimensionality of language ability in school-age children. *Journal of Speech, Language, and Hearing Research, 49*, 1193–1208.

Tranel, D., Grabowski, T. J., Lyon, J., & Damasio, H. (2005). Naming the same entities from visual or from auditory stimulation engages similar regions of left inferotemporal cortices. *Journal of Cognitive Neuroscience, 17*, 1293–1305.

Ullman, M., & Pierpoint, E. (2005). Specific language impairment is not specific to language: The procedural deficit hypothesis. *Cortex, 41,* 399–433.

Van Daal, J., Verhoeven, L., & van Balkom, H. (2004). Subtypes of severe language impairments: Psychometric evidence from 4-year-old children in the Netherlands. *Journal of Speech, Language, and Hearing Research, 47,* 1411–1423.

Wechsler, D. (2003). *Wechsler Intelligence Scale for Children–Fourth Edition* (WISC-IV). San Antonio, TX: Pearson Assessment/PsychCorp.

Weismer, S. E. (2007). Typical takers, late talkers, and children with specific language impairment: A language endowment spectrum? In R. Paul (Ed.), *Language disorders from a developmental perspective* (pp. 83–101). Mahwah, NJ: Erlbaum.

Weismer, S. E., Evans, J., & Hesketh, L. J. (1999). An examination of verbal working memory capacity in children with specific language impairment. *Journal of Speech, Language, and Hearing Research, 42,* 1249–1260.

Weismer, S. E., Plante, E., Jones, M., & Tomblin, J. B. (2005). A functional magnetic resonance imaging investigation of verbal working memory in adolescents with specific language impairment. *Journal of Speech, Language, and Hearing Research, 48,* 405–425.

Wetherby, A. M. (2002) Communication and language disorders in infants, toddlers, and preschool children. In G. H. Shames & N. B. Anderson (Eds.) *Human communication disorders* (6th ed.) (pp. 186–217). Boston: Allyn & Bacon.

Wiig, E. H. (2004). *Wiig assessment of basic concepts.* Greenville, SC: Super Duper Publications.

Wiig, E. H., Langdon, H. W., & Flores, N. (2001). Nominación rápida y automática en niños hispanohablantes bilingües y monolingües. *Revista de Logopedia, Foniatria y Audiologia, 21,* 106–117.

Wiig, E. H., Nielsen, N. P., Minthon, L., & Jacobson, J. (2008). *AQT: Efficacy of a new paradigm for cognitive screening.* Poster presentation. International Conference on Alzheimer's Disease, Chicago, Illinois.

Wiig, E. H., Nielsen, N. P., Minthon, L., & Warkentin, S. (2002). *A quick test of cognitive speed (AQT).* San Antonio, TX: Pearson Assessment/Psych Corp.

Wiig, E. H., & Secord, W. (2003). *Classroom Performance Assessment (CPA).* Sedona, AZ & Arlington, TX: Red Rock Publications, Inc. & Schema Press.

Wiig, E. H., & Wilson, C. C. (1994). Is a question a question? Differential patterns in question answering by students with LLD. *Language, Speech and Hearing Services in Schools, 25,* 250–259.

Wiig, E. H., Zureich, P., & Chan, H. N. (2000). A clinical rational for assessing rapid, automatic naming in children with language disorders. *Journal of Learning Disabilities, 33,* 369–374.

Wilkinson, G. S. (2006). *Wide Range Achievement Test–Fourth Edition* (WRAT4). Lutz, FL: Psychological Assessment Resources.

Wolf, M., Bowers, P. G., & Biddle, K. (2000). Naming-speed processes, timing, and reading: A conceptual review. *Journal of Learning Disability, 33,* 387–407.

World Health Organization (2005). *International statistical classification of diseases and related health problems,* tenth revision (ICD-10). Geneva, Switzerland: Author.

Woodcock, R. W., McGrew, K. W., & Mather, N. (2001). *Woodcock-Johnson III.* Itasca, IL: Riverside.

Zimmerman, I. L., Steiner, V. G., & Pond, R. E. (2002). *Preschool Language Scale Fourth Edition.* San Antonio, TX: Pearson Assessment/PsychCorp.

CHAPTER 6

Al Otaiba, S., & Fuchs, D. (2002). Characteristics of children who are unresponsive to early literacy intervention: A review of the literature. *Remedial and Special Education, 23,* 300–316.

Al Otaiba, S., & Fuchs, D. (2006). Who are the young children for whom best practices in reading are ineffective? An experimental and longitudinal study. *Journal of Learning Disabilities, 39*, 414–431.

Barth, A. E., Stuebing, K. K., Anthony, J. L., Denton, C. A., Mathes, P. G., Fletcher, J. M., & Francis, D. J. (2008). Agreement among response to intervention criteria for identifying responder status. *Learning and Individual Differences, 18*, 296–307.

Bradley, R., Danielson, L., & Hallahan, D. (Eds.) (2002). *Identification of learning disabilities: Research to practice.* Mahwah, NJ: Erlbaum. Available from www.air.org/ldsummit.

Burns, M. K., & Senesac, S. V. (2005). Comparison of dual discrepancy criteria to assess response to intervention. *Journal of School Psychology. 43*(5), 393–406.

Clements, S. D. (1966). *Minimal brain dysfunction in children* [NINDB Monograph No. 3]. Washington, DC: U.S. Department of Health, Education, and Welfare.

Cohen, J. (1983). The cost of dichotomization. *Applied Psychological Measurement, 7*, 249–253.

Connor, C. M., Morrison, F. J., Fishman, B. J., Schatschneider, C., & Underwood, P. (2007). Algorithm-guided individualized reading instruction. *Science, 315*(5811), 464–465.

Donovan, M. S., & Cross, C. T. (2002). *Minority students in special and gifted education.* Washington, DC: National Academy Press. Available from www.nap.edu/catalog/10128.html.

Doris, J. L. (1993). Defining learning disabilities: A history of the search for consensus. In G. R. Lyon, D. B. Gray, J. F. Kavanagh, & N. A. Krasnegor (Eds.), *Better understanding learning disabilities: New views from research and their implications for education and public policies* (pp. 97–116). Baltimore, MD: Brookes.

Fiorello, C. A., Hale, J. B., & Snyder, L. E. (2006). Cognitive hypothesis testing and response to intervention for children with reading problems. *Psychology in the Schools, 43*(8), 835–853.

Fletcher, J. M., Coulter, W. A., Reschly, D. J., & Vaughn, S. (2004). Alternative approaches to the definition and identification of learning disabilities: Some questions and answers. *Annals of Dyslexia, 54*(2), 304–331.

Fletcher, J. M., Lyon, G. R., Fuchs, L. S., & Barnes, M. A. (2007). *Learning disabilities: From identification to intervention.* New York: Guilford.

Fletcher, J. M., Shaywitz, S. E., Shankweiler, D. P., Katz, L., Liberman, I. Y., Stuebing, K.K., et al. (1994). Cognitive profiles of reading disability: Comparisons of discrepancy and low achievement definitions. *Journal of Educational Psychology, 85*, 1–18.

Fletcher, J. M., & Vaughn, S. (2009a). Response to intervention: Preventing and remediating academic deficits. *Child Development Perspectives, 3*, 30–37.

Fletcher, J. M., & Vaughn, S. (2009b). RTI models as alternatives to traditional views of learning disabilities: Response to the commentaries. *Child Development Perspectives, 3*, 48–50.

Francis, D. J., Fletcher, J. M., Stuebing, K. K., Lyon, G. R., Shaywitz, B. A., & Shaywitz, S. E. (2005). Psychometric approaches to the identification of learning disabilities: IQ and achievement scores are not sufficient. *Journal of Learning Disabilities, 38*, 98–108.

Francis, D. J., Shaywitz, S. E., Stuebing, K. K., Shaywitz, B. A., & Fletcher, J. M. (1996). Developmental lag versus deficit models of reading disability: A longitudinal, individual growth curves analysis. *Journal of Educational Psychology, 88*, 3–17.

Fuchs, D., & Deshler, D. K. (2007). What we need to know about responsiveness to intervention (and shouldn't be afraid to ask). *Learning Disabilities Research & Practice, 2*, 129–136.

Fuchs, D., & Young, C. L. (2006). On the irrelevance of intelligence in predicting responsiveness to reading instruction. *Exceptional Children, 73*, 8–30.

Fuchs, L. S., & Fuchs, D. (1998). Treatment validity: A unifying concept for reconceptualizing the identification of learning disabilities. *Learning Disabilities Research & Practice, 13*, 204–219.

Fuchs, L. S., & Fuchs, D. (2004). Determining adequate yearly progress from kindergarten through grade six with curriculum-based measurement. *Assessment for Effective Instruction, 29*(4), 25–38.

Gresham, F. M. (2009). Using response to intervention for identification of specific learning disabilities. In A. Akin-Little, S. G. Little, M. A. Bray, & T. J. Kehl (Eds.), *Behavioral interventions in schools: Evidence-based positive strategies* (pp. 205–220). Washington, DC: American Psychological Association.

Hoskyn, M., & Swanson, H. L. (2000). Cognitive processing of low achievers and children with reading disabilities: A selective meta-analytic review of the published literature. *School Psychology Review, 29*, 102–119.

Individuals with Disabilities Education Improvement Act of 2004, Pub. L. 108-466. *Federal Register*, Vol. 70, No.118, pp. 35802–35803.

Jimerson, S. R., Burns, M. K, & VanDerHeyden, A. M. (2007). *Handbook of response to intervention: The science and practice of assessment and intervention.* Springfield, IL: Charles E. Springer.

Kavale, K. A. & Flanagan, D. P. (2007). Ability-achievement discrepancy, response to intervention, and assessment of cognitive abilities/processes in specific learning disability identification: Toward a contemporary operational definition. In S. R. Jimerson, M. A. Burns, & A. M. VanDerHeyden (Eds.), *Handbook of response to intervention: The science and practice of assessment and intervention* (pp. 130–147). New York: Springer.

Kavale, K., & Forness, S. (1985). *The science of learning disabilities.* San Diego, CA: College-Hill Press.

Mathes, P. G., Denton, C. A., Fletcher, J. M., Anthony, J. L., Francis, D. J., & Schatschneider, C. (2005). An evaluation of two reading interventions derived from diverse models. *Reading Research Quarterly, 40*, 148–183.

Morgan, W. P. (1896). A case of congenital word blindness. *British Medical Journal*, ii, 1378.

Morris, R., & Fletcher, J. M. (1988). Classification in neuropsychology: A theoretical framework and research paradigm. *Journal of Clinical and Experimental Neuropsychology, 10*, 640–658.

Morris, R., Lovett, M. W., Wolf, M., Sevcik, R., Steinbach, K., Frijters, J., & Shapiro, M. (in press). Multiple-component remediation for developmental reading disabilities: IQ, socioeconomic status, and race as factors in remedial outcome. *Journal of Learning Disabilities.*

Nelson, R. J., Benner, G. J., & Gonzalez, J. (2003). Learner characteristics that influence the treatment effectiveness of early literacy interventions: A meta-analytic review. *Learning Disabilities Research & Practice, 18*, 255–267.

Pashler, H., McDaniel, M., Rohrer, D., & Bjork, R. (2009). Learning styles: Concepts and evidence. *Psychological Science in the Public Interest, 9*, 105–119.

Reschly, D. J., & Tilly, W. D. (1999). Reform trends and system design alternatives. In D. Reschly, W. Tilly, & J. Grimes (Eds.), *Special education in transition* (pp. 19–48). Longmont, CO: Sopris West.

Reynolds, C. R. (1984). Critical measurement issues in learning disabilities. *Journal of Special Education, 18*, 451–476.

Reynolds, C. R., & Shaywitz, S. E. (2009). Response to intervention: Ready or not? Or watch-them-fail. *School Psychology Quarterly, 24*, 130–145.

Ross, A. D. (1976). *Psychological aspects of learning disabilities and reading disorders.* New York: McGraw-Hill.

Rutter, M. (1978). Dyslexia. In A. L. Benton & D. Pearl (Eds.), *Dyslexia: An appraisal of current knowledge.* New York: Oxford University Press.

Schatschneider, C., Wagner, R. C., & Crawford, E. C. (2008). The importance of measuring growth in response to intervention models: Testing a core assumption. *Learning and Individual Differences, 18*(3), 308–315.

Siegel, L. S. (1992). An evaluation of the discrepancy definition of dyslexia. *Journal of Learning Disabilities, 25*, 618–629.

Skinner, H. (1981). Toward the integration of classification theory and methods. *Journal of Abnormal Psychology, 90*, 68–87.

Spectrum K12 Solutions/The Council of Administrators of Special Education (2008). *Response to intervention (RTI) adoption survey.* Washington, DC: Council of Administrators of Special Education.

Speece, D. L., Case, L. P., & Molloy, D. E. (2003). Responsiveness to general education instruction as the first gate to learning disabilities identification. *Learning Disabilities Research & Practice, 18,* 147–156.

Stage, S. A., Abbott, R. D., Jenkins, J. R., & Berninger, V. W. (2003). Predicting response to early reading intervention from verbal IQ, reading-related language abilities, attention ratings, and verbal IQ-word reading discrepancy: Failure to validate discrepancy method. *Journal of Learning Disabilities, 36,* 24–33.

Stecker, P. M., Fuchs, L. S., & Fuchs, D. (2007). Using curriculum-based measurement to improve student achievement: Review of research. *Psychology in the Schools, 42,* 795–819.

Still, G. F. (1902). Some abnormal psychological conditions in children. *Lancet, 1,* 1077–1082.

Stuebing, K. K., Barth, A. E., Molfese, P. J., Weiss, B., & Fletcher, J. M. (2009). IQ is not strongly related to response to reading instruction: A meta-analytic interpretation. *Exceptional Children, 76,* 31–51.

Stuebing, K. K., Fletcher, J. M., LeDoux, J. M., Lyon, G. R., Shaywitz, S. E., & Shaywitz, B. A. (2002). Validity of IQ-discrepancy classifications of reading disabilities: A meta-analysis. *American Educational Research Journal, 39,* 469–518.

Swanson, H. L. (2008). *Neuroscience and RTI: A complementary role.* In E. Fletcher-Janzen & C.R. Reynolds (Eds.), *Neuropsychological perspectives on learning disabilities in the era of RTI: Recommendations for diagnosis and intervention* (pp. 14–27). Hoboken, NJ: Wiley.

U.S. Office of Education. (1968). *First annual report of the National Advisory Committee on Handicapped Children.* Washington, DC: U.S. Department of Health, Education, and Welfare.

VanDerHeyden, A., & Burns, M. (2010). *Essentials of response to intervention.* Hoboken, NJ: Wiley.

VanDerHeyden, A. M., Witt, J. C., & Gilbertson, D. (in press). A multi-year evaluation of the effects of a Response to Intervention (RTI) model on identification of children for special education. *Journal of School Psychology.*

Vaughn, S. R., Wanzek, J, Woodruff, A. L., & Linan-Thompson, S. (2006). A three-tier model for preventing reading difficulties and early identification of students with reading disabilities. In D. H. Haager, S. Vaughn, & J. K. Klingner (Eds.), *Validated reading practices for three tiers of intervention.* Baltimore, MD: Brookes.

Vellutino, F. R., Scanlon, D. M., Zhang, H., & Schatschneider, C. (2008). Using response to kindergarten and first grade intervention to identify children at risk for long-term reading difficulties. *Reading and Writing, 21*(4), 437–480.

Walker, H. M., Stiller, B., Serverson, H. H., Feil, E. G., & Golly, A. (1998). First step to success: Intervening at the point of school entry to prevent antisocial behavior patterns. *Psychology in the Schools, 35,* 259–269.

CHAPTER 7

American Institutes for Research. (2002). *Specific learning disabilities: Finding common ground.* Washington, DC: U.S. Department of Education.

Ashman, A. F., & Conway, R. N. F. (1997). *An introduction to cognitive education: Theory and applications.* London: Routledge.

Boden, C., & Kirby, J. R. (1995). Successive processing, phonological coding, and the remediation of reading. *Journal of Cognitive Education, 4,* 19–31.

Brailsford, A., Snart, F., & Das, J. P. (1984). Strategy training and reading comprehension. *Journal of Learning Disabilities, 17,* 287–290.

Carlson, J., & Das, J. P. (1997). A process approach to remediating word decoding deficiencies in Chapter 1 children. *Learning Disabilities Quarterly, 20*, 93–102.

Carroll, J. B. (2000). Commentary on profile analysis. *School Psychology Quarterly, 15*, 449–456.

Ceci, S. J. (2000). So near and yet so far: Lingering questions about the use of measures of general intelligence for college admission and employment screening. *Psychology, Public Policy, and Law, 6*, 233–252.

Cormier, P., Carlson, J. S., & Das, J. P. (1990). *Psychological testing and assessment*. Mountain View, CA: Mayfield.

Das, J. P. (1999). *PASS Reading Enhancement Program*. Deal, NJ: Sarka Educational Resources.

Das, J. P., Kar, B. C., & Parrila, R. K. (1996). *Cognitive planning: The psychological basis of intelligent behavior*. Thousand Oaks, CA: Sage.

Das, J. P., Mishra, R. K., & Kirby, J. R. (1994). Cognitive patterns of dyslexics: Comparison between groups with high and average nonverbal intelligence. *Journal of Learning Disabilities, 27*, 235–242.

Das, J. P., Mishra, R. K., & Pool, J. E. (1995). An experiment on cognitive remediation or word-reading difficulty. *Journal of Learning Disabilities, 28*, 66–79.

Das, J. P., Naglieri, J. A., & Kirby, J. R. (1994). *Assessment of cognitive processes*. Boston: Allyn & Bacon.

Das, J. P., Parrila, R. K., & Papadopoulos, T. C. (2000). Cognitive education and reading disability. In A. Kozulin & Y. Rand (Eds.), *Experience of mediated learning* (pp. 276–291). New York: Pergamon Press.

Davis, F. B. (1959). Interpretation of differences among averages and individual test scores. *Journal of Educational Psychology, 50*, 162–170.

Davison, M. L., & Kuang, H. (2000). Profile patterns: Research and professional interpretation. *School Psychology Quarterly, 15*, 457–464.

Dehn, M. J. (2000). *Cognitive Assessment System performance of ADHD children*. Paper presented at the annual meeting of the National Association of School Psychologists, New Orleans, LA.

Fagan, J. R. (2000). A theory of intelligence as processing: Implications for society. *Psychology, Public Policy, and Law, 6*, 168–179.

Flanagan, D. P., & Kaufman, A. S. (2004). *Essentials of WISC-IV assessment*. Hoboken, NJ: Wiley.

Flowers, L. A. (2007). Recommendations for research to improve reading achievement for African American students. *Reading Research Quarterly, 42*, 424–428.

Foreman, J. (2004). Game-based learning: How to delight and instruct in the 21st century. *Educause Review, 39*(5), 50–66.

Goldberg, E. (2002). *The executive brain: Frontal lobes and the civilized mind*. New York: Oxford University Press.

Goldstein, S., & Naglieri, J. A. (2009). *Autism Spectrum Rating Scale*. Toronto: Multi Health Systems.

Good, R. H., & Kaminski, R. A. (Eds.). (2002). *Dynamic Indicators of Basic Early Literacy Skills-Sixth Edition*. Eugene, OR: Institute for the Development of Educational Achievement.

Haddad, F. A., Garcia, Y. E., Naglieri, J. A., Grimditch, M., McAndrews, A., & Eubanks, J. (2003). Planning facilitation and reading comprehension: Instructional relevance of the PASS theory. *Journal of Psychoeducational Assessment, 21*, 282–289.

Hale, J. B., & Fiorello, C. A. (2004). *School neuropsychology: A practitioner's handbook*. New York: Guilford.

Hale, J. B., Kaufman, A. S., Naglieri, J. A., & Kavale, K. A. (2006). Implementation of IDEA: Integrating response to intervention and cognitive assessment methods. *Psychology in the Schools, 43*(7), 753–770.

Huang, L. V., Bardos, A. N., & D'Amato, R. C. (2010). Identifying students with learning disabilities: Composite profile analysis using the Cognitive Assessment System. *Journal of Psychoeducational Assessment, 28,* 19–30.

Individuals with Disabilities Education Improvement Act of 2004, 20 U. S.C. §§ 1401 *et seq.* (2005).

Iseman, J. S., & Naglieri, J. A. (in press). A cognitive strategy instruction to improve math calculation for children with ADHD: A randomized controlled study. *Journal of Learning Disabilities.*

Kar, B. C., Dash, U. N., Das, J. P., & Carlson, J. S. (1992). Two experiments on the dynamic assessment of planning. *Learning and Individual Differences, 5,* 13–29.

Kaufman, A. S. (1979). *Intelligent testing with the WISC-R.* New York: Wiley.

Kaufman, A. S., & Kaufman, N. L. (1983). *Kaufman Assessment Battery for Children.* Circle Pines, MN: American Guidance.

Kaufman, A. S., & Kaufman, N. L. (2004). *Kaufman Assessment Battery for Children–Second Edition.* Circle Pines, MN: American Guidance.

Kaufman, D., & Kaufman, P. (1979). Strategy training and remedial techniques. *Journal of Learning Disabilities, 12,* 63–66.

Kavale, K. A., Kaufman, A. S., Naglieri, J. A., & Hale, J. B. (2005). Changing procedures for identifying learning disabilities: The danger of poorly supported ideas. *The School Psychologist, 59,* 16–25.

Krywaniuk, L. W., & Das, J. P. (1976). Cognitive strategies in native children: Analysis and intervention. *Alberta Journal of Educational Research, 22,* 271–280.

Lewandowski, L., & Scott, D. (2008). Introduction to neuropathology and brain-behavior relationships. In R. C. D'Amato & L. C. Hartlage (Eds.), *Essentials of neuropsychological assessment: Treatment planning for rehabilitation* (2nd ed.). New York: Springer.

Luria, A. R. (1966). *Human brain and psychological processes.* New York: Harper and Row.

Luria, A. R. (1973). *The working brain.* New York: Basic Books.

Luria, A. R. (1980). *Higher cortical functions in man* (2nd ed.). New York: Basic Books.

Martin, N. A., & Brownell, R. (2005). *Test of Auditory Processing Skills, Third Edition.* Los Angeles: Western Psychological Services.

McDermott, P. A., Fantuzzo, J. W., & Glutting, J. J. (1990). Just say no to subtest analysis: A critique on Wechsler theory and practice. *Journal of Psychoeducational Assessment, 8*(3), 290–302.

Naglieri, J. A. (1999). *Essentials of CAS assessment.* New York: Wiley.

Naglieri, J. A. (2000). Can profile analysis of ability test scores work? An illustration using the PASS theory and CAS with an unselected cohort. *School Psychology Quarterly, 15,* 419–433.

Naglieri, J. A. (2005). The Cognitive Assessment System. In D. P. Flanagan & P. L. Harrison (Eds.), *Contemporary intellectual assessment* (2nd ed.) (pp. 441–460). New York: Guilford.

Naglieri, J. A. (2008a). *Naglieri Nonverbal Ability Test–Second Edition.* San Antonio, TX: Harcourt.

Naglieri, J. A. (2008b). Best practices in linking cognitive assessment of students with learning disabilities to interventions. In A. Thomas and J. Grimes (Eds.), *Best practices in school psychology* (5th ed.) (pp. 679–696). Bethesda, MD: National Association of School Psychologists.

Naglieri, J. A., & Conway, C. (2009). The Cognitive Assessment System. In J. A. Naglieri & S. Goldstein (Eds.), *A practitioner's guide to assessment of intelligence and achievement* (pp. 3–10). Hoboken, NJ: Wiley.

Naglieri, J. A., Conway, C., & Rowe, E. (2010). *An initial examination of the effects of computerized reading instruction on the academic performance of students from Title I schools.* Manuscript submitted for publication.

Naglieri, J. A., & Das, J. P. (1997a). *Cognitive Assessment System*. Itasca, IL: Riverside.

Naglieri, J. A., & Das, J. P. (1997b). *Cognitive Assessment System interpretive handbook*. Itasca, IL: Riverside.

Naglieri, J. A., & Das, J. P. (2005). Planning, Attention, Simultaneous, Successive (PASS) theory: A revision of the concept of intelligence. In D. P. Flanagan and P. L. Harrison (Eds.), *Contemporary intellectual assessment* (2nd ed.) (pp. 136–182). New York: Guilford.

Naglieri, J. A., & Das, J. P. (2006). *Cognitive Assessment System–Adattamento italiano a cura di S. Taddei*. Firenze, Italy: OS.

Naglieri, J. A., & Gottling, S. H. (1995). A cognitive education approach to math instruction for the learning disabled: An individual study. *Psychological Reports, 76*, 1343–1354.

Naglieri, J. A., & Gottling, S. H. (1997). Mathematics instruction and PASS cognitive processes: An intervention study. *Journal of Learning Disabilities, 30*, 513–520.

Naglieri, J. A., & Johnson, D. (2000). Effectiveness of a cognitive strategy intervention to improve math calculation based on the PASS theory. *Journal of Learning Disabilities, 33*, 591–597.

Naglieri, J. A., & Otero, T. (in press) Cognitive Assessment System: Redefining intelligence from a neuropsychological perspective. In A. Davis (Ed.), *Handbook of pediatric neuropsychology*. New York: Springer

Naglieri, J. A., Otero, T., DeLauder, B., & Matto, H. (2007). Bilingual Hispanic children's performance on the English and Spanish versions of the Cognitive Assessment System. *School Psychology Quarterly, 22*, 432–448.

Naglieri, J. A., & Paolitto, A. W. (2005). Ipsative comparisons of WISC-IV index scores. *Applied Neuropsychology, 12*, 208–211.

Naglieri, J. A., & Pickering, E. (2010). *Helping children learn: Intervention handouts for use in school and at home* (2nd ed.). Baltimore, MD: Brookes.

Naglieri, J. A., & Rojahn, J. R. (2004). Validity of the PASS theory and CAS: Correlations with achievement. *Journal of Educational Psychology, 96*, 174–181.

Naglieri, J. A., Rojahn, J., & Matto, H. (2007). Hispanic and non-Hispanic children's performance on PASS cognitive processes and achievement. *Intelligence, 35*, 568–579.

Naglieri, J. A., Rojahn, J. R., Matto, H. C., & Aquilino, S. A. (2005). Black and white differences in intelligence: A study of the PASS theory and Cognitive Assessment System. *Journal of Psychoeducational Assessment, 23*, 146–160.

Naglieri, J. A., Rowe, E. W., & Conway, C. (2010). *Empirical validation of an on-line literacy program using DIBELS for Title 1 students*. Manuscript submitted for publication.

Naglieri, J. A., Salter, C. J., & Edwards, G. (2004). Assessment of ADHD and reading disabilities using the PASS theory and Cognitive Assessment System. *Journal of Psychoeducational Assessment, 22*, 93–105.

Natur, N. H. (2009). *An analysis of the validity and reliability of the Das-Naglieri Cognitive Assessment System (CAS)*, Arabic edition. Unpublished doctoral dissertation. Howard University. Dissertation Abstract International, 70, no. 01B. Retrieved February 8, 2010, from Dissertations and Theses database.

Parrila, R. K., Das, J. P., Kendrick, M., Papadopoulos, T., & Kirby, J. (1999). Efficacy of a cognitive reading remediation program for at-risk children in grade 1. *Developmental Disabilities Bulletin, 27*, 1–31.

Penrose, L. S., & Raven, J. C. (1936). A new series of perceptual tests: Preliminary communication. *British Journal of Medical Psychology, 16*, 97–104.

Pivec, M. (2007). Editorial: Play and learn: Potentials of game-based learning. *British Journal of Educational Technology, 38*, 387–393.

Posner, M. I., & Boies, S. J. (1971). Components of attention. *Psychological Review, 78*, 391–408.

Regulations for the Individuals with Disabilities Education Act, 34 C.F.R. §§ 300.1 *et seq.* (2006).

Roid, G. (2003). *Stanford-Binet Intelligence Scales–Fifth Edition*. Itasca, IL: Riverside.

Rowe, E., Naglieri, J. A., & Conway, C. (2010). *Evaluation of an on-line literacy program for Title I students using DIBELS: A replication and extension study*. Manuscript submitted for publication.

Schneider, W., Dumais, S. T., & Shiffrin, R. M. (1984). Automatic and controlled processing and attention. In R. Parasuraman & D. R. Davies (Eds.), *Varieties of attention* (pp. 1–28). New York: Academic Press.

Segers, E., & Verhoeven, L. (2005). Long-term effects of computer training of phonological awareness in kindergarten. *Journal of Computer Assisted Learning, 21*, 17–27.

Silverstein, A. B. (1993). Type I, Type II, and other types of errors in pattern analysis. *Psychological Assessment, 5*, 72–74.

Suzuki, L. A., & Valencia, R. R. (1997). Race-ethnicity and measured intelligence. *American Psychologist, 52*, 1103–1114.

Taddei, S., & Naglieri, J. A. (2006). L'Adattamento Italiano del Das-Naglieri Cognitive Assessment System. In J. A. Naglieri & J. P. Das, *Cognitive Assessment System–Manuale*. Firenze, Italy: OS.

Wechsler, D. (2001). *Wechsler Individual Achievement Test—Second Edition*. San Antonio, TX: Psychological Corporation.

Wechsler, D. (2003). *Wechsler Intelligence Scale for Children–Fourth Edition*. San Antonio, TX: Psychological Corporation.

Wechsler, D., & Naglieri, J. A. (2006). *Wechsler Nonverbal Scale of Ability*. San Antonio, TX: Harcourt Assessment.

Woodcock, R. (1987). *Woodcock Reading Mastery Test–Revised*. Circle Pines, MN: American Guidance Service.

Woodcock, R. W., & Johnson, M. B. (1989, 1990) *Woodcock-Johnson Psycho-Educational Battery–Revised*. Allen, TX: DLM Teaching Resources.

Woodcock, R. W., McGrew, K. S., & Mather, N. (2001). *Woodcock-Johnson III Tests of Achievement*. Itsca, IL: Riverside.

CHAPTER 8

Aaron, P. G. (1997). The impending demise of the discrepancy formula. *Review of Educational Research, 67*, 461–502.

Alarcon, M., Pennington, B. F., Filipek, P. A., & DeFries, J. C. (2000). Etiology of neuroanatomical correlates of reading disability. *Developmental Neuropsychology, 17*, 339–360.

Anastasi, A., & Urbina, S. (1997). *Psychological testing*. Upper Saddle River, NJ: Prentice Hall.

Artiles, A., & Trent, S. (1994). Overrepresentation of minority students in special education: A continuing debate. *The Journal of Special Education, 27*, 410–437.

Barnett, B. W., Daly, E. J., & Jones, K. M., & Lentz, F. E. (2004). Response to intervention: Empirically based special service decisions from single-case designs of increasing and decreasing intensity. *Journal of Education, 38*, 66–79.

Baron, J. S. (2005). Test review: Weschler Intelligence Scale for Children–Fourth Edition (WISC-IV). *Child Neuropsychology, 11*, 471–475.

Barth, A., Stuebing, K. K., Anthony, J. L, Denton, C. A., Mathes, P. G., Fletcher, J. M., et al. (2008). Agreement among response to intervention criteria for identifying responder status. *Learning and Individual Differences, 18*, 196–307.

Bateman, B. (1964). Learning disabilities—yesterday, today, and tomorrow. *Exceptional Children, 31*, 167–177.

Batsche, G. M., Kavale, K. A., & Kovaleski, J. F. (2006). Competing views: A dialogue on response to intervention. *Assessment for Effective Intervention, 32*, 6–19.

Berninger, V., & Holdnack, J. (2008). Neuroscientific and clinical perspectives on the RTI initiative in learning disabilities diagnosis and intervention: Response to questions begging answers that see the forest and the trees. In: C. Reynolds & E. Fletcher-Janzen (Eds.), *Neuroscientific and clinical perspectives on the RTI initiative in learning disabilities diagnosis and intervention* (pp. 66–81). Hoboken, NJ: Wiley.

Berninger, V., Vaughan, K., Abbott, R., Brooks, A., Begay, K., Curtin, G., et al. (2000). Language-based spelling instruction: Teaching children to make multiple connections between spoken and written words. *Learning Disability Quarterly, 23,* 117–135.

Berninger, V. W. (2006). Research-supported ideas for implementing reauthorized IDEA with intelligent professional psychological services. *Psychology in the Schools, 43,* 781–796.

Berninger, V. W., & Abbott, R. D. (1994). Redefining learning disabilities: Moving beyond aptitude-achievement discrepancies to failure to respond to calibrated treatment protocol. In G. R. Lyon (Ed.), *Frames of reference for the assessment of learning disabilities: New views on measurement* (pp. 163–183). Baltimore, MD: Brookes.

Berninger, V. W., & Richards, T. L. (2002). *Brain literacy for educators and psychologists.* San Diego CA: Academic Press/Elsevier Science.

Bocian, K., Beebe, M., MacMillan, D., & Gresham, F. M. (1999). Competing paradigms in learning disabilities classification by schools and the variations in the meaning of discrepant achievement. *Learning Disabilities Research & Practice, 14,* 1–14.

Brown-Chidsey, R., & Steege, M. (2005). *Response to intervention: Principles and strategies for effective practice.* New York: Guilford.

Castellanos, F. X., Lee, P. P., Sharp, W., Jeffries, N. O., Greenstein, D. K., Clasen, L. S. et al. (2002). Developmental trajectories of brain volume abnormalities in children and adolescents with attention-deficit/hyperactivity disorder. *Journal of the American Medical Association, 288,* 1740–1748.

Caterino, L. C., Sullivan, A., Long, L., Bacal, E., Kaprolet, C. M, Beard, R., & Peterson, K. K. (2008). Assessing school psychologists' perspectives on independent educational evaluations. *APA Division 16 School Psychology, 62,* 6–12.

Ceci, S. J. (1990). *On intelligence . . . more or less: A bio-ecological treatise on intellectual development.* Englewood Cliffs, NJ: Prentice Hall.

Ceci, S. J. (1996). *On intelligence.* Cambridge, MA: Harvard University Press.

Chenault, B., Thomson, J., Abbott, R., & Berninger, V. (2006) Effects of prior attention training on child dyslexics' response to composition instruction. *Developmental Neuropsychology, 29,* 243–260.

Coch, D., Dawson, G., & Fischer, K. W. (2007). *Human behavior, learning, and the developing brain.* New York: Guilford.

Collins, D. W., & Rourke, B. P. (2003). Learning-disabled brains: A review of the literature. *Journal of Clinical and Experimental Neuropsychology, 25,* 1011–1034.

D'Amato, R. C., Fletcher-Janzen, E., & Reynolds, C. R. (2005). *Handbook of school neuropsychology.* Hoboken, NJ: Wiley.

Denckla, M. B. (2007). Executive function: Binding together the definitions of attention-deficit/hyperactivity disorder and learning disabilities. In L. Meltzer (Ed.), *Executive function in education: From theory to practice* (pp. 5–18). New York: Guilford.

Deno, E. (1970). Special education as developmental capital. *Exceptional Children, 37,* 229–237.

Detterman, D. K., & Thompson, L. A. (1997). What is so special about special education? *Special issue: Intelligence & Lifelong Learning, 52,* 1082–1090.

Dombrowski, S. C., Kamphaus, R. W., & Reynolds, C. R. (2004). The demise of the discrepancy: Proposed learning disabilities diagnostic criteria. *Professional Psychology Research and Practice, 35,* 364–372.

Donovan, M. S., & Cross, C. T. (2002). *Minority students in special and gifted education.* Washington, DC: National Academy Press.

Dunn, L. M. (1968). Special education for the mildly retarded—is much of it justifiable? *Exceptional Children, 35,* 5–22.

Elliott, C., Hale, J. B., Fiorello, C. A., Moldovan, J., & Dorvil, C. (in press). DAS-II prediction of reading performance: Global scores are not enough. *Psychology in the Schools.*

Epps, S., Ysseldyke, J., & McGue, M. (1984). Differentiating LD and non-LD students: "I know one when I see one." *Learning Disability Quarterly, 7,* 89–101.

Feifer, S. G., & Rattan, G. (2009). *Emotional disorders: A neuropsychological, pharmacological, and educational perspective.* New York: W. W. Norton.

Fiez, J. A., & Petersen, S. E. (1998). Neuroimaging studies of word reading. *Proceedings of the National Academy of Sciences, 95,* 914–921.

Filipek, P. A. (1999). Neuroimaging in the developmental disorders: The state of the science. *Journal of Child Psychology and Psychiatry, 40,* 113–128.

Fine, J. G., Semrud-Clikeman, M., Keith, T. Z., Stapleton, L. M., & Hynd, G. W. (2007). Reading and the corpus callosum: An MRI family study of volume and area. *Neuropsychology, 21,* 235–241.

Finn, J. D. (1982). Patterns in special education placement as revealed by the OCR surveys. In K. A. Heller, W. H. Holtzman, & S. Messick (Eds.), *Placing children in special education: A strategy for equity* (pp. 322–381). Washington, DC: National Academy Press.

Fiorello, C. A., Hale, J. B., Decker, S. L., & Coleman, S. (2009). Neuropsychology in school psychology. In E. Garcia Vazquez, T. D. Crespi, & C. A. Riccio (Eds.), *Handbook of education, training, and supervision of school psychologists in school and community* (pp. 213–233). New York: Routledge.

Fiorello, C. A., Hale, J. B., Holdnack, J. A., Kavanagh, J. A., Terrell, J., & Long, L. (2007). Interpreting intelligence test results for children with disabilities: Is global intelligence relevant? *Applied Neuropsychology, 14,* 2–12.

Fiorello, C. A., Hale, J. B., McGrath, M., Ryan, K., & Quinn, S. (2001). IQ interpretation for children with flat and variable test profiles. *Learning and Individual Differences, 13,* 115–125.

Fiorello C. A., Hale, J. B., & Snyder, L. E. (2006). Cognitive hypothesis testing and response to intervention for children with reading problems. *Psychology in the Schools, 43,* 835–853.

Fiorello, C. A., Hale, J. B., Snyder, L. E., Forrest, E., & Teodori, A. (2008). Validating individual differences through examination of converging psychometric and neuropsychological models of cognitive functioning. In S. K. Thurman & C. A. Fiorello (Eds.), *Applied cognitive research in K–3 classrooms* (pp. 151–186). New York: Routledge.

Flanagan, D. P., & Kaufman, A. (2009). *Essentials of WISC-IV assessment* (2nd ed.). Hoboken, NJ: Wiley.

Flanagan, D. P., Ortiz, S. O., & Alfonso, V. (2007). *Essentials of cross-battery assessment* (2nd ed.). Hoboken, NJ: Wiley.

Flanagan, D. P., Ortiz, S. O., Alfonso, V., & Dynda, A. (2006). Integration of response to intervention and norm-referenced tests in learning disability identification: Learning from the tower of Babel. *Psychology in the Schools, 43,* 807–825.

Flanagan, D. P., Ortiz, S. O., Alfonso, V. C., & Mascolo, J. (2006). *The achievement test desk reference (ATDR) (2nd ed.): A guide to learning disability identification.* Hoboken, NJ: Wiley.

Flanagan, D. P., Ortiz, S. O., Alfonso, V., & Mascolo, J. (2002). *The achievement test desk reference (ATDR): Comprehensive assessment and learning disabilities.* Boston: Allyn & Bacon.

Fletcher, J. M., Coulter, W. A., Reschly, D. J., & Vaughn, S. (2004). Alternative approaches to the definition and identification of learning disabilities: Some questions and answers. *Annals of Dyslexia, 54,* 304–331.

Fletcher, J. M., Francis, D. J., Morris, R. D., & Lyon, G. R. (2005). Evidence-based assessment of learning disabilities in children and adolescents. *Journal of Clinical Child and Adolescent Psychology, 34,* 506–522.

Fletcher, J. M., Francis, D. J., Shaywitz, S. E., Lyon, G. R., Foorman, B. R., Stuebing, K. K., & Shaywitz, B. A. (1998). Intelligent testing and the discrepancy model for children with learning disabilities. *Learning Disabilities Research & Practice, 13,* 186–203.

Fletcher, J. M., Shaywitz, S. E., Shankweiler, D. P., Katz, L., Liberman, I. Y., Stuebing, K. K., Francis, D. J., Fowler, A. E., & Shaywitz, B. A. (1994). Cognitive profiles of reading disability: Comparisons of discrepancy and low achievement definitions. *Journal of Educational Psychology, 86,* 6–23.

Fletcher, J. M., & Vaughn, S. (2009). Response to intervention: Preventing and remediating difficulties. *Child Development Perspectives, 3,* 30–37.

Fletcher-Janzen, E. (2005). *Handbook of school neuropsychology.* Hoboken, NJ: Wiley.

Fletcher-Janzen, E., & Reynolds, C. R. (Eds.). (2008). *Neuropsychological perspectives on learning disabilities in the era of RTI: Recommendations for diagnosis and intervention.* Hoboken, NJ: Wiley.

Flowers, L., Meyer, M., Lovato, J., Wood, F., & Felton, R. (2001). Does third grade discrepancy status predict the course of reading development? *Annals of Dyslexia, 51,* 49–71.

Francis, D. J., Shaywitz, S. E., Stuebing, K. K., Shaywitz, B. A., & Fletcher, J. M. (1996). Developmental lag versus deficit models of reading disability: A longitudinal, individual growth curves analysis. *Journal of Educational Psychology, 88,* 3–17.

Fuchs, D., & Deshler, D. D. (2007). What we need to know about responsiveness to intervention (and shouldn't be afraid to ask). *Learning Disabilities Research & Practice, 22,* 129–136.

Fuchs, D., & Fuchs, L. S. (2006). Introduction to response to intervention: What, why, and how valid is it? *Reading Research Quarterly, 41,* 93–99.

Fuchs, D., & Fuchs, L. S., & Compton, D. L. (2004). Monitoring early reading development in first grade: Word identification fluency versus nonsense word fluency. *Exceptional Children, 71,* 7–21.

Fuchs, D., Mathes, P., Fuchs, L., & Lipsey, M. (2001). *Is LD just a fancy term for underachievement? A meta-analysis of reading differences between underachievers with and without the label.* Nashville, TN: Vanderbilt University.

Fuchs, D., Mock, D., Morgan, P. L., & Young, C. L. (2003). Responsiveness-to-intervention: Definitions, evidence, and implications for the learning disabilities construct. *Learning Disabilities Research & Practice, 18,* 157–171.

Geary, D. C., Hoard, M. K., & Hamson, C. O. (1999). Numerical and arithmetical cognition: Patterns of functions and deficits in children at risk for a mathematical disability. *Journal of Experimental Child Psychology, 74,* 213–239.

Gerber, M. M. (2005). Teachers are still the test: Limitations of response to instruction strategies for identifying children with learning disabilities. *Journal of Learning Disabilities, 38,* 516–523.

Gottlieb, J., Alter, M., Gottlieb, B. W., & Wishner, L. (1994). Special education in urban America: It's not justifiable for many. *Journal of Special Education, 27,* 453–465.

Gresham, F. (2001). *Responsiveness to intervention: An alternative to the identification of learning disabilities.* Paper presented at the 2001 Learning Disabilities Summit: Building a Foundation for the Future. Retrieved from www.air.org/ldsummit/download, March 8, 2002.

Gresham, F. (2004). Current status and future directions of school-based behavioral interventions. *The School Psychology Review, 33,* 326–343.

Gustafson, S., Ferreira, J., & Ronnberg, J. (2007). Phonological or orthographic training for children with phonological or orthographic deficits. *Dyslexia, 13,* 211–229.

Hain, L. A., Hale, J. B., & Glass-Kendorski, J. (2009). Comorbidity of psychopathology in cognitive and academic SLD subtypes. In S. G. Pfeifer & G. Rattan (Eds.), *Emotional disorders: A neuropsychological, psychopharmacological, and educational perspective* (pp. 199–226). Middletown, MD: School Neuropsychology Press.

Hale, J., Alfonso, V., Berninger, V., Bracken, B., Christo, C., Clark, E., et al. (2010). Critical issues in response-to-intervention, comprehensive evaluation, and specific learning disabilities identification and intervention: An expert white paper consensus. *Learning Disability Quarterly, 33*, 1–14.

Hale, J. B. (2006). Implementing IDEA with a three-tier model that includes response to intervention and cognitive assessment methods. *School Psychology Forum: Research and Practice, 1*, 16–27.

Hale, J. B., & Fiorello, C. A. (2004). *School neuropsychology: A practitioner's handbook*. New York: Guilford.

Hale, J. B., Fiorello, C. A., Bertin, M., & Sherman, R. (2003). Predicting math competency through neuropsychological interpretation of WISC-III variance components. *Journal of Psychoeducational Assessment, 21*, 358–380.

Hale, J. B., Fiorello, C. A., & Brown, L. (2005). Determining medication treatment effects using teacher ratings and classroom observations of children with ADHD: Does neuropsychological impairment matter? *Educational and Child Psychology, 22*, 39–61.

Hale, J. B., Fiorello, C. A., Kavanagh, J. A., Hoeppner, J. B., & Gaither, R. A. (2001). WISC-III predictors of academic achievement for children with learning disabilities: Are global and factor scores comparable? *School Psychology Quarterly, 16*, 31–55.

Hale, J. B., Fiorello, C. A., Kavanagh, J. A., Holdnack, J. A., & Aloe, A. M. (2007). Is the demise of IQ interpretation justified? A response to special issue authors. *Applied Neuropsychology, 14*, 37–51.

Hale, J. B., Fiorello, C. A., Miller, J. A., Wenrich, K., Teodori, A. M., & Henzel, J. (2008). WISC-IV assessment and intervention strategies for children with specific learning disabilities. In A. Prifitera, D. H. Saklofske, & L. G. Weiss (Eds.), *WISC-IV clinical assessment and intervention* (2nd ed.) (pp. 109–171). New York: Elsevier Science.

Hale, J. B., Fiorello, C. A., & Thompson, R. (in press). Implementation of IDEA in neuropsychological report writing: Integrating RTI and cognitive assessment. In E. Arzubi, & E. Mambrino (Eds.), *Practical guide to neuropsychological evaluations*. New York: Springer.

Hale, J. B., Flanagan, D. P., & Naglieri, J. A. (2008). Alternative research-based methods for IDEA (2004) identification of children with specific learning disabilities. *Communiqué, 36*(8), *1*, 14–17.

Hale, J. B., Kaufman, A., Naglieri, J. A., & Kavale, K. (2006). Implementation of IDEA: Integrating response to intervention and cognitive assessment methods. *Psychology in the Schools, 43*, 753–770.

Hale, J. B., & Morley, J. (2009, February). *Combining RTI with cognitive hypothesis testing for effective classroom instruction*. Invited workshop at the Annual Convention of the National Association of School Psychologists, Boston, MA.

Hale, J. B., Naglieri, J. A., Kaufman, A. S., & Kavale K. A. (2004). Specific learning disability classification in the new Individuals with Disabilities Education Act: The danger of good ideas. *The School Psychologist, 58*(1), 6–14.

Helland, T. (2007). Dyslexia at a behavioural and a cognitive level. *Dyslexia, 13*(1), 25–41.

Hosp, J. L., & Reschly, D. J. (2004). Disproportionate representation of minority students in special education: Academic, demographic, and economic predictors. *Exceptional Children, 70*, 185–199.

Hosp, M. K., Hosp, J. L., & Howell, K. W. (2007). *The ABC's of CBM: A practical guide to curriculum-based measurement*. New York: Guilford.

Individuals with Disabilities Education Improvement Act of 2004, 20 U.S.C. §§ 1401 *et seq.* (2004).

Ikeda, M., & Gustafson, J. K. (2002). *Hearland AEA 11's problem-solving process: Impact on issues related to special education.* (Research rep. No. 2002-01). Johnson, IA: Heartland Area Education Agency 11.

Kaufman, A. S. (2008). Neuropsychology and specific learning disabilities: Lesson from the past as a guide to present controversies and future clinical practice. In E. Fletcher-Janen & C. R Reynolds (Eds.), *Neuropsychological perspectives on learning disabilities in the era of RTI: Recommendations for diagnosis and intervention.* Hoboken, NJ: Wiley.

Kavale, K. A. (2005). Identifying specific learning disability: Is responsiveness to intervention the answer? *Journal of Learning Disabilities, 38,* 553–562.

Kavale, K. A., Holdnack, J. A., & Mostert, M. P. (2005). Responsiveness to intervention and the identification of specific learning disability: A critique and alternative proposal. *Learning Disability Quarterly, 28,* 2–16.

Kavale, K. A., Kaufman, A., Naglieri, J., & Hale, J. (2005). Changing procedures for identifying learning disabilities: The danger of poorly supported ideas. *The School Psychologist, 59,* 15–25.

Kavale, K. A., Kaufman, J. M., Bachmeier, R. J., & LeFever, G. B. (2008). Response to intervention: Separating the rhetoric of self-congratulation from the reality of specific learning disability identification. *Learning Disability Quarterly, 31,* 135–150.

Kavale, K., & Forness, S. (1995). *The nature of learning disabilities.* Hillsdale, NJ: Erlbaum.

Kavale, K., Fuchs, D., & Scruggs, T. (1994). Setting the record straight on learning disability and low achievement: Implications for policy making. *Learning Disabilities Research & Practice, 9,* 70–77.

Keith, T. Z., Fine, J. G., Taub, G. E., Reynolds, M. R., & Kranzler, J. H. (2006). Higher order, multisample confirmatory factor analysis of the Wechsler Intelligence Scale for Children–Fourth Edition: What does it measure? *School Psychology Review, 35,* 108–127.

Learning Disabilities Roundtable (2002). *Specific learning disabilities: Finding common ground.* Washington, DC: U.S. Department of Education Office of Special Education Programs.

Learning Disabilities Roundtable (2004). *Comments and recommendations of regulatory issues under the individuals with Disabilities Education Improvement Act of 2004 P.L.108-446.* Washington, DC: U.S. Department of Education Office of Special Education Programs.

Lovett, M. W., Steinbach, K. A., & Frijters, J. C. (2000). Remediating the core deficits of developmental reading disability. *Journal of Learning Disabilities, 33,* 334–358.

Lyon, G. R., Fletcher, J. M., Shaywitz, S. E., Shaywitz, B. A., Torgesen, J. K., Wood, F., et. al. (2001). Rethinking learning disabilities. In C. E. Finn, Jr., R. A. J. Rotherham, & C. R. Hokanson, Jr. (Eds.), *Rethinking special education for a new century* (pp. 259–287). Washington, DC: Thomas B. Fordham Foundation and Progressive Policy Institute.

Machek, G. R., & Nelson, J. M. (2007). How should reading disabilities be operationalized? A survey of practicing school psychologists. *Learning Disabilities Research & Practice, 22,* 147–157.

Machek, G. R., & Nelson, J. M. (2010). School psychologists' perceptions regarding the practice of identifying reading disabilities: Cognitive assessment and response to intervention considerations. *Psychology in the Schools, 47,* 230–245.

MacMillan, D. L., Gresham, F. M., & Bocian, K. M. (1998). Discrepancy between definitions of learning disabilities and school practices: An empirical investigation. *Journal of Learning Disabilities, 31,* 314–326.

Macmillan, D. L., Gresham, F. M., Lopez, M. F., & Bocian, K. M. (1996). Comparison of students nominated for prereferral interventions by ethnicity and gender. *The Journal of Special Education, 30,* 133–151.

Macmillan, D. L., & Hendrick, L. G. (1993). Evolution legacies. In J. I. Goodlad & T. C. Lovitt (Eds.), *Integrating general and special education* (pp. 23–48). Columbus, OH: Merrill/Macmillan.

Macmillan, D. L., Siperstein, G. M., & Gresham, F. M. (1996). A challenge to the viability of mild mental retardation as a diagnostic category. *Exceptional Children, 62*, 356–371.

Macmillan, D. L., & Speece, D. L. (1999). Utility of current diagnostic categories for research and practice. Developmental perspectives on children with high-incidence disabilities. In R. Gallimore, L.P. Bernheimer, D. L. MacMillan, D. L. Speece, & S. Vaughn (Eds.), *Developmental perspectives on children with high-incidence disabilities. The LEA series on special education and disability* (pp. 111–133). Mahwah, NJ: Erlbaum.

Mastropieri, M. A., & Scruggs, T. E. (2005). Feasibility and consequences of response to intervention. *Journal of Learning Disabilities, 38*, 525–531.

Mather, N., & Gregg, N. (2006). Specific learning disabilities: Clarifying, not eliminating, a construct. *Professional Psychology, Research and Practice, 37*, 99–106.

Mather, N., & Roberts, R. (1994). Learning disabilities: A field in danger of extinction? *Learning Disabilities Research & Practice, 9*, 49–58.

McGrew, K. S., & Wendling, B. L. (2010). CHC cognitive-achievement relations: What we have learned from the past 20 years of research. *Psychology in the Schools.*

McKenzie, R. G. (2009). Obscuring vital distinctions: The oversimplification of learning disabilities within RTI. *Learning Disability Quarterly, 32*, 203–215.

Mercer, C. D., Jordan, L., Allsopp, D. H., & Mercer, A. R. (1996). Learning disabilities definitions and criteria used by state education departments. *Learning Disability Quarterly, 19*, 217–232.

Miller, D. C. (2009). *Best practices in school neuropsychology. Guidelines for effective practice, assessment, and evidence-based intervention.* Hoboken, NJ: Wiley.

Miller, D. C., & Hale, J. B. (2008). Neuropsychological applications of the WISC-IV and WISC-IV Integrated. In A. Prifitera, D. Saklofske, & L. Weiss (Eds.), *WISC-IV clinical use and interpretation: Scientist–practitioner perspectives* (2nd ed.). New York: Elsevier.

Miller, J. A., Getz, G., & Leffard, S. A. (2006, February). *Neuropsychology and the diagnosis of learning disabilities under IDEA 2004.* Poster presented at the 34th annual meeting of the International Neuropsychological Society, Boston, MA.

Naglieri, J. A. (1999). *Essentials of CAS assessment.* New York: Wiley.

Naglieri, J. A., & Bornstein, B. T. (2003). Intelligence and achievement: Just how correlated are they? *Journal of Psychoeducational Assessment, 21*, 244–260.

Naglieri, J. A., & Johnson, D. (2000). Effectiveness of a cognitive strategy intervention in improving arithmetic computation based on the PASS theory. *Journal of Learning Disabilities, 33*, 591–597.

National Advisory Committee on Handicapped Children (NACHC) (1968). *First annual report, special education for handicapped children.* Washington, DC: U.S. Department of Health, Education, and Welfare.

National Association of School Psychologists (2007). *Identification of students with specific learning disabilities* (Position Statement). Bethesda, MD: Author.

Nicholson, R. I., & Fawcett, A. J. (2001). Dyslexia, learning, and the cerebellum. In M. Wolf (Ed.), *Dyslexia, fluency, and the brain* (pp. 159–188). Timonium, MD: York Press.

O'Connor, R. E. (2000). Increasing the intensity of intervention in kindergarten and first grade. *Learning Disabilities Research and Practice, 15*, 43–54.

Ofiesh, N. (2006). Response to intervention and the identification of specific learning disabilities: Why we need comprehensive evaluations as part of the process. *Psychology in the Schools, 43*, 883–888.

O'Malley, K., Francis, D. J., Foorman, B. R., Fletcher, J. M., & Swank, P. R. (2002). Growth in precursor and reading-related skills: Do low achieving and IQ discrepant readers develop differently? *Learning Disabilities Research and Practice, 17*, 19–34.

Oswald, D. P., Coutinho, M. J., Best, A. M, & Singh, N. N. (1999). Ethnic representation in special education. *The Journal of Special Education, 32*, 194–206.

Peterson, K. M. H., & Shinn, M. R. (2002). Severe discrepancy models: Which best explains school identification practices for learning disabilities? *The School Psychology Review*, *31*, 459–476.

Pugh, K. R., Mencl, W. E., Shaywitz, B. A., Shaywitz, S. E., Fulbright, R. K., Constable, R. T., et al. (2000). The angular gyrus in developmental dyslexia: Task-specific difference in functional connectivity within posterior cortex. *Psychological Science*, *11*, 51–56.

Reddy, L. A., & Hale, J. B. (2007). Inattentiveness. In A. R. Eisen (Ed.). *Treating childhood behavioral and emotional problems: A step-by-step evidence-based approach* (pp. 156–211). New York: Guilford.

Regulations for the Individuals with Disabilities Education Act, 34 C.F.R. §§ 300.1 *et seq.* (2006).

Reschly, D. J. (2005). Learning disabilities identification. *Journal of Learning Disabilities*, *38*, 510–515.

Reschly, D. J., & Hosp, J. L. (2004). State SLD policies and practices. *Learning Disability Quarterly*, *27*, 197–213.

Reschly, D. J., & Ysseldyke, J. E. (2002). Paradigm shift: The past is not the future. In A. Thomas & J. Grimes (Eds.), *Best practices in school psychology IV* (4th ed.) (pp. 3–20). Bethesda, MD: National Association of School Psychologists.

Reynolds, C. (1984). Critical measurement issues in learning disabilities. *The Journal of Special Education*, *18*, 451–476.

Reynolds, C. (1988). Sympathy not sense: The appeal of the Stanford-Binet: Fourth Edition. *Measurement and Evaluation in Counseling and Development*, *21*, 45.

Reynolds, C. R. (1997). Forward and backward memory span should be not combined for clinical analysis. *Clinical Neuropsychology*, *12*, 29–40.

Reynolds, C. R., & Shaywitz, S. E. (2009). Response to intervention prevention and remediation, perhaps. Diagnosis, no. *Child Development Perspectives*, *3*, 44–47.

Richards, T. L., Aylward, E. H., Field, K. M., Grimme, A. C., Raskind, W., Richards, A. L., et al. (2006). Converging evidence for triple word form theory in children with dyslexia. *Developmental Neuropsychology*, *30*, 547–589.

Schrank, F. A., Miller, J. A., Caterino, L. C., & Desrochers, J. (2006). American Academy of School Psychology survey on the independent educational evaluation for a specific learning disability: Results and discussion. *Psychology in the Schools*, *43*, 771–780.

Semrud-Clikeman, M. (2005). Neuropsychological aspects for evaluating learning disabilities. *Journal of Learning Disabilities*, *38*, 563–568.

Shapiro, E. S. (2006). Are we solving the big problems? *School Psychology Review*, *35*, 260–265.

Shaywitz, B. A., Lyon, G. R., & Shaywitz, S. E. (2006). The role of functional magnetic imaging in understanding reading and dyslexia. *Developmental Neuropsychology*, *30*(1), 613–632.

Shaywitz, S. E., Shaywitz, B. A., Fulbright, R., Skudlarski, P., Mencl, W. E., Constable, R. T., et al. (2003). Neural systems for compensation and persistence: Young adult outcome of childhood reading disability. *Biological Psychiatry 54*, 25–33.

Siegel, L. S. (1989). IQ is irrelevant to the definition of learning disabilities. *Journal of Learning Disabilities*, *22*, 469–478.

Siegel, L. S. (1999). Issues in the definition of and diagnosis of learning disabilities: A perspective on Guckenberger v. Boston University. *Journal of Learning Disabilities*, *32*(4), 304–319.

Simos, P. G., Fletcher, J. M., Sarkari, S., Billingsley, R. L, Francis, D. J., Castillo, E. M., et al. (2005). Early development of neurophysiological processes involved in normal reading and reading disability. *Neuropsychology*, *19*, 787–798.

Smit-Glaude, S. W. D., Van Strien, J. W., Licht, R., & Bakker, D. J. (2005). Neuropsychological intervention in kindergarten children with subtyped risks of reading retardation. *Annals of Dyslexia*, *55*, 217–245.

Speece, D. L. (2005). Hitting the moving target known as reading development: Some thoughts on screening children for secondary interventions. *Journal of Learning Disabilities*, *38*, 487–493.

Spitzer, R. L, & Wakefield, D. S. W. (1999). DSM-IV diagnostic criterion for clinical significance: Does it help to solve the false positives problem? *The American Journal of Psychiatry*, *156*, 1856–1864.

Stage, S. A., Abbott, R. D., Jenkins, J. R., & Berninger, V. W. (2003). Predicting response to early reading intervention from verbal IQ, reading-related language abilities, attention rating, and verbal IQ–word reading discrepancy. *Journal of Learning Disabilities*, *36*, 24–33.

Stanovich, K. E. (1988). The right and wrong places to look for the cognitive locus of reading disability. *Annals of Dyslexia*, *38*, 154–177.

Stanovich, K. E. (1994). Constructivism in reading education. *The Journal of Special Education*, *28*, 259–274.

Stanovich, K. E. (2000). *Progress in understanding reading: Scientific foundations and new frontiers*. New York: Guilford.

Stanovich, K. E. (2005). *The robot's rebellion: Finding meaning in the age of Darwin*. Chicago: University of Chicago Press.

Stanovich, K. E., & Siegel, L. S. (1994). The phenotypic performance profile of reading-disabled children: A regression-based test of phonological core variable-difference model. *Journal of Educational Psychology*, *86*, 24–53.

Stein, S. M., & Chowdbury, U. (2006). *Disorganized children: A guide for parents and professionals*. London: Jessica Kingsley.

Sternberg, R. J., & Grigorenko, E. L. (2002). Difference scores in the identification of children with learning disabilities: It's time to use a different method. *Journal of School Psychology*, *40*, 65–83.

Stuebing, K. K., Fletcher, J. M., & LeDoux, J. M. (2002). Validity of IQ-discrepancy classifications of reading disabilities: A meta-analysis. *American Educational Research Journal*. *39*, 469–518.

Tallal, P. (2006). What happens when "dyslexic" subjects do not meet the criteria for dyslexia and sensorimotor tasks are too difficult even for the controls? *Developmental Science*, *9*, 262–264.

Thomas, A., & Grimes, J. (2008). *Best practices in school psychology, V*. Bethesda, MD: National Association of School Psychologists.

Tilly, W. D. (2008). The evolution of school psychology to evidence-based practice: Problem solving and the three-tiered model. In A. Thomas and A. J. Grimes (Eds.), *Best Practices in School Psychology* (5th ed., vol. 1, pp. 17–36). Bethesda, MD: National Association of School Psychologists.

U.S. Office of Education (1977). *Assistance to states for education of handicapped children: Procedures for evaluating specific learning disabilities*. Federal Register, 42(250), 6508265085.

Vanderheyden, A. M., Witt, J. C, & Gilbertson, D. (2007). A multi-year evaluation of the effects of a response to intervention (RTI) model on identification of children for special education. *Journal of School Psychology*, *45*, 225–256.

Vaughn, S., & Fuchs, L. S. (2003). Redefining learning disabilities as inadequate response to instruction: The promise and potential problems. *Learning Disabilities Research and Practice*, *18*, 137–146.

Vaughn, S., Linan-Thompson, S., & Hickman, P. (2003). Response to instruction as a means of identifying students with reading/learning disabilities. *Exceptional Children*, *69*, 391–409.

Vellutino, F. R., Scanlon, D. M., & Lyon, G. R. (2000). Differentiating between difficult-to-remediate and readily remediated poor readers: More evidence against the IQ-achievement discrepancy definition of reading disability. *Journal of Learning Disabilities*, *33*, 223–238.

Vellutino, F. R., Scanlon, D. M., Sipay, E. R., Small, S. G., Pratt, A., Chen, R., & Denckla, M. B. (1996). Cognitive profiles of difficult-to-remediate and readily remediated poor readers: Early intervention as a vehicle for distinguishing between cognitive and experiential deficits as basic causes of specific reading disability. *Journal of Educational Psychology, 88*, 601–638.

Watkins, M. W., Glutting, J. J., & Lei, P. W. (2007). Validity of the Full Scale IQ when there is significant variability among WISC-III and WISC-IV factor scores. *Applied Neuropsychology, 14*, 13–20.

Wechsler, D. (2009). *Wechsler Individual Achievement Test–Third Edition*. San Antonio, TX: Psychological Corporation.

Wiederholt, J. L. (1974). Historical perspectives on the education of the learning disabled. In: L. Mann & D. Sabatino (Eds.), *The second review of special education* (pp. 103–152). Philadelphia, PA: JSE Press.

Willis, J. O., & Dumont, R. P. (1998). *Guide to identification of learning disabilities* (1998 New York State Ed., p. 104). Acton, MA: Copley.

Willis, J. O., & Dumont, R. P. (2006). And never the twain shall meet: Can response to intervention and cognitive assessment be reconciled? *Psychology in the Schools, 43*, 901–908.

Wodrich, D. L., Spencer, M. L. S., & Daley, K. B. (2006). Combining RTI and psychoeducational assessment: What we must assume to do otherwise. *Psychology in the Schools, 43*, 797–806.

Ysseldyke, J. (2009). When politics trumps science: Generalizations from a career of research on assessment decision making, and public policy. *Communiqué, 38*(4), 6–8.

Ysseldyke, J., Algozzine, B., Shinn, M. R., & McGue, M. (1982). Similarities and differences between low achievers and students classified learning disabled. *The Journal of Special Education, 16*, 73–85.

Ysseldyke, J. E., & Marston, D. (2000). Origins of categorical special education services in schools and a rationale for changing them. In D. Reschly, D. Tilley, & J. Grimes (Eds.), *Functional and noncategorical special education* (pp. 137–146). Longmont, CO: Sopris West.

Zirkel, P. A., & Thomas, L. B. (2009). State laws for RTI: An updated snapshot. *Teaching Exceptional Children, 42*, 56–63.

CHAPTER 9

Altemeier, L., Abbott, R., & Berninger, V. (2008). Executive functions for reading and writing in typical literacy development and dyslexia. *Journal of Clinical and Experimental Neuropsychology, 30*, 588–606.

Amtmann, D., Abbott, R., & Berninger, V. (2007). Mixture growth models for RAN and RAS row by row: Insight into the reading system at work over time. *Reading and Writing. An Interdisciplinary Journal, 20*, 785–813.

Berninger, V. (1998). *Process Assessment of the Learner (PAL). Guides for Intervention. Reading and Writing*. Also, *Intervention Kit with Handwriting Lessons and Talking Letters*. San Antonio, TX: Psychological Corporation/Pearson.

Berninger, V. (2007a). *Process Assessment of the Learner–Second Edition. Diagnostic for Reading and Writing (PAL-II RW)*. San Antonio, TX: Psychological Corporation/Pearson.

Berninger, V. (2007b). *Process Assessment of the Learner Diagnostic for Math (PAL II-M)*. San Antonio, TX: Psychological Corporation/Pearson.

Berninger, V. (2007c). *Process Assessment of the Learner II User's Guide–Second Revision*. San Antonio, TX: Harcourt Assessment/PsychCorp.

Berninger, V. (2008a). *Understanding Dysgraphia*. Available from www.interdys.org.

Berninger, V. (2008b). Defining and differentiating dyslexia, dysgraphia, and language learning disability within a working memory model. In E. Silliman & M. Mody (Eds.), *Language impairment and reading disability: Interactions among brain, behavior, and experience* (pp. 103–134). New York: Guilford.

Berninger, V. (2008c). Evidence-based written language instruction during early and middle childhood. In R. Morris & N. Mather (Eds.), *Evidence-based interventions for students with learning and behavioral challenges* (pp. 215–235). Mahwah, NJ: Erlbaum.

Berninger, V. (2008d). Listening to parents of children with learning disabilities: Lessons from the University of Washington Multidisciplinary Learning Disabilities Center. *Perspectives on Language and Literacy, Fall Issue,* 22–30.

Berninger, V. (in press). Process Assessment of the Learner–Second Edition (PAL II): Comprehensive assessment for evidence-based, treatment-relevant differential diagnosis of dysgraphia, dyslexia, oral and written language learning disability (OWL LD), and dyscalculia. In N. Mather, & L. Jaffe (Eds.), *Comprehensive evaluations: Case reports for psychologists, diagnosticians, and special educators.* Hoboken, NJ: Wiley.

Berninger, V., Abbott, R., Nagy, W., & Carlisle, J. (2010). Growth in phonological, orthographic, and morphological awareness in grades 1 to 6. *Journal of Psycholinguistic Research.* Available from SpringerLink, www.springerlink.com/openurl.asp? genre=article&id=doi:10.1007/s10936-009-9130-6.

Berninger, V., Abbott, R., Swanson, H. L., Lovitt, D., Trivedi, P., Lin, S., Gould, L., Youngstrom, M., Shimada, S., & Amtmann, D. (in press). Relationship of word- and sentence-level working memory to reading and writing in second, fourth, and sixth grade. *Language, Speech, and Hearing Services in Schools.*

Berninger, V., Abbott, R., Thomson, J., & Raskind, W. (2001). Language phenotype for reading and writing disability: A family approach. *Scientific Studies in Reading, 5,* 59–105.

Berninger, V., Abbott, R., Thomson, J., Wagner, R., Swanson, H. L., Wijsman, E. & Raskind, W. (2006). Modeling developmental phonological core deficits within a working-memory architecture in children and adults with developmental dyslexia. *Scientific Studies in Reading, 10,* 165–198.

Berninger, V., Abbott, R., Trivedi, P., Olson, E., Gould, L., Hiramatsu, S., et al. (2009). Applying the multiple dimensions of reading fluency to assessment and instruction. *Journal of Psychoeducational Assessment.* Available from Sage Publications 10.1177/ 0734282909336083 http://jpa.sagepub.com, hosted at http://online.sagepub.com.

Berninger, V., & Abbott, S. (2003). *PAL Research-supported reading and writing lessons.* Also, *PAL Reproducibles for the Lessons.* San Antonio, TX: Harcourt/PsychCorp.

Berninger, V., & Fayol, M. (2008). Why spelling is important and how to teach it effectively. *Encyclopedia of Language and Literacy Development* (pp. 1–13). London, ON: Canadian Language and Literacy Research Network. Available from www.literacyencyclopedia.ca/ pdfs/topic.php?topId=234.

Berninger, V., & Hidi, S. (2006). Mark Twain's writers' workshop: A nature-nurture perspective in motivating students with learning disabilities to compose. In S. Hidi, & P. Boscolo (Eds.), *Motivation in writing* (pp. 159–179). Oxford, UK, and Amsterdam, The Netherlands: Elsevier.

Berninger, V., & Holdnack, J. (2008). Neuroscientific and clinical perspectives on the RTI initiative in learning disabilities diagnosis and intervention: Response to questions begging answers that see the forest and the trees. In C. Reynolds & E. Fletcher-Janzen (Eds.), *Neuroscientific and Clinical Perspectives on the RTI Initiative in Learning Disabilities Diagnosis and Intervention* (pp. 66–81). Hoboken, NJ: Wiley.

Berninger, V., & Nagy, W. (2008). Flexibility in word reading: Multiple levels of representations, complex mappings, partial similarities, and cross-modality connections. In Cartwright, K.

(Ed.), *Flexibility in literacy processes and instructional practice: Implications of developing representational ability for literacy teaching and learning* (pp. 114–139). New York: Guilford.

Berninger, V., Nagy, W., Carlisle, J., Thomson, J., Hoffer, D., Abbott, S., et al. (2003). Effective treatment for dyslexics in grades 4 to 6. In B. Foorman (Ed.), *Preventing and remediating reading difficulties: Bringing science to scale.* (pp. 382–417). Timonium, MD: York Press.

Berninger, V., Nielsen, K., Abbott, R., Wijsman, E., & Raskind, W. (2008a). Writing problems in developmental dyslexia: Under-recognized and under-treated. *Journal of School Psychology, 46,* 1–21.

Berninger, V., Nielsen, K., Abbott, R., Wijsman, E., & Raskind, W. (2008b). Gender differences in severity of writing and reading disabilities. *Journal of School Psychology, 46,* 151–172.

Berninger, V., O'Donnell, L., & Holdnack, J. (2008). Research-supported differential diagnosis of specific learning disabilities and implications for instruction and response to instruction (RTI). In A. Prifitera, D. Saklofske, L. Weiss (Eds.), *WISC-IV Clinical Assessment and Intervention–Second Edition* (pp. 69–108). San Diego, CA: Academic Press (Elsevier).

Berninger, V., & O'Malley, M. (in press). Evidence-based diagnosis and treatment for specific learning disabilities involving impairments in written and/or oral language. For special issue of Journal of Learning Disabilities on Cognitive and Neuropsychological Assessment Data That Inform Educational Intervention (guest editors, B. Hale & D. Fuchs).

Berninger, V., Raskind, W., Richards, T., Abbott, R., & Stock, P. (2008). A multidisciplinary approach to understanding developmental dyslexia within working-memory architecture: Genotypes, phenotypes, brain, and instruction. *Developmental Neuropsychology, 33,* 707–744.

Berninger, V., & Richards, T. (2002). *Brain literacy for educators and psychologists.* New York: Academic Press.

Berninger, V., Winn, W., Stock, P., Abbott, R., Eschen, K., Lin, C., . . . Nagy, W. (2008). Tier 3 specialized writing instruction for students with dyslexia. *Reading and Writing. An Interdisciplinary Journal, 21,* 95–129.

Berninger, V., & Wolf, B. (2009a). *Teaching students with dyslexia and dysgraphia: Lessons from teaching and science.* Baltimore, MD: Brookes.

Berninger, V., & Wolf, B. (2009b). *Helping students with dyslexia and dysgraphia make connections: Differentiated instruction lesson plans in reading and writing.* Baltimore, MD: Brookes.

Cassiday, L. (2009). Mapping the epigenome. New tools chart chemical modifications of DNA and its packaging proteins. *Chemical and Engineering News.* Retrieved from www.cen-online .org, September 14, 2009.

Delis, D., Kaplan, E., & Kramer, J. (2001). *Delis-Kaplan Executive Function System.* San Antonio, TX: Psychological Corporation/Pearson.

Dunn, A., & Miller, D. (2009). Who can speak for the children? Implementing research-based practices in an urban school district. In Rosenfield, S., & Berninger, V. (Eds.), *Implementing evidence-based interventions in school settings* (pp. 385–413). New York: Oxford University Press.

Garcia, N., Abbott, R., & Berninger, V. (2010). Predicting poor, average, and superior spellers in grades 1 to 6 from phonological, orthographic, and morphological, spelling, or reading composites. *Written Language and Literacy, 13,* 61–99.

Gilger, J. (2008). Atypical neurodevelopmental variation as a basis for learning disorders. In M. Mody & E. Silliman (Eds.), *Brain, behavior, and learning in language and reading disorders.* New York: Guilford.

Kaufman, A., & Kaufman, N. (2004). *Kaufman Test of Educational Achievement–Second Edition (KTEA-2).* San Antonio, TX: Pearson.

Pearson Education, Inc. (2009). Webinars on Preventing Reading, Writing, and Math Problems and Differential Diagnosis and Treatment of Dysgraphia, Dyslexia, Oral and Written

Language Learning Disability (OWL LD), and Dyscalculia. Available from http://psychcorp.pearsonassessments.com/pai/ca/training/webinars/RTIWebinarSeries.htm.

Petitto, L. (2009). New discoveries from the bilingual brain and mind across the lifespan and their implications for education. *Journal of Mind, Brain, and Education*.

Prifitera, A., Saklofske, D. H., & Weiss, L. G. (2005). *WISC-IV clinical use and interpretation: Scientist-practitioner perspectives*. San Diego, CA: Elsevier Academic Press.

Richards, T., Aylward, E., Berninger, V., Field, K., Parsons, A., Richards, A., & Nagy, W. (2006). Individual fMRI activation in orthographic mapping and morpheme mapping after orthographic or morphological spelling treatment in child dyslexics. *Journal of Neurolinguistics*, *19*, 56–86.

Richards, T., Aylward, E., Raskind, W., Abbott, R., Field, K., Parsons, A., et al. (2006). Converging evidence for triple word form theory in children with dyslexia. *Developmental Neuropsychology*, *30*, 547–589.

Richards, T., Berninger, V. & Fayol, M. (2009). FMRI activation differences between 11- year-old good and poor spellers' access in working memory to temporary and long-term orthographic representations. *Journal of Neurolinguistics*, *22*, 327–353.

Richards, T., Berninger, V., Stock, P., Altemeier, L., Trivedi, P., & Maravilla, K. (2009). fMRI sequential-finger movement activation differentiating good and poor writers. *Journal of Clinical and Experimental Neuropsychology*, *29*, 1–17.

Richards, T., Berninger, V., Winn W., Stock, P., Wagner, R., Muse, A., & Maravilla, K. (2007). fMRI activation in children with dyslexia during pseudoword aural repeat and visual decode: Before and after instruction. *Neuropsychology*, *21*, 732–747.

Richards, T., Berninger, V., Winn, W., Swanson, H.L., Stock, P., Liang, O., & Abbott, R. (2009). Differences in fMRI activation between children with and without spelling disability on 2-back/0-back working memory contrast. *Journal of Writing Research*, *1*(2), 93–123. Available from www.jowr.org.

Rosenfield, S., & Berninger, V. (Eds.) (2009). *Implementing evidence-based interventions in school settings*. New York: Oxford University Press.

Semel, E., Wiig, E. H., & Secord, W. A. (2003). *Clinical evaluations of language fundamentals* (4th ed.): *Examiner's manual*. San Antonio, TX: Harcourt Assessment, Inc.

Silliman, E., & Scott, C. (2009). *Research-based oral language intervention routes to the academic language of literacy: Finding the right road*. In Rosenfield, S., & Berninger, V. (Eds.), *Handbook on implementing evidence-based academic interventions* (pp. 107–145). New York: Oxford University Press.

Torgesen, J., Wagner, R., & Rashotte, C. (1999). *Test of Word Reading Efficiency*. Austin, TX: PRO-ED.

Wagner, R., Torgesen, J., & Rashotte, C. (1999). *Comprehensive Test of Phonological Processing*. Austin, TX: PRO-ED.

Washington, J., & Thomas-Tate, S. (2009). How research informs cultural-linguistic differences in the classroom: The bi-dialectal African American child. In Rosenfield, S., & Berninger, V. (Eds.), *Handbook on implementing evidence-based academic interventions* (pp. 147–163). New York: Oxford University Press.

Wechsler, D. (2003). *Wechsler Intelligence Scale for Children–Fourth Edition* (WISC-4). San Antonio, TX: Pearson.

Wiederholt, J., & Bryant, B. (2001). *Gray Oral Reading Test–Fourth Edition*. Odessa, FL: Psychological Assessment Resources.

Wodrich, D. (2008). Contemplating the new DSM-V: Considerations from psychologists who work with school children. *Professional Psychology: Research and Practice*, *39*, 626–532.

Wolf, M., & Denckla, M. (2005). *RAN/RAS Rapid Automatized Naming and Rapid Alternating Stimulus Tests*. Austin, TX: PRO-ED.

Woodcock, R. W., McGrew, K. S., & Mather, N. (2001, 2007). *Woodcock-Johnson III Tests of Achievement*. Rolling Meadows, IL: Riverside Publishing.

Yates, C., Berninger, V., & Abbott, R. (1994). Writing problems in intellectually gifted children. *Journal for the Education of the Gifted, 18*, 131–155.

CHAPTER 10

Bateman, B. (1965). An educational view of a diagnostic approach to learning disorders. In J. Hellmuth (Ed.), *Learning disorders:* Vol. 1 (pp. 219–239). Seattle, WA: Special Child Publications.

Carroll, J. B. (1993). *Human cognitive abilities: A survey of factor-analytic studies*. Cambridge, UK: Cambridge University Press.

Della Toffalo, D. (2010). Linking school neuropsychology with response-to-intervention models. In D. C. Miller (Ed.), *Best practices in school neuropsychology: Guidelines for effective practice, assessment, and evidence-based interventions* (pp. 159–184). New York: Guilford.

Flanagan, D. P., & Alfonso, V. C., Ortiz, S. O., & Dynda, A. (2006). Integration of Response-to-Intervention and Norm-Referenced Tests in Learning Disability Identification: Learning from the Tower of Babel. *Psychology in the Schools, 43*(7), 807–825.

Flanagan, D. P., Fiorello, C., & Ortiz, S. O. (2010). Enhancing practice through application of Cattell-Horn-Carroll theory and research: A "third method" approach to specific learning disability Identification. *Psychology in the Schools, 47*, 739–760.

Flanagan, D. P., & Kaufman, A. S. (2009). Essentials of WISC-IV Assessment (2nd ed. Hoboken, NJ: Wiley.

Flanagan, D. P., Kaufman, A. S., Kaufman, N. L., & Lichtenberger, E. O. (2008). *Agora: The marketplace of ideas. Best practices: Applying response to intervention (RTI) and comprehensive assessment for the identification of specific learning disabilities*. [6-hour training program/DVD]. Bloomington, MN: Pearson.

Flanagan, D. P., Ortiz, S. O., & Alfonso, V. C. (2007). Essentials of Cross-Battery Assessment with C/D ROM (2nd ed.). Hoboken, NJ: Wiley.

Flanagan, D. P., Ortiz, S. O., & Alfonso, V. C. (2011). Essentials of Cross-Battery Assessment with C/D ROM (3rd ed.). Hoboken, NJ: Wiley. Manuscript in preparation.

Flanagan, D. P., Alfonso, V. C., Mascolo, J. T., & Hale, J. B. (in press). The Wechsler Intelligence Scale for Children-Fourth Edition in neuropsychological practice. In A. Davis (Ed.), Handbook of pediatric neuropsychology (pp. 397–414). New York: Springer Publishing.

Flanagan, D. P., Ortiz, S. O., Alfonso, V. C., & Mascolo, J. (2002). The Achievement Test Desk Reference (ATDR): Comprehensive Assessment and Learning Disabilities. Boston: Allyn & Bacon.

Flanagan, D. P., Ortiz, S. O., Alfonso, V. C., & Mascolo, J. (2006). The Achievement Test Desk Reference (ATDR), Second Edition: A Guide to Learning Disability Identification. Hoboken, NJ: Wiley.

Fletcher, J. M., Lyon, G. R., Fuchs, L. S., & Barnes, M. A. (2007). *Learning disabilities: From identification to intervention*. New York: Guilford.

Fletcher, J. M., Taylor, H. G., Levin, H. S., & Satz, P., 1995. Neuropsychological and intellectual assessment of children. In: Kaplan, H. and Sadock, B. (Eds.), 1995. *Comprehensive textbook of psychiatry* (6th ed.) (pp. 581–601). Baltimore, MD: Williams & Wilkens.

Fletcher-Janzen, E., & Reynolds, C. R. (Eds.). (2008). *Neuropsychological perspectives on learning disabilities in the era of RTI: Recommendations for diagnosis and intervention*. Hoboken, NJ: Wiley.

Fuchs, L. S., & Fuchs, D. (1998). Treatment validity: A unifying concept for reconceptualizing the identification of learning disabilities. *Learning Disabilities Research and Practice, 13*, 204–219.

Fuchs, D., & Young, C. L. (2006). On the irrelevance of intelligence in predicting responsiveness to reading instruction. *Exceptional Children, 73*, 8–30.

Hale, J., Alfonso, V., Berninger, V., Bracken, B., Christo, C., Clark, E., et al. (2010). Critical issues in response-to-intervention, comprehensive evaluation, and specific learning disabilities identification and intervention: An expert white paper consensus. *Learning Disability Quarterly, 33*, 1–14.

Hale, J. B., & Fiorello, C. A. (2004). *School neuropsychology: A practitioner's handbook.* New York: Guilford.

Hale, J. B., Flanagan, D. P., & Naglieri, J. A. (2008). Alternative research-based methods for IDEA (2004): Identification of children with specific learning disabilities. *Communiqué, 36 (8)*, 1, 14–15.

Individuals with Disabilities Education Improvement Act of 2004, Pub. L. 108-466. *Federal Register*, Vol. 70, No.118, pp. 35802–35803.

Kaufman, A. S. (2008). Neuropsychology and specific learning disabilities: Lessons from the past as a guide to present controversies and future clinical practice. In E. Fletcher-Janzen & C. Reynolds (Eds.), *Neuropsychological perspectives on learning disabilities in an era of RTI: Recommendations for diagnosis and intervention* (pp. 1–13). Hoboken, NJ: Wiley.

Kavale, K. A. (2005). Identifying specific learning disability: Is responsiveness to intervention the answer? *Journal of Learning Disabilities, 38*, 553–562.

Kavale, K. A., & Flanagan, D. P. (2007). Utility of RTI and assessment of cognitive abilities/ processes in evaluation of specific learning disabilities. In Jimerson, S., Berns, M., & Van Der Heyden, A. (Eds.). *Handbook of Response to Intervention: The science and practice of assessment and intervention.* New York: Springer Science.

Kavale, K. A. & Forness, S. R. (2000). What definitions of learning disability say and don't say: A critical analysis. *Journal of Learning Disabilities, 33*, 239–256.

Kavale, K. A., Holdnack, J. A., & Mostert, M. P. (2005). Responsiveness to intervention and the identification of specific learning disability: A critique and alternative proposal. *Learning Disabilities Quarterly, 28*, 2–16.

Kavale, K. A., Kauffman, J. M., Bachmeier, R. J., & LeFever, G. B. (2008). Response-to-intervention: Separating the rhetoric of self-congratulation from the reality of specific learning disability identification. *Learning Disability Quarterly, 31*, 135–150.

Kavale, K. A., Kaufman, A. S., Naglieri, J. A., & Hale, J. B. (2005). Changing procedures for identifying learning disabilities: The danger of poorly supported ideas. *The School Psychologist, 59*, 16–25.

Kavale, K. A., Spaulding, L. S., & Beam, A. P. (2009). A time to define: Making the specific learning disability definition prescribe specific learning disability. *Learning Disability Quarterly, 32*, 39–48.

Keith, T. Z., Fine, J. G., Taub, G. E., Reynolds, M. R., & Kranzler, J. H. (2006). Higher order, multisample, confirmatory factor analysis of the Wechsler Intelligence Scale for Children– Fourth Edition: What does it measure? *School Psychology Review, 35*, 108–127.

Keogh, B. K. (2005). Revisiting classification and identification. *Learning Disability Quarterly, 28*, 100–102.

Lezak, M. (1995). *Neuropsychological assessment*, 3rd edition. New York: Oxford University Press.

Lichtenstein, R., & Klotz, M. B. (2007). Deciphering the Federal Regulations on identifying children with specific learning disabilities. *Communiqué, 36(3)*, 1, 13–16.

McCloskey, G., Perkins, L. A., & Van Divner, B. (2009). *Assessment and intervention for executive function difficulties.* New York: Routledge.

McGrew, K. S. (1997). Analysis of the major intelligence batteries according to a proposed comprehensive Gf-Gc framework. In, D.P. Flanagan, J.L. Genshaft, and P.L. Harrison (Eds.), *Contemporary intellectual assessment: Theories, tests, and issues* (pp. 151–180). New York: Guilford.

McGrew, K. S., & Knopik, S. N. (1996). The relationship between intra-cognitive scatter on the Woodcock-Johnson Psycho-Educational Battery–Revised and school achievement. *Journal of School Psychology, 34,* 351–364.

McGrew, K., & Wendling, B. (2010). Cattell-Horn-Carroll cognitive-achievement relations: What we have learned from the past 20 years of research. *Psychology in the School, 47,* 651–675.

Miller, D. C. (2007). *Essentials of school neuropsychological assessment.* Hoboken, NJ: Wiley.

Miller, D. C. (Ed.) (2010). *Best practices in school neuropsychology: Guidelines for effective practice, assessment, and evidence-based intervention.* Hoboken, NJ: Wiley.

Oakley, D. (2006) *Intra-cognitive scatter on the Woodcock-Johnson Tests of Cognitive Abilities–Third Edition and its relation to academic achievement.* Dissertation Abstracts International: Section B: The Sciences and Engineering, 67, 1199.

Pearson (2010). Wechsler Individual Achievement Test-Third Edition (WIAT-III). San Antonio, TX: Pearson.

Reynolds, C. R., & Kamphaus, R.W. (2004). *Behavior Assessment System for Children–Second Edition.* Circle-Pines, MN: American Guidance Service.

Reynolds, C. R., & Shaywitz, S. A. (2009a). Response to intervention: prevention and remediation, perhaps, diagnosis, no. *Child Development Perspectives, 3,* 44–47.

Reynolds, C. R., & Shaywitz, S. A. (2009b). Response to intervention: Ready or not? Or, from wait-to-fail to watch-them-fail. *School Psychology Quarterly, 24,* 130–145.

Siegel, L. S. (1999). Issues in the definition and diagnosis of learning disabilities: A perspective on Guckenberger v. Boston University. *Journal of Learning Disabilities, 32,* 304–320.

Stanovich, K. E. (1999). The sociopsychometrics of learning disabilities. *Journal of Learning Disabilities, 32,* 350–361.

U.S. Office of Education (USOE). (1977). Assistance to states for education of handicapped children: Procedures for evaluating specific learning disabilities. *Federal Register, 42*(250), 65082–65085.

Vellutino, F. R., Scanlon, D. M., & Lyon, G. R. (2000). Differentiating between difficult-to-remediate and readily remediated poor readers: More evidence against the IQ-achievement discrepancy definition of reading disability. *Journal of Learning Disabilities, 33,* 223–238.

Wechsler, D. (2003). *Wechsler Intelligence Scale for Children–Fourth Edition.* San Antonio, TX: Psychological Corporation.

Woodcock, R. W., McGrew, K. S., & Mather, N. (2001). *Woodcock-Johnson III Tests of Cognitive Abilities.* Itsca, IL: Riverside.

Zirkel, P. A., & Thomas, L. B. (2010). State laws for RTI: An updated snapshot. *Teaching Exceptional Children, 42*(3), 56–63.

CHAPTER 11

Aguera, F. (2006). *How language and culture impact test performance on the differential abilities scale in a pre-school population.* Unpublished manuscript. St. John's University, New York.

American Educational Research Association, American Psychological Association, & National Council on Measurement in Education. (1999). *Standards for educational and psychological testing.* Washington, DC: American Educational Research Association.

American Psychological Association. (1990). *Guidelines for providers of psychological services to ethnic, linguistic, and culturally diverse populations.* Washington, DC: Author.

American Psychological Association (2002). Ethical principles of psychologists and code of conduct. *American Psychologist, 57,* 1060–1073.

Bialystok, E. (1991). *Language processing in bilingual children.* Cambridge, UK: Cambridge University Press.

Braden, J. P., & Iribarren, J. A. (2005). Test Review: Wechsler, D. (2005). Wechsler Intelligence Scale for Children–Fourth Edition Spanish. *Journal of Psychoeducational Assessment, 25,* 292–299.

Brigham, C. C. (1923). *A study of American intelligence.* Princeton, NJ: Princeton University.

Cathers-Schiffman, T. A., & Thompson, M. S. (2007). Assessment of English- and Spanish-speaking Students with the WISC-III and Leiter-R. *Journal of Psychoeducational Assessment, 25,* 41–52.

Cummins, J. C. (1984). *Bilingual and special education: Issues in assessment and pedagogy.* Austin, TX: PRO-ED.

Dynda, A. M. (2008). *The relation between language proficiency and IQ test performance.* Unpublished manuscript. St. John's University, New York.

Esparza-Brown, J. (2007). *The impact of cultural loading and linguistic demand on the performance of English/Spanish bilinguals on Spanish language cognitive tests.* Unpublished manuscript. Portland State University, Portland, Oregon.

Figueroa, R. A. (1989). Psychological testing of linguistic-minority students: Knowledge gaps and regulations. *Exceptional Children, 56,* 145–152.

Figueroa, R. A. (1990). *Assessment of linguistic minority group children.* In C. R. Reynolds and R. W. Kamphaus (Eds.), *Handbook of psychological and educational assessment of children: Vol. 1, Intelligence and achievement.* New York: Guilford.

Figueroa, R. A. & Hernandez, S. (2000). *Testing Hispanic Students in the United States: Technical and policy issues.* Report to the President's Advisory Commission on Educational Excellence for Hispanic Americans. Washington, DC: U. S. Department of Education, Office of Educational Research and Improvement (OERI).

Flanagan, D. P., McGrew, K. S., & Ortiz, S. O. (2000). *The Wechsler intelligence scales and CHC theory: A contemporary approach to interpretation.* Boston: Allyn & Bacon.

Flanagan, D. P., & Ortiz, S. O. (2001). *Essentials of cross-battery assessment.* New York: Wiley.

Flanagan, D. P., & Ortiz, S. O., & Alfonso, V. C. (2007). *Essentials of cross-battery assessment* (2nd ed.). Hoboken, NJ: Wiley.

Flanagan, D. P., Ortiz, S. O., Alfonso, V. C., & Mascolo, J. (2006). *The Achievement Test desk reference (ATDR)–Second Edition: A guide to learning disability identification.* Hoboken, NJ: Wiley.

Goddard, H. H. (1913). The Binet tests in relation to immigration. *Journal of Psycho-Asthenics, 18,* 105–107.

Goddard, H. H. (1917). Mental tests and the immigrant. *Journal of Delinquency, 2,* 243–277.

Goldenberg, C. (2008). Teaching English language learners: What the research does—and does not—say. *American Educator, 32*(2) 8–23, 42–44.

Hakuta, K. (1991). *Mirror of language: The debate on bilingualism.* New York: Basic Books.

Harris, J. G., & Llorente, A. M. (2005). *Cultural considerations the use of the Wechsler Intelligence Scale for children–Fourth Edition.* In A. Prifitera, D. H. Saklofske, & L. G Weiss (Eds.), *WISC-IV clinical use and interpretation: Scientist-practitioner perspectives* (pp. 382–416). San Diego, CA: Academic Press.

Jensen, A. R. (1974). How biased are culture-loaded tests? *Genetic Psychology Monographs, 90,* 185–244.

Jensen, A. R. (1976). Construct validity and test bias. *Phi Delta Kappan, 58,* 340–346.

Jensen, A. R. (1980). *Bias in mental testing.* New York: Free Press.

Lohman, D. F., Korb, K., & Lakin, J. (2008). Identifying academically gifted English language learners using nonverbal tests: A comparison of the Raven, NNAT, and CogAT. *Gifted Child Quarterly, 52*, 275–296.

Mercer, J. R. (1979). *The system of multicultural pluralistic assessment: Technical manual.* New York: The Psychological Corporation.

Mpofu, E., & Ortiz, S. O. (2010). *Equitable assessment practices in diverse contexts.* In E. L. Grigorenko (Ed.), *Assessment of abilities and competencies in the era of globalization.* New York, NY: Springer Publishing Company.

Muñoz-Sandoval, A. F., Woodcock, R. W., McGrew, K. S., & Mather, N. (2005). *Batería III Woodcock-Muñoz: Pruebas de habilidades cognitivas.* Itasca, IL: Riverside Publishing.

Nieves-Brull, A. (2006). *Evaluation of the Culture-Language Matrix: A validation study of test performance in monolingual English speaking and bilingual English/Spanish speaking populations.* Unpublished manuscript. St. John's University, New York.

Oakland, T. (1976). *Non-biased assessment of minority group children: With bias toward none.* Paper presented at the National Planning Conference on Nondiscriminatory Assessment for Handicapped Children, Lexington, Kentucky.

Oakland, T., & Harris, J. G. (2009). Impact of test-taking behaviors on Full Scale IQ scores from the Wechsler Intelligence Scale for Children—IV Spanish edition. *Journal of Psychoeducational Assessment, 27*(5), 366–373.

Oakland, T., & Laosa, L. M. (1976). *Professional, legislative, and judicial influences on psychoeducational assessment practices in schools.* Paper presented at the National Planning Conference on Nondiscriminatory Assessment for Handicapped Children, Lexington, Kentucky.

Ortiz, S. O. (2008). Best practices in nondiscriminatory assessment. In A. Thomas & J. Grimes (Eds.), *Best practices in school psychology V*, (pp. 661–678). Washington, DC: National Association of School Psychologists.

Ortiz, S. O., & Dynda, A. M. (2010). Diversity, fairness, utility and social issues. In E. Mpofu & T. Oakland (Eds.), *Assessment in rehabilitation and health.* Boston: Allyn & Bacon.

Ortiz, S. O., & Ochoa, S. H. (2005). Intellectual assessment: A nondiscriminatory interpretive approach. In D. P. Flanagan & P. L. Harrison (Eds.), *Contemporary intellectual assessment* (2nd ed.) (pp. 234–250). New York: Guilford.

Reynolds, C. R. (2000). Methods for detecting and evaluating cultural bias in neuropsychological tests. In E. Fletcher-Janzen, T. Strickland, & C. R. Reynolds, (Eds.), *Handbook of cross-cultural neuropsychology* (pp. 249–285). New York: Kluwer Academic/ Plenum Publishers.

Rhodes, R., Ochoa, S. H., & Ortiz, S. O. (2005). *Assessment of culturally and linguistically diverse students: A practical guide.* New York: Guilford.

Salvia, J., & Ysseldyke, J. (1991). *Assessment in special and remedial education* (5th ed.). Boston: Houghton-Mifflin.

Sanchez, G. I. (1934). The implications of basal vocabulary to the measurement of the abilities of bilingual children. *The Journal of Social Psychology, 5*, 395–402.

Sandoval, J. (1979). The WISC-R and internal evidence of test bias with minority groups. *Journal of Consulting and Clinical Psychology, 47*, 919–927.

Sandoval, J., Frisby, C. L., Geisinger, K. F., Scheuneman, J. D., & Grenier, J. R. (Eds.). (1998). *Test interpretation and diversity: Achieving equity in assessment.* Washington, DC: American Psychological Association.

Sattler, J. (1992). *Assessment of children* (revised and updated 3rd ed.). San Diego, CA: Author.

Sotelo-Dynega, M. (2007). *Cognitive performance and the development of English language proficiency.* Unpublished manuscript. St. John's University, New York.

Tychanska, J. (2009). *Evaluation of speech and language impairment using the Culture-Language Test Classifications and Interpretive Matrix.* Unpublished manuscript. St. John's University, New York.

Valdes, G., & Figueroa, R. A. (1994). *Bilingualism and testing: A special case of bias.* Norwood, NJ: Ablex.

Vukovich, D., & Figueroa, R.A. (1982). *The validation of the system of multicultural pluralistic assessment: 1980–1982.* Unpublished manuscript, University of California at Davis, Department of Education.

Wechsler, D. (2005). *Wechsler Intelligence Scale for Children–Fourth Edition Spanish.* San Antonio, TX: Psychological Corporation.

Weiss, L. G., Harris, J. G., Prifitera, A., Courville, T., Rolfhus, E., Saklofske, D. H., & Holdnack, J. A. (2006). WISC-IV interpretation in societal context. In L. G Weiss, D. H. Saklofske, & J. Holdnack (Eds.), *WISC-IV advanced clinical interpretation* (pp. 1–57). Burlington, MA: Academic Press.

Woodcock, R. W., McGrew, K. S., & Mather, N. (2001). *Woodcock-Johnson III Tests of Cognitive Abilities.* Itasca, IL: Riverside Publishing.

Yerkes, R. M. (1921). Psychological examining in the United States Army. *Memoirs of the National Academy of Sciences, 15,* 1–890.

Annotated Bibliography

Berninger, V. (2007). *Process assessment of the Learner II User's Guide.* San Antonio, TX: Harcourt/PsychCorp (CD format). Second revision issued August, 2008; decoder for Table of Contents, 2009.

Research-based guidance for making differential diagnoses based on assessment data for dysgraphia, dyslexia, oral and written language learning disability (OWL LD), and dyscalculia, and linking assessment results to instructional interventions.

Feifer, S. G., & Della Toffalo, D. A. (2007). *Integrating RTI with cognitive neuropsychology: A scientific approach to reading.* Middletown, MD: School Neuropsych Press.

This book examines the underlying causes of reading disorders from a brain-behavioral perspective within an RTI service delivery model. There are four main subtypes of reading disorders discussed, with 20 evidence-based intervention programs reviewed as well.

Flanagan, D. P., & Harrison, P. L. (Eds.). (2005). *Contemporary intellectual assessment: Theories, tests, and issues* (2nd ed.). New York: Guilford.

A hard-cover edited book that includes chapters on all major intelligence tests, including the WJ III, WISC-IV, KABC-II, and SB5, as well as the prevailing theories of the structure of cognitive abilities and the nature of intelligence. In addition, a variety of new approaches to test interpretation are included, alongside guidelines for using tests of cognitive ability with different populations (e.g., preschool, learning disabled, gifted, culturally and linguistically diverse, etc.).

Flanagan, D. P., Ortiz, S. O., & Alfonso, V. C. (2007). *Essentials of cross-battery assessment* (2nd ed.). Hoboken, NJ: Wiley.

This volume provides a comprehensive set of guidelines and procedures for organizing assessments based on contemporary CHC theory and research, integrating test results from different batteries in a psychometrically defensible way, and interpreting test results within the context of research on the relations between cognitive and academic abilities and processes. It also includes guidelines for assessing culturally and linguistically diverse populations and individuals suspected of having a specific learning disability. The book includes a CD-ROM containing three software programs for assisting in data management and interpretation, making decisions regarding specific learning disabilities, and discerning difference from disability in individuals whose cultural and linguistic backgrounds vary from the mainstream.

Flanagan, D. P., Ortiz, S. O., Alfonso, V. C., & Mascolo, J. T. (2006). *The achievement test desk reference (ATDR): A guide to learning disability identification* (2nd ed.). Hoboken, NJ: Wiley.

This reference reviews comprehensive, brief, and special-purpose tests of achievement, including the WIAT-II, KTEA-II, and WJ III, and specialized reading, math, and written language tests, and tests of auditory and phonological processing. It explains how to integrate findings from achievement tests with findings from cognitive tests following CHC theory and its research base, offers an operational definition of specific learning disability (SLD), and demonstrates how to incorporate this definition into everyday practice in the schools.

Fletcher, J. M., Lyon, G. R.,Fuchs, L. S., and Barnes, M. A. (2007). *Learning disabilities: From identification to intervention*. New York: Guilford.

This book articulates a classification of LD around academic deficiencies in word reading, reading fluency, reading comprehension, mathematics calculation and problem solving, and written expression. Within each type of LD, it reviews research on identification, cognitive correlates, and neural and environmental factors. In addition to a review of the history of LD, the authors address models of classification and identification, along with assessment issues.

Fletcher-Janzen, E., & Reynolds, C. R. (Eds.). (2008). *Neuropsychological perspectives on learning disabilities in the era of RTI: Recommendations for diagnosis and intervention*. Hoboken, NJ: Wiley.

This book illuminates the contribution of neuroscience and neuropsychology to the identification of specific learning disabilities. It is written with an eye toward the future of education and how it will embrace neuroscientific findings going forward. The contributing authors of this book use research to answer three important questions: (1) How do you reconcile RTI as a means of diagnosis of LD with knowledge from the clinical neurosciences? (2) What role does neuropsychology have to play in the diagnosis of LD? (3) What role does neuropsychology have in designing interventions in the context of RTI?

Hale, James B., & Fiorello, Catherine A. (2004). *School neuropsychology: A practitioner's handbook*. New York: Guilford.

This practitioner-friendly bestselling book provides fundamental knowledge of brain-behavior relationships for interpretation of cognitive and neuropsychology tests, and methods for linking assessment data to intervention.

Mather, N., & Jaffe, L. (Eds.). (in press). *Comprehensive evaluations: Case reports for psychologists, diagnosticians, and special educators*. Hoboken, NJ: Wiley.

This book provides samples of varied assessment reports written by leading experts in the fields of psychology and special education. The reports are written from a variety of perspectives and settings (e.g., clinical, school, and private practice) and by evaluators from varied backgrounds (e.g., test developers, neuropsychologists, university professors, school and clinical psychologists, diagnosticians, and speech language pathologists).

Mather, N., Wendling, B. J., & Roberts, R. (2009). *Writing assessment and instruction for students with learning disabilities*. San Francisco: Jossey-Bass

This book addresses the informal assessment of written language, including CBM measures, as well as how to analyze written products to determine appropriate interventions. Various interventions are described that may be used to address difficulties in handwriting, spelling, and written composition. Numerous writing samples are included that illustrate different types of problems, as well as provide practice with analysis.

Miller, Daniel C. (Ed.). (2010). *Best practices in school neuropsychology: Guidelines for effective practice, assessment, and evidence-based interventions*. Hoboken, NJ: Wiley.

A comprehensive guide to the practice of school neuropsychology, including current assessment and intervention models and clinical applications of school neuropsychology with special populations.

Naglieri, J. A., & Goldstein, S. (2009). *A practitioner's guide to assessment of intelligence and achievement*. Hoboken, NJ: Wiley.

This edited book is a valuable resource for students and practitioners interested in understanding and interpreting all the major intelligence and achievement tests commonly used. Each chapter is written by the test author or a closely affiliated professional using the same basic outline, which includes: the theory behind the test; description; administration and scoring; psychometric characteristics; interpretation; and correspondence to IDEA.

Naglieri, J. A., & Pickering, E. B. (2010). *Helping children learn: Intervention handouts for use at school and home* (2nd ed.). Baltimore, MD: Brookes.

The second edition of Helping Children Learn *takes the successful formula for handouts to a new level. The book now includes several case studies that illustrate how the PASS theory can be used to select interventions from the book. This edition also contains nearly 150 intervention handouts for parents and teachers, including those for the students themselves, as well as handouts in Spanish.*

Rhodes, R.,Ochoa, S. H., & Ortiz, S. O. (2005). *Assessment of culturally and linguistically diverse students: A practical guide.* New York: Guilford.

This volume is an excellent resource that covers all of the major aspects of working with and evaluating culturally and linguistically diverse students. It has chapters that span the prereferral process, special education, bilingual education, acculturation, as well as evaluation of language proficiency, academic skills, and cognitive abilities. It provides a broad and in-depth framework for engaging in nondiscriminatory assessment that constitutes today's best practices in evaluating diverse individuals.

Swanson, H. L., Harris, K. R., & Graham, S. (Eds.). (2003). *Handbook of learning disabilities.* New York: Guilford.

A comprehensive handbook that provides reviews of major theoretical, methodological, and instructional advances in the field of learning disabilities. It also includes a large body of knowledge on the nature of learning disabilities, their relationship to basic psychological and neuropsychological processes, and how students with learning disabilities can be identified and treated.

Wendling, B., & Mather, N. (2009). *Essentials of evidence-based academic interventions.* Hoboken, NJ: Wiley.

This book provides descriptions of instructional techniques that are appropriate for the effective use of evidence-based academic interventions. It includes coverage of phonological awareness, beginning reading, phonics and sight word instruction, reading fluency, vocabulary, reading comprehension, spelling, written expression, basic math skills, and math problem solving. In addition, the general principles of effective instruction and the relevance of cognitive abilities to academic interventions are discussed.

ABOUT THE EDITORS

Dawn P. Flanagan, Ph.D. is Professor of Psychology and Director of the School Psychology Training Programs at St. John's University in New York, and Clinical Assistant Professor at Yale Child Study Center, Yale University, School of Medicine. In addition to her teaching responsibilities in the areas of cognitive assessment, psychoeducational evaluation, specific learning disabilities, and professional issues in school psychology, she serves as an expert witness, learning disability consultant, and psychoeducational test/measurement consultant and trainer for organizations nationally and internationally. She is a widely published author of books, book chapters, and articles. She is Fellow of the American Psychological Association (Division 16) and the American Board of Psychological Specialties. Dr. Flanagan's recent books in the *Essentials* series include *Essentials of Cross-Battery Assessment*, 2nd edition, and *Essentials of WISC-IV Assessment*, 2nd edition.

Vincent C. Alfonso, Ph.D. is Professor and Associate Dean for Academic Affairs in the Graduate School of Education at Fordham University. He is former Coordinator of the specialist- and doctoral-level School Psychology Programs at Fordham and former Executive Director of the Rosa A. Hagin School Consultation Center and the Early Childhood Center. His research interests include psychoeducational assessment, early childhood assessment, training issues, and psychometrics. In November 2003, Dr. Alfonso received the Leadership in School Psychology Award from the New York Association of School Psychologists. More recently, he was elected Fellow of Division 16. He is a certified school psychologist and licensed psychologist in New York State and has provided psychoeducational services to individuals across the life span for more than 20 years.

ABOUT THE CONTRIBUTORS

Vincent C. Alfonso, Ph.D., Graduate School of Education, Fordham University, New York, NY

Drew H. Bailey, Ph.D., Department of Psychological Sciences, College of Arts and Science, University of Missouri, Columbia, MO

Amy E. Barth, Ph.D., Texas Institute for Measurement, Evaluation, and Statistics and Department of Psychology, University of Houston, Houston, TX

Virginia W. Berninger, Ph.D., Department of Educational Psychology, College of Education, University of Washington, Seattle, WA

Steven G. Feifer, D.Ed., School Psychologist, Frederick County Public Schools, Frederick, MD

Catherine A. Fiorello, Ph.D., Psychological Studies in Education, College of Education, Temple University, Philadelphia, PA

Dawn P. Flanagan, Ph.D., Department of Psychology, St. John's University, Jamaica, NY, and Yale Child Study Center, Yale University, School of Medicine, New Haven, CT

Jack M. Fletcher, Ph.D., Department of Psychology, University of Houston, Houston, TX

David C. Geary, Ph.D., Department of Psychological Sciences, University of Missouri, Columbia, MO

James B. Hale, Ph.D., Department of Psychology, Philadelphia College of Osteopathic Medicine, Philadelphia, PA

Mary K. Hoard, Ph.D., Department of Psychological Sciences, University of Missouri, Columbia, MO

Jennifer T. Mascolo, PsyD., Department of Health & Behavior Studies, Teacher's College, Columbia University, New York, NY.

Nancy Mather, Ph.D., Department of Special Education, Rehabilitation, and School Psychology, University of Arizona, Tucson, AZ

Jack Naglieri, Ph.D., Department of Psychology, George Mason University, Fairfax, VA

Samuel O. Ortiz, Ph.D., Department of Psychology, St. John's University, Jamaica, NY

Marlene Sotelo-Dynega, Ph.D., Department of Psychology, St. John's University, Jamaica, NY

Karla K. Stuebing, Ph.D., Texas Institute for Measurement, Evaluation, and Statistics and Department of Psychology, University of Houston, Houston, TX

Barbara J. Wendling, M.A., Education Director, Woodcock-Munoz Foundation, Dallas, TX

Elizabeth Wiig, Ph.D., Professor Emerita, Boston University, Boston, MA

Kirby L. Wycoff, Ed.M., Graduate School of Applied and Professional Psychology, Rutgers University, New Brunswick, NJ

Author Index

Subject Index

CPSIA information can be obtained at www.ICGtesting.com
Printed in the USA
BVOW08s0458200715

409012BV00016B/42/P